THE AVENUES OF SALT LAKE CITY

THE
AVENUES
OF ·SALT LAKE CITY·

Karl T. Haglund and Philip F. Notarianni

Second Edition

Cevan J. LeSieur

The University of Utah Press | Utah State Historical Society
Salt Lake City

First edition published 1980 by the Utah State Historical Society.
Second edition is a copublication of the University of Utah Press
and the Utah State Historical Society.

 The Defiance House Man colophon is a registered trademark
of the University of Utah Press. It is based upon a four-foot-tall,
Ancient Puebloan pictograph (late PIII) near Glen Canyon, Utah.

16 15 14 13 12   1 2 3 4 5

Haglund, Karl T.
  The Avenues of Salt Lake City / Karl T. Haglund and Philip F. Notarianni ; revised
and updated by Cevan J. LeSieur. — Second edition.
     pages cm
  First edition published 1980 by the Utah State Historical Society. Second edition is a
copublication of the University of Utah Press and the Utah State Historical Society.
     Includes bibliographical references and index.
     ISBN 978-1-60781-181-7 (pbk. : alk. paper)
1. Architecture—Utah—Salt Lake City. 2. Avenues (Salt Lake City, Utah)—
Buildings, structures, etc. 3. Salt Lake City (Utah)—Buildings, structures, etc.
I. Notarianni, Philip F. II. LeSieur, Cevan J., 1969- III. Title.
  NA735.S34H3 2012
  720.9792'258—dc23
               2011050450

Printed in China

ACKNOWLEDGMENTS
Historical photographs courtesy of Utah State
     Historical Society
Contemporary photographs of significant sites
     by Heather and Cevan LeSieur
Map data courtesy of Salt Lake City CED
     Department/Engineering Division/GIS Team
Maps by XNR Productions
Interior book design by Jessica A. Booth
Frontispiece photo by Elizabeth Cotter

Contents

Preface to the Second Edition

Growing up in the suburbs of Salt Lake City in the 1970s, it was clear to me even at a young age that the Avenues neighborhood was different from the rest of the city. I was fascinated with the eclectic blend of architecture and people. My father purchased the original edition of this book when it was published in 1980 and I read it for the first time soon after, at the age of eleven. I knew that if I ever lived in Salt Lake City "when I grew up," I wanted to live in the Avenues. When my wife and I returned to the city in 1999, we purchased a bungalow on Ninth Avenue and our first restoration project was underway. I soon found myself digging out the old blue Avenues book to read the history of my new neighborhood once again. Sadly, the book was so worn that all of the pages were falling out of the binding. I looked for a new copy but discovered that the book was out of print.

A few years ago, I started thinking it was time to write a new book on the area that would reflect all the changes that had occurred since 1980. It seemed every block in the neighborhood had at least one extensive restoration project underway. I expressed my interest to Kirk Huffaker, director of the Utah Heritage Foundation. Kirk put me in touch with Peter DeLafosse at the University of Utah Press. As we shared ideas on which way to proceed, we agreed that the best course to take was to update and revise the original Avenues book. Peter and I met with Philip Notarianni, Kent Powell, and Barbara Murphy at the Division of State History. The Utah State Historical Society had been the original publisher. It was agreed that I could proceed with the research and writing needed to create a new edition of this book.

I felt strongly that the Significant Sites section should be greatly expanded. As in the original edition, my primary source of information on the homes listed in the book came from extensive records accumulated on Avenues historic sites. These records are located at the State Preservation Office. I was then able to add or correct the information with more recent historical findings. I also tried to include when a property had been recently restored.

In addition to revising the original text of the first two chapters, a section was added to the book that describes the many changes that have occurred in the area during the past thirty years.

I could not have completed this project without the support of several persons I want to mention. Kirk Huffaker gave me encouragement and direction. Peter DeLafosse had faith that a ship captain who has never written any kind of book could complete this revision. Barbara Murphy and the State Historic Preservation Office allowed me to spend countless hours digging through their files. Kent Powell provided support from the Division of State History. Former director of the Division of State History and one of the original authors, Philip Notarianni, granted us permission to proceed with this book. Finally, I thank my wife, Heather, for allowing me to spend precious family time researching, taking pictures, and writing this update.

Preface to the First Edition

Travel to the heart of Salt Lake City and you will see the State Capitol dominating the hills to the north. East of the capitol and climbing farther up the slopes of the Wasatch Range is an area known to Salt Lakers as the Avenues, one of the city's oldest and most important residential areas. Besides boasting some of Utah's best examples of residential architectural styles, the Avenues include several significant public and commercial buildings.

Turreted, ornamented, or plain, the houses stand as a reminder of a truly unique neighborhood. Some are statuesque—tall and well proportioned—portraying poise and dignity. Others, through the use of natural materials, reflect the graceful simplicity of the pioneer era. Most are single-family or two-family structures, though three- and four-story dwellings, built at the turn of the twentieth century, dot the area's southwest corner.

The Avenues district lacks the broad, spacious look of other parts of the city. The pioneers who built their homes on the Avenues were mostly businessmen, not farmers, and so had no need for farmland about their homes. Instead of following the city's traditional system of ten-acre blocks with 132-foot-wide streets, they employed a system of two-and-a-half-acre blocks with streets 82 ½ feet wide. Their gridiron plan platted on rather steep slopes further accentuates the special visual elements of the Avenues.

The heights, setbacks, styles, spacing, and design of the buildings produce a sense of continuity along many avenues and streets. Small side yards and the dense pattern of structures create an almost rowhouse-like feeling—a feeling reinforced by the repetition of narrow house ends facing the street. Other visual features, such as front porches, retaining walls, fences, and landscaping, complete the sense of place that makes the Avenues Historic District such a remarkable facet of Salt Lake City's past and present.

This book, divided into three sections, deals with both the history and the architecture of the Avenues. Over 140 significant structures are presented in detail to allow the reader to understand this district's special sense of place. The area outlined in the book contains some of the most remarkable early architecture to be found in the West. Although it is impossible to drive the complete perimeter of the district, all of the sites can be approached by car. Because of the stairway at the end of Canyon Road, it is necessary to backtrack Canyon Road to Second Avenue (one way east). One of the most stirring views of the Mormon Temple occurs while driving west along First Avenue. Approaching F Street, two spires of the temple come into view on the western horizon, framed by the rows of houses on either side of First Avenue. Climbing the rise to B Street the spires momentarily drop from sight, only to reappear as the temple seems to rise out of the ground until it stands completely revealed.

The information included in this book was gathered primarily by the research personnel of the Utah State Historical Society. An architectural survey conducted by a private firm, Historic Utah, Inc., was also utilized. The historical society devised a structure-site information form to include data on the status, use, architecture, and history of each significant structure. Forms were completed on 2,100 sites identified by the Historic Utah, Inc., survey as well as on an additional 200 structures. Less complete structure-site forms were produced by the Utah State Tax Commission's Local Valuation Office on 2,974 buildings in the survey area. Photographs of these sites were attached to their corresponding forms to aid in architectural identification and description. As research progressed, survey procedures were further refined to include a title search of each property up through the 1940s, biographical data on owners, and, where appropriate, tenant information. The researchers scrutinized building permits, newspaper building lists, Sanborn maps, city directories, obituary indices, and other related sources.

Nominations to the National Register of Historic Places were also prepared from this research. These included the Avenues Historic District and the City Creek Canyon Historic District as well as individual building nominations. Although the

Avenues neighborhood extends from A Street to Virginia Street and from First to Eighteenth avenues, the majority of the significant sites are located within a smaller boundary. Thus the nominated Avenues Historic District lies within the following boundary: beginning at State Street and South Temple, the line proceeds north to Canyon Road, east to the set of steps on Fourth Avenue, north on A Street to Ninth Avenue, including both sides of A Street to Sixth Avenue, east along the south side of Ninth Avenue to B Street, then south to the McIntyre house at 259 Seventh Avenue. From that point the northern boundary proceeds east, including both sides of Seventh Avenue and excluding a parking terrace next to 259 Seventh Avenue, to N Street, and drops south, including both sides of Fourth Avenue, to Virginia Street. Following Virginia Street south to the First Avenue–South Temple block, the boundary traces the South Temple property lines back to the starting point.

This area was selected primarily because of its concentration of sites of historical and/or architectural significance. Within the historic district boundary are 134 of the 143 identified significant sites on the Avenues: 55 of the 63 architecturally significant sites, all 31 of the historically significant buildings, and 48 of the 49 sites significant for both architectural and historical reasons. It also contains over 90 percent of the two- and two-and-one-half-story dwellings, an important visual feature of the Avenues. Augustus Koch's 1870 map of Salt Lake City gives historical support for the boundary by clearly showing Seventh Avenue as the uppermost point of Avenues settlement.

The City Creek Canyon Historic District, because of its distinctive geography, was nominated separately. It begins at Third Avenue and Canyon Road and is bounded by the roads on the east and west slopes of lower City Creek Canyon.

The Historic Preservation Office of the Utah State Historical Society researches properties and districts for listing in the National Register. Sites listed in the National Register are eligible for development funding that is used to ensure their protection, allow the reuse of valuable resources, and make the state's communities and rural areas more attractive for both resident and tourist.

This book reflects the efforts of many different individuals both within and outside of the historical society. The architectural firm of Wallace Cooper Associates worked with the Historic Preservation Office to prepare reports on the architectural styles on the Avenues, historic district ordinances in other major cities, and design guidelines for the Avenues, City Creek Canyon, and Capitol Hill historic districts. The work of Wally Cooper, Allen Roberts, and Kip Harris contributed substantially to this publication. The researchers involved in the survey project also deserve recognition and profound thanks for their excellent work. Jessie Embry, Thomas Hanchett, Lois Harris, Mark Lundgren, Kathryn MacKay, John McCormick, and Henry Whiteside all share in this book's production. Special thanks must be extended to Linda Edeiken, Salt Lake City preservation planner, for her help and support, and to the officials of Salt Lake City for their aid and foresight in participating in this venture. The book has benefited from the organizational touch of Sybil Clays, and Katherine G. Morrissey, Yale University graduate student and historical society publications intern during the summer of 1980, did a superlative job of editing the manuscript for publication and completely rewriting the Significant Sites section.

Historical photographs are from the Utah State Historical Society collections. Contemporary photographs of significant sites are by Richard Menzies.

THE PATTERNS OF THE PAST

Beginnings

In July 1847, Mormon pioneers descended into the Salt Lake Valley to establish their city by the Great Salt Lake. Its founding stemmed from the Mormons' religious purpose to build a community free of extensive secular restraints that would hinder their plans to bring about the kingdom of God. There followed a well-planned settlement where the original pioneers and those who came afterward could go about their business without fear of persecution. The massive migration was conceived and executed with care and skill.

The city itself was deliberately planned, with streets and buildings laid out according to a definite scheme patterned after the City of Zion plat drawn in 1833 by Joseph Smith, founder and first president of the Church of Jesus Christ of Latter-day Saints (Mormon). The city's ten-acre blocks lay east-west and north-south to provide for well-spaced houses on lots large enough to allow for lawns, vegetable gardens, trees, and orchards. Houses were set well back from wide streets that would eventually be lined with shade trees, and each street was to contain an irrigation ditch to which all would have water rights. Fields were platted in a belt around the town lots and their owners, who lived in town, were obliged to journey out daily to farm them. Ultimately, the unique characteristics of the city brought about an alliance among the people that fostered both religious and social institutions.

In his work on Utah history, Charles S. Peterson tells of the colonizing efforts of the frontier Mormons:

Responding in part to the Great Basin environment and in part to the teachings and experiences that made them a chosen people, Mormons developed their most distinctive institutions and practices in the...colonizing process—the call, the move, group control over land and water, and the farm village life. Developed to bring a raw environment into harmony with God's will on the one hand, and to protect the independence that its rawness permitted on the other, the practices of colonization proved impossible to perpetuate indefinitely, but until 1890 they distinguished Mormon culture and served as the vehicle of the church's geographic expansion.[1]

Expansion of settlement into the Avenues aided in marking the end of certain settlement practices, at least in Salt Lake City.

The Avenues neighborhood is the northernmost arc of a crescent formed by the foothills of the Wasatch Mountains north and east of Salt Lake City. Unlike the longer eastern section of the crescent, which flattens out part way up the slope to form what Utahns call the East Bench, the Avenues area is relatively steep from South Temple north to the crest of the foothills where it ends at the visible shoreline of ancient Lake Bonneville, the remnant of which is now the Great Salt Lake. Settlement of the upper Avenues area was delayed until the end of the nineteenth century because of the difficulty in getting water up the slopes.

Surveyed in the early 1850s as Plat D of Salt Lake City, the Avenues was the first section to deviate from the original plan of ten-acre blocks. Possibly because of the slopes and lack of water, the Avenues have narrower streets and smaller blocks than those of Salt Lake City proper. Instead of forty-rod squares for city blocks, Plat D contained fifty-six blocks, each twenty rods square (two and one-half acres). Blocks were then subdivided into four lots instead of eight as in the greater Salt Lake City area; streets were five rods wide, and sidewalks were to be ten feet wide as opposed to twenty feet wide as in the rest of the city. Plat D was formally recorded on February 7, 1857.[2] The Avenues' deviation from the city's original platting violated the law and required enactment of an additional survey ordinance by the territorial legislature on January 20, 1860.[3]

Expansion into the Avenues became necessary with the city's steady growth in population. In addition, the discovery of gold in California in 1848 placed Salt Lake

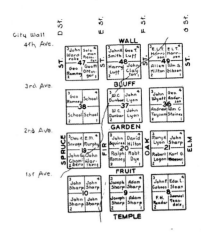

Early property owners are indicated on this Plat D map compiled by Nicholas Morgan Sr. The portion shown includes the area presently bordered by D Street, Fourth Avenue, G Street, and South Temple.

OPPOSITE. In this 1870 bird's-eye view of Salt Lake City, the Avenues extend as far as Mountain Street, present-day Seventh Avenue. Drawn by Augustus Koch, the map looks northeast toward the Wasatch Mountains and shows the cemetery on the upper right. A completed version of the LDS temple emerges on the lower left even though the project was still under construction.

The old city wall is visible in the foreground of this southeast view of the LDS Eighteenth Ward chapel.

City in a strategic position to supply gold rush prospectors and others headed for the coast. The increased economic activity boosted local business and manufacturing. Early tradesmen came to prefer the Avenues area for residences because of its proximity to the city's business center and the splendid view of the valley offered by the bench lands.[4]

Originally, the streets in the Avenues were named rather than numbered. The north-south streets were named for trees and the four east-west avenues were called Fruit, Garden, Bluff, and Wall Streets. Tree names on what are now A through N Streets were initially Walnut, Chestnut, Pine, Spruce, Fir, Oak, Elm, Maple, Locust, Ash, Beech, Cherry, Cedar, and Birch, respectively. Early on the area was referred to as "the dry bench" because of its paucity of water. By 1885 the east-west streets had become First, Second, Third, and Fourth Avenues and the north-south streets had been given alphabetical titles: A Street through V Street. (V Street later became

Virginia Street.) Changing the word "street" to "avenue" for the numerical titles marked the beginning of the current appellation—the Avenues. In 1907 the city council approved the street name changes that remain to this day.[5]

The early designation of Fourth Avenue as Wall Street is explained by the existence of a city wall that ran east along Fourth Avenue to N Street, then veered south. Built of mud mixed with straw, hay, vegetation, and gravel, the wall was constructed by the public works department during 1853–1854 and measured twelve feet in height and six feet thick at its base, tapering to two and a half feet thick near its rounded top.[6] Its purpose was not only to control livestock but to furnish public works employment for incoming immigrants. An opening existed at present D Street and Fourth Avenue where cattle were herded through each day to graze.[7]

Scarcity of water plagued the Avenues area until the LDS Twentieth Ward ditch diverted water from City Creek to supply the western section with water sufficient to influence development of the area. The ditch ran along Fourth Avenue from Sudbury Mill to K Street, where water was then distributed via a series of ditches and pipelines to residents south to South Temple. The eastern section of the Avenues was supplied from Red Butte Canyon until 1862 when water was diverted to newly constructed Fort Douglas.[8] For the next fifteen to twenty years, residents of the northeastern corner of the area had to haul water for everyday use.[9] Eventually, in 1884, protests from Avenues citizens over lack of facilities prompted the city to install about twelve thousand feet of pipeline from reservoirs in City Creek near Sudbury Mill along Sixth Avenue to the city cemetery.[10]

Meanwhile, the upper avenues and streets continued to suffer from lack of water until the early decades of the twentieth century. In 1908 the Twentieth Ward water system was hooked into a large reservoir in City Creek. Three years later an eighteen-inch water main was installed from City Creek to Thirteenth Avenue and J Street, allowing for further development of the northern section.[11] One scholar contends that "had water facilities been more accessible during this period…the North Bench would have been built up to a far greater extent, for it held an elevated position above the city proper and lay close to the business center."[12]

Homes began to dot the Avenues as early as the 1850s, despite the lack of water. Usually built of adobe and typical of pioneer homes throughout Utah Territory, these early houses were constructed in the platted portion from A to N Streets and First to

Fourth Avenues. Then, in 1860 the slaughter yards were moved from Eighth South and State Streets to the East Bench near the mouth of Dry Canyon so that water from both Dry and Red Butte Canyons could be utilized. An area known as Butcherville sprang up near the eastern Avenues in what is now known as Federal Heights, and men who worked for the slaughter yards lived there to be nearer their place of work.[13] For example, in 1866 butcher John Picknell built a typical pioneer vernacular home which still stands at 1216 First Avenue. Water from Dry Canyon was used to make adobes from excellent clay found in the vicinity. Later, a brickyard at Fourth Avenue and V Street was built and operated by Edward Brain in the 1880s. Farther north, Mark and Birthiah Lindsey established a pleasure resort during the 1860s called Lindsey Gardens.[14]

In February 1857 Jesse W. Fox, as city and territorial surveyor, issued land certificates to Brigham Young for the fifty-six blocks in Plat D, and in 1859, as territorial surveyor, issued land certificates to Young covering the same tract and listing him as "lawful claimant." Beginning in 1871 these certificates were either confirmed or supplemented by mayoral deeds issued by Mayor Daniel H. Wells and his successors. Titles thus obtained were deemed legal.[15]

The first owners of lots in Plat D received nearly all deeds from Brigham Young or his executors, with but a few obtaining title by mayoral deeds. Of the 192 homeowners indexed in Nicholas Morgan's "Pioneer Map," 151 received titles from Young, 11 had mayoral deeds, 21 were squatters, and 7 received titles with no recorded dates.[16] Clearly, Mormons were predominant in this portion of the area, at least during the Avenues' early existence. Butcherville also housed a sizable number of Mormons. Not until the late nineteenth century would so-called Gentiles (non-Mormons) settle in larger numbers in the Avenues, obtaining deeds primarily from Mormons.[17]

A pattern of home ownership illustrating the Mormon character of the southwestern Avenues is manifest in polygamous construction—houses built by one man for his several wives; 379 and 385 Fifth Avenue are good examples. These homes were built for the sisters Henrietta Woolley Simmons and Rachel Emma Woolley Simmons, respectively, who had both married Joseph M. Simmons.[18] In this case, the homes were built by Edwin D. Woolley, father of Simmons's wives. The home at 379 Fifth Avenue is a small, one-story, gable-roofed dwelling, while the structure at 385 is a two-story frame house with Georgian detailing. Both homes reflect early

vernacular styles employed before the
use of professional architects.

Transportation and Transition

Transportation to and from the Avenues and the downtown business district soon became a factor important to
settlement. The first rail line was constructed to haul sandstone from Red
Butte Canyon to a stone yard at South
Temple and U Street.[19] The Salt Lake
Railroad Company was organized in
1872, and rides on the mule-drawn cars
cost five cents. By 1875, a track ran east
on South Temple to E Street, then north
to and along Third Avenue. In 1889, the
first five miles of the system were elec-
trified. The following year a competing
company, the Salt Lake Rapid Transit
Company, was incorporated. Competi-

1875 AVENUES RAIL SYSTEM
1890 AVENUES RAIL SYSTEM
1921 AVENUES RAIL SYSTEM

This map represents the routes of the Salt
Lake City rail system as it extended up the
Avenues. Map by Kip K. Harris.

tion between the companies was often bitter, and competing lines were sometimes
run along the same streets. Several smaller companies were also started.

In 1890 Salt Lake Railroad trolleys climbed E Street to Third Avenue, went over to
F Street, climbed north to Sixth Avenue, and ran east to N Street. An alternate route
climbed from I Street and South Temple to Third Avenue and then east to P Street.
A Rapid Transit Company line ran along First Avenue to T Street. There it met one of
Salt Lake's shortest lines, the Popperton and Fort Douglas Rapid Transit Company
track, which ran only a mile and a half to Fort Douglas.[20]

The two large companies bought out the smaller ones during the 1890s and in
1903 merged as the Consolidated Railway and Power Company. Because the transit companies either ran their own power plant or leased electric power from other

companies, their history parallels the development of the city's electric utilities. In 1903, Utah Light and Power merged with Consolidated to become Utah Light and Railway. With its purchase by E. H. Harriman, the company expanded rapidly and became the Utah Light and Traction Company in 1914.

The Traction Company's increased service to the Avenues reflected the northward growth of the area. By 1915 one route followed Second Avenue to B Street, then to Ninth Avenue, turning east to K Street. Another route turned east at Sixth Avenue and B Street and ended at N Street. A feeder system that provided electricity connected the Ninth and Sixth Avenue routes at K Street. Another rail line serviced South Temple. At E Street, a spur continued north to Third Avenue, running east to Virginia Street, eventually winding its way north, east, and then south to Fort Douglas. Feeder lines existed at M between P and Q, and at S Street.[21]

Though trolley rails in the Avenues were removed in the 1940s, their existence has left a permanent mark on the area's physical environment. Third, Sixth, and Ninth Avenues are wider and flatter than the others and receive a heavier traffic flow.[22] Even E Street, which flattens out at Third Avenue, reflects the prior existence of the trolley system.

Avenues settlement patterns reflect the transition that occurred in Salt Lake City during the latter decades of the nineteenth century. With the advent of the mining industry in 1863 and the coming of the transcontinental railroad in 1869, Salt Lake City's character began to undergo a gradual transition from that of a large farm village to that of a regional commercial center. With the development of industry came secondary and tertiary functions that contributed to even more diversification of the city's social milieu. From the founding of Salt Lake City in 1847 to 1910, the proportion of Mormons declined from 100 percent of the population to less than 45 percent, with the greatest change occurring between 1885 and 1891.[23] Non-Mormons came to form a representative portion of the population, injecting into the once-dominant Mormon city a force that would lead to changes and adjustments in a number of institutions and areas including the physical environment.[24]

Because of titles issued by Brigham Young or his executors, Mormons were initially the majority landholders in the southwestern portion of the Avenues, with some dominance in the eastern section (Butcherville) as well. But as the population diversified, the proximity of the Avenues to the city center and its geographical

OPPOSITE. A Utah Light and Traction Company streetcar on B Street near First Avenue. The car is bound for Ninth Avenue.

location on the rising north bench became increasingly attractive. Consequently, the Avenues evolved into one of the city's most prestigious neighborhoods and became a middle- and upper-middle-class streetcar suburb. Ronald B. Boyce argues that the transition of Salt Lake City from village to city required the reorganization of space to accommodate both a concentration of population and a commuter population.[25] It was during this transition period that the Avenues district began to assume the characteristics of its present state. One such characteristic is diversity, both in population and in architecture.

Salt Lake City directories illustrate the changing occupational composition of the Avenues. Scrutiny of the city directory for 1869 reveals some 48 occupations represented by Avenues residents.[26] By 1889 about 145 occupations were found in the neighborhood.[27] The changes in occupation during that twenty-year period reflect the economic transition of Salt Lake from village to city. In 1889, for example, Avenues residents in the field of mining included miners, mine owners, mine operators, and assayers, while only one miner was recorded in 1869. Those in crafts and trades increased substantially as did those employed in industries supportive to mining and railroading and in service enterprises. Builders and contractors increased from only one, George Romney, in 1869, to William L. N. Allen Jr., John C. Dowlin, W. J. Tuddenham, and A. R. Wright Jr., in 1889. In addition, architect William S. Hedges resided

at Fourth Avenue between Canyon Road and A Street in 1889. Hedges's presence reflects the increasing use of professional architects in Salt Lake City during the late decades of the nineteenth century.

Avenues builder and businessman George Romney stands in his garden.

Other professionals had begun to reside in the Avenues by 1889. Dr. Ellen B. Ferguson, 121 B Street, was one of the first physicians to settle in the area. She was also active in political affairs, serving as the only woman delegate to the Democratic National Convention in 1896. Other doctors included Mrs. M. E. Van, at 167 Third Avenue, and Mr. and Mrs. J. M. Holland, at 316 E Street. Dentists, nurses, veterinary surgeons, and attorneys were also numbered among the Avenues residents of 1889. At least one lawyer was specializing in land and mining law, further illustrating the growing influence of the mining industry.

The pattern of living in the Avenues and working in the downtown commercial business district was firmly established by the 1890s. However, it began much earlier. For instance, in 1869 Charles R. Savage, a prominent Utah photographer, lived at the corner of Garden and Spruce (Second Avenue and D Street) but maintained his studio on Main Street downtown.[28]

Not all Avenues residents commuted to jobs downtown. Various service-related businesses grew up in the area to accommodate residents. Of these, grocery stores were the most typical. An example is found in the Twentieth Ward Store, located at 423–425 Fourth Avenue, owned by William and Elizabeth Willes. This still-existing structure illustrates the house-store combination popular in many communities. These neighborhood stores functioned as a valuable part of local life. Other local markets in 1889 included the Evans Meat Market, at Sixth Avenue and B Street, and a grocery owned by Mrs. Thomas McIntyre at 39 I Street. Gibson's Tailor Shop could be found at the corner of Q Street and Second Avenue, with Goddard and Company, hatters, housed at 304 Sixth Avenue. By 1889, the Avenues was well established as a popular residential area with a growing number of community amenities such as stores, shops, schools, and churches.

Prominent Salt Lake City photographer and Avenues resident Charles R. Savage is pictured with his wife and nine children in about 1880. Kneeling: Lenny Louise; sitting: Annie Amelia, Charles R. Savage, Ray T., Annie Adkins Savage, Roscoe E., Ida May; standing: Luacine Annette, George L., Ralph G., Fannie.

The twentieth century ushered in a period of continued growth in Salt Lake City, with the Avenues experiencing the vicissitudes of that process. Diversity continued to characterize the area as occupational, housing, and land-use patterns adapted to the changing times. The increasing industrialization and diversification of the city's economy account for the variety of occupations represented in the Avenues as well as for the patterns of home ownership. In 1895, Mormons accounted for some 60 percent of the population living in the Avenues. By 1917, the figure was down to about 50 percent.[29] Diversity of architecture, occupations, and ownership continued to increase in the district.

As Utah became a leader in the mining of gold and silver, the increasing prosperity significantly altered Salt Lake City's physical environment. Prominent mining entrepreneurs turned Brigham Street (South Temple) into a street of palatial residences.[30] Gill S. Peyton built a large two-and-one-half-story Classical Revival mansion, probably designed by architect Walter E. Ware, at 259 Seventh Avenue. William McIntyre, cattleman and owner of the fabulous Mammoth gold mine in the Tintic Mining District, purchased the residence in 1901. The structure sits in the northwestern part of the Avenues, symbolizing the new wealth of the age, especially evident in the use of a professional architect.

The Charles Felt–Richard R. Lyman–Amy Brown Lyman house at 1084 Third Avenue represents another home built by an entrepreneur, and its owners illustrate the Avenues' changing social dynamics. Charles Felt, a strong anti-Mormon member of the American Party and a force in Salt Lake City politics from 1905 to 1911, sold the home to Richard R. Lyman, a Mormon apostle of twenty-five years. Other representative residences built by the wealthy include the George Wallace house, 584 Third Avenue; the William Cunningham and Elizabeth Dern Cunningham house, 18 U Street; and the Rhoda Chase Welcher–J. C. Penney house, 371 Seventh Avenue.

Physicians, attorneys, and architects enjoyed the amenities offered by the Avenues neighborhood. Dr. Alice E. Houghton built a one-and-one-half-story Dutch Colonial residence in 1906 at 911 Third Avenue. She practiced in the city from 1905 until her death in 1968. Likewise, Dr. Ellis R. Shipp, active in the medical profession for more than sixty years, lived in a home built in 1903 at 711 Second Avenue. She trained nurses and midwives in her own school and also served on the staff of the Deseret Hospital. The home at 903 First Avenue was built during the 1890s, and in 1912 Dr. Panagestes Kassinikos purchased it. A native of Greece, he immigrated to Utah in 1905 and became the publisher of a Greek weekly, *The Light*. Samuel H. Allen, one of Utah's notable physicians, built a two-story Prairie-style residence at 206 Eighth Avenue in 1910. A trend toward investment properties, common in the Avenues in the twentieth century, can be seen at 224 M Street. Representing the legal profession, William H. McCarty, chief justice of the Utah State Supreme Court from 1902 to 1919, built an American Four Square–type home at 1053 Third Avenue in 1903.

Architect Walter E. Ware designed and built a two-story, gambrel-roofed Colonial Revival home on First Avenue in 1906. Lewis Telle Cannon, another Salt Lake City architect and senior partner in the firm of Cannon and Fetzer, constructed a one-and-one-half-story English cottage–inspired bungalow.[31] Several other prominent turn-of-the-century architects built or rented homes in the Avenues.

Mormon ecclesiastical leaders influenced trends in housing in the Avenues through their church positions, through the value attached to home ownership by the church, and by their involvement in Avenues real estate. George F. Richards, a member of the Quorum of Twelve Apostles and church historian, purchased a residence at 1010 Third Avenue in 1905. The large, two-story Victorian home was built in 1898 by William H. Needham. Brigham H. Roberts, a General Authority in the church, mission president, and historian, lived at 77–79 C Street. Of particular significance was Heber J. Grant's 1915 bungalow residence at 201 Eighth Avenue. Grant became the seventh president of the LDS church in 1918 and served until his death in 1945. During those years he continued to live on Eighth Avenue, and as president of the Heber J. Grant and Company real estate and insurance agency, he exerted influence in the building of structures and the acquisition of land in the Avenues.

The move of the University of Utah to its present location stimulated additional growth in the Avenues area. In 1894, sixty acres west of Fort Douglas were granted to the Utah Territory for the university.[32] Subsequently, faculty members found the Avenues a suitable residential area. Typifying this trend is the Orson Howard house at 1105 First Avenue, a two-story brick Victorian home constructed about 1904 for the professor of natural history and curator of the Museum of Natural History. Howard moved into the area in 1898 upon receiving his appointment and Sadie Tripp Howard, his wife, worked as a part-time teacher for the experimental William Stewart

Dr. Ellis Reynolds Shipp was president of the Utah Women's Press Club and editor of the *Salt Lake Sanitarian*, a monthly medical journal. Dr. Shipp, one of Utah's first prominent woman physicians, resided at 711 Second Avenue.

School at the university. For about twenty years Noble Warrum, journalist and historian, lived at 1153 Second Avenue in a home built in 1905. Warrum, a non-Mormon, authored the four-volume work *Utah Since Statehood*. Educator Christian N. Jensen also resided at an Avenues address. His one-and-one-half-story dwelling was built in 1908 at 1202 Fourth Avenue as a rental unit. In 1921, Jensen became the first resident-owner and in that year was named state superintendent of public instruction. Orson F. Whitney, teacher, historian, politician, and apostle of the Mormon Church, lived in two different Avenues homes, 160 Fourth Avenue, built in about 1903, and 764 Fourth Avenue, constructed in 1923.

Noteworthy in the mix found in the Avenues neighborhood were the politicians residing there, both state and local officials including governors, mayors, councilmen, and key political party figures. Heber M. Wells, governor of Utah from 1896 to 1905, lived for a time at 182 G Street. This one-story Victorian home was constructed in 1889 and remained the Wells residence until 1897. Wells then moved to 61 First Avenue, which is now the site of the Wells Apartments. Wells served in many political capacities prior to his election as the state's first governor.[33] George Dern, governor from 1925 to 1933, and U.S. Secretary of War from 1933 to 1936, lived at 36 H Street until 1922 when he moved to South Temple. Architect Richard K. A. Kletting was employed by him to design the substantial two-story home, built in 1899, that shows influences of the Colonial Revival style then popular. Dern became a renowned mining figure who, with Theodore P. Holt, developed the Holt-Dern roaster—a method for treating a certain grade of silver ore. He maintained interests in Mercur, Park City, and Tintic, three of Utah's richest mining areas, and also served in the Utah State Senate before being elected governor. Another political figure, Lydia D. Alder, purchased a home at 320 First Avenue in 1905. Active in women's movements, she served as the first president of the National Women's Congress in London in 1899 and also became the first president of the National Women's Suffrage Association in Utah. In addition, she was an active member of the LDS Church, helping organize the Relief Society in Utah.

Utah's cultural development also became entwined with Avenues history as artists, poets, actors, and musicians began to move into the area. Numbered among the artists are Mahonri Young, Lee Greene Richards, and Alma B. Wright, who all grew up together in the LDS Twentieth Ward during the 1880s. Earlier artists included George

The family of architect Richard K. A. Kletting is shown about 1917. CLOCKWISE FROM THE TOP: Richard K. A. Kletting, Mary, Mary Elizabeth Kletting, Helen, Walter.

M. Ottinger, Henry L. A. Culmer, and Alfred Lambourne. When Utahn Mary Teasdel returned in 1903 from her successful three-year sojourn in Paris, she established a private art studio and residence on C Street.[34] One year earlier Anton Pedersen, who directed the Salt Lake Philharmonic Orchestra, had purchased a Victorian residence at 509 Third Avenue. An immigrant from Norway in 1875, he formed military bands in Salt Lake City and organized the first symphony orchestra in Utah. His son, Arthur Pedersen Freber, lived in the house until 1951. Freber, who adopted his stepfather's name, was a child prodigy on the violin. He soloed at the Salt Lake Tabernacle at the age of four and in 1913 became conductor of the Philharmonic. Two musicians who exerted strong influence upon the Mormon Tabernacle Choir were John J. McClellan and Joseph J. Daynes. McClellan purchased the home at 688 First Avenue in 1906. An accomplished musician, he became the organist for the choir in 1906, holding that position for twenty years. He also founded the Utah Conservatory of Music and conducted the Salt Lake Opera Company and the Salt Lake Symphony Orchestra. Daynes, the first Salt Lake Tabernacle organist, commissioned John A. Headlund to design his home. Built in 1904 by the Salt Lake Building Company at 38 D Street, the two-story, Four Square dwelling served as the Daynes residence until 1920.[35]

The majority of residents in the early Avenues were clerks, laborers, and other functionaries. The list is long, but an example can be found in the home of Orvin Morris, 129 G Street, built in 1894. Morris was the chief rate clerk for the Oregon Short Line Railroad and traffic manager for the U & I Sugar Company. Farther east, Oscar H. Cook, a teamster, lived at 83 Q Street.

Changing Patterns: Ownership and Development

Occupational diversity was one characteristic that defined the Avenues area and illustrated the city's transition from Mormon village to regional center. Another trend identifiable with the Avenues was the changing pattern of property ownership. Of special note in the late nineteenth century was the growing practice of hiring houses. In 1900 Salt Lake City, 4,391 homes were owned by their occupants, whereas 6,700 were hired or rented.[36] Mingled with the trend toward rental housing was the greater longevity of women that made widowhood a reality for many and affected, to an extent, property ownership.

Musician John J. McClellan is pictured three years after purchasing his home on First Avenue.

The 1889 city directory reveals the presence of many widows in the Avenues. Research indicates that the building of homes as residences and income-producing properties by widows as well as by families became common. Several examples illustrate this point. Juliette O. Croxall, the widow of musician Mark Croxall, built a home for herself at 425 Sixth Avenue in 1902 at a cost of two thousand dollars and lived in this cottage until 1913. Oliver A. and Georgia Jennings, who lived at 353 Sixth Avenue, built three other dwellings as investments at 361 and 367 Sixth Avenue and 320 D Street. All were constructed in the 1890–1891 period. Elizabeth E. Martin, widow of mining entrepreneur Lewis Martin, who died in 1902, resided at 128 B Street but maintained rental units at 124 and 132 B Street.

This movement toward rental and speculative properties accelerated in the early decades of the twentieth century. The enthusiastic efforts of development companies and those in the home-building industry, as well as the popularity of the Avenues, may account for this acceleration. However, Charles Brooks Anderson observes that by 1912 in the housing industry "not only did vacancies cease to increase in certain areas of the city although new dwellings increased, but the greater proportion of the new residences were owned by their occupants," indicating the purchase of many of these houses from the developer.[37] In the Avenues the activities of investors, developers, and speculators centered on the construction of speculative properties and rental units. Residential additions were often laid out on large tracts of land and sold to home-seekers. An early and successful example is Darlington Place, encompassing the area from approximately N to S Streets and First to Third Avenues. Promoted by Elmer E. Darling, who lived at 1031 First Avenue, Darlington Place was begun in 1890 and by 1892 was "one of the most popular residence portions of the city."[38] As a publication of the period described it:

House after house was reared with energetic rapidity. Then streetcar companies...extended thru electric lines on First and Third Streets, giving the residents a double service of rapid transit....In two years this locality has grown from a few scattered houses to a thriving community represented by countless homes, every one of which has been built with an eye to the special comfort and convenience of its occupants. The residents of Darlington Place are now building in their midst their own church. The promoters have pursued a most judicious course,...giving the option to buyers of building themselves, or furnishing their own plans, besides making the terms of purchase easy....This, together with the choice location, is the keynote to the situation, and such is the present popularity of Darlington Place, that new buildings may be seen in all stages of construction from the foundation to the last finishing touch.[39]

Darling announced in an 1892 newspaper article that the growth of the addition was steady, due largely to the acquisition of natural gas. Business had been good in 1891, with fifty homes built. He predicted that the number would double by 1893. "Salt Lake is my kind of a town," the developer said, "it is a go-ahead city, full of golden opportunities for enterprising rustlers and will be the metropolis of the intermountain region."[40] Darling worked in partnership with Frank E. McGurrin in 1891, but by 1893 they apparently had gone their separate ways.[41] Nevertheless, Darlington Place continued to thrive as other real estate developers such as Frank A. Grant built homes in the area.[42] Grant himself lived at 963 Third Avenue for a time but also built a home at 967 Third Avenue, which was purchased by Joseph P. Bache, the territorial librarian and a court clerk.[43]

The panic of 1893, and the subsequent depression, eventually affected the Darlington project, and building in the area slowed.[44] By 1898 Darling had moved to 934 East South Temple, and McGurrin had established F. E. McGurrin and Company. By 1905, when real estate activity again entered a boom period, McGurrin formed the Salt Lake Security and Trust Company which built many homes in the Avenues.[45]

Building and construction firms greatly influenced Avenues development. As a result, pattern-book homes became significant. Usually constructed from architectural pattern books, these dwellings were repetitious in design—much the same as homes found in many of today's suburbs. However, the earlier developments were smaller in scale. Similar pattern-book houses can be seen scattered throughout the Avenues area. Construction firms could build pattern-book homes at a lower cost, since the expense of having an architect was eliminated.

Among the firms involved in Avenues construction were the Modern Home Building Company, the National Real Estate and Investment Company, the Aaron Keyser Investment Company, Deseret Savings and Loan, the George Romney and

Sons Company, the Taylor-Armstrong Lumber Company, and Heber J. Grant and Company. The Modern Home Building Company first appeared in the city directory in 1907, with William H. Tibbals as president and R. S. Pritchard as secretary and treasurer. Tibbals lived at 1006 Third Avenue.[46] The National Real Estate and Investment Company was cited in the city directory in 1909, with G. H. Wallace as president, Theodore Tobiason as vice-president, M. E. Crandall Jr. as secretary, W. J. Burton as treasurer, and W. T. Atkins as manager. Three of these officers lived in the area: Crandall and Wallace at 676 and 584 Third Avenue, respectively, and Atkins at 90 N Street.[47] Apparently, many corporate officers chose to live and build in the Avenues, attesting to the desirable living conditions of the district.

The patterns of family ownership, especially evident in specific blocks, also attest to the popularity of the Avenues. Numbered among the families with ties in the area were those of Grant, Romney, Brain, Hansen, Glade, and Wells. These ties were often solidified by intermarriage between prominent Mormon families as well as by the business firms of the Grants and Romneys. Heber J. Grant functioned as a successful businessman, and his company actively developed the Avenues. In addition, he helped organize the Home Benefit Building Society in 1915, encouraging Mormon families, especially young couples, to acquire their own homes.[48]

ELIJAH GRIFFITHS' RESIDENCE.

RESIDENCE OF ERNEST G. ROGNON.

HOUSE OF JAMES A. ROBINSON.

EDWARD D. WOODRUFF'S RESIDENCE.

RESIDENCE OF E. C. COFFIN.

THE NEWELL BEEMAN HOUSE.

DARLINGTON PLACE RESIDENCES.

The block between A and B Streets and Eighth and Ninth Avenues illustrates family ties at work. Elizabeth Holland Anderson, wife of Robert R. Anderson, originally owned most of the land. Grant purchased much of the south half in 1908, selling lots to others but providing property for his own family. Mary Grant Judd, Heber's daughter, owned the property at 201 Eighth Avenue and in 1915 acquired the property at 420 A Street from her half-sister, Anne Grant Midgley. In 1909 Grant deeded land at 207 Eighth Avenue to his son-in-law, Willard Richards Smith, husband of Florence Grant Smith. The bungalow at 219 Eighth Avenue was built in 1908 by Fannie F. and Albert E. Neslen, who had purchased the land from Grant. Grant moved into 201 Eighth Avenue in 1916. In 1924 Brigham Frederick Grant acquired the property at 418 B Street, giving it to his son.[49] Descendents of the Smith and Grant families continued to live on this block ninety years later.[50]

As the twentieth century approached, more individuals developed Avenues properties. John A. Anderson Jr., a Salt Lake City contractor, built dozens of homes in the Avenues during the 1890s. One example of an Anderson home is 681 Third Avenue. In a similar manner, Lillias T. Staines erected Avenues dwellings. She built, among others, homes at 135 F Street and 434 Third Avenue. By the mid-1930s the availability of lots in the lower Avenues had diminished. A few smaller residences were built by individual builders into the 1950s. In the second half of the century, development would continue in the upper Avenues above Tenth Avenue, as desirability of the lower Avenues neighborhood began to decline.

OPPOSITE. These six Darlington Place homes are all still standing. Clockwise from upper left, they are located at 953 Third Avenue, 959 Third Avenue, 986 Third Avenue, 1007 First Avenue, 1037 First Avenue, and 70 P Street.

Avenues developer Heber J. Grant heads this gathering of LDS Church General Authorities and their wives in 1930. Many of these people, such as Anthony W. Ivins, the first man sitting on the right, resided in the Avenues.

Shops, Churches, Schools, and Hospitals of the Avenues

Adding to the popularity of the Avenues as a residential area were the convenient amenities such as neighborhood stores in the district. Merchants William and Elizabeth Willes constructed a house and store at 423–425 Fourth Avenue during 1886–1887. The one-story cottage with an attached Mission-style store in front was known as the Twentieth Ward Store or the W. and E. Willes Grocery Store. Through various owners, the structure continued to operate as a neighborhood grocery, one of many in the area. In about 1905, Albert and Serena Olson built a frame commercial building at 480 Sixth Avenue. Known as Bert M. Olson Groceries and Provisions, it was more popularly called the Sixth Avenue Meat Market and the Sixth Avenue Grocery. The Castleton Brothers General Merchandise Store, a two-story corner building, was founded at 736–740 Second Avenue. The Castleton brothers operated their store for many years as the largest business of its kind in the Avenues. Charles L., William J., Frank M., James S., Arthur R., and Wallace C. Castleton established the business in 1891, and operated from this location until about 1920. The building continued in use as a meat market and grocery store until 1940.[51]

National grocery store chains came to the Avenues after World War II. A Safeway market operated at 118 First Avenue behind the Hillcrest Apartment building.[52] After Safeway moved out, the store became the Hillcrest Market. Demand for larger shopping amenities in the area led to the construction of the Avenues Plaza Shopping Center in 1967 between E and F Streets and Fifth and Sixth Avenues. Among the original businesses in the complex were Smith's Grocery and Zion's First National Bank.[53] Unfortunately, construction of this project caused the demolition of about twenty-six homes on the block.

Churches, schools, and hospitals were among the other amenities that created a sense of neighborhood. The LDS Eighteenth Ward was one of the original nineteen wards created in Salt Lake City. An early member of the ward was William Bell Barton whose Gothic Revival cottage, built about 1865, stands at 157 B Street. By 1877 the ward was bounded by South Temple, the northern city limits, Main Street, and C Street. Its Gothic Revival chapel, designed by Obed Taylor and dedicated in 1883, sat high on the bench at A Street between Second and Third Avenues. The Eighteenth Ward Independent School was constructed adjacent to the chapel in 1884 but was razed in 1907 to make way for Whitney Hall, a recreation hall for the ward.[54] This

OPPOSITE. The Sixth Avenue Drug Store stood on the corner of Sixth Avenue and E Street. This 1939 photo shows the store advertising air conditioning.

architecturally significant early Mormon church was razed in the late 1970s along with Whitney Hall. Some remnants of the old chapel were used in a reconstruction of the building across from the Utah State Capitol.

In October 1856 the first LDS expansion ward in Salt Lake City, the Twentieth Ward, was created with John Sharp as its first bishop. According to the original plat of the Avenues, three-quarters of the block between D and E Streets and Second and Third Avenues was set aside for a school. The first meetinghouse for the Twentieth Ward was built on this block. By 1884 the congregation had moved to a new building on the same block and continued to meet there until 1923. In the meantime, the Lowell School was erected next to the church and, when school expansion was needed, the church decided to sell the ward building and construct a new meetinghouse. The firm of Cannon and Fetzer received a commission to design the chapel, and in 1924 the cornerstone was laid for the Twentieth Ward building that still stands at Second Avenue and G Street. The Classical Revival building with some Mannerist details has an ell plan with the open side to the street corner, a layout that breaks with the rhythm of Avenues house lots.[55]

The expansion and division of the LDS wards in the Avenues continued as the area grew. The Twenty-first Ward was formed from the Twentieth on July 5, 1877. Eventually a large ward building was erected on First Avenue between J and K Streets next to the Longfellow School. The ward boundary encompassed the area east of H Street between South Temple and the northern limit of settlement at Seventh Avenue. The original building was demolished in 1977 and replaced by a modern Latter-day Saints Stake Center. The Twenty-first Ward was further subdivided in January 1902 as population increased. The newly created Twenty-seventh Ward was built at 187 P Street. This Gothic Revival structure and 1927 compatible recreation hall addition continues to serve as a ward house and is well maintained. A later addition to the Avenues' wards was the Ensign Ward. Members came from the Eighteenth, Twentieth, and Twenty-first Wards that lay north of Seventh Avenue. The imposing Prairie-style structure built in 1914 stood at the corner of Ninth Avenue and D Street.[56] The building was severely altered in the 1950s with a new front that destroyed the structure's architectural integrity. The number of ward buildings in the Avenues peaked in 1953 with the construction of an additional ward building at K Street and Ninth Avenue. Late in the twentieth century the percentage of LDS Avenues residents

LDS Bishop John Sharp was deeded the city block between D and E Streets and First and Second Avenues.

declined. This led to a realignment of
wards and the demolition of two ward
buildings. The Ensign Ward was demolished in the late 1980s and replaced by
townhome condominiums. The white
concrete mid-century ward building
built in 1953 was demolished in 2005
and has been replaced by new homes.[57]

Other religious denominations were
also represented in the Avenues. Members of the Catholic Church worshipped
at the Cathedral of the Madeleine, 331
East South Temple, dedicated in 1909.
The First Presbyterian Church, an edi-
fice designed by Walter E. Ware, was
completed in 1906 at 347 East South
Temple. Although these two church
buildings are not in the Avenues proper
but lie on the perimeter, they are noteworthy here because of their exquisite architecture and their historical value.[58]

The only non-Mormon church built in the Avenues was the Danish Evangelical Lutheran Church at 387–389 First Avenue. The first Danish mission in Utah was
established by Rev. F. W. Flohm who ran the Lutheran Mission in the Avenues in the
1890s. A small church was built at 760 First Avenue in 1890. The building was later
converted to a home and still stands.[59] Lack of support contributed to its demise, but
in 1902 the United Danish Evangelical Lutheran Church formulated plans to begin a
Utah Mission. Harold Jensen served as an early missionary and in 1907 built a one-
and-one-half-story residence at 61 E Street which was later connected to the church.
That same year the Church of Denmark purchased property from Ashby Snow and
provided $14,330 of the $17,330 needed to erect a church. Theodore Lauridsen, a
draftsman for architect Richard K. A. Kletting, designed the Gothic Revival building
and Jens Huid was the mason. The basement was completed in 1909, followed by the
exterior, interior, and tower. The entire building was dedicated August 20, 1911. The

The old Eighteenth Ward chapel stood on A
Street between First and Second Avenues.
The building was designed by Obed Taylor.
After it was demolished, portions of the
structure were used to build a replica
chapel across the street from the Utah State
Capitol.

Tabor Lutheran Church used the structure until 1963 when it was sold to the Central Baptist Church.[60] In 1987, the Central Baptist Church sold the building to a local business, Mahood Engineering, which converted it into offices.[61]

Neighborhood schools were built to complement growth and development in the Avenues. The earliest schools were LDS ward schools. The Eighteenth Ward School had been built in 1884, and a year later the city directory listed the Twentieth District School at the corner of E Street and Third Avenue. By 1894 Lowell School, 379 Second Avenue, and Wasatch School, corner of R Street and South Temple, had been built. Work on the buildings started in 1892, two years after the consolidation of the city school system under the Salt Lake City Board of Education.[62] Longfellow School at the corner of J Street and First Avenue, the site of the Twenty-first District School, was in full operation by 1900.[63] Ensign School was built in 1912 at the corner of Ninth Avenue and F Street. Construction of Ensign School

and the Ensign Ward documents the northward growth into the upper Avenues.

For a brief period after World War II, the Avenues schools served residents outside of the neighborhood. School construction in Salt Lake City could not keep up with the postwar building and population boom. Students were bused to the existing Avenues' schools.[64] All of the early public school buildings in the Avenues have since been torn down. The designs for Lowell, Wasatch, and Longfellow were typically eclectic and related to other early school buildings in Salt Lake City. Lowell School was replaced with a mid-century structure in the late 1960s and has since closed. The building is currently used by a charter school. Ensign School was a reserved Classical Revival design by Utah Capitol architect Richard Kletting. Ensign School was replaced by a new building above Twelfth Avenue. Wasatch remains open in an almost windowless mid-1970s structure.[65]

A 1916 photo of Longfellow School. The building stood on the corner of First Avenue and J Street.

A group of women play
tennis in the yard of
Rowland Hall School
in 1908.

One of the many female homeowners in the
Avenues, Priscilla Paul Jennings served on
the LDS Relief Society general board.

The castle-like structure of LDS Hospital
stands prominently on Eighth Avenue
between C and D Streets in 1912. Over the
next seventy-five years the hospital would
grow to cover several of the surrounding
blocks.

The Rowland Hall–Saint Mark's School at 205 First Avenue represents an important development in Utah's educational and religious history. Although never numerically strong in Utah, the Episcopal Church figured among the first non-Mormon denominations to assign clergymen to the area, with priests sent to Utah in 1867. Saint Mark's Grammar School for Boys was organized first, followed by the Saint Mark's School for Girls. In 1880 a school for girls was endowed by Virginia L. Rowland and was operated exclusively for boarders. The two girls' schools eventually merged. The greater availability of free public schools in the post-1896 years caused the closing of the school for boys. It was reestablished in 1956.[66]

The campus includes four homes originally built as single-family residences. The George D. Watt–Thomas W. Haskins house was built in 1862, making it one of the oldest dwellings in the Avenues. This adobe structure was enlarged about 1871 in the Georgian style, with a truncated hip roof, and in 1880 was again remodeled. Changes were made by Haskins, an Episcopal missionary, but in 1880 the residence became the home of Rowland Hall. The Joseph L. Rawlins house, 231 First Avenue, became part of the school in 1922. In 1956 both the Joseph E. Caine Mansion at 67 B Street and the Priscilla Paul Jennings house were added to the complex. The Priscilla Paul Jennings house, built about 1901 at 87 B Street (on the corner of Second Avenue), shows influences of the Classical Revival style. The cornerstone for the school classroom building was laid in 1906 by newly appointed Bishop F. S. Spalding, and

A 1916 view of the original Wasatch School standing at 1155 South Temple. The school served the southeast portion of the Avenues.

The first Lowell School, with its large windows and heavy construction, contrasts sharply with the single-story structure built in the 1970s.

the chapel was completed in 1910.[67] City directories note the presence of Rowland Hall students residing on in the Avenues. All academic grades at Rowland Hall–Saint Mark's School remained at this location until 1984 when the "upper school" (upper grades) moved to the former Roosevelt Junior High School at 843 Lincoln Street outside of the Avenues.[68] In 2002, the remaining grades were moved to a new property near the University of Utah. The original campus and all buildings were acquired by the Catholic Salt Lake Diocese, which moved the Madeleine Choir School to the campus in 2003.[69] The Madeleine School is undertaking an extensive restoration of the historic buildings.

Significant to the northward development of the Avenues and to the entire city was the construction in 1904 of the LDS Hospital on Eighth Avenue between C and D Streets. Money to purchase the site and begin construction came from a bequest of Dr. William H. Groves, a dentist. Additional funds were raised by the LDS Church.[70] The site, high on the bench, was then remote from the noise, pollution, and congestion of the city. Since its inception, LDS Hospital has been continually expanded. The alterations and additions have left the original castellated structure indistinguishable. At times the expansion has been a source of friction between the hospital and the community. Just as historic preservation began reversing the decline of the Avenues neighborhood in the mid-1970s, new hospital construction resulted in the demolition of over fifty homes around the hospital and the closure of Eighth Avenue between C and D Streets. The Greater Avenues Community Council unsuccessfully protested the construction of the dominating clinic building and parking complex on the north side of Ninth Avenue.[71] The metal-screened parking structure built west of the main hospital campus unfortunately dominates the adjacent historic McIntyre house.

Two additional hospitals were located in the upper portion of the Avenues. The Veterans Administration Hospital was built at Twelfth Avenue at the top of E Street in 1932, but the VA would move to a larger facility on Foothill Boulevard in 1962. Primary Children's Medical Center built a new hospital in 1952 below the Veterans Hospital. In 1994, the children's hospital relocated to a building near the University of Utah, and the grounds of the old hospital were developed into residential housing in 1996.[72] The Veterans Hospital building has been converted into condominiums.

A Suburban Cityscape

During the first generation of settlement in Great Salt Lake City, the largest and most fashionable houses were built near Temple Square on the original three plats of the city. Surveyed as Plat D in 1855, the Avenues were only sparsely developed before 1880 due to the lack of water. By the time ample water was available to this northern bench land, substantial changes had occurred in residential construction and in the architectural preferences of the populace. These changes are mirrored in the houses built on the Avenues between 1880 and 1930. From vernacular dwellings like the Barton house at 157 B Street to the Art Moderne Miller house at 711 Tenth Avenue built during the 1930s, homes changed dramatically. Straightforward architectural configurations based on traditional patterns, limited in form, massing, and ornamentation, became "machines for living." In the years between, a wide range of domestic styles that closely followed national trends were employed in the Avenues. After World War II, the popular common American ranch-style home was built in the area now known as the upper Avenues. These homes also filtered into the few remaining lots of the lower historic Avenues.

Changing architectural fashions were only part of the residential evolution of this north bench neighborhood. The popularity of pattern-book homes accelerated changes in taste. A growing concern for family life and more efficient domestic arrangements became a primary consideration, as the installation of utilities—water, gas, and electricity—altered the working environment in the home. In addition, professional architects came to Utah in the late nineteenth century and designed homes for wealthy clients in the Avenues.

OPPOSITE. The Barton residence stands at 157 B Street. It is a central-hall cottage and includes a steeply pitched Gothic Revival cross gable.

Outside the home, the public landscape reflected the changes taking place in the Avenues. The development of parks, the public improvement of streets and sidewalks, and the increase in commercial enterprises occurred as part of the expansion of this residential area.

Although the Avenues thrived for two generations, growth slowed after 1910 as new neighborhoods developed to the south and east. A steady increase of rental and investment properties occurred in the twentieth century. This trend culminated in the demolition of many older homes and the construction of large, out-of-scale apartment and condominium blocks between 1950 and 1977. Since the late 1970s, historic preservation, historic designations, and critical zoning changes have led to neighborhood renewal.

Developing the Avenues and Architectural Styles

Development patterns in the Avenues are a significant part of the neighborhood's architectural history. The population of the Avenues generally expanded up the north bench from Temple Square and South Temple. Architectural styles in the Avenues reflect this northward and eastward expansion. Most of the remaining vernacular dwellings are located between Canyon Road and E Street. The majority of the later, two-and-one-half-story Victorian homes are found south of Fourth Avenue. This area also includes most of the large, often architect-designed homes in the Eastlake, Queen Anne, or Shingle styles and, later, the Prairie and Craftsman-style homes. Although they account for less than one

Prominent Salt Lake City architect Walter E. Ware designed these First Avenue homes near S Street in 1903. They are examples of speculation properties built by a real estate developer. A Wasatch School parking lot currently occupies the site.

percent of all Avenues residences, these landmark structures greatly influence the general perception of the Avenues. The majority of houses north of Seventh Avenue are one-and-one-half-story bungalows built after the turn of the century. Often constructed by developers, these modest homes reflect the growing neighborhood population.

Salt Lake City's early builders brought a number of traditional house-plan types with them from the East. Often called "Nauvoo houses," after the city settled by the Mormons from 1839 to 1845 in Illinois, these house types were in fact derived from English Georgian architecture via the American Federal and Greek Revival styles.[1]

Although few early residents of the city could afford the elaborate, double-depth house type, a similar plan half as large could be built. Depending on the width of city lots, either the broad side or the narrow side of the house faced the street. The one-story house built for Henrietta Simmons at 379 Fifth Avenue and the two-story house built next door for her sister Rachel Simmons are examples of these vernacular plans.

In the eastern United States a variation of the narrow, gable-façade plan which utilized a side hall was introduced. Although rarely employed in vernacular or Federal or Greek Revival houses in Utah, this plan became at least as popular as the earlier hall-and-parlor and central-hall house plans during the Victorian era of house construction. The popularity of this new plan resulted largely from the enormous impact of house-pattern books on the builders' tradition.

The nineteenth-century house builder often used builders' guides that showed scale drawings of all the decorative detailing—moldings, doorways, balustrades, mantels—required in a proper residence. The Utah Territorial Library catalogue of 1852 listed several of the most popular builders' guides, including works by Minard Lafever, Asher Benjamin, and Peter Nicholson.[2] By midcentury these builders' guides had been supplanted by the so-called pattern books that consisted almost entirely of complete house plans and façades. Potential homeowners or builders could browse through these books, in the same way they examined the new mail-order catalogues of the period, to choose the type of house they wanted. There was no longer the need for measured drawings of ornamental trim, since it, too, could now be ordered from catalogues. By 1890 even mail-order houses, ready to assemble, could be bought from large cities in the East or California.[3]

Many homes in the Avenues are copies or simplified versions of plans from the popular pattern books. The Sainsbury house at 206 E Street is a close copy of a plan found in A. J. Bicknell's book of Victorian designs, *The Village Builder*.[4] The two single windows on each façade have been changed to paired windows framed in a single opening, but the plan and most of the other details are copied directly from Bicknell's book.

Most of the homes built before 1900, perhaps a third of all Avenues residences, are much plainer than most pattern-book houses of the period. Although incorporating a few elements of various styles, for example the irregular plans and massing of the Queen Anne style, most homes lack elaborate detailing and decorative trim. These homes might more accurately be called Builders' Victorian Eclectic. Such a phrase lacks the definition of traditional stylistic categories of the period, but it does indicate the more casual approach to house design reflected in most Avenues homes. These eclectic designs are not landmarks themselves but they do form a consistent background for the more intricate examples of pattern-book and architect-designed homes.

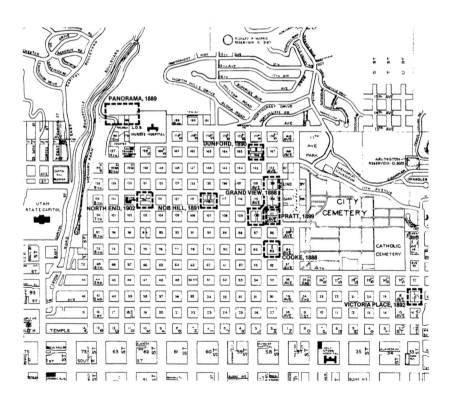

By the 1880s, real estate developers were active in the growth of the neighborhood. The early Sanborn maps of the Avenues from 1898 show a large number of the original quarter-block lots still intact, but later, as the city's population increased and as the original Avenues lots were sold, the dividing of lots became more frequent.[5] Lots were increasingly sold to developers, who served a new function as brokers between builders and home buyers.

The history of Darlington Place, described earlier, is one example of Avenues development. Because of existing patterns of ownership, Elmer Darling and Frank McGurrin were unable to buy whole blocks or formally plat their "subdivision." They nonetheless succeeded in buying a large number of lots in the area between P and T Streets and built at least fifty houses on the Avenues. Development concerns and streetcar companies affected the growth of each other's business; improved transit and expanded utility lines accelerated the pace of house construction east of N Street on Plat G and north above Seventh Avenue.[6]

Nine subdivisions were formally platted and recorded on the northern and eastern edges of the Avenues. All but two of these subdivisions occupied only one Avenue block, and all of them tried to solve two problems that had become apparent throughout the Avenues: confusing right-of-ways and unused land in the center of blocks that had been divided piecemeal by separate owners. For most of these subdivisions the solution was a simple alley, formally platted down the middle of the block. The Nob Hill subdivision, platted in 1891 between H and I Streets and Eighth and Ninth Avenues, provided a court in the center of the block by adding an east-west alley down the center of the block interrupted by two alleys running north.[7] The use of alleys such as these on Avenues blocks increased the number of lots per block and provided access to the block interior. The alleys would later become the access for many garages. Ultimately, these right-of-ways would cause some problems. Controversy over garage right-of-ways persists today.

Early in the twentieth century, fashionable neighborhoods were developed east and south of the Avenues and near the new University of Utah campus. These neighborhoods include Federal Heights, Gilmer Park, and the "Harvard-Yale" area. The Avenues saw a decline in the building of large elaborate homes. However, developers continued to build in the upper Avenues. Some subdividing of large lots continued. Modest bungalows were built on the vacant lots on the blocks

OPPOSITE. The first drawing comes from A. J. Bicknell's *The Village Builder* as a design for a French cottage. The second architect's drawing is from the late-1970s restoration of the Sainsbury house at 206 E Street.

OPPOSITE. Eight subdivisions were platted in the Avenues between 1888 and 1902. The historic base map comes from the Salt Lake City Engineer's office.

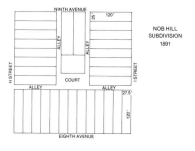

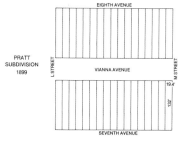

Alleys dividing some of the Avenues blocks were created by the Nob Hill and Pratt subdivisions during the 1890s.

below Seventh Avenue and filled the blocks between Seventh and Eleventh Avenues.

These early twentieth-century bungalows comprise about a fourth of all the homes in the Avenues. Although styles and floor plans had changed, these homes, like the Builders' Eclectic houses built before the turn of the century, represent the filtering down of contemporary architectural ideas to local contractors, carpenters, and developers. At least one local real estate firm, Frank McGurrin's Salt Lake Security and Trust Company, published its own small "pattern book" in 1908. Two-thirds of the homes pictured in their booklet, *Owning Your Own Home*, were in the Avenues. Besides photographs and house plans of recently constructed dwellings, endorsements were included from satisfied home buyers. The owners were pleased with the "substantially built homes with every modern improvement," whose materials and workmanship were "far superior to those of the average cottage built for sale." Owning a home offered contentment, satisfaction, "an anchor in times of adversity," and a "mainstay in old age."

Even though such enterprising publications boasted that "America is distinguished among the nations of the world as a land of home owners," there remained a large population who could not afford the "easy monthly installments" offered by promoters.[8] To meet the demand for rental housing, apartment projects multiplied. At the western edge of the Avenues near the city's central business district, the concentration of large apartment buildings increased markedly after 1900. Built with elements of various early twentieth-century styles including Prairie, Mediterranean, Spanish Colonial Revival, Tudor, and Art Moderne, these apartments comprise almost all of the historic buildings taller than two and a half stories. Together with the single-family dwellings converted into small apartments, they illustrate the trend toward higher-density rental properties in the twentieth century.

Most of these apartments were of ordinary design, but a few are fine examples of architectural styles applied to larger-scale buildings. The Gateway Apartments stood at 28–38 North State Street as an important architectural landmark in Utah. Probably influenced by several published projects of Prairie-style architects William Purcell

The exterior of the Prairie-style Caithness Apartments at Second Avenue and B Street is shown just after completion in 1909. Its design is similar to one of Frank Lloyd Wright's published (but never built) Chicago projects.

OPPOSITE. The Covey Apartments reach up a steep portion of A Street between South Temple and First Avenue in 1916. The Covey was one of several apartment complexes built close to downtown in the western Avenues during the first two decades of the twentieth century.

and George Elmslie, the design of the Gateway was distinguished by the large, fan-shell cast panels above the entries. Unfortunately the Gateway apartments were demolished along with the neighboring Canyon and Eagle Gate Apartments in 1984. Preservation groups led by the Utah Heritage Foundation fought unsuccessfully to save these buildings.[9] The Caithness Apartments (now converted to condominiums) at 86 B Street still stand as one of Utah's Prairie-style landmarks. It is rare not just in Utah but nationwide to find such a large building built with clinker-style brickwork. The Villa Andrea Apartments at 265–269 First Avenue are unique to the Avenues with their Spanish Colonial Revival style. Built in 1929, this building was designed by Slack W. Winburn,[10] who is better known for his later modernist structures around Salt Lake City. One of the best Art Moderne apartments in the city, the Wymer, is at 603–607 First Avenue. The Hillcrest Apartments, at 155–189 First Avenue, is the largest apartment complex of a popular local type. Otherwise unadorned, the apartment balconies are connected by three-story, square Classical columns. The large U-shaped blocks provide enough open space to give the whole complex a satisfying residential scale.

Building Technology and the Middle Class

The transformation in building technology that took two centuries in the eastern United States occurred in Utah in two generations. From the vernacular adobe buildings of the 1850s and 1860s to the two-story brick Victorian homes of the 1880s and 1890s, a revolution had taken place in home building. The "well-tempered environment" became a common feature of most middle-class homes. Coinciding with this technological revolution was the rise of the middle class. Increasing affluence meant improvements in the design and function of the house.[11]

The new home environment included central heating, gas ranges, gas and later electric lighting, and indoor plumbing. The development of the Avenues' water supply and the introduction of gas and electricity to Salt Lake City and the Avenues by the 1890s contributed to a greater variation in floor plans. Earlier homes of adobe and brick were commonly built with wood-frame extensions for the kitchen at the rear, following patterns used in the Midwest and New

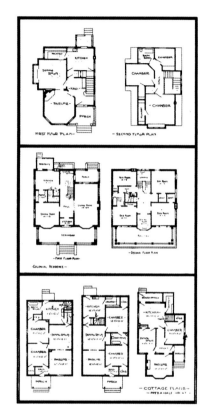

These drawings from architect Frederick A. Hale's published portfolio illustrate popular house plans. The side-hall plan at the top and the central-hall plan in the middle both include two floors. The three bottom plans show the compressed spatial arrangements of small Victorian cottages.

England. In the later side-hall plans, the kitchens were located within the body of the house, to the rear of the parlors.

The use of adobe rather than the heavy timber brace frame in early homes was a consequence of the scarcity of local timber. Brick later supplanted adobe as the primary building material, and wood-frame houses are uncommon in the Avenues. By the 1870s, when railroads made cheap lumber available in Utah, the brace frame had become obsolete, succeeded by the balloon frame. This new construction method, developed in the Midwest during the 1830s, involved "the substitution of thin plates and studs running the entire height of the building and held together only by nails, for the ancient and expensive method of construction with mortised and tenoned joints. To put together a house, like a box, using only nails, this must have seemed utterly revolutionary to carpenters."[12] Even in brick homes, the balloon frame replaced masonry walls and interior partitions. The expressive forms, massing, and wall surfaces of the Victorian, Colonial Revival, and Craftsman styles were made possible by the freedom of this new construction method.

Technological improvements in house construction were mirrored by the development of the "domestic economy," the new science of home management. These efforts suggested the impact of a growing middle class whose attitude toward domestic life was expressed in the ideal of "Home Religion," an accepted part of American Christianity in 1860.[13]

In *The American Woman's Home*, published in 1869, Catherine Beecher and her sister Harriet Beecher Stowe asserted that "the family state...is the aptest earthly illustration of the heavenly kingdom and in it woman is its chief minister." Women assumed this role, they said, not as "men-pleasers" but to properly train the young, either their own or the neglected children of the world. The Beecher sisters introduced their discussion of domestic science with plans and drawings for an ideal home. Although the basic plan is a New England central-hall house with a Gothicized exterior, their adjustments and modifications to the plan were intended to create "a house contrived for the express purpose of enabling every member of a family to labor with their hands for the common good, and by modes at once healthful, economical, and tasteful."[14]

The philosophical basis for writings like the Beechers' is found in the sermons and popular writings of the day's Protestant ministers, perhaps best outlined by

Congregationalist Horace Bushnell: In developing a theory of what he called "Christian Nurture," Bushnell recognized that American society had changed profoundly in the generation before the Civil War. The era of home manufacture, what he termed the "Age of Homespun," was over. The opportunities in the "Day of Roads" that replaced it were numerous, but for most families the father's work was now permanently separated, by the road to his office or factory, from the home. No longer primarily a place for work and sleep, the home, Bushnell argued, should reflect instead the ideals of family and nurture.[15]

This emphasis on domestic family life was symbolized by three elements of home—the lawn, the porch, and the roof. The leisure that the middle-class father worked so hard for, and the invention of the lawnmower, made possible the development of the lawn and the home grounds. The lawn became the proper place for family activities and games like croquet and was connected to the house by the porch. Originally only a shelter for the front steps, the porch had grown to become a covered outdoor living room. The family's living space now extended from the tree-shaded public sidewalks and the more private areas of the lawn and the porch, to the completely private spaces of the home itself, wrapped protectively by the massive roof forms of the Victorian home.

Although most Avenues homes from 1880 to 1900 were built with the side-hall plan, the great variety in exterior massing, most often reflected in the large and irregular roof, gives a distinctive character to the entire neighborhood. The suburban ideal, with its emphasis on the porch and the roof, may also suggest class-conscious social

This Queen Anne–style cottage located at 1059 Third Avenue was built for Salt Lake City educator Arthur O. Clark in 1895. The octagonal tower and elaborate ornament are representative of this style.

aspirations—"a compromise between the city townhouse and the country estate. Both were models of great affluence, combining rich materials and textures, especially brick and stone. The stylistic treatment of the average suburban house was a reflection of these two upper-class ideals, but adjusted to the social aspirations of the owner and the limitations of suburban lot sizes."[16] Homes like the Coffin house at 1037 First Avenue and the Tibbals house at 1006 Third Avenue with their large porches, complex roof geometry, and wrought iron fences outlining the lawn illustrate this new middle-class ideal.

Unfortunately, the machine-cut wood-shingle roofs and the elaborate porches of Avenues homes were generally the first exterior elements to suffer from lack of maintenance and general age. The wood-shingle roof, unoiled and curling, was often covered with multiple layers of asphalt shingles. The porch would originally be ornamented to the limit of the owner's means. During the second half of the twentieth century, these elaborate porches were often removed, filled in, or rebuilt in a manner that damaged the original architectural integrity of the home.

When the reaction to the architectural extravagance of the Victorian era finally set in, it came in the form of house designs inspired by Craftsman-style architects such as Charles and Henry Greene in California and the Prairie-style designs of Frank Lloyd Wright and his midwestern contemporaries. These new styles were widely circulated in journals like the *Craftsman* magazine published by Gustav Stickley from 1901 to 1916. New magazines for the homemaker, like *House Beautiful*, also published works by Wright and other architects. Such magazines included not only residential architecture but also furniture and decorations appropriate to the new styles.[17]

A number of fine bungalows were built in the Avenues. The Patrick house at 427 First Avenue provides a good example of the exposed framing that characterizes Craftsman bungalows. Cobblestone was a popular natural material and was often used in bungalows like the Kienke house at 307 M Street for foundations, retaining walls, and porch columns. Bungalows were advertised in many types and variations such as Chicago, Colonial, and California. They were often associated with regional styles. A fine and unique example of a large Swiss bungalow is the Beesley house at 533 Eleventh Avenue. A row of four small bungalows, at 754, 758, 764, and 768 Fourth Avenue, provides examples of a common Utah bungalow with Prairie-style influence. Although the Prairie style was more popular in newer areas like Federal Heights, the Allen house at 206 Eight Avenue and the Keyser house at 381 Eleventh Avenue are good examples of the style designed by local architects. The 1920s brought the Tudor style to the Avenues. Returning veterans from World War I preferred historic European styling for homes, thus putting a quick end to the popularity of Craftsman architecture. Tudor is characterized by steeply pitched roofs and half-timber surfaces, as seen in the small home at 158 Third Avenue.

Demand for new housing after World War II created new neighborhoods throughout Salt Lake City. Infill construction[18] of small ranch-style homes occurred on the few remaining lots in the historic lower Avenues while more extensive new construction stretched into the upper Avenues. Even though the neighborhood was suffering from an extended period of decline, its location near downtown still attracted new residents and new construction.

Architects and the Avenues

Architecture as a profession developed in the last third of the nineteenth century, coinciding with the major period of house construction in the Avenues. Until the turn of the century few academically trained architects worked in Utah; most had been trained as apprentices to engineers or builders. Self-styled "builder-architects," whose training and approach to house design fell somewhere between the carpenter-builders of vernacular dwellings and professional architects, were also responsible for many house designs during this period. A number of architects

Architect Richard K. A. Kletting designed and resided in his 280 A Street home for more than fifty years before his death in 1943. The home has since been demolished.

lived in the Avenues, and several of them designed distinguished residences there.[19] Although local architects supervised the construction of many modest homes, their greatest impact on the visual character of the Avenues came from the elaborate residences they designed at the height of the neighborhood's popularity.

Herman H. Anderson, a Danish immigrant to Salt Lake City in 1881, was listed in city directories first as a carpenter and later as a builder-architect. He built his own house at 207 Canyon Road. A modest one-story house, its intricate, wooden ornament is still intact. Anderson's most flamboyant documented work is the Murdoch house at 73 G Street, perhaps the Avenues' most elaborate example of

The Peyton-McIntyre residence is the Avenues' most prominent mansion. It was most likely designed by Walter E. Ware prior to his partnership with Alberto Treganza.

Builders' Victorian Eclectic. Without adhering to a single style, the Murdoch house design is held together by sheer exuberance.

Richard K. A. Kletting, at the other end of the professional spectrum, received academic training in architecture in his native Germany. Best known for his design of the State Capitol, he arrived in Utah in the mid-1880s and built a house at 280 A Street soon after. Many of Utah's next generation of architects were trained in his office. Kletting's own house incorporated the side-hall plan and eclectic decorative detailing of the period but reflects his skill in applying the current style. Kletting also designed the Dern house at 36 H Street, another house marked more by its refinement of established convention than by extravagance or innovation.

The firm of Ware and Treganza was probably second only to Kletting's office in its impact on domestic Utah architecture between 1890 and 1910. A native of Massachusetts, Walter E. Ware came to Salt Lake City about 1890 after working for the Union Pacific Railroad in Omaha and Laramie and establishing a private practice in Denver. During the 1890s his office designed at least nine residences still standing in the Avenues. The Beeman house at 1007 First Avenue, designed by the firm of Ware and Cornell, shows a deft use of the Shingle style. The style was a reaction against the florid ornament of the most elaborate Victorian styles and a precursor of the more restrained Colonial Revival and Craftsman styles. Ware was probably the architect for the house at 259 Seventh Avenue, built for the family of Gill S. Peyton in 1896. The Peytons lived there only about three years, selling the house to William S. McIntyre in 1901. The McIntyre family owned the home until 1946. Set on a podium with a large, two-story pediment framed by four fluted columns, the McIntyre house, in its setting and design, is the most extravagant and pretentious house in the Avenues. The home is currently used as reception facility by Intermountain Corporation, owners of LDS Hospital.

In 1904 Ware established a partnership with Alberto O. Treganza, who became the firm's principal designer. Treganza had studied architecture at Cornell University and had worked in the well-known California firm of Hebbard and Gill in San Diego. At least four Avenue landmarks were designed by Ware and Treganza. The Georgian Revival style of the Ellis home, built in 1906 at 607 Second Avenue, contrasts strongly with the Prairie-style Allen house at 206 Eighth Avenue, finished four years later. The Caithness Apartments at 86 B Street, in some ways similar to Frank Lloyd Wright's design for the McArthur Apartments in Chicago, also show Ware and Treganza's talent in this new twentieth-century style.[20] Ware's own house, at 1184 First Avenue, was built about 1905. Treganza's influence on the design is not known. The house stands unquestionably as the most pleasing essay in the Dutch Colonial style in the Avenues. Although many gambrel-roofed homes were built about this time, none matches the grace

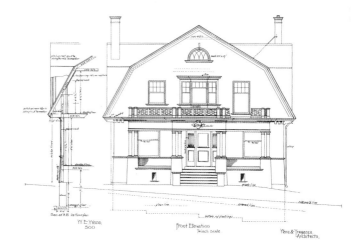

Front elevation of the Ware house, from the architect's original drawings.

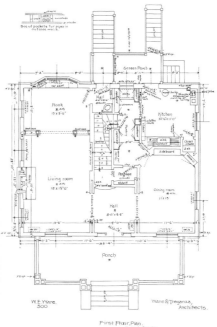

First-floor plan of the Ware house, from the architect's original drawings.

The Dutch Colonial–style Walter E. Ware house is shown soon after completion at 1184 First Avenue.

of Ware's detailing or the balance of the cross-gambrel roof which responds to the house's corner lot. Ware and Treganza's best effort in the Craftsman style is the home at 111 O Street. The home's steeply pitched roof, exposed beams, and half-timber work also shows influence of a more European Arts and Crafts style. The home is fully restored and the impressive heavy woodwork of the interior remains intact.

Another architect, Frederick A. Hale, is best known for the houses he designed for others. He rented a succession of houses in the Avenues but never, apparently, designed a house for himself.[21] A native of New York, Hale enrolled at Cornell University in 1875 and completed the course in architecture, which had been established four years before. Cornell's architecture program was only the second of its kind in the United States, Massachusetts Institute of Technology having established the first in 1869. Hale designed the restrained, Classical Box house at 361 Seventh Avenue, as well as a number of smaller houses in Darlington Place.

Architect Lewis Telle Cannon, of the firm Cannon and Fetzer, built his house at 376 Second Avenue in 1920. Cannon lived in the home until his death in 1946, and his wife continued to live there until 1968. Although best known for larger structures like the now-demolished Prairie-style Salt Lake Technical School and the old First Security Bank tower at First South and Main Street, Cannon and John Fetzer were the architects for the family home of Lewis's brother, Radcliffe Q. Cannon, at 86 H Street, a competent essay in the Prairie style. The most academically classical public building in the Avenues is Cannon and Fetzer's Twentieth Ward chapel at 107 G Street. Cannon and Fetzer designed several Mormon wards outside of the Avenues as well.

A number of other architects also made important contributions to the architecture of the Avenues. The most prolific architect in the neighborhood may have been David C. Dart, who designed the downtown Judge Building and the Covey Apartments on South Temple. He also designed a shingle-clad one-and-one-half-story bungalow at 909 Second Avenue. Its façade is dominated by a unique arching front porch that extends the full width of the home. He was also the architect of record for numerous other Avenues homes of varying styles from 1895 to around 1912. His own cobblestone and shingle bungalow was built just

OPPOSITE. 925 First Avenue was designed by architect David C. Dart for Martin E. Lipman, a prominent business leader in Salt Lake City. The home exhibits elements of both the Craftsman and Tudor styles.

outside of the Avenues at 206 Douglas Street. Other architects included former Frank Lloyd Wright apprentice Taylor Wooley, who designed the Prairie-style gate to the Salt Lake City cemetery. Bernard Mecklenburg probably designed the home at 69 S Street that his family occupied for about three years. He also completed the Cathedral of the Madeleine after the death of Carl M. Neuhausen, the principal architect. At least sixteen homes remain in the Avenues that were designed by John Headlund of the firm Headlund and Wood. The firm of Young and Son (Joseph Don Carlos Young and Don Carlos Young Jr.) did several homes in the Avenues, the best of which is a Craftsman bungalow with unusual scroll-sawn ornament on the dormer balcony rail at 18 U Street. Carl

The gate and planter at the southwest entrance to the Salt Lake City Cemetery were designed in the Prairie style by architect Taylor Wooley. Wooley had apprenticed with Frank Lloyd Wright in Chicago.

Scott, whose architectural work included the Masonic Temple and the Elks Building on South Temple, built his own house at 765 Eighth Avenue in 1920.

Although the two hundred or so architect-designed homes seem like a small proportion of all the homes built in the Avenues, one must also include the several hundred more pattern-book houses whose original drawings were also done by architects. The impact of architects on the neighborhood helps explain the Avenues' streetscape with contrasting home styles and sizes.

Public Spaces of the Avenues

Beyond its residential architecture, the visual characteristics of the district's public landscape include setbacks, fences, retaining walls, landscaping, and public parks.

These features evolved through both regulation and development. As early as 1848 Brigham Young prescribed twenty-foot setbacks for Salt Lake City residences.[22] The original quarter-block lots in the Avenues were slowly divided into long, narrow lots as the population grew. When the blocks filled in, the setbacks were generally maintained, even though the construction dates of most of the buildings in the lower Avenues range from the early 1860s to after 1930. The combination of long-term development and large setbacks produced the important visual characteristics of the Avenues neighborhood.

Another early regulation was the 1851 city ordinance that required the fencing of all property. Originally a necessity in what was predominantly an agricultural village, a tradition of fences continued long after the city ordinance was forgotten.[23] Where the lots on the north sides of streets required retaining walls to establish level building lots, sandstone, occasionally cobble walls, and later concrete separated the yards from the street.

Set in an enormous valley near forested canyons, Salt Lake City did not experience the same pressure for the development of public parks and open spaces as did the more dense and rapidly industrializing cities of the East. Early parks were developed as pleasure resorts or commemorative sites. In the Avenues, public spaces in the early years consisted of the few large grounds of the neighborhood's schools and churches. One example, now gone, was the Eighteenth Ward Square located south of the old ward building on A Street. Not until the organization of local civic improvement groups after the turn of the century did active public support emerge for the acquisition of such parks as Lindsey Gardens and Memory Grove.

First Avenue, shown prior to city paving efforts and sidewalk installation. The Drayton Apartments located at 1119 First Avenue are visible on the right.

During the 1860s Mark and Birthiah Lindsey built a home near today's First Avenue and K Street. Close to a natural spring in the vicinity of present-day Ninth Avenue and M Street, they homesteaded 160 acres in 1865 and developed Lindsey Gardens, one of the territory's first pleasure resorts, which included gardens, picnic areas, playgrounds, and bathhouses. Lindsey began selling lots in 1872, only two years after he received the federal patent to the homestead, and in 1875 he mortgaged the gardens to finance a dance hall. After Lindsey's death in 1878, his family was unable to hold onto the resort and Auerbach Realty took over the land. A few small subdivisions were opened on part of the original homestead.

Several groups were responsible for the eventual development of a city park on the site of the old resort. In 1921 the Federation of Women's Clubs petitioned the city to obtain the property as a playground, and the city leased the land the following year. The North Bench Improvement League constructed a shelter there in 1924 and four years later petitioned the city to purchase the available open land. At the request of Lindsey's daughter Emma, the city officially named the new fifteen-acre park Lindsey Gardens.[24]

Memory Grove Park in City Creek Canyon also has a long history. The mouth of City Creek Canyon, in the area of Third Avenue and Canyon Road, was one of the first campsites used by the Mormons when they came to the valley in 1847. Ten years later this area was deeded by the territorial legislature to Brigham Young, who developed several industrial enterprises there. City Creek was used to power a saw mill and a flour mill. During the 1860s and 1870s Brigham Young gave and sold sections of the area to family members and friends. Several of these people built houses in the lower section of the canyon mouth, probably because the canyon was wider at that point. The upper section of the canyon remained undeveloped since it was narrower and more difficult to reach.

The city began to acquire some of the land in 1902 and eventually developed three parks in the area. The land that became Memory Grove was set aside in 1902 but not improved until 1914. After World War I the first memorial monument was established and in 1924 the area was dedicated as a memorial park. South of Memory Grove there are two small parks down the center of Canyon Road. When lower City Creek was put underground in 1909, the filled-in creek bed was developed into park areas.[25]

Mark and Birthiah Lindsey, pictured in this photo, resided near First Avenue and K Street. Lindsey established Lindsey Gardens pleasure resort in 1865.

Other city projects reflected the growing population of the Avenues. In 1893 a citywide program of improvements was begun to grade streets and build sidewalks. While providing better transportation, this development also removed or damaged a number of large shade trees. The *Deseret Evening News* reported that "on F Street and E Street near First Street, there is a complete blockade of trees which have gone down in a frantic endeavor to make the hilly sections over into flat sections when laying sidewalks."[26] Perhaps as a belated response to such criticism, the Salt Lake Shade Tree Commission was established by city ordinance seventeen years later, in 1923. After studying similar commissions in other cities, it recommended a list of trees appropriate for the city. In 1932, the numbered avenues and the lettered cross streets were alternately assigned London plane, Norway maple, linden, and white ash.

By 1947 the earliest trees in the Salt Lake Valley had become rare enough that the Daughters of Utah Pioneers, as part of the state's centennial celebration, hung plaques on all the trees whose genealogy could be traced back before 1869. The oldest living trees in the Avenues were European lindens originally brought from England for William C. Staines. They stood on the grounds of the Twentieth Ward chapel.[27]

The concern for shade trees and landscaping declined with the increase in absentee ownership of Avenues homes. Large gaps in the tree canopy developed as older trees were removed and not replaced. Sandstone walls deteriorated and were patched or replaced with concrete. Broken wrought-iron fences were removed or left to fall down. The prohibitive expense of replacing sandstone walls has often

The construction of the Fourth Avenue stairs between Canyon Road and A Street was one of the city's earliest public landscaping efforts. The stairs were recently restored.

meant the substitution of incompatible materials like concrete or railroad ties to maintain existing yards. During the period of Avenues decline, another contributing factor was the failure of the city to enforce the maintenance of the parking strip. As a result, in many places the original expanses of grass and shade trees were broken up by gravel and boulders. Failure to adequately irrigate the parking strips has led to disease and death for many older trees.

Decline, Renewal, and Preservation

The mid-1970s Master Plan for the Avenues declared that there was a startling level of blight below Sixth Avenue and dramatically spelled out the level of decline that affected the neighborhood.[1] The Avenues had long since ceased being the premier area of Salt Lake City to live. Fortunately the late 1970s brought about a movement throughout America to "return to the cities." A growing interest in preserving historic architecture, changes in zoning laws, and a desire by city residents to live near downtown and the University of Utah spurred a renewal effort that continues to this day.

Newer neighborhoods were built in the Salt Lake Valley beginning before World War I. A growing pool of homeowners moved to the newer developments such as the Sugar House area. A trend toward multifamily housing in the Avenues started early in the twentieth century, and the first apartment blocks and duplex units were built as early as 1908. City government reacted to the decline of the Avenues by changing zoning and encouraging these larger multifamily buildings. City leaders desired to increase the available residential units near the city's downtown. Also, older homes were not considered a valuable commodity. Unfortunately such measures only accelerated the neighborhood's decline as numerous homes were demolished to make room for large, out-of-scale apartment blocks. Long-time Avenues' residents tell stories of developers walking door to door with handfuls of cash trying to buy blocks of homes in order to redevelop the area. As late as 1969, 10 percent of all property demolition permits granted in Salt Lake City were for Avenues homes.[2] Absentee ownership of properties was another early trend in the neighborhood that would also lead to decline. Many Avenues homes of all sizes were converted to apartments during the Great Depression by homeowners as a means to

Robert Anderson built his three-story tower in 1884 on a small promontory at Sixth Avenue and A Street. Although he expected to profit from tourists who would pay for the view from the top, the base of what became known as "Anderson's Folly" offered the same attraction for free. Anderson's Tower stood until 1932.

gain additional income. As a matter of real estate economics the increasing number of rental units drove down the price of real estate and the desirability of the neighborhood. The trend accelerated after World War II. Owner-occupied residential units declined 47 percent while renter-occupied units increased by 61 percent from 1960 until 1974. The district lost 915 single-family units and gained 1,261 multifamily units during that same time period.[3]

By the mid-1970s the first "urban pioneers" were discovering the benefits of this older neighborhood and its location in the city. The new residents that entered the area realized the need for local leadership to change the neighborhood's course. The Greater Avenues Community Council was formed in response to out-of-scale development and the expansion of LDS Hospital. The group was instrumental in accelerating the preservation of the neighborhood. A landmark victory occurred for the group in 1976 as they helped block the demolition of the entire block bordering I Street, J Street, Second Avenue, and Third Avenue. A local developer intended to build a strip mall containing a Safeway grocery store.[4] Salt Lake City's city council soon became more favorable to efforts stopping additional large-scale construction projects.[5] A six-month demolition moratorium was imposed in February 1977.[6] This would eventually lead to city historic district designation and new zoning laws that put an end to apartment and condominium construction. The Avenues master plan was completed in 1979 by the Salt Lake City Planning Commission. Work on the master plan proved the major impetus for declaring the Avenues a historic district, including A to Virginia Street and First to Sixth Avenues. In 1980 the Avenues would receive its designation as a National Historic District. The designated area was the first major residential historic district in Utah and one of the largest at the time in the United States. Restoration of Avenues properties accelerated through the 1980s and 1990s, and increasing property values and tax incentives aided the restoration efforts.

Community efforts to expand the preservation of the Avenues outside of the historic district continue to the present day. A critical rezoning effort by the compatible housing committee of the Greater Avenues Community Council was undertaken to prevent the spread of out-of-scale single-family homes on small Avenues' blocks outside of the defined historic district. Ironically, these "monster homes" are a result of the renewed desirability of the neighborhood. In December 2005 the city council approved new zoning rules that limited the amount of each lot that could be built upon and also limited the height of structures on the block.[7] Economic conditions first led to the decline of Salt Lake City's Avenues neighborhood. Rising real estate prices in the neighborhood have had the opposite effect. Since 1990 home prices in the lower Avenues have more than doubled.[8] These increased home values have made it easier for citizens to get loans, use historic tax credits, and restore their homes. The Avenues has become a neighborhood of well-preserved, diverse architectural styles reflecting Salt Lake City's unique history.

Architectural Styles and Types

In the following pages the styles of architecture most common in the Avenues are briefly outlined. Longer guides to architectural styles are widely available, and the descriptions here are intended only as a starting point.

While the language of architecture may be unfamiliar, it begins with Sloan's division of horizontal and vertical and with the distinction between symmetry and asymmetry. These two aspects of architectural form underlie changing architectural fashions. Vernacular architecture is balanced and usually symmetrical. Victorian styles are vertical and asymmetrical, with picturesque façades and irregular floor plans. The Prairie and Craftsman style emphasize the horizontal in the relationship of building to the landscape whether the designs are symmetrical and formal or asymmetrical and open. Without any architectural training it is possible to look at a house and determine whether it is horizontal or vertical, symmetrical or asymmetrical. This is the first step in reading the vocabulary of its design.

Vernacular

Vernacular architecture includes most of the remaining residences built in the Avenues during the pioneer period. In plan and massing they reflect East Coast traditions based on the formal, symmetrical Georgian architecture of the eighteenth century and modified by the Federal and Greek Revival styles. These square or rectangular houses are one or two rooms wide and one or two rooms deep. The most common plan is the hall-and-parlor; occasionally a central passage plan is used.

117 C Street, *ca. 1872*

Vernacular homes are sometimes misunderstood to be a crude imitation of academic architecture. Vernacular construction, however, is distinct from both the popular pattern-book building culture and the academic architectural high culture. All three modes of building do influence each other but tradition is the major determinant of the form, construction, and use of this style of architecture.

Gothic Revival

Imported to the United States from England about 1800, the Gothic Revival style was first used in Utah by Truman O. Angell for his 1853 design of the Salt Lake LDS Temple. This style was also popular for residential buildings. Angell's design for the Lion House on South Temple used buttresses, steeply pitched dormers, and pointed arched windows. The cottages designed by John Watkins in Midway, Utah, sometimes mistakenly referred to as "Swiss," are examples of the Gothic cottages made popular by the pattern books of Gervase Wheeler, Andrew Jackson Downing, and others. Because of the scarcity of both lumber and nails in Utah before the completion of the transcontinental railroad, "carpenter Gothic" houses were often built of adobe or brick. Often a vernacular dwelling, like the Barton house at 157 B Street, employed a few Gothic Revival elements such as the steeply pitched roof and finial.

157 B Street, *ca. 1865*

A later, high-culture form, usually called Victorian Gothic, was popularized in midcentury by John Ruskin and others. The style was especially popular for religious buildings. The Twenty-seventh LDS Ward and the Danish Lutheran Church in the Avenues are descendants of the later Gothic Revival.

Italianate

The Italianate, like other Victorian styles, came to Utah after the peak of its popularity in the eastern United States and before the advent of professional architects. Local examples tend to be plainer than their eastern counterparts. In the Avenues, there are two distinct manifestations of the style. The two-story Italianate house usually follows the style more carefully, with box-like massing, wide bracketed eaves, tall narrow windows, and low-pitched hip roofs. The elaborate cut-stone arch-window

474 Second Avenue, *1888*

treatment typical of the high-style Italianate is usually reduced in the Avenues houses to straight-sided arch with corbelled brick drip molding.

The Italianate cottage is a smaller popular version of the style. All that usually remains of the style in its cottage form are the hip roof and the corbelled brick window trim.

Second Empire

The most prominent element of the Second Empire style is the Mansard roof, often originally covered with slate or metal. The style was widely used for public architecture in France during the reign of Napoleon III. One of the best-known local examples of the style is the Devereaux House at the Triad Center in downtown Salt Lake City. The home received a Second Empire addition to the original Gothic cottage in the 1860s. The most elaborate example in the city was the now-demolished Gardo House on the corner of South Temple and State Street. These elaborate homes employed many of the other characteristics of the style, including projecting pavilions and heavily molded classical ornament.

33 C Street, *ca. 1881*

Early photographs of Salt Lake City show a number of Second Empire houses, most of which were demolished to make way for later historical styles. Only a few examples of the style remain in the Avenues.

Queen Anne

Developed in the work of English architect Richard Norman Shaw, the Queen Anne style became known to a large American public at the Philadelphia Centennial Exposition of 1876 where the British government built two extravagant Queen Anne structures. In its most elaborate form, the style is highly decorative, asymmetrical, and exuberant. Towers, bays, and porches are added to the form of the house, which is covered in a rich variety of surface materials.

The Queen Anne was the most popular American residential style in the late nineteenth century and is one of the more dominant Victorian styles in the Avenues. The height of popularity for the style coincided with one of Utah's building booms

1037 First Avenue, *1896*

in the late 1880s and 1890s. For many Avenues residents, the two-story brick Queen Anne symbolizes the character of the neighborhood. Smaller examples of the style, often lacking the towers and expansive porch, were also popular in the area.

Eastlake

This style is named for Charles Locke Eastlake, whose book, *Hints on Household Taste*, included the decorative turned and carved woodwork that became the hallmark of the style. Eastlake himself found the American style of architectural ornament which developed from his furniture designs "extravagant and bizarre." Eastlake architecture is distinguished from other Victorian styles by its massive, three-dimensional ornament. Unlike the scroll-sawn ornaments of Queen Anne and Stick styles, Eastlake brackets, spindles, knobs, and posts were turned on a lathe or carved.

There is only one fully realized example of Eastlake style in the Avenues. However, Eastlake ornamentation can be found on many Victorian homes in the area.

30 J Street, *1892*

Victorian Eclectic

Most of the homes built in the Avenues during the twenty years prior to the turn of the century cannot be described by a single style. Referred to in this book as Victorian Eclectic, these simplified versions of pattern-book houses usually follow a side-hall plan with a complex hip, gable, or hip-and-gable roof. A limited range of ornament is most often concentrated on the porch.

A few examples described as Victorian Eclectic are architect designed and highly decorative. These more elaborate houses may include Eastlake, Queen Anne, and Stick-style ornament, with several types of window openings. Some are asymmetrical Victorian in plan and massing but also include Colonial or Classical Revival detailing.

1006 Third Avenue, *1898*

Shingle

Henry Hobson Richardson and the firm of McKim, Mead, and White were the leading architects in development of the Shingle style. The most important characteristic

1007 First Avenue, *ca. 1892*

of the style is the uniform covering of wood shingles. A reaction against the diverse surface textures of the Queen Anne style, the use of shingles was the first sign of a return to American colonial precedents. The style is simpler and more horizontal than the Queen Anne. In Utah, the style found few adherents. Often elements of Shingle style were combined with Colonial Revival elements.

Colonial Revival

An academic style promoted by McKim, Mead, and White, as well as other prominent East Coast architectural firms, the Colonial Revival was popular in several different modes. In larger and more correct versions, the style was symmetrical and formal. Several roof types including hipped and gambrel were used with classically detailed cornices.

In the Avenues the most common variant is the Dutch Colonial house characterized by a gambrel roof. House-pattern books, like *Radford's Bungalows*, include a number of Dutch Colonial designs typical of Avenues homes.

1184 First Avenue, *ca. 1905*

American Four Square

A residential type rather than a style, this two-story house plan is found in several plain and ornamented variations. These residences provide extensive interior space where it is impossible to face the broad side of the house to the street, as the Colonial and Classical Revival styles required. This type of home was popular throughout the United States between 1890 and 1920. Most Avenues examples are built of brick with a full-width front porch. They most commonly exhibit elements of the Craftsman style or Colonial Revival style.

361 Seventh Avenue, *1905*

Bungalow

This type of home has become the most popular historic type of residence in the past fifteen years. The term *bungalow* is borrowed from the Hindustani and was used by British colonials in the early part of the nineteenth century to refer to a low house surrounded by a veranda. The American bungalow was popular in this country between 1905 and 1925.

166 Q Street, *ca. 1916*

The home represents the persistence of the single-family home in its smallest realization. Because bungalows became popular during the peak of the Arts and Crafts Movement in the United States, it can be considered both a home type and a style. Bungalows can be found in many styles including Prairie, Craftsman, Tudor, and Colonial Revival. Most Avenues bungalows are either Prairie style or a variation of the California Craftsman style. Utah bungalows tend to be plainer than those in other parts of the country but are found in large numbers in neighborhoods built in the early twentieth century.

Prairie

Frank Lloyd Wright, the master of the Prairie style, was greatly influenced by the Arts and Crafts Movement and Japanese architecture. In describing this uniquely American style of architecture, Wright spoke of "gently suppressed, heavy set chimneys and sheltering overhangs, low terraces and outreaching walls sequestering private gardens." The LDS Church became a patron of the style as several Utah architects worked or studied in Chicago during the peak of the Prairie style's popularity. Several LDS church buildings throughout the Intermountain West were designed by local architects in the Prairie style. Avenues homes in this style tend to exhibit many of the horizontal design characteristics but follow a traditional, often symmetrical plan and massing. The large numbers of rather plain bungalows built in northern Utah with Prairie-style characteristics reveal the extent of the design's popularity in the state.

381 Eleventh Avenue, 1913

Craftsman

Craftsman or Arts and Crafts–style architecture was popularized in the early twentieth century by architects and designers such as Gustav Stickley, Frank Lloyd Wright, and Charles and Henry Greene. The use of natural materials and the expression of the wood structure were common characteristics of many of their projects. Exposed rafter tails and purlins, broad sloping roofs, cobblestone, clinker brick, and extensive interior woodwork are frequently used in Craftsman or Arts and Crafts homes. The style included not only an approach to structure and materials, but an ideal union of architecture and decorative art. Copper fixtures, tiled fireplaces, and heavy wood furniture were very much a part of Craftsman design.

453 C Street, 1909

Tudor Revival

After World War I architectural styles related to European design regained popularity with Americans. In Utah both large Tudor and Historical Revival–style homes of varying size can be found. This style of home was not built in large numbers in the Avenues as most of the historic neighborhood had been built up by 1920.

Tudor-style homes typically present an asymmetrical design. Half-timber façades, steeply pitched rooflines, and decorative brickwork are found on the exterior of these homes.

528 Fifth Avenue, *1936*

Art Moderne

Strongly influenced by the new International style, Art Moderne expressed the machine aesthetic of early modern architecture. Also known as Streamline Moderne or Art Deco in its more decorative form, the style was widely used in Los Angeles and Miami. Metal was a major building material in the style, and metal factory-sash windows and aluminum or stainless steel railings were common. Windows often continued around square or round corners, showing the designer's freedom from structural constraint. Stucco was the most common exterior material.

Because of the Depression's harsh effect in Utah, few Art Moderne structures were built in the state. A few examples can be found in the upper Avenues scattered among many bungalows.

711 Tenth Avenue, *1936*

The John F. Bennett house at 176 D Street is pictured in 1906 after a remodel that added a second story. The children on the porch are future U.S. senator Wallace F. Bennett, Harold H. Bennett, and Elizabeth Bennett Winters.

The Significant Sites

Most of the individual structures and sites in the Avenues contribute to the district's historic character. A brief history and photos of some of these significant sites are listed in this section.

The judgment of significance was based on three categories: resident history, architectural importance, and state of restoration. While all historic properties in the Avenues have a unique history, it was impossible to include a full listing in this publication. Even if a home was not listed in this section, it does not diminish the property's value to the historic neighborhood. A brief history of each contributing property is available from the State Historic Preservation Office.

Information on each of these sites came from a variety of sources. Original owners listed for each site are either the individual for whom the house was constructed, a developmental company, or a private speculator. The date of construction was determined by building permits, Sanborn maps, building lists, and sale prices from the title abstracts.

The architectural descriptions include information on notable Utah designers as well as on the characteristics of the structures. Architectural style is a category easily misunderstood. Most of the homes in the Avenues do not represent formal academic essays in particular styles. Frequently they are the products of local adaptations of popular styles.

The letter in the square given with each entry corresponds to the map on which the significant site appears. Maps are lettered A through D, and they begin on page 345.

CANYON ROAD

183 Canyon Road [A]

BUILT: 1888
STYLE: Victorian Eclectic
ORIGINAL OWNER: George Blair

This two-story, stone-and-brick Victorian home includes a large arched window on the second floor. The segmented arched windows, Eastlake trim around the windows, and gable roof exhibit excellent design and craftsmanship. A massive porch added in the early twentieth century dominates the façade.

Real Estate investor George E. Blair, who worked as a deputy county clerk and a manager of the White Star Oil Company, originally owned this home. According to family tradition, his wife, Nellie May Thatcher, designed the house in consultation with her uncle, Salt Lake City LDS Temple architect Truman Angell. The home has recently been completely restored and the original red brick painted white.

207 Canyon Road [A]

BUILT: 1892
STYLE: Victorian Eclectic/Eastlake
ARCHITECT: H. H. Anderson
ORIGINAL OWNER: H. H. Anderson

Excellent Eastlake detailing characterizes this one-story frame cottage. The front gable and bay window retain most of the original trim, but a balustrade along the edge of the hip roof has been removed and the front porch altered.

H. H. (Herman Holstein) Anderson, a native of Denmark, came to Utah as a member of the LDS Church in 1881. He initially worked as a laborer and carpenter before becoming an architect and builder. Mr. Anderson designed more than seventy buildings and homes in the city including several in the Avenues between 1891 and 1897. His daughter, Rose Wilhelmina, and her husband, Clarence Herrick, later owned the residence.

233 Canyon Road [A]

BUILT: 1900
STYLE: Victorian Eclectic
ORIGINAL OWNER: Veteran Volunteer Fireman's Association

A bell tower set on a parapet gable dominates this two-story brick building. The Roman-arched entry includes a fanlight transom. The façade is enlivened by corbelled brick and raised segmental arched window openings. The northern section of the building is a later addition.

Ottinger Hall was constructed by members of the Veteran Volunteer Fireman's Association as a social hall in 1900. From about 1850 until 1883 Salt Lake City had a volunteer fire department. George M. Ottinger, a former volunteer chief, was appointed as the first paid fire chief. He organized the Veteran Volunteer Fireman's Association in 1890 and served as its president until 1917.

252 Canyon Road   A

BUILT: 1880
STYLE: Second Empire
ORIGINAL OWNER: Helaman Pratt

Built before the construction of Canyon Road, this early one-and-one-half-story home faces downtown Salt Lake City. The Mansard roof, paired gabled dormers, wide-bracketed frieze, and Roman-arched window bays are characteristic of the Second Empire style.

Helaman Pratt acquired this property from Joseph I. Kinsburg who ran a mill in City Creek Canyon. Mr. Pratt had helped settle the Muddy River area of Arizona and the Sevier area of Utah. In 1883 he left to serve on an LDS Church mission in Mexico. Franklin Richard Snow, a businessman and son of LDS Church apostle Erastus Snow, purchased the home in the early 1890s.

A STREET

140 A Street   A

BUILT: 1889
STYLE: Victorian Eclectic
ORIGINAL OWNER: Hannah Wells

This two-story brick Victorian home has a complex gable roof. Each gable is faced with patterned-wood shingles. The front porch is supported by Doric columns.

Hannah Wells was the sixth plural wife of Salt Lake City mayor and LDS Church leader Daniel H. Wells when she had this home built. Initially her son Victor P. Wells resided in the home. In 1900 Mrs. Wells moved to the residence with her son Gershom. Gershom Wells was the private secretary of his half-brother, Heber M. Wells, who was the governor of Utah. The home remained in the family into the 1940s. It was converted into a duplex in 1936.

165 A Street   A

BUILT: 1903
STYLE: Classical Revival
ARCHITECT: John A. Headlund
ORIGINAL OWNER: Joseph T. Richards

This is a good example of a shingle-sided, Classical Revival–style home. It has a front pedimented gable with flared ends and a Palladian window. There is a curved, first-floor, front bay window, and a front porch with paired Ionic columns that extends out the south side of the house under a conical roof.

This home was designed by noted Utah architect John A. Headlund and built for prominent Salt Lake City attorney Joseph T. Richards. Mr. Richards was an assistant United States attorney for the Utah Territory. After his death in 1909, his wife, Mattie Richards, continued to own the home until 1921. At that time the residence was purchased by Philo T. Farnsworth Jr., who also practiced law in Salt Lake City. In 1945 the home was converted to apartments.

174 A Street   A

BUILT: 1883
STYLE: Italianate
BUILDER: Charles J. Brain
ORIGINAL OWNER: Charles J. Brain

This home shows Italianate-style influence in its massing and decoration. The windows on the first floor have elaborate, round-topped pediments with carved panels. The second story has fish-scale-patterned shingles. The porch appears to be a later addition as it awkwardly cuts off the top of one of the window pediments.

This home was built by Charles J. Brain, who built several properties in the Avenues. He was married to the daughter of prominent LDS Church leader and Avenues developer George Romney. Mr. Brain lived here briefly before selling the home to David R. Allen, who served as secretary-treasurer of the University of Utah. In 1890, Phineas Young, a nephew of Brigham Young, bought the home. From 1889 until 1969 members of the William Shepherd family lived here. In 1970 the home was converted into apartments.

175 A Street   [A]

BUILT: 1884
STYLE: Queen Anne
ORIGINAL OWNER: Franklin D. and Emily S. Richards

This is a two-story, brick Queen Anne Victorian–style home. A center tower over the entry has a steep gable roof, heavy cornice, and fish-scale, wood-shingle siding. The one-story, flat-roofed porch, with paired Ionic columns on brick piers, has been partially enclosed.

This home was built for Franklin and Emily Richards. Mr. Richards was the general counsel for the LDS Church from 1880 until 1934. He pleaded several prominent polygamy cases before the United States Supreme Court. He is also known for settling Brigham Young's estate. As a leading Utah suffragette, Mrs. Richards attended and represented Utah at many conventions for women's suffrage. The home was divided into apartments in 1925.

178 A Street   [A]

BUILT: 1885
STYLE: Queen Anne
ARCHITECT: H. H. Andersen
BUILDER: Charles E. Brain
ORIGINAL OWNER: James M. and Jane F. Barlow

This Queen Anne–style home features a southwest tower with carving and dentil molding in the tower cornice. Later additions blend well with the original structure. The original Crager Iron Works fence surrounds the property.

This home was designed by H. H. Andersen and built by Charles E. Brain for James and Jane Barlow. Mr. Brain built several homes in the Avenues. Alonzo B. and Rosanah Irvine purchased the property in 1905. Mr. Irvine was an attorney and member of the Utah State Senate from 1920 until 1928. He added a kitchen in 1916 and converted part of the home to an apartment in 1925. The home was split into more apartments in 1948. In 1994 the home was restored by Roland and Sandy Held.

183 A Street   [A]

BUILT: 1913
STYLE: Bungalow
BUILDER: G. H. Adamson
ORIGINAL OWNER: Walter T. and Della Pyper

This is a one-and-one-half-story brick bungalow with a gable roof. The noncompatible addition to the original dormer adversely affects the architectural integrity of the home.

This bungalow was built for Walter and Della Pyper. Mr. Pyper was the assistant secretary-treasurer of the Utah and Idaho Sugar Company. He also served as the Salt Lake County auditor. In 1920 he sold the residence to Lafayette Whitney, who owned a brokerage firm in Salt Lake City. In 1934 the home was converted into apartments.

214 A Street · A

BUILT: 1912
STYLE: Craftsman Bungalow
ARCHITECT: Charles B. Onderdonk
BUILDER: Frank Schuyler
ORIGINAL OWNER: Daniel J. Lang

This one-and-one-half-story, gable-roofed Craftsman bungalow has an extended, shed-roofed center dormer. The wide front porch has large, wood-paneled corner columns on a cobblestone railing wall. The small perch atop the roof is not original to the home.

This home was designed by Charles B. Onderdonk and built as part of the Cobble Knoll development, named after the cobble-stones used for various exterior elements in the homes. The stones were taken from Salt Lake City streets. This home was sold to Daniel J. Lang, an employee of the ZCMI department store for thirty-seven years. In 1931 he started his own company by the name of Langko Modern Electric Company.

220 A Street · A

BUILT: 1912
STYLE: Craftsman Bungalow
ARCHITECT: Charles B. Onderdonk
BUILDER: J. M. Selmas
ORIGINAL OWNER: Frank M. and Eva Whitney

This gable-roofed Craftsman bungalow has a hip-roofed center dormer. The wide front porch has heavy corner columns of corbelled brick with wooden decoration at the tops.

This home was designed by Charles Onderdonk and built as part of the Cobble Knoll development. The development was named after the cobblestones used for various exterior elements in the homes. It was sold to Frank M. and Eva Whitney. He was an agent for the U.S. Fidelity and Guaranty Company. In the 1930s, Hyrum and Lillian Lee purchased the home. Hyrum Lee was a mechanic for the Denver, Rio Grande, and Western Railroad. In 1985, David Richardson and Amy Wadsworth bought the home. Mr. Richardson is an architect and builder and Amy Wadsworth is an educator. They have been restoring the home for the past twenty-five years.

224 A Street · A

BUILT: 1911
STYLE: Bungalow
BUILDER: Bettilyon Home Building Company
ORIGINAL OWNER: George D. and Emmaretta W. Pyper

This is a one-story, gable-roofed bungalow with a hip-roofed, front-center dormer. The wide front porch has been partially enclosed. Dense front foliage makes the home difficult to see.

The first resident owners of this property were George and Emmaretta Pyper. Mr. Pyper, a well-known arts promoter in Salt Lake City, was manager of the Salt Lake Theater and the Mormon Tabernacle Choir. He was also heavily involved in the LDS education system. In 1935 he became superintendent of the LDS Sunday School.

232 A Street [A]

BUILT: 1911
STYLE: Bungalow
ORIGINAL OWNER: Sidney G. and Hattie Saville

This one-and-one-half-story, gable-roofed bungalow has a shed-roofed, front center dormer. The noncompatible dormer ridge was added in the mid-1970s.

This bungalow was built for Sidney and Hattie Saville. Hattie was the sister of Emaretta Whitney Pyper, who lived next door at 224 A Street. Mr. Saville worked for twenty years with McCornick and Company bankers. He was also a sales manager for the Electronic Products Corporation and director of the Utah Department of Motor Vehicles. In 1922 the home was sold to George E. Marr, an attorney, for $3,500.

235 A Street [A]

BUILT: 1924
STYLE: Period Revival
ARCHITECT: Georgius Y. Cannon
ORIGINAL OWNER: Alfred and Elizabeth McCune

This Period Revival–style home has a unique, random-course wood-shingle roof. There is an elaborate terracotta sculpture relief around the front door featuring owls, flowers, and leaves.

Georgius Cannon designed this home for Alfred and Elizabeth McCune. Mr. Cannon, a great-grandson of Brigham Young, had a long and successful career as a residential architect. The McCunes never lived in this home as Elizabeth died before its completion. Henry A. Schweikhart, the vice president and general manager of the Salt Lake Hardware Company, was the first resident owner. Over the years, the basement of the home had been divided into several apartments. The interior has been restored to near original condition.

238 A Street [A]

BUILT: 1909
STYLE: Bungalow
BUILDER: B. G. Smith
ORIGINAL OWNER: Henry F. and Gertrude Kimball

This one-and-one-half-story bungalow has a bay window on the front gable. The art glass in the window next to the front door and in the north windows is probably original to the home. A small gable on the porch marks the entry.

This bungalow was built for Henry and Gertrude Kimball for three thousand dollars. Mr. Kimball was an art glass designer for the Bennett Glass Company for sixty-two years. He is known to have designed many church windows throughout the West. The Kimball family lived in the home into the 1950s.

330 A Street   A

BUILT: 1911
STYLE: Pueblo Revival
ARCHITECT: Nils E. Liljenberg and Alvin F. Sundberg
ORIGINAL OWNER: Benjamin F. and Ardella Tibby

This home is a rare example of Pueblo Revival style for Utah. The battered stucco walls, parapeted flat roof, and stepped-back upper-story tower are typical of this style.

The firm of Liljenberg and Sundberg designed this home for Benjamin and Ardella Tibby. Mrs. Tibby was a teacher at the Latter-day Saints College and later became a prominent educator in Southern California. Herbert Z. and Emma J. Lund purchased the home in 1920. Mr. Lund was a surgeon at LDS Hospital. The home was a rental property from 1952 until 1976. The exterior of the home has been restored over the past fifteen years. The adjacent cottage south of the home was built in 2005 after a small bungalow was demolished on the site.

370 A Street   D

BUILT: 1916
STYLE: Spanish Colonial Revival
ORIGINAL OWNER: Grant and Catherine Hampton

This two-story, hip-roofed, stucco home has Spanish Colonial Revival design elements. The symmetrical front façade includes fan lights over the first-floor windows and fan patterns in the second-floor transoms.

This home was built for a successful Salt Lake City investment broker, Grant A. Hampton. Mr. Hampton worked for nearly thirty-five years for the Consolidated Wagon and Machine Company before joining the investment firm of Ross Beason and Company. He was also a member of the Rotary Club, the Salt Lake Country Club, and the University Club. The Hampton family remained in this home until 1957.

420 A Street   D

BUILT: 1915
STYLE: Spanish Colonial Revival/Bungalow
BUILDER: Grant and Bower Building Company
ORIGINAL OWNER: Mary Grant Judd

This one-story bungalow exhibits elements of Spanish Colonial Revival style. For many years the building was covered in siding that hid many of the original architectural elements. The siding was removed and the exterior restored in the late 1990s.

Heber J. Grant's Grant and Bower Building Company built this home for Mary Grant Judd, Mr. Grant's daughter. Heber J. Grant, who would later become president of the LDS Church, built his own home at the adjacent 201 Eighth Avenue. Mary Grant Judd was a writer and board member of the LDS Relief Society.

442 A Street

BUILT: 1923
STYLE: Art Moderne/Bungalow
ORIGINAL OWNER: Alfred C. and Vera T. Callister

This is a one-story, hip-roofed bungalow with an Art Moderne front addition. There is a projecting gable over the entrance.

This home was built for Alfred and Vera Callister. Mr. Callister was a prominent physician and surgeon in Salt Lake City and the founder of the Salt Lake Board of Plastic Surgery. He practiced at both LDS Hospital and Primary Children's Hospital. He also served as chairman of the Utah Board of Health. In 1942 Mr. Callister was instrumental in the founding of the four-year medical school at the University of Utah and was dean of the school from 1942 until 1945.

B STREET

67 B Street A

BUILT: 1888
STYLE: Victorian Eclectic
ORIGINAL OWNER: Joseph E Caine

Composed of a small, main, hip-roofed block with three projecting two-story bays and a gabled, one-and-one-half-story rear wing, this house is notable for its unusual brick and stone decorations. A corbelled brick parapet runs around the edge of the roof. At the peak of the gables, the cornice rises into a single corbelled step above the ridgeline of the roof with checkerboard-pattern brickwork.

This home was built for Joseph E. Caine. He was the manager of the Caine and Hooper Company, an insurance firm. He later became secretary and manager of the Salt Lake Commercial Club. In 1956, the Episcopal Church purchased the home for additional classroom space for the St. Mark's School for Boys. The school would eventually become Rowland Hall–St. Mark's School. Since 2003, the home has been part of the Madeline Choir School.

76 B Street A

BUILT: 1905
STYLE: Craftsman
ARCHITECT: Walter E. Ware and Alberto O.
   Treganza
ORIGINAL OWNER: Levi Riter

This two-story home has hip roofs with broad eaves supported by oversized brackets. The building is similar to 87 U Street, having been designed by the same architects during the same time period.

Levi Riter, a mining engineer, hired the prominent Salt Lake City architectural firm of Ware and Treganza to design this home. Mr. Riter assisted in developing the adjacent Riter-Caithness Apartments. In 1932 the home was purchased by Harold C. and Elsie Brandley. Mr. Brandley was a salesman for the Hogle Investment Company. Mrs. Brandley was an author for and editor of LDS women's publications. The home is currently divided into apartments.

86 B Street A

BUILT: 1908
STYLE: Prairie Style
ARCHITECT: Walter E. Ware and Alberto O.
   Treganza
BUILDER: E. R. W. Terrion
ORIGINAL OWNER: Lynville C. and Isabella M. Riter

This apartment block is one of the best examples of Prairie-style architecture in Utah. The clinker brick exterior adds to the unique presence of this structure. The projecting eaves, flat roofline, and bands of art glass windows are typical of the style. A roof garden graced the building until 1964. Most of the interior architectural details have been removed over the past century.

Scottish immigrants Lynville C. Riter and his mother, Isabella M. Riter, had this apartment building built. The family had been successful in business and engineering, and they hired the firm of Ware and Treganza as architects. Upon completion the structure was recognized by local media as "one of the finest in the Intermountain West." The Riter family lost ownership of the building during the Great Depression. In 2005 the apartments were converted to condominiums.

87 B Street   A

BUILT: 1900
STYLE: Colonial Revival
ORIGINAL OWNER: Priscilla Paul Jennings

Three gabled bays and three chimneys project from the main hip-roofed block of this three-story home. The gables are finished with stucco and decorative wood framing. The pediments are ornamented with modillion brackets. Two porches extend from the building.

Priscilla Paul Jennings had this house built fourteen years after the death of her husband, businessman and former mayor William Jennings. She served on the general board of the Relief Society for the LDS Church. After her death in 1918, Charles E. and Pearl Pinkerton bought the property. Mr. Pinkerton was a physician. Several different owners occupied the home from 1938 until 1956. It was then purchased by the Episcopal Church for use by Rowland Hall–St. Mark's School. The home has been part of the campus of the Madeleine Choir School since 2003.

116 B Street   A

BUILT: 1891/1896
STYLE: Victorian Eclectic
ORIGINAL OWNER: John Cornelius Edwards

Several early renovations changed the street face of this Victorian home. Originally built as a one-story structure, a second story and the front bay window were added in 1896. Portions of the original one-story home can be seen in the changing tone of exterior brick. A 1924 remodel converted the home into a duplex and added the Bungalow-style porch.

This home was built for John Cornelius and Frances Woodmansee Edwards. Mr. Edwards was a salesman and later a traveling agent for both the Walker Brothers and ZCMI department stores. Frances continued to own the home after John's death, residing in one side of the duplex until her own death in 1962.

119 B Street   A

BUILT: 1881
STYLE: Vernacular/Bungalow
BUILDER: Joseph Chapman
ORIGINAL OWNER: Joseph Chapman

This home was originally a one-story vernacular cottage. It was remodeled into its current architectural style in the early 1920s.

Brick mason and builder Joseph Chapman built this home for himself. In 1887 he sold the property to Jane A. Young Robbins, the niece of Brigham Young, who had been renting 129 B Street. She had a frame addition put on the home that year. Her son Joseph B. Robbins inherited the home after Jane's death. Mr. Robbins was one of the founders of Keeley Ice Cream and Keeley's Restaurant in Salt Lake City. The Robbins family remained in this home until 1958.

121 B Street A

BUILT: 1887
STYLE: Victorian Eclectic
ORIGINAL OWNER: Ellen Brooke Ferguson

This Victorian cottage has a three-sided front bay window. Alterations have been made to the front entrance porch. The stucco finish is most likely not original to the home.

Ellen Brooke Ferguson settled in St. George, Utah, with her husband, William Ferguson, in the late 1870s. There she established the Utah Conservatory of Music. When her husband died, she studied medicine and returned to Salt Lake City, moving into this home in 1887. Mrs. Ferguson was a physician at the old Deseret Hospital. She was also the only female delegate to the 1896 national Democratic Party Convention. She was a Salt Lake County deputy sheriff in the late 1890s, the first female deputy sheriff in the United States. In 1900 the home was sold to members of the Robbins family, who owned Keeley Ice Cream and Keeley's restaurant in Salt Lake City.

126–128 B Street A

BUILT: 1883/1908
STYLE: American Four Square
BUILDER: Oscar M. Engdahl
ORIGINAL OWNER: Lewis and Elizabeth Martin

The Four Square–type duplex incorporates an earlier 1883 vernacular structure. The earlier structure can be clearly seen from the side of the building. A broad, reconstructed porch covers the front façade.

The oldest portion of this home was built for Lewis and Elizabeth Martin. Mr. Martin was vice president of the Cane Spring Consolidated Gold Mining Company operating in Tooele County. In 1901 the Martins had 124 and 132 B Street built as rental homes. In 1908 builder Oscar M. Engdahl purchased the home and converted it into a duplex. The two sides of the building would remain rental properties for the balance of the twentieth century.

129 B Street A

BUILT: 1890
STYLE: Victorian Eclectic
ORIGINAL OWNER: Enos Daugherty Hoge

This two-story Victorian home has a gabled front bay window and a wood-paneled south-side bay window. The upper portion of the home is covered in patterned wood-shingle siding which flares out over the brick first story.

This home was built for a prominent early Utah attorney. Enos Daugherty Hoge came to Utah after serving in the Union Army during the Civil War. In 1868 he was appointed associate justice of the Utah Territory. In 1874 he was one of the defense lawyers for accused and convicted director of the Mountain Meadow Massacre, John D. Lee. Mr. Hoge owned the home for ten years before selling it to R. W. Sloan, who ran an insurance company and invested in several properties in this portion of the Avenues. This home has remained a rental property since 1900. It is currently divided into five apartments.

140 B Street   A

BUILT: 1892
STYLE: Victorian Eclectic
ARCHITECT: Samuel C. Dallas and William S. Hedges
BUILDER: Shaw and Roakidge
ORIGINAL OWNER: Henrietta D. Ellerbeck

This home has a main hip-roofed block with two large chimneys. There is a projecting, rectangular center bay on the west side and an octagonal northwest corner bay. The home's original cast-iron fence runs along the street.

This home was built for Henrietta D. Ellerbeck, a plural wife during the end of the polygamy period in Utah history. Her husband, Thomas W. Ellerbeck, was Brigham Young's chief clerk. She remained in the residence until 1903 when it was sold to William F. Armstrong, who lived in the home until 1958. Involved in the banking and furniture business, Mr. Armstrong founded the Standard Furniture Company. The building has been a bed and breakfast inn for several years.

157 B Street   A

BUILT: 1865
STYLE: Gothic/Vernacular
ORIGINAL OWNER: William Bell Barton

This rare, well-preserved example of Gothic Revival–style pioneer architecture is the oldest remaining home in the Avenues. The house is also known as the oldest remaining home in the city that could boast of argon gas lighting and indoor plumbing. The building has a steeply pitched roof and a protruding bay window supported by brackets. The foundation is granite left over from the Salt Lake LDS Temple construction. Stucco covers the original adobe walls, and several additions have been made to the structure.

William Bell Barton, an accountant, lived in this home with his two wives, Ellen Birchall and Sarah Foster. Mr. Barton, an immigrant from England, worked as a clerk in the presiding bishop's office of the LDS Church. Members of the family lived here until the 1950s.

167–169 B Street   A

BUILT: 1900
STYLE: Victorian Eclectic
ARCHITECT: David C. Dart
ORIGINAL OWNER: Robert and Rachel Patrick

This two-story Victorian duplex building has two projecting bays with a recessed entry section. The front porch has dentil molding and Doric columns.

Early Avenues merchant Robert Patrick hired prolific Avenues architect David C. Dart to design this duplex. Mr. Patrick lived on one side while he rented out the other. He also served as a city alderman and was in charge of early public tree plantings including those in the City Cemetery. The Patricks emigrated from Scotland to Utah as LDS converts in 1863. In 1923 John and Laura Nicholson purchased the property. Mr. Nicholson was the manager of the men's department at the ZCMI department store. In 1954 the duplex was divided into additional apartments.

174 B Street

BUILT: 1889
STYLE: Queen Anne
ARCHITECT: Richard K. A. Kletting
ORIGINAL OWNER: John A. and Florence N. Evans

A central tower is the main feature of this one-story Queen Anne home. The tower has a four-sided bell-shaped roof.

John and Florence Evans had Utah Capitol architect Richard Kletting design their home. Mr. Evans was the general manager of the *Deseret News*. Two of the Evans's children achieved prominence in Utah. David L. Evans founded Evans Advertising while Richard L. Evans was a member of the Quorum of the Twelve Apostles for the LDS Church. He was also a writer, producer, and announcer for Music and the Spoken Word on KSL radio. The home was split into a duplex in the 1930s. Reed Warnick purchased the property in 2000 and restored the home. The restoration included raising the ceilings back to original height and returning the floor plan back to a single-family home.

181 B Street [A]

BUILT: 1899
STYLE: Victorian Eclectic
ARCHITECT: Richard K. A. Kletting
BUILDER: William Crabbe
ORIGINAL OWNER: William Beer

This large, sandstone-and-brick Victorian home has complex roof geometry including multiple dormers, metal ornamentation, and a fish-scale domed partial turret. Some of the home's extensive original art glass is still present.

William Beer hired prominent Utah architect Richard Kletting to design this home. Mr. Kletting was the architect of the Utah State Capitol building. Mr. Beer was an influential Utah physician but also had mining interests. He was the physician in charge of German POWs held at Fort Douglas during World War I. Mr. Beer was a founding member of the Utah Medical Society. In 1925 he divided the home into apartments and continued to live in one of the apartments. The home remained in the Beer family until 1975.

216 B Street [A]

BUILT: 1908
STYLE: Bungalow
ORIGINAL OWNER: Orvin Morris

This one-and-one-half-story bungalow exhibits elements of both the Craftsman and Neoclassical styles. The rafter ends are left exposed for decorative effect. The low, hip roof has two front dormers as well as two south-side dormers.

Orvin Morris, an employee of the Utah-Idaho Sugar Company, built this home on speculation but chose to live in the residence until 1918. The lower level was a separate apartment and rented out for most of the home's existence. In 1929 Dr. W. Creed Haymond, a dentist, purchased the property. From 1950 until about 2003 members of the DeVroom family owned the home. The home was extensively restored in 2003.

226–228 B Street

A

BUILT: 1907
STYLE: Victorian Commercial
ORIGINAL OWNER: William and Louise Stoneman

This commercial structure and residence are typical of those found in early twentieth-century neighborhoods throughout Utah. Unlike this building, most of these stores were located on corner lots in the Avenues. The residential wing is set back from the street on the south side. Both structures have corbelled brick parapets around their flat roofs.

English immigrants William and Louise Stoneman opened this store after initially operating a similar business at 444 West Fourth North. Three generations of the family kept this business in operation. The original signage remained on the building into the early 1990s. It read "Stoneman's Grocery, Our Motto 'Live and Let Live.'"

238 B Street

A

BUILT: 1911
STYLE: Craftsman Bungalow
BUILDER: Modern Home Building Company
ORIGINAL OWNER: Modern Home Building Company

This one-story home exhibits the classic low profile of a bungalow. The hip roof has a front center dormer, and the rafter ends are left exposed for decorative effect.

The Modern Home Building Company built this home as an investment for $4,500. It was initially leased to John D. and Clarissa Y. Spencer, who bought the home five years later. Mr. Spencer worked for the New York Life Insurance Company and was the first manager of the Salt Lake Symphony. In 1922 C. Bicknell Robbins purchased the residence. Mr. Robbins was the general manager of Keeley Ice Cream Company which had been founded by his father. The family also owned the popular Keeley's Restaurant in downtown Salt Lake City.

251 B Street

A

BUILT: 1911
STYLE: Italian Classical
ARCHITECT: John H. Magdiels
BUILDER: John H. Magdiels
ORIGINAL OWNER: Mary A. and William J. Robinson

This home was one the first large, poured-concrete residences built in Utah. The home alludes to the Italian Renaissance style. A balustrade rings the nearly flat roof, and the broad eaves have modillion brackets for decoration. The enclosed east porch has a tile roof and cornice with elaborate cast ornament.

Mary and William Robinson had this home built at a cost of $4,500. They hired John H. Magdiels to design and construct the residence. He worked with his brother Daniel H. Magdiels in developing reinforced concrete "fireproof" buildings. Mr. Robinson was involved in mining. Members of the Robinson family remained in the home until 1942. The home was divided into several apartments in the 1950s but has since been restored back to a single-family residence.

269 B Street A

BUILT: 1908
STYLE: Transitional Bungalow
BUILDER: Carmon Brothers Builders
ORIGINAL OWNER: Winslow F. and Emily Smith

This home was built during a period when architectural styles in Utah were transitioning from Victorian Eclectic to the various bungalow styles. The Doric columns and small gable above the front porch carry forward some earlier architectural elements into this bungalow layout.

Winslow and Emily Smith had this home built in 1908. Mr. Smith was the president of the LDS Ensign Stake for seventeen years. He spent most of his professional life as a life insurance agent for the Equitable Life Assurance Society. He also served on the board of LDS Hospital for many years. In 1936 the home was sold to Richard P. Condie, a music professor at the University of Utah and director of the Mormon Tabernacle Choir. He remained in the home until 1963.

271 B Street A

BUILT: 1915
STYLE: American Four Square/Prairie
BUILDER: Young and Son
ORIGINAL OWNER: Olaf Thommasen

This two-story, Four Square–type home shows Prairie-style influence in its massing and decoration. It has a low-pitch hip roof with projecting eaves. The front porch is supported by brick columns. Most of the front porch has been enclosed.

Olaf Thommasen, an accountant for the Singer Sewing Machine Company, was killed in an automobile accident soon after moving into this home. Fred W. Alkire, owner of the Alkire-Smith Auto Company, purchased the property in 1921. In 1925 the home was purchased by Orson J. Hyde, the grandson of two early LDS Church leaders, John Taylor and Orson Hyde. Mr. Hyde was a long-time employee of the Rocky Mountain Bell Telephone Company. From 1944 until 1973 Clarence S. Barker, a reporter for the *Deseret News*, lived in the home.

280 B Street A

BUILT: 1883
STYLE: Italianate
ORIGINAL OWNER: Elizabeth Allredge Evans

This is a large, two-story, early Avenues home with Italianate detailing. A cornice with paired brackets runs under the eaves. The central front porch has been altered but retains a similar cornice.

A widow, Elizabeth Allredge Evans, had this home built. Her husband, David W. Evans, had been an employee of the *Deseret News*. Elizabeth's daughter, Annie Evans, inherited the house. She and her husband Era Lamberson converted the home into apartments in 1914. This home is an example of an early apartment conversion in the Avenues. The building has been known as both the Lamberson and the Jeanette Apartments.

283 B Street   A

BUILT: 1929
STYLE: Tudor Revival
BUILDER: Noall Building Company
ORIGINAL OWNER: Loren W. and Mary Godbe Cibbs

This Tudor-style residence features a steep-gabled entry bay. The arched front casement window has diamond panes of leaded glass. A chimney dominates the southeast corner of the home. The built-up front porch is a late-1950s addition.

Loren and Mary Godbe Cibbs had this home and 277 B Street built as rental properties by the Noall Building Company. Frank E. and Anna K. Hungate purchased the home in 1937. Mr. Hungate was a conductor for the Oregon Short Line Railroad. William K. McDonald acquired the property in 1943 and rented it to Sam Sakutaro Kawakami. Mr. Kawakami was a Japanese immigrant and prominent member of the local Japanese community. He owned the Wester and Tuxedo Cafes and the Tuxedo Hotel.

301 B Street   A

BUILT: 1912
STYLE: Prairie
ORIGINAL OWNER: Murray C. and Alta Y. Godbe

The rectangular plan and hip roof has the general lines of a Prairie-style home. Over the front door is a curvilinear pedimented hood. The south end porch has been enclosed, and the northern attached garage is not original to the home.

Murray and Alta Godbe had this home built on land originally owned by Robert Russell Anderson and Elizabeth Holland. Mr. Godbe was the general manager of the Ophir Mono Mining Company in Tooele County. Alta Young Godbe was the granddaughter of Brigham Young and was born in the Beehive House. The Godbes owned the home until 1926 when it passed to their daughter, Mary Godbe Gibbs. Mrs. Gibbs owned the home until 1976.

377 B Street   D

BUILT: 1926
STYLE: Cape Cod
BUILDER: Vincent and Peterson Company
ORIGINAL OWNER: Christian L. Schettler

This one-story, brick, Cape Cod–style home is unique to both the Avenues and Salt Lake City. During the 1920s small Tudor-style homes were more commonly built in the area.

This home was built for Christian Schettler, whose brother lived next door at 385 B Street. Several members of the Schettler family lived in this portion of the Avenues. Mr. Schettler was a member of the Salt Lake City Police Department and later served as deputy sheriff for Salt Lake County. In 1938 he sold the home to Heber J. Grant. Mr. Grant, president of the LDS Church and a real estate developer, maintained the property as a rental house. In 1942 he transferred ownership of the home to his business partner, J. George Midley.

385 B Street [D]

BUILT: 1909
STYLE: Bungalow
ARCHITECT: David C. Dart
BUILDER: George Gray
ORIGINAL OWNER: G. Hermann Schettler

This one-and-one-half-story bungalow has a hip roof and front center dormer. The front porch is supported by wood-paneled columns. The window pattern in the dormer is a recent alteration.

Notable Salt Lake City and Avenues architect David C. Dart designed this home, which was built by George Gray for Herman and Nettie Schettler. Several members of the Schettler family lived in this portion of the Avenues. Mr. Schettler was an accountant for U.S. Fidelity and Guarantee Company. In 1919 Samuel C. Parkinson, a livestock dealer, purchased the home. Dr. Dennie O. Martin, an orthodontist, bought the home in 1924.

407 B Street [D]

BUILT: 1909
STYLE: Craftsman Bungalow
BUILDER: Effie R. Maddison
ORIGINAL OWNER: Lucian Ray

This one-story home with hip roof and front center dormer window is typical of the Bungalow style found throughout Utah. The roof flares out at the eaves. The full-faced front porch is supported by square wood columns. The rafter ends are left exposed for decorative effect, a typical feature found in Craftsman bungalows.

Heber J. Grant, president of the LDS Church and a real estate developer, sold this lot and 403 B Street to Effie R. Maddison. She had this home built for investment and sold it to Lucian Ray, who was the owner of a brokerage firm in Salt Lake City.

421 B Street [D]

BUILT: 1911
STYLE: Bungalow
ORIGINAL OWNER: Karl L. Schettler

This one-story bungalow has a hip roof and front center dormer window typical of the style found throughout Utah. The paneled-wood columns supporting the full-faced front porch have diamond-shaped decoration at the tops.

Karl L. Schettler purchased this lot from Elizabeth Holland Anderson in 1908 and built this home for himself in 1911. He moved here from his family home at 215 B Street. Several members of the Schettler family lived in this portion of the Avenues. Mr. Schettler was a salesman, clerk, and purchasing agent for the Crane Company. The property was maintained as a rental home for many years in the twentieth century.

C STREET

33 C Street   [A]

BUILT: 1881
STYLE: Second Empire
ORIGINAL OWNER: William Harrison Culmer

Ornate details, such as the bell-curved Mansard roof, the mahogany entrance doors with hand-etched panes, and the carved sandstone lintels and pediments, characterize this home. The interior includes stencils and murals by artist Henry L. A. Culmer, the brother of the first owner. The ironwork on the towers and porches was added in the early 1900s.

This home was built for William H. Culmer. He and his brothers were successful entrepreneurs in a variety of fields including retail distribution of paints, oils, varnishes, ironwork, and art glass. They also managed several rock quarries and a pavement company responsible for paving the city's streets. The home, once divided into apartments, was restored by Donald and June Stromquist in the 1980s. It is currently owned by the Catholic Archdiocese of Salt Lake City.

68 C Street   [A]

BUILT: 1908
STYLE: Bungalow
BUILDER: John W. A. Timms
ORIGINAL OWNER: Joseph M. and Clarissa Howell

This hip-roofed bungalow is a common Utah design. The original front windows have been removed and replaced with large picture windows. The front porch columns have been replaced by iron posts.

John W. A. Timms built several homes in the Avenues. Joseph and Clarissa Howell were the first owners of this residence. Clarissa Howell was a granddaughter of Brigham Young. Joseph M. Howell, an owner of mines in Park City and Big Cottonwood Canyon, was the son of a Utah congressman. Extended members of the Howell family maintained ownership of the home until 1929, when the property was purchased by Frank and Jeanette Nelden. Mr. Nelden was a salesman.

75 C Street   [A]

BUILT: 1903
STYLE: American Four Square
ORIGINAL OWNER: Emma Spence Ellerbeck

This residence is a Four Square–type home with some Craftsman details. The home has a hip roof with a front center dormer and exposed rafter tails. The front porch columns were replaced by iron posts in the 1960s. The front bay window has also been altered. The window shutters are not original to the home.

This home was built for Emma Spence Ellerbeck, widow of Thomas Witton Ellerbeck. A clerk for Brigham Young, Mr. Ellerbeck had negotiated contracts between Young and the Union Pacific during the construction of the Transcontinental Railroad. In 1909, after Emma's death, ownership of the home passed to the three Ellerbeck daughters, who shared the residence until 1920. A later owner, Charles W. Reese, was a surveyor in Tooele County and was heavily involved in the development of the Tintic Mining District.

77–79 C Street A

BUILT: 1903
STYLE: Dutch Colonial Revival
ORIGINAL OWNER: Brigham H. Roberts

This well-preserved two-story home has a hip roof and front gable with a unique stepped-up façade. There is also a two-story front porch supported by Doric columns. The exterior brick has been stripped and restored.

This residence was built for Brigham H. Roberts. When Mr. Roberts moved into this home, he was a General Authority for the LDS Church. He served as a mission president in several locations and as head of numerous LDS organizations. In 1895 he was elected to the U.S. House of Representatives but was denied his seat due to his polygamist past. Mr. Roberts was also an LDS historian and wrote the *Documentary History of the Church*. During World War I, he was one of only three LDS chaplains in the U.S. Army. The home was divided into a duplex in 1926 by then-owner William E. Rands.

85 C Street A

BUILT: 1904
STYLE: American Four Square
ORIGINAL OWNER: Alphonso H. Snow

This residence is a good example of an American Four Square–type home. The home has a hip roof with a front center dormer. The full-faced front porch has paired wooden columns. The second floor has a unique open corner porch which has since been enclosed.

This home was built for Alphonso H. Snow, son of LDS Church president Lorenzo Snow. Mr. Snow owned the A. H. Snow Development Company and served in the Utah State Legislature. He was also involved in the peach industry. He owned the first peach orchard in northern Utah and founded Brigham City's Peach Days. After 1920 the home was held as a rental property, then was converted to apartments in 1937. In 2004 the residence was restored to a single-family home.

86 C Street A

BUILT: 1876
STYLE: Vernacular
ORIGINAL OWNER: Charles F. and Mary Ann Sansom

This adobe home has several additions. The two-story north wing has a simple, built-up cornice on the gable roof. Its massing is typical of the Federal style which is rare in Salt Lake City. The second-floor windows have Italianate pedimented lintels. The south wing has a Victorian Eclectic, projecting second-story bay window.

The oldest portion of this residence was built for Charles F. and Mary Ann Sansom. Mr. Sansom was the manager of the Twentieth Ward Co-op Mercantile Store. They remained in the home until 1888 when it was sold to Richard W. Young, a retired military officer and grandson of Brigham Young. He served in the Philippines and returned to Utah in 1901. He sold the home in 1905 and moved to the now demolished 305 First Avenue.

111 C Street A

BUILT: 1900
STYLE: Victorian Eclectic
BUILDER: George Morrow
ORIGINAL OWNER: William H. and Eunice Neslen Foster

This pattern-book design is common in two-story, Victorian-style Avenues homes. The gable has fish-scale-pattern, wood-shingle siding and is supported at the corners by large decorative brackets. There is a diamond-shaped window above the front porch.

The home was built for William H. Foster, renowned as a highly skilled wood-worker. A convert to the LDS Church, Mr. Foster came to Utah in 1852. He also sang in the Mormon Tabernacle Choir for forty-five years. Following his death in 1906, his wife, Eunice Neslen Foster, remained in the home until she died in a fire at the residence in 1924. After 1930 the home was maintained as a rental property for many years.

117 C Street A

BUILT: 1872
STYLE: Vernacular
BUILDER: Samuel F. Neslen
ORIGINAL OWNER: Samuel F. and Eunice F. Neslen

This Vernacular home is one of the oldest standing structures in the Avenues. The one-story south wing and two-story north wing were most likely built at different times. Stucco covers the original adobe walls, and the current porch railings and supports are not original to the home.

Samuel F. and Eunice F. Neslen were LDS converts from England. A skilled carpenter, Mr. Neslen built this home, and the Neslen family maintained ownership until 1925. After that time the home was a rental property for much of the rest of the century.

122 C Street A

BUILT: 1887/1892
STYLE: Victorian Eclectic
BUILDER: Joseph V. Brain
ORIGINAL OWNER: Heber J. and Vilate E. Romney

A two-story front bay with segmented roof is found on this Victorian home. Dentil molding runs under the eaves of the roof. The first-story windows have brick arches with projecting drip molding.

Polygamist Heber J. Romney built this home for the first of his three wives, Vilate Ellen Romney. Originally the home was one story. In 1892 a second story was added by Mr. Romney's brother-in-law, Joseph V. Brain, who also may have been the original builder of the home. Heber J. Romney operated a store with his brothers at 89 D Street. He was later vice president of the George Romney Lumber Company. The home is currently split into three apartments.

138 C Street [A]

BUILT: 1926
STYLE: Tudor Revival
BUILDER: Thomas L. Newton
ORIGINAL OWNER: John and Barbara Rosell

This Tudor cottage is a good example of in-fill development in the Avenues in the late 1920s. The home has a small, gabled, arched entry. The walls are covered in random red and yellow bricks.

Salt Lake City contractor Thomas L. Newton built this cottage, along with 130 and 134 C Street, on speculation. He sold this home to John and Barbara Rosell. Mr. Rosell owned the Rosell School of Music at 44 South Main Street in Salt Lake City, and Barbara taught at the school. John and Barbara divorced in the early 1940s and she became sole owner of the property. She later worked as matron of the Wasatch Plunge pool just north of Salt Lake City.

153 C Street [A]

BUILT: 1895
STYLE: Queen Anne
ARCHITECT: Richard K. A. Kletting
BUILDER: Wright and Bonnerud
ORIGINAL OWNER: William T. Dinwoodey

The massing of this home is typical of the Queen Anne style. A one-story turret on the southeast corner of the building dominates the façade.

Utah Capitol architect Richard K. A. Kletting designed this home for William T. Dinwoodey, who was the son of Henry Dinwoodey, the founder of Dinwoodey Furniture. William worked for his father for many years before starting a mining brokerage firm. In 1900, he sold the home to Joseph Enzensperger, who operated the Oxford Saloon. Lucy and Otto Branning purchased the home in 1908. Mr. Branning owned the Chili Parlor Restaurant and was known as the "Chili King" of Salt Lake City. From 1932 until 1958 the home was owned by Albert J. Southwick, an assistant director of the Mormon Tabernacle Choir. A retirement home operated out of this residence from 1959 into the 1980s.

161 C Street [A]

BUILT: 1878
STYLE: Vernacular
ORIGINAL OWNER: John H. Rumel Jr.

This is a Vernacular cottage with several additions. The original home is one story with two gable-roofed wings forming an L-shaped pattern.

John H. Rumel Jr. built this cottage for himself. Mr. Rumel was originally a carpenter for the Union Pacific Railroad but later became a teller for the Deseret National Bank. From 1890 until 1901, several members of the Beatie family resided here. In 1901 Elis H. Pierce purchased the property. Mr. Pierce worked in the insurance industry and was also the business manager for the Mormon Tabernacle Choir.

167 C Street [A]

BUILT: 1873/1887
STYLE: Vernacular
ORIGINAL OWNER: Edward E. Shoebridge

This is a simple Vernacular structure. The off-center front porch with Doric columns was a later addition to the home. The glass block sidelights date to the 1940s.

The oldest portion of the home was built for Edward Shoebridge, an English immigrant who was successful in local business and in the mining industry. He added the 1887 addition to the rear of the home. In 1907 Frank A. Beckwith purchased the property. Mr. Beckwith worked as a clerk for several banks throughout the Intermountain West. He was also a journalist, eventually serving as editor of the Millard County Chronicle. In 1940 the home was purchased by Joseph F. Willes, who was the local leader of the New Deal Reconstruction Finance Corporation.

175 C Street [A]

BUILT: 1906
STYLE: Dutch Colonial Revival
ORIGINAL OWNER: Andrew M. Gordon

The gambrel roof of this one-and-one-half-story cottage is typical of the Dutch Colonial Revival style. There is unusual stick work in the gable.

Andrew M. Gordon, a tailor, was the first resident of this home. Upon his death, the property was sold to Richard H. Jones in 1916. Mr. Jones was an executive with the Utah Power and Light Company for forty-two years. He was a Mason and was very active in civic affairs, serving as a board member of the Salt Lake Chamber of Commerce. Jesse and Cecil Bean purchased the home in 1931 and lived here until 1953. Mr. Bean was in the cattle business.

176 C Street [A]

BUILT: 1873
STYLE: Vernacular/Greek Revival
ORIGINAL OWNER: John Wardrobe Jr.

This is a heavily remodeled vernacular cottage. The gable roof has returns on the ends. The rear adobe structure was built in 1887. A 1970s remodel is responsible for the aluminum siding, metal windows, rock façade, and front door.

John Wardrobe Jr. built this home for himself. Mr. Wardrobe, a carpenter, was known to have driven the final nail in the Nauvoo (Illinois) Temple for the LDS Church. In 1884 Agnes M. Young purchased the home. Mrs. Young was the widow of Mahonri Young, who was a son of Brigham Young. Their son, Mahonri Young, a nationally renowned sculptor, grew up in this home.

177–181 C Street [A]

BUILT: 1873/1910
STYLE: Vernacular
BUILDER: William Robinson
ORIGINAL OWNER: William Robinson

These attached vernacular structures were heavily remodeled in 1910, including the addition of the casement windows and heavy columned porch.

Carpenter William Robinson was responsible for some of the interior woodwork of the Salt Lake City LDS Temple. Mr. Robinson, a polygamist, built this residence for himself and his two wives. Frank and Elizabeth Sugden bought the property in 1905. Mr. Sugden made several changes to the home in 1910 and split the building into apartments in 1923.

217 C Street [A]

BUILT: 1905
STYLE: Victorian Eclectic
BUILDER: Goddard Investment Company
ORIGINAL OWNER: William and Hannah Hardy

The design of this Victorian cottage was mostly likely taken from a pattern book. The home is similar in style to many other Avenues cottages from this time period.

This home and 215 C Street were built by the Goddard Investment Company for William and Hannah Hardy, who had the homes built for their two sons. The Hardy family lived at a now-demolished adobe home at 281 Fourth Avenue. These homes are an example of the breaking up of the original quarter-blocks in the Avenues. The first resident owner of the home was Raphael Brown, who was a clerk at George Mullet Company, a men's clothing store. George and Pamela Cochrane purchased the property in 1913. Mr. Cochrane was successful in the sheep industry in Tooele County.

218 C Street [A]

BUILT: 1889
STYLE: Vernacular
ORIGINAL OWNER: Esther F. N. Dean

This small, adobe vernacular cottage is a good example of the earliest housing type in the Avenues. The windows have arched openings with corbelled drip molding. The original porch columns have been replaced by iron posts.

This home was built for Esther Dean, the widow of Samuel Dean. Mrs. Dean had been a convert to the LDS Church and came to Utah in 1853. She remained in this home until her death in 1916. Daniel S. and Margaret C. Spencer purchased the home from Mrs. Dean's estate. Mr. Spencer worked for the Union Pacific railroad for fifty-three years. The home was maintained as a rental property by the Spencer family. John S. and Pearl Olive Speier bought the home in 1939 and lived in the residence for over fifty years.

229 C Street

BUILT: 1896
STYLE: Italianate
ORIGINAL OWNER: Brigham J. and Edith Hyde
Clayton

This two-story home is a good example of Italianate architecture. The hip roof has a bracketed cornice with dentil molding.

This residence was built for Brigham J. and Edith Hyde Clayton, who maintained ownership of the property until 1903. Arthur and Hannah Winter purchased the home in 1906. Mr. Winter was a clerk for the LDS Church and later in life served on boards of several church-owned businesses. Tess Harper Anderson bought the home in 1979. She restored the property which included converting it back to a single-family home.

265 C Street

A

BUILT: 1903
STYLE: Victorian Eclectic
ORIGINAL OWNER: Richard and Emma Latimer

This two-story Victorian home has a projecting, gabled front bay. The front gable has wood-shingle siding and a half-round window. The front porch, which had been severely modified, has been recently restored.

This home was built for Richard and Emma Latimer. Mr. Latimer was an employee of the ZCMI department store for fifty-three years. After his death the home was sold to Clyde B. and Nedra J. Freeman. Mr. Freeman was the local superintendent for AT&T. In 1960 he ran for U.S. Senate on the American Independent Party ticket. Salt Lake City planner Douglas H. Campbell owned the property in the 1970s.

268 C Street

A

BUILT: 1909
STYLE: Classical Revival
ARCHITECT: Joseph Jensen
BUILDER: George Trobridge
ORIGINAL OWNER: Washington W. Taylor

This flat-roofed, two-story apartment block shows Classical Revival decoration. The front façade is topped by a brick parapet and has modillion brackets. The central entry is flanked by two heavy, one-story porches. An early example of apartment construction in the Avenues, this building also represents the shift to multifamily housing in the area.

Washington W. Taylor developed this apartment block as an investment. Mr. Taylor was successful in the Idaho sheep industry. The original construction cost of these apartments was eight thousand dollars.

272 C Street [A]

BUILT: 1895
STYLE: Victorian Eclectic
BUILDER: Pacific Lumber Company
ORIGINAL OWNER: Edward L. and Mary E. Sloan

A 1917 Prairie-style porch dominates the façade of this one-and-one-half-story Victorian home. The front gable has wood-shingle siding and a round window.

The home was built for Edward and Mary Sloan. Mr. Sloan, a prominent insurance executive in Salt Lake City, worked for several companies before starting the Sloan Insurance Agency. He also served as secretary of the first Independent Telephone Company in Utah. After the death of Mr. and Mrs. Sloan, the home was inherited by their son, J. Spafford Sloan, who was also involved in the insurance industry after a career in art sales. A third generation of the Sloan family lived in this home after 1974.

317 C Street [A]

BUILT: 1898
STYLE: Victorian Eclectic
ORIGINAL OWNER: Henry C. and Emma C. Barrell

This one-story Victorian cottage was heavily remodeled in the mid-twentieth century. The exterior is covered in asbestos siding and the windows have been replaced.

This home was built for Henry and Emma Barrell. Mr. Barrell was the bodyguard for LDS Church president John Taylor. He later worked as a foreman for the Utah Central Railroad and a security guard at the Denver and Rio Grande Railroad shops. He was also an organizer of marching bands in Salt Lake City. In 1919 the home was sold to James H. and Marie M. Deakin. Mr. Deakin was a janitor in the Salt Lake City public school system.

327 C Street [A]

BUILT: 1893/1910
STYLE: Victorian Eclectic
BUILDER: William S. Glade
ORIGINAL OWNER: William S. and Annie Glade

This home is an example of an early Avenues remodel. The residence was originally built as a Victorian cottage. The jerkin-head roof was added in 1910 to try to give the home a Dutch Colonial bungalow look.

William S. Glade built this home for his family. Mr. Glade was a clerk for several Salt Lake City stores in his career. He and his wife, Annie, were also early members of the Mormon Tabernacle Choir.

331 C Street

BUILT: 1879/1921
STYLE: Eclectic
BUILDER: James Glade
ORIGINAL OWNER: James Glade

This structure incorporates an 1879 vernacular home set back from the street. A 1921 addition converted the home into apartments. Behind the brick, two-story enclosed porch is an early concrete block wall with large, plain-faced blocks and panel-faced quoins at the corners. At least ten homes in this portion of the Avenues are partially or completely built of concrete blocks. This may indicate an early manufacturer of this material may have lived in the area.

The original structure was built by James Glade for his family. Mr. Glade, a confectioner and baker, died in the mid-1880s. His wife, Eliza M. Glade, remained in the home until her death in 1921. Her son, William J. Glade, completed the 1921 addition and conversion to apartments.

337 C Street A

BUILT: 1905
STYLE: Victorian Eclectic
ORIGINAL OWNER: Hyrum H. and Margaret E. Derrick

This one-and-one-half-story Victorian house has a main hip roof with a gabled front dormer. The front porch has barge boards covered in wood-shingle siding and is supported by Doric columns.

This Victorian cottage was built for Hyrum and Margaret Derrick. Mr. Derrick was a clerk for the ZCMI department store. Margaret Derrick was a member of the Glade family, which built several homes in this area including 321, 323, 329, and 337 C Street. The Derricks remained in this home until 1948.

453 C Street D

BUILT: 1909
STYLE: Craftsman/American Four Square
BUILDER: Salt Lake Security and Trust Company
ORIGINAL OWNER: Elof N. Engberg

This Four Square home exhibits detailing typical of the Craftsman style. The unique second-story corner bay windows are a common design element found in Craftsman homes in the northwestern part of the United States. The home at 1176 Second Avenue is similar in design.

Elof Engberg, a framing carpenter, bought this home from the Salt Lake Security and Trust Company, which built this home and the two heavily altered homes immediately to the north. A rare tornado that passed through the neighborhood in 1999 severely damaged this building. The exterior was restored after the storm. Homes on the opposite side of this street were demolished prior to the construction of the Physicians Tower. The home is currently owned by Intermountain Corporation.

D STREET

38 D Street

BUILT: 1904
STYLE: American Four Square
ARCHITECT: John A. Headlund
BUILDER: Salt Lake Building Company
ORIGINAL OWNER: Joseph John Daynes

This is a brick, Four Square–type home. At the corners of the home, every fourth brick course has been corbelled out suggesting pilasters. They are topped by carved wooden capitals.

John A. Headlund designed this home for Joseph John Daynes, a prominent early Utah musician. He became the first organist for the Mormon Tabernacle Choir at the age of sixteen. He played at Brigham Young's funeral and composed many popular LDS hymns. He also owned the duplexes to south of this home and maintained the buildings as rental properties. After his death in 1920, Henry I. Moore purchased the home. Mr. Moore was the vice president of the Salt Lake and Utah Railroad and also held mining interests in Nevada. The home was converted into apartments in the 1930s.

66 D Street

BUILT: 1892
STYLE: Queen Anne
ARCHITECT: Vin Crola
BUILDER: Warren Brothers
ORIGINAL OWNER: John Farrington Cahoon

This large, ornate, Queen Anne home features a second-story turret. The domed roof was restored in the late 1990s. Art glass can be found in several transoms and on a first-floor window under the porch.

Contractor John F. Cahoon was the home's first owner. His father had also been a contractor and worked on the LDS Temple in Nauvoo, Illinois. He sold the home in 1895 to Henry R. Brown, vice president of the Utah National Bank and owner of the Salt Lake Saddlery Company. He built a two-story barn to the rear of the home. The home was purchased in 1910 by Emerson Root, who was the chief of staff at Holy Cross Hospital. He sold the home to Ivor and Marianne Sharp in 1940. Mr. Sharp was vice president of KSL Radio and Television. Mrs. Sharp remained in the home until the late 1970s. The home was extensively restored in the 1990s.

69 D Street

BUILT: 1908
STYLE: Craftsman Bungalow
ARCHITECT: David C. Dart
BUILDER: Jacob Jensen
ORIGINAL OWNER: Culbert L. Olson

This Craftsman bungalow has a porch supported by wooden columns. Rafter tails are left exposed as is typical of this style.

Noted architect David C. Dart designed this home for Culbert L. Olson, an attorney and political activist. From 1916 until 1920, Mr. Olson served in the Utah State Senate as a Democrat and fought for many Progressive causes. He relocated to California in 1920 and was elected governor of California in 1938. He continued to own this home and rent it out after he left Utah. Glenn and Edna Anderson purchased the property in 1942. Mr. Anderson was a teacher at Bryant Junior High School. Mrs. Anderson lived here until the early 1980s. Chris Krueger and Lisa Thompson became owners in 1994 and have restored the home.

80 D Street

A

BUILT: 1871
STYLE: Italianate
ORIGINAL OWNER: Charles R. Savage

This home shows elements of Italianate design. It has the characteristic rectangular massing, low roof pitch, and a strong paneled and bracketed cornice of wood. This home began as a small adobe vernacular structure.

Charles R. Savage sold his oxen when he arrived in Utah in 1860 to buy this lot near the corner of Second Avenue and D Street. Eleven years later he built his home here, adding on to the original structure as his wealth grew. He was a prominent photographer in the Intermountain West, and was the official photographer at the driving of the Golden Spike uniting the Transcontinental Railroad in 1869. His son-in-law, J. Reuben Clark, purchased the home in the 1920s. He was the U.S. ambassador to Mexico, assistant solicitor general of the United States, and member of the LDS Church's First Presidency.

83 D Street

A

BUILT: 1922
STYLE: Bungalow
BUILDER: T. L. Newton
ORIGINAL OWNER: Niels Anthon

This brick bungalow has a main jerkin-head roof and jerkin-head front porch. The front porch is supported by paired brick columns. It was built as an over-under duplex.

This home was built for Niels Anthon, a cabinetmaker. About 1942, the home was rented and eventually purchased by Henry Kasai, who came to Utah to work for the New York Life Insurance Company. He became a respected leader of Salt Lake City's Japanese community. He and his family were transferred to a relocation camp after the attack on Pearl Harbor. They returned to this home after World War II. Mr. Kasai received an award from the Japanese government in 1965 for cultivating good relations between Japanese-Americans and Caucasians in Utah. His wife remained in the home until the late 1970s.

86 D Street

A

BUILT: 1905
STYLE: Victorian Eclectic
ORIGINAL OWNER: William D. and Susan D. Ritter

This is a two-story, late Victorian home most likely of pattern-book design. A two-story segmental bay projects from the front façade. There is a small bay window on the second story. The front porch has been removed from the structure.

This home was built for William and Susan Ritter. Mrs. Ritter was the daughter of prominent Salt Lake City photographer C. R. Savage, who lived at the adjacent 80 D Street. Mr. Ritter, an attorney, was appointed assistant attorney general for the United States during the Warren G. Harding administration in 1921. He sold the home when he moved to Washington, D.C. In 1929 Sybella Clayton Bassett, a leading Utah pianist, moved into the home.

89 D Street [A]

BUILT: 1890
STYLE: Commercial
ORIGINAL OWNER: Romney Brothers and Company

This commercial structure is representative of many small grocery stores that served the Avenues from the late nineteenth century until the 1950s. This building has remained open as some type of store since its construction.

Romney Brothers and Company opened this general store about 1890. The company was led by three brothers, Heber J., George J., and Miles A. Romney, and family friend, Nephi Y. Scofield. In 1898 the Romney family sold the store. A later owner was William Lloyd, who was an early professional baseball player in Salt Lake City. He lived at 357 Second Avenue when he purchased the business. He lost the store during the Great Depression. In the 1930s and 1940s the store was known as the Peoples Market.

121 D Street [A]

BUILT: 1890
STYLE: Victorian Eclectic
ORIGINAL OWNER: George L. Savage

This Victorian cottage has a truncated hip roof and a projecting front bay. The bay has a bracketed cornice and bay window.

This home was built for George L. Savage, who was the son of Salt Lake City's leading early photographers, Charles R. and Annie A. Savage. He eventually worked in the family business. Mr. Savage remained in the home until 1900. For most of the next century, several owners maintained the home as a rental property.

167 D Street [A]

BUILT: 1883
STYLE: Victorian Eclectic
ORIGINAL OWNER: Margaret A. T. and George Romney

This home has a two-story, gable-roofed main section with the gable facing the street. Much of the home's decoration was covered in asbestos siding in the 1950s. The siding has since been removed and the exterior restored. The wooden front bay window retains its Victorian detailing.

Prominent Avenues leader and businessman George Romney built this home for Margaret Ann Thomas Romney, one of his plural wives. She died in the home in 1915. Numerous owners maintained the property as a rental unit for much of the rest of the twentieth century.

176 D Street   A

BUILT: 1888/1902
STYLE: American Four Square
BUILDER: James Sabine
ORIGINAL OWNER: James Sabine

This large, two-story Avenues home has a hip roof and broad eaves. The upper walls have wood-shingle siding while the first story is red brick. The second story of the current structure was added in 1902.

A local contractor, James Sabine, built this home for his family. He sold the property in 1897 to John F. Bennett. Mr. Bennett became the principal owner of the Sears Paint and Glass Company that same year and soon changed the name to Bennett Paint and Glass Company. The company would remain a prominent Utah business for the next ninety years. The home would also remain in the Bennett family. Former U.S. senator Wallace F. Bennett grew up in this home. He was the father of U.S. senator Robert Bennett.

188 D Street   A

BUILT: 1908
STYLE: Craftsman Bungalow
ARCHITECT: David C. Dart
ORIGINAL OWNER: James P. Sharp

This Craftsman bungalow has a center balcony dormer and half-timber decoration on both the north and south gables. The first-floor porch is supported by paired wooden columns and has exposed brackets that are typical of the style.

The home was designed by noted architect David C. Dart for James P. Sharp, a Utah historian and authority on the Pony Express. Mr. Sharp served as director for several companies including the Pleasant Grove Canning Company, Standard Furniture, and the State Bank of Park City. He was also an early and long-time leader of the Boy Scouts in the state. He remained in the home until his death in 1968. Dennis R. Phillips, owner of the Phillips Gallery, purchased the home in 1973. He has maintained and restored the residence.

214 D Street   A

BUILT: 1908
STYLE: American Four Square
BUILDER: W. J. Dean
ORIGINAL OWNER: George F. and Susannah Hill Evans

This two-story, Four Square–type home exhibits Neoclassical influences. Doric columns support the front porch that covers the face of the home.

George F. and Susannah Hill Evans hired W. J. Dean to build this home soon after they were married. The land was acquired from Mr. Evans's father. George was the manager of the Souvenir Novelty Company and is credited with inventing the salt bag postcards. The Evans family moved next door to the now-demolished 208 D Street in 1920 and sold this property to William and Isabella Grace. They maintained the property as a rental until 1935. At that time their tenants, Charles and Emma Whitehead, purchased the home. Mr. Whitehead was a mechanical arts teacher at West High School for thirty years.

215–217 D Street [A]

BUILT: 1885/1905
STYLE: Greek Revival
ORIGINAL OWNER: George Reynolds

The heavy cornice and returns on the gables of this adobe house show the influence of the Greek Revival style. Additions were made to this home in 1905 and 1920.

The home's first owner was George Reynolds, who served as secretary to LDS president Brigham Young. Amelia Jane Schofield became Mr. Reynolds's second wife in 1874, and this marriage became a test case for the 1862 federal antibigamy law. Mr. Reynolds was convicted and sentenced to one year in prison. His case was appealed to the U.S. Supreme Court, which upheld the ruling in 1879. Amelia Jane Schofield mainly resided in this residence. Mr. Reynolds' third wife lived at the now-demolished 333 Fourth Avenue. Members of the Reynolds family lived in this home until 1927. The building is currently split into several apartments.

225 D Street [A]

BUILT: 1905
STYLE: Victorian Eclectic
BUILDER: Anderson Realty Company
ORIGINAL OWNER: William P. and Florence Fowler

This Victorian cottage has a hip roof that flares out at the eaves. A segmental dormer projects from the front of the roof. The front porch is supported by Doric columns.

The Anderson Realty Company constructed and sold numerous homes throughout the Avenues. This home was sold to William and Florence Fowler. Mr. Fowler was an employee of the Salt Lake Hardware Company. In 1923 they sold the residence to Harold Bennett, who worked for the family business, Bennett Paint and Glass Company. He also later served as president of the ZCMI department store. In 1930, ownership of the property transferred to Wellington B. and Elizabeth Stafford. Mr. Stafford, Harold Bennett's uncle, also worked for Bennett Paint and Glass Company.

231 D Street [A]

BUILT: 1912
STYLE: Bungalow
ARCHITECT: Lewis Telle Cannon and John Fetzer
BUILDER: J. R. Singleton
ORIGINAL OWNER: Edwin Quayle Cannon

This bungalow has a hip roof and front center dormer typical of the style. The front porch is supported by brick pillars and square columns with Prairie-style decoration on top.

The home was built for Edwin Quayle Cannon, son of LDS Church president George Q. Cannon. Edwin was the president of the Salt Lake Stamp Company and also served as director of the Utah Manufacturers Association and president of the Salt Lake Exchange Club. His brother, Lewis Telle Cannon, who designed the home, was a prominent architect in the city. His firm, Cannon and Fetzer, designed several notable buildings including West High School and the University of Utah's Park Building.

236 D Street A

BUILT: 1866
STYLE: Vernacular
ORIGINAL OWNER: Henry and Ann S. Puzey

This vernacular structure may contain an earlier adobe home. The one-story, stucco-covered wing is most likely the 1866 portion of the home. The two-story portion of the home was covered in aluminum siding in the 1950s. The siding has been removed and stucco covers the original adobe.

Henry and Ann Puzey came to Utah as Mormon converts in 1866 and acquired a quarter of this block. Mr. Puzey, a blacksmith and wheelwright, later became a carriage and wagon builder. The Puzey sons built homes on the lot at 222, 230, and 234 D Street. All homes were built by the Taylor, Romney, and Armstrong Company. This home remained in the Puzey family for over seventy-five years.

254–256 D Street A

BUILT: 1913
STYLE: Second Renaissance Revival
ORIGINAL OWNER: Clayton T. Thatcher and Martha J. Hines

This is a two-story apartment block representing the early trend toward multifamily housing in the neighborhood. The flat roof has a brick parapet. The second story has narrow, corbelled-brick belt courses resembling rustications, and a wider belt course separates the first and second stories.

Clayton Thatcher was secretary-treasurer of Clayton Piano Company and Martha Hines was the wife of Frank Hines. They built this building as a joint investment project. The relationship between Thatcher and Hines is not known. This structure was originally a duplex but was converted into multiple apartments in 1966.

275 D Street A

BUILT: 1906
STYLE: Victorian Eclectic
BUILDER: William D. Pinney
ORIGINAL OWNER: William D. and Sophia Pinney

This one-and-one-half-story Victorian home is of pattern-book design. The small, projecting front gable has large returns with a carved sunburst panel above framing a small window. The original wood front porch columns were replaced with wrought iron ones in the 1960s. The porch has now been restored.

William D. Pinney was a patternmaker at Silver Brothers Iron Works Company when this home was built. Mr. Pinney most likely constructed the home himself, as he was also a building contractor. He would serve as building inspector for Salt Lake City until 1935. He died in 1940 and the home was purchased by a school teacher named Joseph Andrew Anderson.

289 D Street A

BUILT: 1909
STYLE: Craftsman Bungalow
ARCHITECT: William J. Cannonville
BUILDER: W. Scott Weiler
ORIGINAL OWNER: William D. and Alice N. Harris

A scalloped cornice runs along the front of the main roof on this one-story Craftsman bungalow.

Developer W. Scott Weiler built this home and 287 D Street as investments. This home was sold to William D. Harris, who was a clerk for the Oregon Short Line Railroad and later a controller for the Portland Cement Company. The Harris family remained in the home until 1962.

E STREET

75 E Street A

BUILT: 1906
STYLE: Craftsman/American Four Square
ORIGINAL OWNER: Thomas Marioneaux

This home is one of the earliest in the Avenues to show Craftsman detailing. The roof of the house flares out to form broad eaves which are supported by oversized exposed brackets. The front porch has paired wood columns on a sandstone foundation.

This home was built for Thomas Marioneaux, a prominent attorney in Salt Lake City who served briefly as district attorney. Ralph D. Pomeroy purchased the property in 1917. Mr. Pomeroy was employed by the Utah Coal Company and would eventually be vice president of the firm. Walter B. LeSueur, owner of the LeSueur Market at 752 Sixth Avenue, lived in the home from 1953 until 1963. Hyrum C. Cieslak converted the building into a fourplex in 1965.

77 E Street A

BUILT: 1911
STYLE: Craftsman/Tudor Revival
ARCHITECT: Lewis Telle Cannon and John Fetzer
ORIGINAL OWNER: Martha T. Cannon

The design of this gable-roofed home is a mix of popular styles. The front façade includes half-timbered gable decoration typical of the Tudor Revival style. The front porch is supported by Craftsman-style, battered wood columns.

Lewis Telle Cannon's architecture firm designed this home for his mother, Martha Telle Cannon. She was a widow and fourth wife of former LDS Church president George Q. Cannon. She lived in the home until 1917. Son-in-law and Salt Lake City mayor C. Clarence Nelson lived here after Mrs. Cannon moved to 313 Third Avenue. In 1925 the home was converted into apartments. In the 1930s the property was owned by J. Reuben Clark, who was an ambassador to Mexico and a prominent LDS Church leader.

78 E Street A

BUILT: 1874
STYLE: Vernacular
ORIGINAL OWNER: John Squires

This plain, one-story vernacular cottage is devoid of almost all stylistic ornament with the exception of the Greek Revival returns on the gables. The shutters on the façade and the columned entrance pergola are not original to the home.

John Squires was deeded this property from the mayor's office in 1870. Mr. Squires was a barber, serving as Brigham Young's personal barber. He had four wives. In the early 1890s he sold the home to Thomas G. Allen, an electrician who eventually opened his T. G. Allen Electrical Supply Store in 1909 in the adjacent commercial structure. Mr. Allen installed some of the first electrical wiring in the Salt Lake LDS Temple. William O. Bennett purchased the home and store in 1934 and converted the store into a grocery business.

82 E Street

A

BUILT: 1909
STYLE: Commercial
ORIGINAL OWNER: Thomas G. Allen

This is a two-story commercial structure that has had residential use. An older adobe section at the rear of the building most likely dates back to the 1870s.

Thomas G. Allen was a contracting electrician who did a variety of electrical wiring repair and installations. He is known to have installed some of the original wiring for the Salt Lake LDS Temple. This building housed the T. G. Allen Electric Supply Company until 1934 when William O. Bennett purchased this building and the home at 78 E Street. He operated Bennett's Market from this site until 1956. The building was later converted into apartments and housed a dry cleaning business. In 1999 Cruser Rowland restored the structure. It housed an art gallery for several years before becoming a coffee business.

87 E Street

A

BUILT: 1890
STYLE: Queen Anne
ORIGINAL OWNER: Parley L. Williams

When this home was built, it was one of the largest mansions in the Avenues. It has extensive carved stonework and an elaborate wraparound porch with knob-and-spindle balustrades. Leaded glasswork can be found in the major windows. The home was condemned in the late 1980s due to an advanced state of disrepair but has since been restored.

The first owner of this mansion was Parley L. Williams, a general counsel for the Oregon Short Line Railroad. Later residents included drama critic Glen Miller and mining developer Ernest L. Godbe. Jennie L. Cohn, owner of Cohn Dry Goods Store, converted the home to apartments in the 1920s. Eventually eighteen apartments were located in the building. Breck Anderson purchased the home in 1990 and undertook its extensive restoration.

162 E Street

A

BUILT: 1911
STYLE: Victorian Eclectic/Bungalow
BUILDER: Henry Luff
ORIGINAL OWNER: Henry and Lovina Luff

This one-story, gable-roofed cottage was built as a bungalow with Victorian detailing. The year 1911 was very late to be adding Victorian style to a home. The front porch has been altered.

Henry Luff built this home for his family. Mr. Luff was a carpenter and had worked on the Salt Lake City LDS Temple and Tabernacle. Members of the Luff family owned several different homes on this block. From 1925 until 1936 Fanny Hatfield resided in the home. Mrs. Hatfield was employed by the ZCMI Department Store.

167 E Street

BUILT: 1903
STYLE: Victorian Eclectic
ORIGINAL OWNER: George E. and Elizabeth O.
Romney

This is a Victorian home with a projecting front bay. The front gable is covered in wood-shingle siding. The front porch has been removed from the home.

George E. and Elizabeth O. Romney moved from 359 Third Avenue to this new home upon its completion in 1903. He was a son of prominent Avenues businessman and church leader George Romney. George E. Romney became a leading lumber distributor in Utah. Three of his sons who grew up in this home were successful athletes. D. L. Romney coached football at Utah State. Milton Romney was an All-American football player at Chicago University. George O. Romney was athletic director at Brigham Young University. Mr. Romney's second wife, Ardelle D. Romney, owned the home until 1949.

168 E Street

BUILT: 1903
STYLE: Victorian Eclectic
ORIGINAL OWNER: William W. and Hermia P.
Rogers

This is a one-and-one-half-story Victorian cottage. The complex roof massing shows the influence of the Queen Anne style. The multiple gables are covered in wood-shingle siding. The front porch is supported by Doric columns. The original fencing from Salt Lake City's Crager Iron Works runs along the street.

The home was built for William and Hermia Rogers. He was a part owner and bookkeeper for the Rogers Cigar Company. Mrs. Rogers was a fur furnisher at Auerbachs Department Store. Mr. Rogers died in the home in 1947. Their son, Wallace Rogers, a salesman for the Bennett Paint and Glass Company, owned the home until 1958.

178 E Street

BUILT: 1873
STYLE: Queen Anne
ORIGINAL OWNER: William and Martha Lambourne

A tall, rectangular tower with pyramidal roof is the main architectural feature of this Queen Anne mansion. The elaborate front gable has a metal finial, carved-panel fascia boards, and a large sunburst panel.

It took five years to complete construction of this home for William and Martha Lambourne, who came to Utah in 1866. Mr. Lambourne was a wallpaper hanger and designer. Joseph J. Daynes, the first LDS Tabernacle organist, lived here briefly in 1889 before moving to 38 D Street. Mining engineer Benjamin W. Tibby purchased the property in 1900. His family retained ownership of the property until 1925 when Frank H. Coulter bought the house. Mr. Coulter, building manager for the Continental Bank Building, converted the home into apartments in 1932.

185–187 E Street   A

BUILT: 1875–1879/1909
STYLE: Italianate/Commercial
ORIGINAL OWNER: William W. Salmon

This is a two-story, gable-roofed house in the Italianate style. The house has heavy, bracketed cornices with returns. The one-story, wooden front bay has pilasters, dentil molding, and delicate brackets. The north side of the home is cut off by the adjoining commercial structure which was added in 1909.

William W. Salmon lived in this residence and operated a meat market from a frame building on the corner of the block. Mr. Salmon was a former Salt Lake City police officer. In 1909 the larger commercial structure incorporated the home. It has been a rental property since Mr. Salmon moved to 183 E Street in 1909, and was converted into a duplex around 1920. Recently several successful Avenues businesses have occupied the commercial building.

188 E Street   A

BUILT: 1889
STYLE: Victorian Eclectic
ORIGINAL OWNER: Martha Wernham Lambourne

This one-story Victorian cottage has multiple hip roofs. Several additions have been made to the home.

The first resident of this home was Martha Wernham Lambourne, widow of William Lambourne, and the mother of thirteen children. She lived here until her death in 1912. Eugene A. Lambourne inherited the home from his mother. Mr. Lambourne was a musician and paperhanger, and played steel guitar and banjo. From 1921 until 1974 Warren J. Thomas owned the property. Mr. Thomas was a clerk for the Union Pacific Railroad.

206 E Street   A

BUILT: 1881
STYLE: Second Empire
BUILDER: Brice W. Sainsbury
ORIGINAL OWNER: Brice W. and Martha Z. Sainsbury

The mansard roof of this home is a common trait of the Second Empire style. Homes with large mansard roofs are rare in the Avenues. The design of this home was taken from a popular pattern book of the period, A. J. Bicknell's *The Village Builder*. The original fence by Crager Iron Works of Salt Lake City runs along the street.

Music is a common theme running through the history of this home. Brice W. Sainsbury built the home for his family. He was a carpenter and sang in the Mormon Tabernacle Choir. William Nelson Morris obtained ownership in 1935. Mr. Morris was a musician. He sold musical instruments for the Beesley Music Company. He also played violin for the Utah Symphony and became president of the Utah Federation of Musicians.

277 E Street A

BUILT: 1908
STYLE: Bungalow
ARCHITECT: William J. Cannonville
BUILDER: Goddard Investment Company
ORIGINAL OWNER: Orson D. Romney

This bungalow has a hip roof and a front center dormer. The front porch is supported by square wooden columns. It is similar to 279 E Street which was built by the same developer.

Architect William J. Cannonville designed this home and several others on this block for Orson D. Romney and the Goddard Investment Company. Mr. Romney, part of the prominent Romney family of Avenues business and church leaders, owned the George Romney Lumber Company. The home was a rental unit until 1920. His son, Melbourne Romney, moved into the home at that time. He was also involved in the local lumber industry. Mary Rose Reese Mosley purchased the home in 1927 and maintained ownership of this home until 1968.

307 E Street A

BUILT: 1890
STYLE: Victorian Eclectic
BUILDER: Taylor, Romney, and Armstrong
ORIGINAL OWNER: James W. Wright

This one-story Victorian cottage is most likely from a pattern-book design. The bay has a large front window with elaborate Italianate decoration and a sunburst carving. The house is covered with aluminum siding and the porch columns have been replaced by iron posts. 303 E Street was built by the same developer.

James W. Wright was a carpenter employed by the Taylor, Romney, and Armstrong construction firm. He had done a lot of carpentry work on the Salt Lake City LDS Temple. His second wife, Sarah L. Wright, a schoolteacher, lived in this home until the late 1950s.

321 E Street A

BUILT: 1907
STYLE: Victorian Eclectic
ORIGINAL OWNER: Van D. and Elizabeth Spalding

This two-and-one-half-story late Victorian home has two projecting gables, each faced with wood-shingle siding. A projecting belt course runs around the house at the top of the second story.

Built in 1907, this home was one of the last Victorian-style residences built in the Avenues. Van D. and Elizabeth Spalding had the home built for four thousand dollars. Mr. Spalding was involved in mining, real estate, and the manufacturing of farm equipment. The Spaldings lived here until their deaths, at which time their daughters inherited the home. The home is currently split into a duplex.

322 E Street [A]

BUILT: 1888/1914
STYLE: Victorian Eclectic
ORIGINAL OWNER: Andrew J. Clift

The rear, two-story, gable-roofed section was added in 1914 to this Victorian cottage. The home is covered in shiplap wood siding. The original front porch columns have been replaced by iron posts.

This home was built for Andrew J. Clift, who was the first Caucasian child born at Cove Fort, Utah. At age fourteen he became a stage driver, and later drove the first mule-drawn streetcars in Salt Lake City. He eventually organized the Clift Investment Company, a real estate firm. He owned this property until his death in 1952.

337 E Street [A]

BUILT: 1905
STYLE: Victorian Eclectic
ORIGINAL OWNER: Edward R. and Bertha P. Phelps

This one-story Victorian cottage has been heavily remodeled. An oversized picture window has replaced the original bay window. The home's original entry has also been glassed in.

This home was built for Edward and Bertha Phelps. Mr. Phelps was the traffic manager and assistant manager for the Continental Oil Company, freight and passenger agent for the Oregon Short Line Railroad, and manager for the Tooele County Railroad. Edward and Bertha lived in this home until 1909 when it was sold to John B. Dunn, a buyer for the Kahn Brothers Company, a dry goods store. After 1928 the home would be a rental property for an extended period of time.

F STREET

34–40 F Street   A

BUILT: 1901
STYLE: Victorian Eclectic
ORIGINAL OWNER: Rebecca B. Daynes

This duplex features a U-shaped gable roof. The front façade's two gables have fish-scale, wood-shingle siding.

The duplex was built in 1901 for Rebecca B. Daynes, a plural wife of John Daynes. Mr. Daynes, a pioneer music and jewelry dealer, was the founder of the Daynes Jewelry and Optical Store. Mrs. Daynes lived on one side of the duplex. The Daynes family also owned 28–30 F Street. This building has had numerous owners and been maintained as a rental since it was sold in 1913.

35 F Street   A

BUILT: 1928
STYLE: Mediterranean
BUILDER: McGregor Brothers Construction Company
ORIGINAL OWNER: Charles R. McGregor

This six-story apartment building exhibits elements of Mediterranean style. It has a broken parapet with a red tile cornice. The attached garage was one of the first such structures built in Utah.

Charles R. McGregor built this apartment block at a time when multifamily residential construction was accelerating in the Avenues. The brick exterior of the structure has been well maintained.

64 F Street   A

BUILT: 1883
STYLE: Victorian Eclectic
ORIGINAL OWNER: Charles W. and Fanny Steed Stayner

Several additions to the front of this home's façade have obscured the home's original appearance.

Charles W. Stayner returned from an LDS Church mission in 1883 and moved into this home. He was a practicing attorney and one of the founders of the Utah and Idaho Sugar Company. He lived in this home only briefly before moving to the now-demolished 465 First Avenue. He maintained this home as a rental until it was sold to Mary V. Hempstead in 1894. The home has had multiple absentee owners since that time. In 1923 the home was converted into a duplex.

70 F Street

BUILT: 1908
STYLE: Commercial
ORIGINAL OWNER: David L. and William Murdoch

This one-story commercial building was built as a neighborhood grocery store. The façade remains in original condition with the exception of some mid-twentieth-century stone veneer on the lower wall. The building is representative of many small stores built throughout Salt Lake Valley in residential areas prior to the advent of the supermarket.

David L. and William Murdoch opened the Murdoch Grocery here in 1908. The grocery, known to be popular with the owners of the large mansions on nearby South Temple, operated until 1942. In 1946 Nephi Jensen purchased the building and opened Jensen Grocery, which remained in operation until 1977.

78 F Street A

BUILT: 1902
STYLE: American Four Square
ORIGINAL OWNER: Perry J. Anson

This classic Four Square home replaced an earlier adobe structure. The home has had its original porch removed, and the entrance details and shutters are later additions.

Perry J. Anson, owner of Anson Real Estate, was the first owner of the home. William Murdoch, owner of the adjacent Murdoch Grocery, purchased the residence in 1923. He was also active in the Utah Retail Grocers Association and the Salt Lake Chamber of Commerce. In 1946 the home was bought by Joseph A. Kopp, who had been a miner in Park City and Eureka. Robert W. Sorenson converted the home to apartments in 1952.

118 F Street A

BUILT: 1905
STYLE: American Four Square
BUILDER: Anderson Realty Company
ORIGINAL OWNER: Lillias Staines

This Four Square–type home has a main hip roof with a front center dormer. A corbelled belt course of rough-faced brick runs along the bottom of the second-story windows, with another course running along the top of the first-story windows. The front porch has Doric columns.

The Anderson Realty Company was one of the largest developers of Avenues homes. They built this home and several others nearby. Lillias Staines purchased the residence upon completion, and members of the Staines family maintained the property as a rental until 1947. Musa S. Tellier and Jeanne Tellier Leeson purchased the house at that time. Jeanne's husband, Delmar, was the sales manager at KDYL television.

119 F Street   A

BUILT: 1905
STYLE: American Four Square
BUILDER: Anderson Realty Company
ORIGINAL OWNER: Ella and Milton E. Price

This yellow brick, Four Square–type home has a main hip roof with a front center dormer. Corbelled brick quoin topped with carved wooden Ionic capitals grace the corners.

The Anderson Realty Company, owned by John G. and James M. Anderson, was a prolific development company in the Avenues. Ella and Milton Price purchased the home upon completion. Horace H. Walker, city editor for the *Deseret News*, purchased the property in 1921. Birdie E. Brey Hara bought the home in 1954, moving from 107 F Street. She owned several retirement homes in the Avenues including those at 539 Third Avenue and 425 Second Avenue. She converted the two Four Squares, 107 and 113 F Street, into a single, midcentury building as an additional retirement home.

121 F Street   A

BUILT: 1904
STYLE: Victorian Eclectic
BUILDER: Anderson Realty Company
ORIGINAL OWNER: Fred A. Price

The roofline of this home flares out over the boxed eaves. The front gable has patterned, wood-shingle siding. There is a wood segmental bay window above the Doric-columned front porch.

The Anderson Realty Company, owned by John G. and James M. Anderson, was a prolific development company in the Avenues, building several homes in this area. Fred A. Price purchased this home upon completion and maintained it as a rental property. The home was later purchased by a tenant named Ruth Blumenthal, who was the branch manager for the Metro-Goldwyn-Mayer Distributing Company. She and her husband also owned the Texas Motor Company at 120 South Temple. The property was divided into three apartments in the 1930s. It has since been restored to a single-family home.

129 F Street   A

BUILT: 1911
STYLE: Craftsman Bungalow
ORIGINAL OWNER: William J. and Inez Leaker

This Craftsman bungalow has walls covered in wood-shingle siding. There is clinker brickwork on the chimney and lower façade. The extensive original woodwork remains on the interior of the home.

William and Inez Leaker replaced an older frame cottage with this home. Mr. Leaker was a real estate agent. They defaulted on the loan and the property was maintained as a rental by investment companies between 1917 and 1925. Benjamin and Walley Stanley purchased the property in 1925. Having changed their name from Morzelewski after emigrating from Poland, the Stanleys owned numerous businesses in Salt Lake City including the Stanley Shoe Store, the Headlight Bar, and the Pioneer Inn. Walley Stanley maintained ownership of this residence until her death in 1975.

134 F Street A

BUILT: 1909
STYLE: American Four Square
ARCHITECT: John A. Headlund
BUILDER: Hess Builders
ORIGINAL OWNER: Mary L. Parke

The hip roof of this classic Four Square flares out at the eaves. The front center dormer is also typical of the style. A corbelled brick course separates the first and second floors.

Prominent Salt Lake City architect John A. Headlund designed this home for Mary L. Parke, the widow of William H. Parke, a farmer. She lived here with her children until 1919 when she started renting out the home. She sold the residence to tenants Louis C. and Lucretia Kimball in 1923. Mr. Kimball was secretary for the Kimball and Richards Land and Securities Company. In 1946 Ruth A. and Paul H. Sutton purchased the property. Mr. Sutton was an inspector for the Union Pacific Railroad.

170 F Street A

BUILT: 1880
STYLE: Vernacular
ORIGINAL OWNER: Amanda M. Worthen

This small cottage has an L-shaped floor plan with extensions across the rear of the building. The front windows are framed by raised brick arches, and the arch keystones are ornamented with a star design.

This home was built for Amanda Worthen, the widow of John Worthen. They had previously lived at 170 D Street. In 1923 Thomas Latimer, a metallurgist, purchased the property and constructed the rear additions. Upon his death in 1933, his daughter Clara inherited the home. She was the first female graduate of the University of Utah's School of Engineering and for many years was the only licensed female engineer in Utah. She would eventually teach at the university.

174 F Street A

BUILT: 1909
STYLE: American Four Square
ARCHITECT: G. W. Eldredge
BUILDER: J. G. Briggs
ORIGINAL OWNER: Charles A. and Emma Lambourne

This is a two-story, brick Four Square with a hip roof and front center dormer. The front porch is supported by wood Doric columns.

The home was built for Charles and Emma Lambourne. Mr. Lambourne was an employee of the U.S. Postal Service. Several homes in the Avenues were built for members of the Lambourne family. This home was converted into apartments in 1948 but has since been restored to a single-family residence.

179 F Street [A]

BUILT: 1904
STYLE: Victorian Eclectic
BUILDER: Fred S. Luff
ORIGINAL OWNER: Fred S. Luff

The circular porch with conical roof is the prominent feature of this Victorian home. The front gable has fish-scale, wood-shingle siding. The home is nearly identical to 187 F Street.

Fred Luff tore down his family home and built this house and 187 F Street as investments. John and Irene Pursell were the first resident owners. Mr. Pursell was an employee of the Shilling Company. In 1926 the home was sold to Thomas and Bertha Holt. Mr. Holt was a guide at the Utah State Capitol and the treasurer of the state Democratic Party.

186 F Street [A]

BUILT: 1902
STYLE: Victorian Eclectic
ORIGINAL OWNER: Richard Royal Romney

This one-and-one-half-story, yellow brick Victorian home has a gable roof with a front dormer window and a projecting front bay. The dormer and side gables are covered in wood-shingle siding.

This home was built for Richard Royal Romney, who was the secretary of the Daynes and Romney Piano Company. Mr. Romney also worked on a design for an automobile wheel and organized a company called the Ellis Resilient Wheel Company. He died three days after he was to begin production of the wheels. The home was converted into several apartments in 1974. It has since been converted back to a single-family residence.

188 F Street [A]

BUILT: 1922
STYLE: Prairie Bungalow
ORIGINAL OWNER: Leonard J. and Mabel Bratager

This brick, one-story bungalow is typical of the Prairie design commonly found throughout Utah.

Leonard and Mabel Bratager were the first owners of this home. Mr. Bratager was a clerk at Woolworth's and Mrs. Bratager was an assistant manager at Auerbachs Department Store. They only lived here briefly before selling the property to Edward Hughes Miller, manager of the Tracy Loan and Trust Company. From 1935 until 1942, J. Frank Cookson, who owned the Modern School of Music, lived in the home. The home was split into apartments during the Great Depression but appears to have been converted back to a single-family residence.

217–219 F Street [A]

BUILT: 1902
STYLE: American Four Square
ORIGINAL OWNER: Alfred H. Meredith

This unique Four Square was an early Avenues duplex signaling the beginning of the trend toward multifamily residences in the neighborhood. The front corners of the home are notched out for the entries.

Alfred H. Meredith was partners with J. William Guthrie in a bicycle business. He later opened and managed the Meredith Automobile Company at 68 West 300 South in Salt Lake City. After he had this duplex built, he and his wife, Anna, lived in one side of it and rented out the other.

218 F Street [A]

BUILT: 1889
STYLE: Victorian Eclectic
ORIGINAL OWNER: Walter Reynolds

This Victorian cottage has a hip roof and a large, segmental, projecting front bay. The bay has corbelled brickwork, including arched drip molding above the windows.

This modest home is an example of the many residences built for working-class families in the area during the late nineteenth century. The first owner, Walter Reynolds, was a janitor for the Zion's Savings Bank and Trust. Richard T. and Caroline Haag purchased the home in 1892. Mr. Haag was a German instructor at Latter-day Saints College. In 1902 Thomas F. Thomas, who worked at the *Salt Lake Herald* newspaper, became the home's owner. He was active in Democratic Party political campaigns and was the first federal appointee from Utah in the Franklin D. Roosevelt administration, serving with the U.S. Land Board Office.

238 F Street [A]

BUILT: 1906
STYLE: Dutch Colonial Revival
BUILDER: Midgley-Boedel Company
ORIGINAL OWNER: Etta F. and Rufus C. Hill

This Dutch Colonial Revival home has elaborate Classical Revival ornament on the gable of the gambrel roof. The porch has egg-and-dart molding under the front eaves. The three-part window has a leaded glass transom. The adjacent home at 234 F Street is identical but was stripped of its details in the 1950s or 1960s.

The Midgley-Boedel Company built this home and 234 F Street. Etta and Rufus Hill purchased the home for $3,500 a year after completion. Mr. Hill was an agent for the New York Life Insurance Company. Alvin E. and Zita M. Niles became the owners in 1922. Mr. Niles was secretary-treasurer of the Valley Market at 24 West 100 South. Lewis E. Abbot, a claims agent for the Oregon Short Line Railroad, purchased the home in 1924.

274 F Street   A

BUILT: 1922
STYLE: Prairie Bungalow
ORIGINAL OWNER: Edward R. Johnson

This one-story, hip-roofed, Prairie bunga-low was built in a style commonly found throughout Utah neighborhoods from the late 1910s through the early 1920s. The walls are brick below the windows and stucco above. The lava rock on the lower front porch and the iron rails on the lower part of the windows are noncompatible modifica-tions made to the home.

This home, built for Edward R. John-son, replaced a pre-1898 Vernacular struc-ture owned and occupied by George D. and Sarah Luff. Mr. Johnson was a tinsmith and treasurer for the J. A. Johnson and Sons tin company. From 1923 until 1936 several dif-ferent people occupied the home. In 1936 it was purchased by J. Allan Crockett, who lived in the home until 1961. Mr. Crockett served on the Utah Supreme Court from 1951 until 1981.

320 F Street   A

BUILT: 1893
STYLE: Victorian Eclectic
ORIGINAL OWNER: Lucius L. Woodruff

This Victorian home of pattern-book design is similar to many other homes of the period in the Avenues. The gabled front porch has been partially enclosed. The original Doric porch columns have been replaced by iron posts.

This home was maintained as a rental property from 1893 until 1907. Among the owners during this period was Aaron Key-ser of A. Fisher Brewing Company. Eliza Partridge Kingsbury was the first resident owner. Mrs. Kingsbury was the fourth wife and widow of Joseph C. Kingsbury, who had been a close associate of LDS Church presi-dent Joseph Smith.

G STREET

21 G Street   A

BUILT: 1911
STYLE: American Four Square
ORIGINAL OWNER: Richard D. Millet

This is a popular Four Square–type home with some unique detailing. The cornice is decorated with heavy modillion brackets. Brick piers set on the diagonal support the front porch and dormer window.

Richard D. Millet, a mining engineer, lived at 559 South Temple and owned this portion of the block. He built a corral on this lot in 1889, then replaced the corral with a home in 1911 and maintained it as a rental property. Mary T. Sorenson bought the home in 1924 and continued to rent out the property. One of the renters, Reuben E. Farr, lived in the house from 1925 until 1942. He owned and operated the Hillcrest Pharmacy in the Avenues. In 1963 the home was converted into a nursing home. Terracor bought the building in the 1970s and converted it into offices.

25 G Street   A

BUILT: 1896
STYLE: Victorian Eclectic
ARCHITECT: Samuel C. Dallas
BUILDER: Salt Lake Building Company
ORIGINAL OWNER: John W. Jenkins

This two-story Victorian home has a low, main hip roof and two-story ornate porch. The heavy cornice has modillion brackets and dentil molding. Leaded glass windows can be found around the home.

Salt Lake City architect Samuel C. Dallas designed this home for John W. Jenkins, a harness maker who ran a shop at 76 East 200 South. The store became one of the first sporting goods stores in the region. Mr. Jenkins continued to live in this home until his death in 1920. The building was converted into apartments in 1923. The home is now used as an office building.

68 G Street   B

BUILT: 1888
STYLE: Victorian Eclectic
BUILDER: Lewis P. Kelsey
ORIGINAL OWNER: Charles M. and Minnie Priscilla Bell

This home is a good example of Victorian architecture influenced by the Shingle style. The front gable has an elaborate, curved, wood-shingle fascia and gable end. The second-story, shingle-covered walls flare out over the brick first story.

The home was built by Lewis P. Kelsey of the Kelsey, Gillespie, and Pomeroy Company. The home had numerous owners during its first twenty years. In 1902 James X. Ferguson, manager of the Keith-O'Brien Department Store, purchased the property. He was the brother-in-law of store owner David Keith. William and Eva Armstrong purchased the home in 1903. Mr. Armstrong was the president of the First National Bank of Park City and in 1910 became president of the National Copper Bank of Salt Lake City.

73 G Street

BUILT: 1892–1894
STYLE: Victorian Eclectic
ARCHITECT: H. H. Anderson
BUILDER: William Aspen and Company
ORIGINAL OWNER: David Lennox Murdoch

This house with its projecting towers, gabled bay, and ornate front porch is an elaborate example of Victorian eclecticism. Fascia boards with rosettes and ornately carved lintels on the windows fill the northwest gabled bay. The southeast tower has a four-sided, bell-shaped roof. Much of the original woodwork in the interior remains today.

This home was built for Scottish immigrant David Lennox Murdoch. A prominent businessman in the Avenues, he managed the LDS Church's Twentieth Ward Co-op Store and worked as an accountant for the ZCMI department store. This home remained in the Murdoch family until 1954. It was used as a retirement home during the late 1950s and 1960s. It has also been used as an office building and apartment building since that time.

76 G Street

BUILT: 1891
STYLE: Victorian Eclectic
BUILDER: A. Wade and Company
ORIGINAL OWNER: Jeanette Gibson

This is a Victorian cottage with a truncated hip roof. The small front porch is supported by Doric columns.

This home was built for Jeanette Gibson, the widow of John Gibson. She only remained in the home for five years. The residence changed hands several times and was maintained as a rental unit until 1949. From that year until 1962, Harry H. Rose, owner of the Rose Printing Company in Salt Lake City, owned and resided in the home. In 1964 and 1965 the home was occupied by Jane Leona Ashton, who started the Pink Ladies Voluntary Auxiliary at LDS Hospital.

77 G Street

BUILT: 1880–1884
STYLE: Vernacular/Tudor Revival
ORIGINAL OWNER: Janet Barnard

This one-story vernacular cottage was heavily remodeled in the 1930s. A steeply pitched, Tudor Revival–style entry gable was added, reflecting features found in period cottages that were popular at the time.

This home was built for Janet Barnard, a widow. She sold it in 1887 to her sons, Joseph and James. It was sold in 1928 to Richmond Young who worked for Mountain States Telephone.

83 G Street   [A]

BUILT: 1914
STYLE: Prairie Style Bungalow
BUILDER: H. Henderson
ORIGINAL OWNER: Thomas Richard Robins

The design of this one-story, hip-roofed bungalow is commonly found throughout neighborhoods built in Utah between 1910 and 1925.

The home was built for Thomas Richard Robins as an investment. A prominent local businessman and broker, Mr. Robins was president of the Fabian Brokerage Company and vice president of the Robins Canning Company of Roy, Utah. He sold the home in 1917 to James H. Dunkley, who worked for the Decker and Patrick Dry Goods Company. From 1918 until 1920 Heber Nielson lived in the home. Mr. Nielson was president of the Utah-Idaho School Supply Company. A later owner, Kathryn D. Cummings, taught at East High School for thirty-two years.

89 G Street   [A]

BUILT: 1914
STYLE: Bungalow
ARCHITECT: Monson and Price
BUILDER: H. Henderson
ORIGINAL OWNER: Thomas Richard Robins

The large front dormer dominates this brick bungalow. The front porch is supported by paired brick columns. The original main front window and dormer windows have been replaced.

The home was designed by Joseph Monson and Arthur Price. Mr. Monson was supervising architect for Utah state schools for many years, and Arthur Price was known for his work on the Utah State Capitol, the Walker Bank Building, and the Alta Club. The home's original owner, Thomas R. Robins, was president of the Fabian Brokerage Company and vice president of the Robins Canning Company of Roy, Utah. He was also an amateur horticulturist, bird watcher, and member of the Alta Club. From 1925 until 1948, the home was owned by William J. Morrison, superintendent of the Utah division of the Union Pacific Railroad.

107 G Street   [A]

BUILT: 1924
STYLE: Neoclassical
ARCHITECT: Lewis Telle Cannon and John Fetzer
ORIGINAL OWNER: Church of Jesus Christ of Latter-day Saints

This Neoclassical-style church building also exhibits Renaissance Mannerist influences, found in the double gable, discontinuous cornice, and Palladian-style entry.

The Twentieth LDS Ward's original meetinghouse was on Second Avenue between D and E Streets. They moved to this new, larger facility in 1924. Lewis Telle Cannon and ward member John Fetzer were hired to design the building, which was dedicated by LDS Church president and Avenues resident Heber J. Grant on April 17, 1927. Several additions have been made over the years to the basic L-shaped plan. The addition of new classrooms and a new entry on the southeast corner occurred in 1941. The stained-glass windows were added in the 1970s.

115 G Street   A

BUILT: 1909
STYLE: American Four Square
BUILDER: Coulan and White
ORIGINAL OWNER: Alexander Ryan

This is a two-story Four Square with a hip roof. The one-story front porch is supported by Doric wood columns.

The Coulan and White Construction Company built this home for Alexander Ryan, who was a partner in Lyon and Richards Groceries. He later opened his own store on 400 South. In 1924 the home was sold to Glenn Logan, treasurer of the Kinney Coal Company. John L. A. Schilperoort, a salesman with the J. V. Bucke Electric Company, bought the house in 1939. In the 1980s this home faced demolition to make way for additional parking for the adjacent LDS Church. Community leadership saved the home.

129 G Street   A

BUILT: 1894
STYLE: Queen Anne
BUILDER: E. T. Ashton
ORIGINAL OWNER: Orvin Morris

An octagonal tower with a segmental hip roof can be found on the southeast corner of this Queen Anne–style home. The dormer window and third story of the tower have wood-shingle siding. A dentiled cornice runs under the eaves.

Orvin Morris was the chief rate clerk for the Oregon Short Line Railroad and an Avenues property speculator when he moved into this home upon completion. Mr. Morris lost the home in a tax sale in 1904 and it was purchased by Arthur E. Snow, who was then secretary-treasurer of the Columbus Consolidated Mining Company.

168 G Street   B

BUILT: 1902
STYLE: Victorian Eclectic
ORIGINAL OWNER: Albert H. and Laura W. Adkison

This Victorian home is most likely a pattern-book design. It has a tall main hip roof, a gabled front dormer window, and a hip-roofed, three-sided front bay. The original porch columns have been replaced by iron posts, and the trim around the front door is not original.

This home was built for Laura and Albert Adkison. Mr. Adkison was a cashier at Western Loan and Savings Company. In 1904 the home was sold to Orville A. and Inez R. Honnald for $3,400. Mr. Honnald was an electrical engineer for the Utah Light and Railway Company. A later owner, Angus I. Nicholson, was the manager of television and houseware sales for the Salt Lake district of Graybar Electric.

175 G Street [A]

BUILT: 1903
STYLE: Victorian Eclectic
BUILDER: James Sabine
ORIGINAL OWNER: John A. and Selina Maynes

This large Victorian home has a two-story bay on the southeast corner. The northeast front corner has a round bay window faced in rough brick. There is an oval window at the front entrance. Iron posts have replaced the original porch columns.

John Sabine built this home for his son-in-law and daughter, John A. and Selina Maynes. Mr. Maynes was assistant manager of the J. H. Leyson Jewelry Company. He died while serving an LDS Church mission in his native England. Selina Maynes remained in this home until 1932. It was converted into five apartments in 1935.

176 G Street [B]

BUILT: 1890
STYLE: Victorian Eclectic/Bungalow
ORIGINAL OWNER: Joseph S. Wells

This home was originally built as a Victorian cottage. It was remodeled in the early twentieth century into a bungalow-style home. Another attempt to modernize the home in the 1950s resulted in the replacement of the front windows and removal of the original porch posts.

This home was built for Joseph S. Wells, brother of Utah's first state governor, Heber M. Wells. Joseph S. Wells was a bookkeeper working for several firms including the Utah Light and Railway Company, Salt Lake Railway Company, and the Consolidated Railway and Power Company. He lived in this home until 1893, and later lived at his brother's home at 182 G Street. A third Wells brother, Luis R. Wells, moved into this home next. He was employed by the ZCMI department store and was known as a genealogy expert.

182 G Street [B]

BUILT: 1889
STYLE: Victorian Eclectic
ORIGINAL OWNER: Heber M. Wells

This is a rambling, one-story Victorian home. The north wing has a hip roof and an unusual chimney, while the south wing has a transverse gable roof.

The home was built for Heber M. Wells, who became Utah's first governor after statehood. He also held several elected positions with the Salt Lake City government after serving as governor. He moved from this home in 1897, and his brother Joseph S. Wells lived here until 1909. He was a bookkeeper working for several firms including the Utah Light and Railway Company, Salt Lake Railway Company, and the Consolidated Railway and Power Company. In 1909 he sold the home to Ole C. Hansen, owner of the Salt Lake Tailoring Company, who maintained the property as a rental unit. The home is currently split into a duplex.

229 G Street [A]

BUILT: 1892
STYLE: Victorian Eclectic
BUILDER: Oliver B. Greene
ORIGINAL OWNER: Oliver B. Greene

This one-story Victorian cottage features excellent exterior woodwork. There was a large rear addition made to the home in the 1970s.

Oliver B. Greene was a carpenter and built this home for his family. He lived here only briefly before selling the residence to Eleanor Rebecca Keep in 1896. Mrs. Keep, a seamstress, lived in the home with her mother, Susannah B. Keep, and brother Alfred J. Keep. Mr. Keep was a barber.

263 G Street [A]

BUILT: 1898
STYLE: Victorian Eclectic
BUILDER: William H. Clayton
ORIGINAL OWNER: William H. Clayton

This structure was originally a one-story Victorian cottage. It has been heavily remodeled several times over the past hundred years.

William H. Clayton, a member of the Volunteer Fireman's Association, built several homes on this block. In 1905 he sold the home to Oliver G. Workman, who was also a fireman. From 1916 until 1926 the residence was owned by David A. Straasbach, a watchmaker for various jewelers in Salt Lake City. The property was bank owned through most of the Great Depression. Albert A. and Carla J. Eitner owned the home from 1935 until 1961. Mr. Eitner was a pharmacist at the Sixth Avenue Drug Store and also served as president of the Utah Pharmacological Association.

267 G Street [A]

BUILT: 1902
STYLE: Victorian Eclectic
BUILDER: William H. Clayton
ORIGINAL OWNER: Georgianna and James Mickelson

This is a one-and-one-half-story, gable-roofed Victorian home. The front gable is covered in wood-shingle siding and has a Palladian window. The original front porch columns had been replaced by iron posts in the 1960s but have since been restored.

William H. Clayton built this home as an investment property. Georgianna and James Mickelson became the first resident owners in 1903. Mr. Mickelson was a shoemaker for Hirschnen Shoes. Sarah R. Dodge purchased the property in 1907 but Mr. Mickelson continued to live here until 1923. Several members of the Dodge family lived in this home after 1923. Mrs. Dodge converted the house into multiple apartments in 1936.

270 G Street [B]

BUILT: 1905
STYLE: Victorian Eclectic
ORIGINAL OWNER: Thomas Emanuel Harper

This one-story Victorian cottage has a hip roof, side dormers, and a gabled front bay. The front gable has wood-shingle siding. This home was an early Avenues restoration project. The porch was completely restored in 1977.

Thomas E. Harper lived at 280 G Street and built this home as a rental property. A grocer with the Harper Brothers Store, Mr. Harper established the first delicatessen in Utah. He was also a long-time music teacher and choir leader at Saint Mark's Episcopal Church. His son, Thomas E. Harper Jr., lived in the residence between 1918 and 1923. He was a chemist and assayer with United States Steel. In 1931 the home was bought by Elizabeth Jackson Moffitt, who was associate editor of the LDS Church magazine, *The Improvement Era*.

280 G Street [B]

BUILT: 1892
STYLE: Victorian Eclectic
ORIGINAL OWNER: Thomas Emanuel Harper

The design of this two-story Victorian home was commonly found throughout the Avenues for this time period. The front gable has a lattice-work panel supported by scroll-sawn brackets. The house was covered in asbestos shingles in the mid-twentieth century, but the siding has since been removed.

The original owner, Thomas E. Harper, was a grocer with the Harper Brothers Store and established the first delicatessen in Utah. He was also a long-time music teacher and choir leader at Saint Mark's Episcopal Church. He lived in this home until his death in 1939. From 1939 until 1949 his daughter, Jessie L. Billingsley, lived in the home. She was a school nurse for the Salt Lake County Board of Health. She converted the home into a duplex in 1949. In 1974 additional apartments were added to interior.

283 G Street [A]

BUILT: 1911
STYLE: Craftsman Bungalow
ORIGINAL OWNER: Albert M. and Serena Olson

This gable-roofed Craftsman bungalow has a second-story dormer that shelters a small balcony. Large, square wood columns support the first-floor front porch.

The home was built for Albert M. and Serena Olson, who also owned the Sixth Avenue Grocery Store which stood at 480 Sixth Avenue. Mr. Olson was the founder of the Builder's and Grocer's Association and the Associated Retail Credit Organization. He was also a Salt Lake City schoolteacher. The home was converted into a duplex in 1936. It is currently a single-family home.

328 G Street

BUILT: 1893
STYLE: Victorian Eclectic
ARCHITECT: Richard K. A. Kletting
ORIGINAL OWNER: Ernest Alonzo and Georgianna
  Kitz Tripp

This Victorian home has a large bay window and a continuous band of sandstone extending across the width of the house. The hipped roof features two eyebrow windows looking south and west. The original stone front porch was removed in the 1950s.

The home was designed by prominent Utah architect Richard K. A. Kletting, who was also the architect of the Utah State Capitol. It is very similar to his own now-demolished home that stood on A Street. The residence was built for Ernest A. and Georgianna Tripp. Mr. Tripp practiced dentistry in Salt Lake City for sixty years. He served on several state health boards and was a member of the Alta and University Clubs. Mr. Tripp lived here until his death in 1948.

H STREET

22 H Street   B

BUILT: 1912
STYLE: Craftsman Bungalow
ARCHITECT: David C. Dart
ORIGINAL OWNER: Daniel W. Lipman

Cobblestone columns support the porch of this gable-roofed Craftsman bungalow. The rear section of the home has clipped gables. The porch has been partially enclosed.

Prominent Avenues and Salt Lake City architect David C. Dart designed this bungalow for Daniel W. Lipman, who was president of a wholesale grocery business. Jane M. Skolfield bought the home in 1920. After a successful career in the development of early childhood education in Utah and Colorado, Mrs. Skolfield became a physician and practiced at LDS Hospital for twenty-five years. She was elected to the Utah State Legislature in 1912. Her son, Mazel Skolfield, also a physician at LDS Hospital, bought the home in 1932. The bungalow has since been split into several apartments.

36 H Street   B

BUILT: 1899
STYLE: Victorian Eclectic
ARCHITECT: Richard K. A. Kletting
ORIGINAL OWNER: George H. Dern

This Victorian home shows the influence of the Colonial Revival style popular at the beginning of the twentieth century. The front porch has paired Doric columns on wood-paneled posts.

Utah State Capitol architect Richard K. A. Kletting designed this home for George H. Dern. Mr. Dern was a well-known Utah mining figure, governor of Utah from 1925 until 1933, and U.S. Secretary of War from 1936 until 1940. In 1922 Mr. Dern moved to a larger home at 715 South Temple but maintained ownership of this property until 1929. The home was a rental property for much of the rest of the century.

67 H Street   B

BUILT: 1908
STYLE: Craftsman Bungalow
ARCHITECT: Bernard O. Mecklenberg
BUILDER: Eardley and Ball
ORIGINAL OWNER: Hoffmar H. and Nellie H. Bitner

This one-and-one-half-story Craftsman bungalow has overhanging eaves supported with large brackets in the gables. Rafter ends are left exposed for decorative effect. The gabled front porch is supported by heavy wood columns.

Prominent Salt Lake City architect Bernard O. Mecklenberg designed this bungalow for Hoffmar and Nellie Bitner. Mr. Bitner was involved in livestock. In 1955 they sold the property to Sten H. Swenson, who operated his business, Swenson Golden Crown Furniture Polish, out of the home until the late 1970s. The bungalow was restored in 2005.

75 H Street [B]

BUILT: 1904
STYLE: American Four Square
BUILDER: William H. Jones
ORIGINAL OWNER: William H. Jones

This two-story, Four Square–type home has a hip roof and front center dormer window. The original front porch had been removed in the 1960s but was restored in the past ten years.

William H. Jones built this home for three thousand dollars. In 1907 Annie Mc-Murray became the home's owner, maintaining the property as a rental unit. From 1921 until 1923 the First Methodist Episcopal Church used the home as a rectory. Peter and Mary E. Rasmussen purchased the property in 1923. Mr. Rasmussen repaired rail cars for the Oregon Short Line Railroad.

78 H Street [B]

BUILT: 1899
STYLE: Victorian Eclectic
ORIGINAL OWNER: Harry S. Joseph

This Victorian has a main hip roof with front- and south-side gabled wall dormers and a projecting, gable-roofed front bay. The gables are covered in patterned, wood-shingle siding. The original front porch columns had been replaced by iron posts in the 1960s. The porch has since been restored.

Original owner Harry S. Joseph maintained the home as a rental. Leslie H. and Hazel Alice Calder Groesbeck were the first resident owners of this property. Mr. Groesbeck was an engineer for the Utah Power and Light Company. He had also worked for the precursor of the company, as did his father and brother. Alice Groesbeck died in 1942. Leslie married Ella Brown May in 1946 and remained in the home until his death in 1961.

80 H Street [B]

BUILT: 1894
STYLE: Victorian Eclectic
ORIGINAL OWNER: Harry S. Joseph

This Victorian home has a large, arched first-floor front window with corbelled drip molding. There is a heavy, two-story northwest front porch supported on the first story by heavy square columns.

The home was built for Harry S. Joseph, a well-known mining man, civil engineer, and politician. He was initially employed by his uncle and eventual Utah governor, Simon Bamberger. It was through Mr. Bamberger that he became involved in mining and railroad development. Mr. Joseph also developed several Utah water companies. He served in the Utah State Legislature and as speaker of the Utah State House of Representatives in 1907. In the mid-1920s Mr. Joseph and his wife, Mamie, moved to the Hotel Utah but maintained ownership of this property until 1942.

83 H Street [B]

BUILT: 1905
STYLE: American Four Square
BUILDER: Aaron Keyser
ORIGINAL OWNER: Sarah J. Wilson

This is a two-story, Four Square–type home with a hip roof, front center dormer window, and side chimneys. A corbelled brick belt course runs below the second-floor windows. The original front porch had been removed in the 1950s but was restored in the past ten years.

Avenues property developer Aaron Keyser built this home on speculation. Upon completion it was purchased by Sarah J. Wilson, widow of Patrick Judge and mother-in-law of mining millionaire Thomas Kearns. After her death, her daughters Anna M. Conlon and Frances W. Gallivan lived in the home, along with Frances's husband, Daniel J. Gallivan. Long-time *Salt Lake Tribune* president Jack Gallivan, Frances and Daniel's son, lived in this home as a young boy.

86 H Street [B]

BUILT: 1911
STYLE: Prairie
ARCHITECT: Lewis Telle Cannon and John Fetzer
BUILDER: F. W. Carpenter
ORIGINAL OWNER: Radcliffe Q. Cannon

Designed by the architectural firm of Cannon and Fetzer in the second year of their partnership, this hip-roofed house is stuccoed on the second story. The influence of the Prairie style is found in the stucco-brick split, the leaded art glass with geometric patterns, and horizontal bands of casement windows. The two planters are replicas of a Frank Lloyd Wright design. This home is one of the better examples of Prairie style in the area.

Radcliffe Q. Cannon was a son of George Q. Cannon, a counselor to the LDS Church's first presidency during the late nineteenth century. Radcliffe, a long-time accountant for the ZCMI department store, owned the home until 1937.

115 H Street [B]

BUILT: 1915
STYLE: Prairie/American Four Square
BUILDER: M. Kjergaard
ORIGINAL OWNER: Lorenzo and Hattie Jensen

This two-story Four Square exhibits elements of Prairie-style architecture. The home has a low hip roof, two second-story belt courses of brick, and casement windows. The porch columns have Prairie-style stone decorations. The plaque between the second-floor front windows has a monogram "J" for the original owner.

Lorenzo and Hattie Jensen had this home built. Mr. Jensen was an insurance agent for the Beneficial Life Insurance Company. Joseph P. and Loy M. Mayer purchased the property in 1950. Mr. Mayer was employed by the University of Utah. After his death in 1954, Mrs. Mayer split the home into three apartments.

125 H Street [B]

BUILT: 1896
STYLE: Tudor Revival
ORIGINAL OWNER: Salt Lake College

This large home exhibits elements of the Tudor Revival style. It has a one-and-one-half-story wing with a long, sloping gable roof that covers porches on the north and south sides. Behind the front wing is a two-and-one-half-story wing that runs east to west giving the house a T shape.

The structure was built for the Salt Lake College operated by the Congregational New West Education Committee as rental housing. The college was located on Third South between Third and Fourth East. The contracting firm of Alexander and McDonald moved into this building soon after completion. They developed several lots in this area of the Avenues. In 1906 Helena C. Gleason purchased the home and maintained the property as rental units.

126 H Street [B]

BUILT: 1883
STYLE: Victorian Eclectic
ORIGINAL OWNER: George and Clare Cameron

This one-story Victorian cottage has a truncated hip roof and projecting, gabled front bay. The front porch has turned wood columns. The exterior of the home was covered in asbestos shingles and imitation brick during the 1960s, but those modifications have since been removed.

The home was built for George and Clare Cameron. Mr. Cameron found success in Utah mining, owning the Calumet and Utah Queen mines. In 1904 the Cameron family moved into a larger home at 132 H Street but continued to own this home and maintain it as a rental property until 1921. Marie Newmann bought the residence that year and lived in the house until the late 1950s.

132–134 H Street [B]

BUILT: 1903
STYLE: Victorian Eclectic
ARCHITECT: Walter E. Ware
BUILDER: George A. Fisher
ORIGINAL OWNER: George and Clare Cameron

This Victorian duplex has a main gable roof with a front dormer and two projecting gable front bays, creating a symmetrical, U-shaped plan. The large front porch was enclosed and covered in Permastone during the 1960s. The exterior has since been restored.

This home was designed by prominent architect Walter E. Ware just before he formed his partnership with Alberto O. Treganza. The home was built by George A. Fisher for George and Clare Cameron. Mr. Cameron owned the Calumet and Utah Queen mines. The Camerons lived on one side of this duplex until Mr. Cameron's death in 1913. His wife remained there until her death in the 1920s. Their daughter Cliffie converted the duplex into several apartments during the Great Depression. The home was converted into a single-family home in the past ten years.

168 H Street [B]

BUILT: 1884
STYLE: Victorian Eclectic
ORIGINAL OWNER: Frederick O. Webb

This single-story cottage was completely covered in aluminum siding in the 1950s. Other changes included metal awnings, iron porch posts, and new windows, all typical of mid-twentieth-century attempts to modernize Avenues homes. Some of these alterations have since been removed from the structure.

This house had six different owners between 1884 and 1940. It was originally built for Frederick O. Webb, a long-time clerk for the Oregon Short Line Railroad and the Union Pacific Railroad. Leopold Goldsmith purchased the home in 1908. An owner of several Salt Lake City bars, Mr. Goldsmith was known to be involved in the city's prostitution business as well.

176 H Street [B]

BUILT: 1891
STYLE: Victorian Eclectic
ORIGINAL OWNER: John and Sarah Sheriff

This two-story home is an example of a cube-shaped Victorian that was a forerunner of the popular American Four Square–type home. The front porch is supported by Doric columns.

This home was built for John Sheriff, a pioneer stonecutter and builder who may have also been the builder. Among the projects he worked on were the Salt Lake Temple, the Salt Lake City and County Building, and the LDS Church's Cardston Temple in Alberta, Canada. He lived here until his death in 1932. Sarah Sheriff remained in the home until the mid-1940s.

177 H Street [B]

BUILT: 1883
STYLE: Italianate
ORIGINAL OWNER: Alfred A. Isom

The façade of this home is dominated by a unique, two-story front porch supported by cobblestone columns. The porch, which may have been added in the early twentieth century, hides the simple Italianate form and detailing of the original home.

The home was built for Alfred A. Isom. He and other members of his family worked for the Salt Lake Mattress and Manufacturing Company. The family moved from the home in 1904 but continued to own the property until 1952. It was converted into a duplex in the 1950s but in the mid-1990s was restored to a single-family home.

187 H Street

BUILT: 1903
STYLE: Victorian Eclectic
ORIGINAL OWNER: William A. Isom

This well-preserved, one-and-one-half-story, gable-roofed Victorian home has a small, Doric-columned front porch. The upper walls are covered in patterned, wood-shingle siding. The lower walls are yellow brick.

This home was built for William A. Isom, who was a foreman for several furniture companies while he lived here. In 1932 he moved to Portland, Oregon, and sold the property to Truman Burke, a physiotherapist for the Veterans Administration. A later owner, John E. Wright, was the auditor and office manager of the Highland Dairymen's Association. He lived in this property from 1948 until 1962.

270 H Street   B

BUILT: 1906
STYLE: Dutch Colonial Revival
BUILDER: Davis M. Leland
ORIGINAL OWNER: Davis M. Leland

The gambrel roof of this home is typical of the Dutch Colonial Revival style. The front porch is supported by square wood columns. The stucco railing is most likely not original.

Davis M. Leland, a contractor, built this home for himself. Five years later he sold the property to William F. Jacobson. From 1924 until 1928 it was owned by Arthur B. Cadman, the manager of Salt Lake City's branch of W. P. Fuller and Company. E. Le-Roy and Ethel Bourne purchased the home in 1934. Mr. Bourne was a prominent newspaper man, serving over the years as editor of the *Deseret News* and *Salt Lake Telegram*. Ethel Bourne remained in the home until her death in 1970.

275 H Street   B

BUILT: 1880
STYLE: Vernacular
BUILDER: Charles L. Castleton
ORIGINAL OWNER: William J. Castleton

This well-preserved, one-story vernacular cottage has an early twentieth-century addition. The wide front porch is supported by square wood columns.

Charles L. Castleton built this home for his brother William, who was a clerk for several mercantile businesses in Salt Lake City. He later worked with his brothers in a dry goods business at 736 Second Avenue. In 1890 he moved to 735 Third Avenue and maintained this home as a rental property until 1903.

283 H Street `B`

BUILT: 1880
STYLE: Vernacular
BUILDER: Charles L. Castleton
ORIGINAL OWNER: Charles L. Castleton

This one-story vernacular cottage has had several early additions. The gabled roof has wood-shingle siding and fascias. The southeast front porch has unusual square wooden columns with curving, tapered tops.

Charles L. Castleton, a carpenter and builder, built this home for himself. He is known to have also worked on the Salt Lake LDS Tabernacle and LDS Temple. He was a member of the Salt Lake Theater for nearly twenty years. His widow, Mary Ann Luff Castleton, lived in the home until 1949. Her daughter, Lucille C. Savage, remained in the home until 1977. This home represents a rare case of a century of single-family ownership. Charles L. Castleton also built 275 H Street for his brother William.

323 H Street `B`

BUILT: 1899
STYLE: Victorian Eclectic
ORIGINAL OWNER: Zion's Benefit Building Company

This is a brick Victorian cottage of pattern-book design. The front gable has patterned, wood-shingle siding and a three-part Palladian window. The original front porch has been removed from the home.

This home was built as an investment property by the Zion's Benefit Building Company. They maintained the home as a rental unit until John F. Gunn, who had rented the house since it was built, purchased it in 1906 for one thousand dollars. Mr. Gunn worked for forty-five years as a mechanic and painter for the Utah Light and Railway Company. Solomon D. and Mary M. Chase owned the home from 1917 until 1929. Mr. Chase was a rancher.

I STREET

75 I Street　[B]

BUILT: 1908
STYLE: American Four Square
BUILDER: B. G. Smith
ORIGINAL OWNER: Walter A. Wallace

This is a two-story, American Four Square–type home with a hip roof and front center dormer. The front porch has been removed from the home. All the front windows have been replaced in the past hundred years.

This home was built for Walter A. Wallace, who lived here until 1956. He was a long-time office manager for the National Biscuit Company, and also sang in the Mormon Tabernacle Choir.

76 I Street　[B]

BUILT: 1891
STYLE: Victorian Eclectic
ORIGINAL OWNER: David W. Teachenor

This two-story Victorian home has a front bay with unique, rounded corner windows.

David W. Teachenor built a brick Victorian cottage here for twelve hundred dollars. George Q. Coray bought the cottage from him in 1896 and expanded it to the size of the present home. He was the head librarian from 1892 until 1906 at the University of Utah. He founded the economics department in 1917 and also was responsible for introducing the seminar method of instruction in the sociology and anthropology departments. Grant and Evelyn Snyder bought the home in 1906. Mr. Snyder was assistant manager of the National Development Company. In 1925 Clara S. and Stephen M. Walton purchased the property. Mr. Walton was secretary-treasurer for the Utah Soap Company. Mrs. Walton remained in the home until her death in 1955.

78 I Street　[B]

BUILT: 1899
STYLE: Victorian Eclectic
ORIGINAL OWNER: Harry C. Edwards

This two-story Victorian home has a Prairie-style front porch which was added around 1910. The front gable has returns and curved bargeboards. The corners of the home are accented by rough-faced brick.

The home was built for a Salt Lake City lawyer named Harry C. Edwards, who sold the home in 1903 to Gustof Schulte. Mr. Schulte was the United States deputy mineral surveyor for Utah. After 1911 the home changed hands several times until 1921 when it was purchased by Alice B. and Norton Ross. The Ross family owned the home until 1961.

118 I Street   [B]

BUILT: 1890
STYLE: Victorian Eclectic
ORIGINAL OWNER: Joseph V. and Harriet S. Smith

This is a well-preserved, small Victorian home with multiple hip roofs. There are front- and south-side bay windows with small decorative gables above. The rounded front porch has a dentiled cornice. The original iron fence and gate, produced by Crager Wire and Iron Works of Salt Lake City, graces the front of the home.

Joseph V. Smith was the assistant depot ticket agent for the Union Pacific Railroad when this home was built. He later worked as an agent for the New York Life Insurance Company. His wife, Harriet S. Smith, was a member of the Timms family, who built numerous early Avenues homes. This home faced demolition along with the rest of the block for construction of a Safeway grocery store in 1976, but community opposition stopped the project.

128 I Street   [B]

BUILT: 1901
STYLE: American Four Square
ORIGINAL OWNER: Walter G. Tuttle

This home was originally located at 368 First Avenue. It was moved to this location when several homes on that block were demolished for a parking lot in the 1970s. An iron rail tops the front porch, and cresting still remains on the truncated hip roof. The chimney was originally brick before the house was moved.

Walter G. Tuttle sold this house to Governor William and Mary Spry in 1911. William Spry served as governor from 1909 until 1917. The State Capitol Building was completed during his term. Twice men attempted to blow up this house after Governor Spry refused to intervene in the death sentence of labor leader Joe Hill despite pleas from President Woodrow Wilson in December 1915. He remained in the home until 1921. The home was divided into three apartments during the Great Depression. When the building was moved, it was restored to a single-family home.

156–168 I Street   [B]

BUILT: 1917
STYLE: Prairie
ORIGINAL OWNER: State Loan and Trust Company

These are three-story apartment buildings with Prairie-style decoration. The façades of all three structures are dominated by the enclosed front porches. Arched pediments mark the center front entryways.

These apartment blocks help document the trend toward multifamily housing in the Avenues. Each block was built for twelve thousand dollars by the State Loan and Trust Company.

175 I Street   B

BUILT: 1889
STYLE: Vernacular
ORIGINAL OWNER: Isadore E. Greenwald

This one-story, simple, gable-roofed home has a Greek Revival frame and pedimented entrance which was most likely added at a later date. Next to the door is a wooden, segmental bay window with a bracketed cornice.

This home was built for Isadore E. Greenwald, whose husband owned and managed the Brooks Arcade building at State Street and Third South. She maintained this home as a rental property. Enoch A. Nock, a clerk for the Rio Grande Western Railroad, became the first resident owner of this property in 1901.

183 I Street   B

BUILT: 1900
STYLE: Victorian Eclectic
BUILDER: Elijah B. Burt
ORIGINAL OWNER: Elijah B. Burt

This Victorian has a main hip roof and a projecting, gabled front bay. The gable has carved rope molding in the cornice. Fish-scale-pattern, wood-shingle siding covers the gable. The original front porch has been removed from the home.

Elijah Burt built this home as an investment. He lived at 177 I Street. Mary G. Gamble was the first person to rent the home and purchased it in 1909. She was a practicing physician in Salt Lake City for twenty-two years and also sang for the Mormon Tabernacle Choir. George F. Williams, an inspector for the Oregon Short Line Railroad, purchased the home in 1915. He lived in the residence until 1935 when he sold it to Edward P. and Ethel Carter. Mr. Carter was a gardener at the Salt Lake City Cemetery.

186 I Street   B

BUILT: 1895
STYLE: Victorian Eclectic
ORIGINAL OWNER: Claudius V. Wheeler

This one-story Victorian home with projecting, gabled front bay is most likely a pattern-book design. Asbestos shingles were added in the 1950s to cover the original exterior. Currently the home is covered in stucco. The front porch has also been removed from the structure.

Claudius V. Wheeler was president of the South Swansea Mining Company in Silver Reef, Utah, when this home was built. The Wheeler family moved into the home in 1898. Their son, Claudius Jr., a clerk with the Pacific Express Company, purchased the home in 1908.

206 I Street   B

BUILT: 1899
STYLE: Victorian Eclectic
BUILDER: E. W. Druce
ORIGINAL OWNER: Deseret Savings and Loan Company

A wide cornice runs around this Victorian home of pattern-book design. The front gable is covered in patterned, wood-shingle siding. The current porch is supported by iron posts from the 1960s. The same developer also built 210 and 214 I Street.

The Deseret Savings and Loan Company built this home and maintained the property as a rental home until 1932. In that year, the residence was purchased by James J. Bunsey, a clerk for the American Smelting and Refining Company. George and Amelia Pitts became the owners in 1949 and remained in the home until the early 1980s.

219 I Street   B

BUILT: 1903
STYLE: Victorian Eclectic
BUILDER: Joseph G. Wilkes
ORIGINAL OWNER: Joseph G. and Elizabeth W. Wilkes

This pattern-book-designed Victorian home has a high gabled roof with wood-shingle siding and curved fascia boards. The front porch is supported by Doric columns.

This home was built by early trade union organizer Joseph G. Wilkes. He was the first secretary of the Building Trades Council in Salt Lake City and eventually served as president of the Utah State Federation of Labor. The family maintained ownership of this home until Elizabeth Wilkes's death in 1959.

222 I Street   B

BUILT: 1900/1940
STYLE: Art Moderne
ORIGINAL OWNER: Salt Lake City Fire Department

This fire station was remodeled in 1940 into the Art Moderne style. Scalloped sheet-metal trim runs along the cornice, above the original garage door, and along the edge of the entrance canopy. There is glass brick in the front window.

From 1900 until the 1980s this building served as the Salt Lake City fire station for the Avenues neighborhood. Salt Lake City fire Chief James Devine lived around the corner from this building when the station, designated Engine House No. 4, was built. An immediate consequence of the opening of this station was a 15 percent decrease in the insurance rates for Avenues' homes in 1900. The building has been converted into a residence.

227 I Street   `B`

BUILT: 1888/1912
STYLE: Vernacular/Bungalow
ORIGINAL OWNER: William J. and Maria Burnett

This home was built originally as a small, one-story vernacular cottage with a gable roof, end chimneys, and modified saltbox at the rear. A one-and-one-half-story, Bungalow-style addition was added to the front of the building in 1912. This building represents an example of an early remodel and style change for an Avenues home.

William and Maria Burnett were emigrants from England. This home was built for them in 1888. Mr. Burnett was an operator of a mule-drawn streetcar and later a conductor for the Utah Light and Traction Company. From 1908 until 1912 they maintained the home as a rental property. Marinus Anderson, a fellow conductor for the Utah Light and Traction Company, bought the home that year. The Anderson family maintained ownership of the home into the 1980s.

234 I Street   `B`

BUILT: 1895
STYLE: Federal/Colonial Revival
BUILDER: Alonzo Heber Worthen
ORIGINAL OWNER: Elizabeth Sholes and Alonzo Heber Worthen

This brick, gable-roofed, two-story house was significantly altered in 1925 and now exhibits elements of Federal style that is rare in Salt Lake City. Its tall, narrow windows are framed with stone sills and lintels. The front porch has a gable roof with arched cutout supported by slender, paired columns.

The home was built by contractor Alonzo Heber Worthen, and he and his wife, Elizabeth, were the first owners of the property. Celestia J. Grace Hudson and Frank A. Gregory each owned the house for thirty years.

236 I Street   `B`

BUILT: 1892
STYLE: Victorian Eclectic
ARCHITECT: H. H. Anderson
BUILDER: H. H. Anderson
ORIGINAL OWNER: John Burt

Well-preserved Eastlake ornamentation, such as the carved panels and elaborate woodwork of the porch, characterizes this two-story brick house. The house includes much decorative wood and brickwork along with multiple roofs and an octagonal corner tower.

Builder-architect Herman H. Anderson was responsible for numerous Salt Lake City buildings in the late nineteenth century. In addition to this home, he also designed 73 G Street. This home was built for John Burt, a well-known plasterer who worked on major building projects. He died at the age of forty and his family maintained ownership of the home until 1946.

273 I Street   B

BUILT: 1890
STYLE: Victorian Eclectic
ORIGINAL OWNER: Henry C. Hoffman

Scroll-sawn brackets and turned wooden columns are the Victorian characteristics of this cottage. Imitation brick siding added in the 1950s once covered the first floor exterior but has since been removed.

Henry C. Hoffman built this home, along with 271 and 275 I Street, as an investment property. George Dent, a motorman for the Salt Lake City Railroad, became the first resident owner of the home. Annie L. Bayliss purchased the property in 1908 and maintained it as a rental for the next forty years.

280 I Street   B

BUILT: 1891
STYLE: Victorian Eclectic
ORIGINAL OWNER: Sarah Barton

This two-story Victorian home is a type known as a central block with projecting bays. At the front of the house is a paired second-story window with a brick, first-story bay window. The original porch has been removed.

Sarah Barton was the first owner of the home and lived here until 1911. From 1912 until 1921 George and Ruth Eldredge owned the home. Mr. Eldredge was a streetcar motorman for the Utah Light and Traction Company. In the 1950s the home was divided into three apartments. Art and Marla Ashton purchased the house in 1958 and restored it to a single-family residence in the 1980s.

288 I Street   B

BUILT: 1905
STYLE: Bungalow
ORIGINAL OWNER: Thomas M. Mumford and John W. Moore

This is an early, one-story brick bungalow. Rafter ends are exposed at the eaves for decorative effect. The front porch is supported by Doric columns. The same developers built 286 I Street at the same time, and the two homes may be the oldest bungalows showing Craftsman detailing in the Avenues.

Thomas M. Mumford and John W. Moore built this home and 286 I Street as investment properties. Michael Drum, a conductor for the Oregon Short Line Railroad became the first resident owner in 1915. The home then became a rental property from 1918 until 1950.

333 I Street ◼ B

BUILT: 1901
STYLE: Victorian Eclectic
ORIGINAL OWNER: William M. and Ella J.
McConahy

This one-and-one-half-story Victorian cottage of pattern-book design was heavily remodeled in an attempt to modernize it in the early 1970s. The front of the house was covered with vertical siding and a large picture window.

William and Ella McConahy were the first resident owners of this property. Mr. McConahy was a jeweler in partnership with John Sharp. Harwood M. and Daisy Cushing purchased the home in 1930. They had been tenants in the home since 1915. Mr. Cushing was an employee of the Denver and Rio Grande Railroad for fifty years. In 1896 he was elected to Utah's first state legislature. After his death in 1932, his wife and daughter remained in the home until 1940.

565 I Street ◼ D

BUILT: 1915
STYLE: Craftsman Bungalow
BUILDER: Enoch Smith
ORIGINAL OWNER: Enoch Smith

The exposed rafter ends and heavy, bracketed gables of this one-and-one-half-story home are characteristic elements of the Craftsman Bungalow style. The steep gables are covered in half-timbering. Short, square, tapered wooden columns on high brick posts frame the recessed front porch.

Contractor Enoch Smith built this bungalow high in the Avenues for the time period. It was held as a rental property until 1921 when it was purchased by Mr. Smith's brother, Charles.

568 I Street ◼ D

BUILT: 1915
STYLE: Tudor Revival Bungalow
BUILDER: Enoch Smith
ORIGINAL OWNER: Enoch Smith

This one-and-one-half-story bungalow exhibits elements of the Tudor Revival style. The large dormer and south-side bay window exhibit half-timbering typical of the style. The front porch was partially enclosed with glass in the 1970s. There is a large addition off the rear of the home.

This home was built by developer Enoch Smith, who maintained the property as a rental unit until 1920. Edward R. and Bertha P. Phelps bought the home at that time.

J STREET

30 J Street B

BUILT: 1892
STYLE: Eastlake
ORIGINAL OWNER: Jeremiah Beattie

This home is the only complete example of Eastlake style in the Avenues. The house is decorated with turned ornamental wood-work that is the style's hallmark. This home may also be the largest wood-framed house in the historic district. Wood framing was a necessity in achieving the three-dimensional feel of the style. An octagonal tower with sunburst panels and a tapered conical roof stands over the gabled front entry. Eastlake posts brace the front façade gable, porch roof, and bay. The home matches a design from the pattern books of George F. Barber and Company 1891–1905. However, there is no evidence to confirm that the home was copied from the book.

Physician Jeremiah Beattie held this home as a rental unit until 1915 when it was purchased by Henry A. Sims. Mr. Sims and his children were pioneers in the local motion picture industry. One son owned the Isis Theatre.

77 J Street B

BUILT: 1875
STYLE: Victorian Eclectic
BUILDER: William J. Tuddenham
ORIGINAL OWNER: George W. Reed

This one-and-one-half-story Victorian home has a truncated hip roof, front dormer window, and projecting, gabled front bay. The front gable has returns and a circular window. Floral designs adorn the arched lintels on the first-story windows.

This home was held by one family from construction until 1982. George W. Reed was the first business manager of the *Deseret News* and one of the earliest owners of the rival *Salt Lake Tribune*. Mr. Reed died at this home in 1909 while recovering from being hit by an automobile. The home was built by Mr. Reed's brother-in-law, William J. Tuddenham, who also built 114 J Street. He was the contractor for the Hotel Utah.

114 J Street B

BUILT: 1903
STYLE: Victorian Eclectic
BUILDER: William J. Tuddenham
ORIGINAL OWNER: William J. Tuddenham Jr.

The front gable of this Victorian home covers a projecting segmental bay and is supported at the corners by scroll-sawn brackets. A cor-belled brick cornice runs along the bottom of the second-floor windows.

Contractor and builder William J. Tuddenham built this home for his son, who lived at the now-demolished 665 Second Avenue and maintained this home as a rental property. George N. Curtis, a physician and surgeon, bought this residence and 120 J Street in 1918. In 1936 he was secretary of the Utah State Medical Association and the following year served as its president. He also served as superintendent of the Salt Lake City General Hospital from 1939 until 1944.

115 J Street   B

BUILT: 1901
STYLE: Victorian Eclectic
ARCHITECT: David C. Dart
ORIGINAL OWNER: Frances J. Pascoe

This is a one-and-one-half-story Victorian cottage with a front dormer window and gabled front porch with wood Doric columns. A corbelled brick belt course runs around the house at the tops of the windows.

The home was built for Frances J. Pascoe, who was a clerk for the Oregon Short Line Railroad. He lived in this home until his death in 1950. The home's architect, David C. Dart, designed numerous homes in the Avenues of varying styles over a fifteen-year period. A large Safeway grocery store was to occupy this entire block in 1976, but community resistance led Safeway to abandon its plans.

122 J Street   B

BUILT: 1888
STYLE: Victorian Eclectic
ORIGINAL OWNER: William S. Owens

This one-story Victorian cottage has turned-wood columns supporting the front porch and a bracketed, wood-paneled, south-side bay window. The paired front windows have corbelled brick arches with stone keystones that are carved with abstract designs recalling faces.

William S. Owens, a salesman, purchased this land from his father and had the home built. In 1903 he sold the house to his father, William D. Owens Jr., who was a salesman for the ZCMI department store from its inception in 1869 until his death in 1916.

123 J Street   B

BUILT: 1873
STYLE: Vernacular
BUILDER: Thomas Goodman
ORIGINAL OWNER: Thomas Goodman

This one-story vernacular home has a T-shaped plan and gable roofs. The small front porch is supported by turned-wood columns.

Thomas Goodman and his wife, Harriett, came to Utah from England in 1866 and built this small home in 1873. Thomas was a carpenter. After his death, Harriet Goodman remained in this home until 1912 when it was sold to John C. Eaby, a gardener. The home remained in the Eaby family until 1966 when it was bought by developers for demolition. A large Safeway grocery store was to occupy this entire block, but community resistance led Safeway to abandon its plans. Gregory Walker bought the home in 1977, restored the residence, and sold the home to Ilene Kamsler.

166 J Street   B

BUILT: 1898
STYLE: Victorian Eclectic
ARCHITECT: Edgar Druce
BUILDER: Orville E. Hartwell
ORIGINAL OWNER: Geneva A. Kimball

This Victorian home has a segmental, two-story bay window. Rough-faced brick accents the corners of the house and forms a belt course across the front façade. The original porch columns were replaced by iron posts in the 1960s but have since been restored.

This home was built as a rental property, documenting the shift to absentee ownership of homes in the Avenues. Geneva A. Kimball, widow of Edwin Kimball, had this home and 172 J Street built. The first tenant in the property was Clarence Warnock owner of the Warnock Insurance Company. Another early tenant was Royal Daynes, who was a member of the prominent Daynes Music Company family. Mr. Daynes eventually became president of the company. His brother, Joseph J. Daynes, was the first organist for the Mormon Tabernacle Choir.

175 J Street   B

BUILT: 1891
STYLE: Victorian Eclectic
ORIGINAL OWNER: Alexander Lyon

This pattern-book-designed Victorian cottage has a front porch supported by Doric columns and a front gable covered in wood-shingle siding.

Alexander Lyon operated a grocery store at the corner of 400 South and West Temple when this home was built for him. In 1908 he sold the residence to James Barton, a machinist at Silver Brother Iron Works. Thomas Snedden, owner of the Hyland Bakery, bought the home in 1922.

183 J Street   B

BUILT: 1907
STYLE: Craftsman Bungalow
BUILDER: Lee Christopher
ORIGINAL OWNER: Lee and Melissa Christopher

This home is one of the earliest Craftsman bungalows in the Avenues. The gabled dormer shelters a second-floor porch with triple wooden columns. The dormer gable and the main side gables have bracketed barge-boards and wood-shingle siding. The recessed front porch has wooden, arched openings with paneled corner columns.

Lee Christopher, a contractor, built this home for his family. He and his wife, Melissa, lived here until 1921 when it was purchased by Charles N. Ray. Mr. Ray had been the physician for the Utah Copper Company in Bingham. He set up a private practice in Salt Lake City in 1913 and was appointed Salt Lake County Physician in 1916. He owned this home through the 1930s.

218 J Street   B

BUILT: 1924
STYLE: Prairie Bungalow
ORIGINAL OWNER: Harry James

This one-story, brick, hip-roofed bungalow is of the Prairie style, a common design found throughout Utah. The square posts supporting the porch eaves are a recent addition.

Harry James, the former owner of the market at 220 J Street, had this home built. The James family had originally owned most of this block. Mr. James was an employee of the Salt Lake Streets Department at the time of the home's construction. The James family owned the home until 1939. In 1967 the home was divided into apartments, but the building is now once again a single-family residence.

220 J Street   B

BUILT: 1892
STYLE: Commercial
ORIGINAL OWNER: A. G. Gardiner

This one-story commercial structure set close to the street has several gable-roofed rear wings. The building was remodeled with a new porch, windows, aluminum siding, and Permastone decoration in the 1950s.

This building was constructed by A. G. Gardiner for the Utah Candy Factory. He and his father-in-law, Richard James, operated the business together. Mr. Gardiner lived at 723 Fifth Avenue. Harry James, the son of Richard, operated a grocery store from this building between 1903 and 1919. He later took a job with the Salt Lake Streets Department. From 1920 until the early 1980s, various stores operated here, including the Cottage Grocery Store and the J Street Grocery Store.

227 J Street   B

BUILT: 1889/1906
STYLE: Dutch Colonial Revival
ORIGINAL OWNER: John F. Gunn

This one-and-one-half-story house with gambrel roof was originally built as a one-story Victorian cottage.

The home was originally built for John F. Gunn, an employee of the Utah Light and Traction Company. He maintained this property as a rental house and lived at the now-demolished 237 J Street. Anna T. Piercy purchased the home in 1906 and expanded it into its current size and design. A champion of women's rights, Mrs. Piercy, while a member of the Utah House of Representatives, authored bills to allow women to sit on juries and to limit the work day to eight hours. She founded the Woodrow Wilson Club in Utah and was a delegate to the 1930 Democratic Convention. Her son, J. K. Piercy, was a veteran fireman and served as fire chief for sixteen years. The Piercy family owned this home until 1966.

230 J Street   B

BUILT: 1900
STYLE: Victorian Eclectic
ORIGINAL OWNER: John M. Reinsimars

A corbelled brick course separates the first and second floors of this Victorian home. There is a large, arched first-floor front window. The front porch has been partially enclosed.

John M. Reinsimars, a manager at the Davis Shoe Company, was the original owner of this property. After his death in 1933, his wife, Nettie, continued to reside here until 1937. A later owner, Douglas D. Freeman, lived here from 1938 until 1945. He owned the J Street Grocery located at 220 J Street. The home is currently split into four apartments.

236 J Street   B

BUILT: 1904
STYLE: Dutch Colonial Revival
BUILDER: Louis Kjergard
ORIGINAL OWNER: Joseph W. Townsend

The gambrel roof on this home is characteristic of the Dutch Colonial Revival style. The front end of the roof is covered in wood-shingle siding. The recessed front porch is supported by Doric wood columns.

Louis and Anna Kjergard developed several homes in the Avenues. They completed this residence in 1904 and sold it to Joseph W. Townsend, a clerk at the Walker Brothers Department Store and A. Cohn and Company. William and Fannie Brother owned the home from 1908 until 1926. Mr. Brother was the secretary and treasurer for C. R. Savage and Company, which was the prominent photography and art firm located at 12 Main Street in Salt Lake City.

262 J Street   B

BUILT: 1903
STYLE: Victorian Eclectic
BUILDER: Charles W. Midgley
ORIGINAL OWNER: Charles W. Midgley

This pattern-book-designed Victorian home has a front gable covered in wood-shingle siding. The front porch's tapered wood columns have recently been replaced by round Greek columns.

Charles W. Midgley built this home and four others on the block as investment properties. This home is nearly identical to 252, 258, 264, and 270 J Street. Mr. Midgley, one of Salt Lake City's first theatre operators, owned the American Theater Company. The first resident owner of this home was Charles A. Johnson, who owned the home from 1907 until 1923. He was a manager and buyer of men's clothing for several Salt Lake City stores including the Auerbach's Department Store. The Dennis W. Black family purchased the home in 1929 and maintained ownership for more than fifty years.

264 J Street   `B`

BUILT: 1903
STYLE: Victorian Eclectic
BUILDER: Charles W. Midgley
ORIGINAL OWNER: Charles W. Midgley

This pattern-book-designed Victorian home features a front gable covered in wood-shingle siding. The front porch is supported by tapered wood columns.

Charles W. Midgley built this home and four others on the block as investment properties. The home is nearly identical to the other four, which are 252, 258, 262, and 270 J Street. Mr. Midgley was one of Salt Lake City's first theatre operators, owning the American Theater Company. Walter Bryant, a realtor, purchased the home soon after completion and maintained ownership until 1909. J. Herman Johnson, a civil engineer for the Union Pacific Railroad, purchased the property that year. From 1919 to 1940 the William R. H. Paxman family owned the house.

270 J Street   `B`

BUILT: 1903
STYLE: Victorian Eclectic
BUILDER: Charles W. Midgley
ORIGINAL OWNER: Charles W. Midgley

This pattern-book-designed Victorian home's front gable had been covered in aluminum siding. The original porch columns have been recently restored, replacing 1960s iron posts.

Charles W. Midgley built this home and four others on the block as investment properties. 252, 258, 262, and 270 are nearly identical houses. Mr. Midgley, one of Salt Lake City's first theatre operators, owned the American Theater Company. He never lived in this home but maintained it as a rental property. From 1907 until 1934 Orson P. and Abba G. Rumel owned the home. Mr. Rumel was an accountant and tax expert, and was also the purchasing agent for the Tintic Standard Mining Company.

281 J Street   `B`

BUILT: 1904
STYLE: Victorian Eclectic
ORIGINAL OWNER: Lorenzo and Althea Jensen

The pronounced gable roof of this Victorian home extends down to cover the front porch. The dormers and side gables have wood-shingle siding.

Lorenzo Jensen opened a grocery store in the commercial block at 285 J Street the same year he moved into this home. He lived here from 1904 until 1915. From 1922 until 1938 the home was owned by Fred Pinbourough, a butcher employed by the Palace Meat Market, Utah Packing Company, and Hoskisson and Swell's Market.

285 J Street `B`

BUILT: 1903
STYLE: Victorian Eclectic/Commercial
ORIGINAL OWNER: Myron Jensen

This large, two-story commercial block has a wooden cornice with decorative panels and a band of double-hung windows across the second story.

Myron Jensen built this structure to house a grocery store. Lorenzo Jensen, possibly Myron's brother, operated the store and owned the building from 1904 until 1910. That year Leo Dykes purchased the property for four thousand dollars and added living quarters for his family. He operated a meat market from this site. In 1939 the building was converted into apartments.

326 J Street `B`

BUILT: 1880/1913
STYLE: Victorian Eclectic
ORIGINAL OWNER: Alfred F. and Anne B. Oliver

Originally this house was built as a modest Victorian cottage. In 1913 a second story was added to the home. The Doric-columned front porch had a second story and stairwell added to it in the 1970s. The front bay has a triangular gable window, a three-part, second-story bay window with leaded glass, and a pair of first-story windows that have corbelled brick arches and carved keystones.

Alfred and Anne Oliver, who also owned 334 J Street, were the first owners of this property. Mr. Oliver was a tailor. For twenty-five years, the family lived variously at both homes. In the mid-1920s the home was converted into apartments. Mrs. Oliver continued to live in one of the apartments until her death in 1939.

334 J Street `B`

BUILT: 1901
STYLE: Victorian Eclectic
ARCHITECT: John A. Headlund
ORIGINAL OWNER: Alfred F. and Anne B. Oliver

A diamond-shaped pattern can be found in the second-story brick of this Victorian home. A corbelled belt course separates the first and second stories. The wide front porch is supported by Doric columns.

Salt Lake City architect John A. Headlund designed this home for Alfred F. Oliver, a tailor, and his wife, Anne. Mr. Oliver owned this property until 1925. During the twenty-four years of his ownership, he resided here and at 326 J Street for varying periods of time. From 1925 until 1948 John A. Beck, a carpenter, owned and resided in this home.

335 J Street   B

BUILT: 1898/1911
STYLE: Victorian Eclectic
BUILDER: C. Larson
ORIGINAL OWNER: John W. and Sarah E. Kenar

This one-story Victorian cottage was heavily remodeled in an attempt to modernize the home in the 1950s. The rectangular window in the bay and the pipe porch supports were added at that time.

John W. Kenar was an electrician for the Salt Lake Light and Traction Company when this home was built for him and his wife. In 1911 he added an additional two rooms to the home. Mr. Kenar began a twenty-five-year career as chief engineer for the ZCMI department store in 1922 and lived in this home until his death in 1947. He was survived by his wife and ten children. Sarah E. Kenar lived in the home until her death in 1959.

K STREET

27 K Street   B

BUILT: 1922
STYLE: Spanish Revival
BUILDER: C. R. Houghton
ORIGINAL OWNER: John A. Houghton

This home's red tile roof, stucco finish, arched entryway, and wide, overhanging eaves are characteristics of the Spanish Revival style.

John A. Houghton owned this home for one year but did not live in it. Jesse Jay Thompson owned the property from 1923 until 1935. Mr. Thompson was a member of the Salt Lake City Chamber of Commerce and the founder of the Hunter-Thompson Shoe and Hosiery Company, which operated until his retirement in 1943.

62 K Street   B

BUILT: 1890
STYLE: Victorian Eclectic
ORIGINAL OWNER: Arthur Foulger

This Victorian home has a jerkin-head roof with hip-roofed, side-dormer windows. The front gable is covered in fish-scale, wood-shingle siding. At the lower corners of the gable are elaborate beam-and-bracket decorations with sunburst panels. A second-story fire escape has been added to the home.

This home was built as a rental property for Arthur Foulger, who was variously employed as a druggist, a salesman at the ZCMI department store, a grocer, a root beer manufacturer, and an office manager at the Fisher Brewing Company. The first resident owners of the home were Thomas R. and Alma Buttrey. They resided in the home from 1920 until 1930. The home was converted into apartments in the 1940s.

68 K Street   B

BUILT: 1899
STYLE: Victorian Eclectic/Commercial
ORIGINAL OWNER: Herbert J. Foulger

This Victorian commercial building has a flat roof with a corbelled brick cornice on top. The original four second-story windows were bricked in and two horizontal windows added in the 1950s. The first-floor façade retains much of its original detailing.

This building originally housed the Peoples Equitable Institution, a general merchandise store. Herbert J. Foulger, the store manager, had previously been a construction manager for Brigham Young. He supervised the work on the Salt Lake LDS Temple and the ZCMI department store. Later, the Foulger Brothers Grocery Company was housed in this building. In 1921, Herman Uffens began operating the Golden Top Baking Company from here. The Utah Lace Curtain Cleaning Company occupied the building from 1929 through 1940. An early attempt at restoration was undertaken on this structure in 1968.

133 K Street | B |

BUILT: 1902
STYLE: Victorian Eclectic
ORIGINAL OWNER: Harrison A. Hull

The complex roof massing on this Victorian home shows the influence of the Queen Anne style. The tall, main hip roof flares out at the eaves. All the walls above the first story are covered in wood-shingle siding.

Real estate developer Harrison A. Hull had this home, 125, 127, and 139 K Street built as investments. The first resident owner was Albert H. King in 1907. Mr. King was a foreman for the Oregon Short Line Railroad. J. Warren Beless, manager of the Brigham Street Pharmacy, bought the home in 1918. Earl W. Harmer, a realtor, purchased the property in 1925.

187 K Street | B |

BUILT: 1908
STYLE: Bungalow
BUILDER: Dorius and Erickson
ORIGINAL OWNER: Austin and Son's Livestock Company

This one-story bungalow features a hip roof with a front center dormer. The rafter ends were originally left exposed for decorative effect, but the eaves have since been covered with aluminum siding. The wide front porch is supported by brick columns with corbelled decorations.

The real estate firm of Dorius and Erickson built this house and 183 K Street. They sold this one upon completion to the Austin and Sons Livestock Company as a residence for the company's president, George Austin, who lived here until 1910. Four other families occupied this home until 1928 when it was purchased by a carpenter named John Goodfellow. He lived here through the 1930s and his son and daughter-in-law, Lynn and Dorothy Goodfellow, remained in the home into the late 1990s.

188 K Street | B |

BUILT: 1908
STYLE: Bungalow
ARCHITECT: J. A. Headlund and Nord
BUILDER: W. C. Hawley
ORIGINAL OWNER: Eugene B. Palmer

This transitional bungalow exhibits elements of the Victorian design at a time when the Craftsman style was gaining popularity. The Doric columns and gabled front façade with fish-scale, wood-shingle siding are more commonly found on Victorian cottages.

The home was designed by the firm of Headlund and Nord and constructed by W. C. Hawley for Eugene B. Palmer. Mr. Palmer, a realtor, lived in the home until 1928 but maintained ownership of the property until 1938.

219 K Street

BUILT: 1900
STYLE: Victorian Eclectic
ORIGINAL OWNER: Franklin H. Pickering

This is a one-and-one-half-story Victorian cottage of pattern-book design. It has a hip roof and a gable-roofed front bay. The front gable has a Palladian window. The original porch columns were removed from the home in the early 1970s.

Franklin Pickering had this home built on land originally owned by his father, Simeon Pickering. Mr. Pickering drove mule cars, horse cars, and streetcars in Salt Lake City for forty-five years. He lived in this home with his wife until 1919. His son-in-law and daughter, Thomas B. and Mary Brighton, lived in the home after 1909. Mr. Brighton was a chemist in the local mining industry and would later become a chemistry professor at the University of California and the University of Utah. He died in 1934. Mary Brighton continued to live here until 1947.

222 K Street

B

BUILT: 1893
STYLE: Victorian Eclectic
ORIGINAL OWNER: Thomas A. Mulholland

This well-preserved, wood-frame Victorian home has an unusual H-shaped floor plan. A wood-columned front porch runs along the façade of the house, and a wrought-iron balustrade above the porch creates a second-floor balcony.

The Mulholland family owned a large portion of this lot in the nineteenth century. Thomas A. Mulholland acquired this property from his mother in 1893 and built the home. The manager of the Wheeler Publishing Company, he lived in this home until 1900 and maintained ownership until 1912. Eleanor K. Crawford purchased the house in 1914. She was a music teacher and used the house as her music studio. Her husband, Thomas C. Crawford, worked for the *Herald-Republican* newspaper. Sidney and Elizabeth L. Peek purchased the home in 1934 and lived here until 1976. Mr. Peek was a contractor.

223 K Street

B

BUILT: 1909
STYLE: Craftsman Bungalow
ORIGINAL OWNER: Frank M. Houghton

This is a one-and-one-half-story, hip-roofed bungalow with a front center dormer. The recessed front porch is supported by heavy wood columns. The home has exposed rafter tails typical of the Craftsman style.

Although there is no architect of record for this home, the residence may have been designed by David Dart, as it is very similar to a home he designed at 69 D Street. This house replaced an earlier structure and was built for Frank M. and Adelia T. Houghton. Mr. Houghton had a long career with ZCMI's drug department, eventually becoming assistant manager there. Mrs. Houghton remained in the home after Frank's death in 1934. The Houghton family maintained ownership of the home until 1969.

268 K Street B

BUILT: 1923
STYLE: Tudor Revival Bungalow
BUILDER: Walter Romney
ORIGINAL OWNER: Thomas E. and Laura Steele

This one-and-one-half-story bungalow exhibits elements of the Tudor Revival style popular in the 1920s. The stuccoed gable ends and dormers have half-timber decoration typical of the style. The front bay window has been altered.

This home and 707 Fifth Avenue were built for Thomas and Laura Steele the same year. They rented out this home until 1928. After residing in it for two years, they once again maintained the property as a rental until 1935. Mr. Steele was a vulcanizer for the Sims Tire Company. David H. and Mary H. Jordan purchased the property in 1935. Mr. Jordan was the registrar for LaSalle Extension University.

278 K Street B

BUILT: 1910
STYLE: Bungalow
ARCHITECT: Liljenberg and Sundberg
BUILDER: Quinn and Schmierer
ORIGINAL OWNER: John B. Quinn

This one-story bungalow has a recessed front porch supported by heavy brick columns. The hip roof has a front center dormer.

Contractors John B. Quinn and William Schmierer built the home, and Mr. Quinn assumed ownership after completion. Mr. Quinn lived here with his son Leo. After 1913 Mr. Quinn left contracting and became a champion bowler. He operated a bowling alley and trailer park in Salt Lake City. Stephen A. Stanford, a plumber and contractor, bought the home in 1914 and lived here until 1922.

284 K Street B

BUILT: 1878
STYLE: Vernacular
ORIGINAL OWNER: Henry F. Clark

This is a vernacular home with an L-shaped floor plan. A box cornice runs under the eaves. A one-room addition was made in 1889. The garage addition is not original to the home.

Henry F. Clark came to Utah from England in 1852 and operated a tailor shop at 69 State Street from 1886 until 1926. He died in the home that year. His wife, Margaret M. Clark, continued to live here until 1937. In 1938 Jay W. Wright, an engineer with KSL Radio, bought the property.

287 K Street [B]

BUILT: 1898
STYLE: Victorian Eclectic
BUILDER: M. D. Kearns
ORIGINAL OWNER: Thomas W. and Millicent Halliday

The front gable of this Victorian cottage was covered in aluminum siding in the 1960s. The shingle exterior has been restored along with the front porch columns. A corbelled brick belt course runs around the arched lintels of the first-story windows.

This home was built for Thomas and Millicent Halliday. Mr. Halliday was a civil engineer. They sold the home in 1900 to John Griffin, who was an accountant for the Internal Revenue Service. Mr. Griffin lived in the home until he built the adjacent 289 K Street in 1905.

314 K Street [B]

BUILT: 1902
STYLE: Queen Anne
BUILDER: Harrison Hull
ORIGINAL OWNER: Harrison and Mary E. Hull

Excellent decorative elements are found on this Queen Anne cottage. The front gable is covered in bands of fish-scale, wood-shingle siding and latticework. Below the bay gable is a large, arched front window with small decorative border panes around the upper sash.

Harrison Hull built this home as an investment and sold it to John and Mary Napper soon after completion. Mr. Napper was a shipping clerk at the National Biscuit Company. Avenues real estate developers Lucy and Adolf Richter purchased the property in 1908 and held it as a rental unit until 1930. George A. and Mary L. Derrick moved into the house in 1929 and became owners in 1947. They lived here until their deaths in 1963 and 1966, respectively.

317 K Street [B]

BUILT: 1923
STYLE: Bungalow
BUILDER: P. T. Harmon
ORIGINAL OWNER: Jacob P. and Emma C. Sorenson

Heavy brick columns support the recessed front porch of this hip-roofed bungalow.

The home was built for Jacob and Emma Sorenson. Mr. Sorenson was a postal clerk. He died at this address in 1947. Emma lived in the home until her death in 1958. A basement apartment was added to the home in 1961 by John W. Albrecht, who was a clerk.

326 K Street [B]

BUILT: 1888
STYLE: Vernacular
BUILDER: Charles Caldwell
ORIGINAL OWNER: Charles Caldwell

This is a vernacular cottage with an L-shaped floor plan and an addition on the south side. The front porch, windows, and siding were changed in the 1950s. The exterior has since been restored.

Charles Caldwell, a carpenter, built this home for himself. He lived in the home until 1898 but maintained ownership until 1905. Prominent Utah physician William F. Beer bought the home as a rental property that year. He lived at 181 B Street. Daniel Weller, a portrait artist, moved into the home in 1906, purchased it from Mr. Beer in 1912, and lived here until his death in 1923. Members of his family continued to own the property into the 1980s.

334 K Street [B]

BUILT: 1889
STYLE: Victorian Eclectic
BUILDER: Charles Caldwell
ORIGINAL OWNER: Charles and Emily Caldwell

This is a one-story Victorian cottage with a main hip roof and a projecting, gabled front bay. The gable is covered in asbestos shingles dating to the 1940s or 1950s.

Charles Caldwell, a carpenter, built this home for his family. His son, also named Charles, built his house at 326 K Street. The elder Mr. Caldwell sold this home in 1894 to Alfred M. Derrick. Mr. Derrick was a conductor for the Salt Lake Railway and later became superintendent for the Utah Light and Railway Company. He lived here until his death in 1934.

337 K Street [B]

BUILT: 1907
STYLE: Dutch Colonial Revival
ORIGINAL OWNER: Burton J. and Sarah Ann Hardy

This home was originally built as a one story Victorian cottage. At a later date it was remodeled in the Dutch Colonial Revival style. It has a main gambrel roof and a small, decorative front gambrel bay. The first floor is built from concrete blocks, an early example of this type of construction.

This home was built for Burton J. and Sarah Ann Hardy. Mr. Hardy was an engineer for the Leyson-Pearsall Company. Petrear Giles purchased the home in 1923, and several different members of the Giles family occupied the home for the next seventy-five years.

339 K Street

B

BUILT: 1907
STYLE: Bungalow
BUILDER: William Mantle
ORIGINAL OWNER: William Mantle

This is a transitional bungalow, exhibiting the floor plan of the Bungalow style while still carrying some Victorian detailing. The front gable has returns, wood-shingle siding, and a Palladian window. The original Crager Wire and Iron Works fence runs along the street. Iron posts have replaced the original porch columns.

William Mantle, a contractor, built this home and resided in it for one year. Lloyd P. and Martha Thomas were the next resident owners. Mr. Thomas was a travel agent. In 1919 the home was purchased by Leander J. Parce, a pattern maker for the Utah Copper Company. He lived in the house until his death in 1939.

L STREET

24 L Street   B

BUILT: 1888/1909
STYLE: American Four Square/Craftsman
ORIGINAL OWNER: John W. and Catherine M. King

This Four Square home, originally built as a brick Victorian cottage, was heavily remodeled in 1909. The wide, one-story front porch is supported by heavy square columns. The exposed rafter tails are typical of the Craftsman style. The 1909 alterations to this home are representative of modifications made to early Avenues houses to meet the needs of subsequent owners.

John and Catherine King were the first owners of this home. He was a freight agent for the Rio Grande Western Railroad. In 1907 the home was purchased by Joseph E. and Violet Galligher. Mr. Galligher was the manager of the Utah Mining Machinery and Supply Company. He was responsible for the major remodel of the home. Max Ottenheimer purchased the home in 1914 and lived here through the 1940s.

63 L Street   B

BUILT: 1891/1899
STYLE: Victorian Eclectic
ARCHITECT: Joseph J. Paul
BUILDER: G. Trobridge
ORIGINAL OWNER: William J. Heckman

This one-story Victorian cottage has a main hip roof with a gable and a projecting, front gabled bay.

William J. Heckman built this home in two stages. The rear section was built for two hundred fifty dollars in 1891. The front brick section was added in 1899. Mr. Heckman served in the U.S. Army at Fort Douglas and stayed in Salt Lake City after leaving the army. In 1902 he opened a small grocery and moved from the L Street house. John T. and Isabella H. Nattress bought the home in 1904. Mr. Nattress was variously employed as a clerk for the Peoples Cash Store, as a deputy sheriff, and as an inspector for the Board of Health.

70 L Street   B

BUILT: 1897
STYLE: Victorian Eclectic
ORIGINAL OWNER: Herbert J. and Charlotte M. Foulger

A decorative, corbelled brick arch in the gable and two corbelled brick belt courses around the house are features of this well-preserved Victorian home. The first-story front porch has a dentiled cornice and is supported by Doric wood columns.

The home was built for Herbert and Charlotte Foulger. Mr. Foulger began as a carpenter and rose to be supervising carpenter on the construction of the Salt Lake LDS Temple and original ZCMI department store. He later opened several grocery stores including the Twentieth Ward Co-op, Peoples Equitable Cooperative Store, and the Foulger Brothers General Store. Mrs. Foulger was active in LDS Church affairs. She remained in this home until her death in 1938. Her daughter, Edith M. Foulger, inherited the property.

73 L Street   B

BUILT: 1901
STYLE: Victorian Eclectic
ORIGINAL OWNER: Wallace C. and Alice B.
Castleton

This is a pattern-book-designed Victorian cottage. The front porch is supported by Doric wood columns.

This home was built for Wallace C. and Alice Bitner Castleton. Mr. Castleton served for several years as Brigham Young's personal gardener. He later operated the Castleton Brothers General Merchandise store on the corner of L Street and Second Avenue with his brothers. Mr. Castleton also worked for the ZCMI department store and as a director for the Patrick Dry Goods Wholesalers. He died in 1932. His son, Wallace Lowell Castleton, inherited the home from his mother in 1940. He founded the Castleton's Department Stores that were found throughout Utah from the 1960s through the 1980s.

75 L Street   B

BUILT: 1890
STYLE: Vernacular
ORIGINAL OWNER: Frank M. and Eleanor H.
Castleton

This is a small, hip-roofed vernacular cottage with some Victorian detailing. The simple front porch is supported by Doric wood columns.

This home was built for Frank M. and Eleanor H. Castleton. Mr. Castleton was part of the prominent Avenues family of retailers and operated the Castleton Brothers General Merchandise Store on corner of L Street and Second Avenue. His brother and sister in-law, Wallace C. and Alice B. Castleton, lived in this house prior to the construction of their home at 73 L Street. After 1900, the Castleton brothers' mother, Frances B. Castleton, occupied the residence. Louis Hyrum Booth purchased the home in 1928 and remained here until 1944. He was a cabinet maker for the Salt Lake Cabinet and Fixture Company.

125 L Street   B

BUILT: 1900
STYLE: Victorian Eclectic
ARCHITECT: John A. Headlund
ORIGINAL OWNER: John R. Hardman

This Victorian home, designed by prominent architect John A. Headlund, has complex roof massing. There is a main gable roof with an added front gable, a projecting front bay window with a segmental hip roof, and a hip-roofed front porch.

This home was built for John R. Hardman, who was a clerk at the ZCMI department store. He lived here only briefly. From 1901 until 1925 the home was a rental property. In 1930 Henry L. and Mima J. Jackson bought the property. Mr. Jackson operated a small grocery store in Salt Lake City. The house remained in the Jackson family until 1951.

128 L Street B

BUILT: 1910
STYLE: Bungalow
ORIGINAL OWNER: Thomas H. Lawson

This bungalow has a long gabled roof with a front, center shed-roofed dormer. Heavy wood columns support the recessed front porch.

Thomas H. Lawson, the home's original owner, was a clerk for Auerbach's Department Store when this home was built. He lived here until 1925 when John S. and Nellie Pasey purchased the residence. Mr. Pasey worked as a clerk for the Strevell Paterson Hardware Company.

168 L Street B

BUILT: 1907
STYLE: Bungalow
BUILDER: William C. Steers
ORIGINAL OWNER: William C. Steers

This is a one-story, gable-roofed bungalow. The front gable has fascia boards supported by heavy purlins and wood-shingle siding. The recessed front porch is supported by brick columns.

The home was most likely built by William C. Steers. He was the owner of a good portion of this block and owned this property until 1919. Charles J. and Effie Thomas purchased the home that year. Charles, whose father was a well-known musician in England, was a furniture dealer most of his life and a partner in the Thomas and Madsen Furniture Company. The Thomas family remained in the home until 1949.

174 L Street B

BUILT: 1897
STYLE: Victorian Eclectic
ORIGINAL OWNER: John W. and Laura Smith Walker

This is a one-story Victorian home with a main hip roof and a hip-roofed front bay. The original front porch columns have been replaced by iron posts.

This home was built for John W. Walker the year he married Laura Smith, daughter of LDS Church president Joseph F. Smith. Mr. Walker was in the insurance business for many years and served a four-year term as insurance commissioner for Utah. Hans Christensen purchased the property in 1915 and maintained it as a rental property.

177 L Street   B

BUILT: 1900
STYLE: Victorian Eclectic
ORIGINAL OWNER: Arthur and Gertrude E. Hulbert

A truncated hip roof and boxed cornice are found on this two-story Victorian home. There is a wood-paneled, one-story front bay window. The original front porch had been removed and replaced by a canopy, but the porch has since been restored.

Arthur and Gertrude Hulbert were the first owners of this property. Mr. Hulbert, who came to Utah from England as an LDS convert in 1888, was a trunk manufacturer. With his brother Henry, they operated the Hulbert Brothers Trunk Factory. The Hulbert family maintained ownership of this home until 1948.

183 L Street   B

BUILT: 1890
STYLE: Victorian Eclectic
BUILDER: Alma Caffall
ORIGINAL OWNER: Charles G. Lutz

This Victorian home has a projecting front bay. The tall, narrow paired windows in the bay have corbelled brick arches. The existing front porch is not original to the home.

Alma Caffall built this home and 187 L Street. He sold this residence upon completion to Charles G. Lutz. As a young man, Mr. Lutz was a freight driver between Salt Lake City and Park City. He later worked as a builder under William Tuddenham in the construction of the LDS Hospital on Eighth Avenue. He owned the home until 1932 when his son, Clarence O. Lutz, became the owner.

187 L Street   B

BUILT: 1890
STYLE: Victorian Eclectic
BUILDER: Alma Caffall
ORIGINAL OWNER: Alma and Annie Caffall

This Victorian home has a small, projecting, gabled front bay from a central block, a design that was popular in the Avenues. The tall, narrow paired windows in the bay have corbelled brick arches. The wood front porch is supported by Doric wood columns.

Alma Caffall built this home for his family. Mr. Caffall was a mason and emigrated from England as a convert to the LDS Church. His wife, Annie, remained in the home after Alma's death in 1926. Annie Caffall owned the home until 1941.

230 L Street B

BUILT: 1894
STYLE: Victorian Eclectic
ORIGINAL OWNER: Arthur and Ellen VanMeter

This one-story, gable-roofed Victorian cottage was heavily remodeled in the 1970s. Few of the original architectural details remain on the home.

This home was built for Arthur and Ellen VanMeter, who moved from 24 H Street in 1894. Mr. VanMeter was employed by the Utah Nursery Company and was later a partner in VanMeter, Harness, and Company Nursery. Mr. and Mrs. VanMeter remained in the home until 1904. William and Edith McKee purchased the home in 1908. Mr. McKee worked as a clerk for the Oregon Short Line Railroad before becoming a janitor for the Salt Lake City schools. The McKee family lived here until 1941.

253 L Street B

BUILT: 1935
STYLE: Art Moderne
BUILDER: Carl W. Buehner
ORIGINAL OWNER: Ervin N. and Ruth B. Dahl

This home is an excellent and rare example of streamlined Art Moderne design in the Avenues. Glass brick, steel sash corner windows, rounded exterior corners, and a flat roof are common features. It was originally built as a one-story, one-bedroom home.

Carl W. Buehner used concrete blocks covered in stucco to build this home. Erwin and Ruth Dahl purchased the home upon completion. Mr. Dahl was a salesman for the Hoffman Hardware and Sporting Goods Company. The front porch was enclosed in 1959. Tony J. Quesinberry made compatible modifications to the structure in 1998. A second-story master bedroom and bath were added, the garage basement was enclosed, and the driveway was moved to L Street. Alan and Linda Danielson created a carport over the drive and further expanded the second story addition in 2009.

268 L Street B

BUILT: 1927
STYLE: Period Revival
ARCHITECT: Swen Hansen
BUILDER: Henry B. Whitman
ORIGINAL OWNER: Henry B. Whitman

This is a Period Revival cottage with a small, gable-roofed front porch. The original porch columns had been replaced by iron posts, but they were recently restored. The bay window on the north end of the façade was added in the 1950s.

Henry B. Whitman, a contractor, built this house and maintained it as rental property until 1933. Howard A. and Dora C. Hanks purchased the home that year. Mr. Hanks was a salesman for the Acme White Lead and Color Works Company. In 1939 the home was purchased by Derell McCullough, who owned McCullough's Market at the corner of Sixth Avenue and L Street. He was also the president of the local Audubon Society. He remained in this home until his death in 1963.

274 L Street ◼B

BUILT: 1915
STYLE: Bungalow
ORIGINAL OWNER: Peter N. Rourke

The front gable on this bungalow has plain fascia boards supported by purlins. The home was originally covered in wood siding, but has recently been resurfaced in stucco.

George A. Cooke purchased the north half of this block in 1888 and it became known as Cooke's Subdivision. Peter N. Rourke bought the property in 1911 and built 274, 278, and 282 L Street. Henry and Leona Schranz purchased this home upon completion in 1915. He was then employed as a member of the Salt Lake City Police Department. He worked on the traffic squad stationed on the corner of Main Street and South Temple and was a well-known fixture in the intersection in the 1920s. After Henry's death, Mrs. Schranz remained in the home until 1936. Floyd Goodson, a Salt Lake City fireman, was the owner from 1938 until 1956.

319 L Street ◼B

BUILT: 1902
STYLE: Victorian Eclectic
ORIGINAL OWNER: Willard H. Lyman

An unusual gabled roof characterizes this Victorian home. The roof of the south-side wing is higher than that on the front wing. Gables are covered in patterned, wood-shingle siding. The corners of the home are accented with rough-faced brick. An addition was added to the home in 1921.

Willard H. Lyman was a salesman for the ZCMI department store when he became owner of this home. His wife, Hildegard S. Lyman, was an active leader of the Daughters of Utah Pioneers and the Twenty-first Ward Relief Society. The Lymans lived in this home until 1963.

338 L Street ◼B

BUILT: 1910
STYLE: Bungalow
BUILDER: L. S. Hoglund
ORIGINAL OWNER: John K. Hardy

This is a gable-roofed bungalow with a front center dormer. The gable ends and dormer are covered in wood-shingle siding. The recessed front porch is supported by brick columns.

John K. Hardy was a prominent banker and Utah state official when he had this bungalow built. Mr. Hardy had been appointed deputy U.S. Marshal for the state of Utah at the age of seventeen in 1897. From 1909 to 1917 he was the personal secretary for Governor William Spry and supervised the construction of the Utah State Capitol. He also served as an executive with several prominent Utah banks in his life. He lived in this home until his death in 1930. His wife, Clare Hardy, remained in the home until 1948.

M STREET

70 M Street B

BUILT: 1891
STYLE: Victorian Eclectic
ORIGINAL OWNER: Rachel McMaster

This large, two-story Victorian home has a gabled, segmental front bay. The gable is faced with patterned, wood-shingle siding. The two-story enclosed front porch was added in the 1950s.

This home was built for Rachel McMaster, a conductor on the Salt Lake City Railway. In 1901 the residence was sold to real estate agent Charles A. Groeber, who owned the property briefly before selling it to Charles H. and Lillian Reilley. The building would remain a rental property for most of the rest of the century. Mr. Reilley owned several bars in Salt Lake City including the Elk Saloon, the Buffalo Saloon, and the Flagstaff Bar. Lillian Reilley lived at times in the adjacent homes at 72 and 80 M Street, both of which have been demolished.

71 M Street B

BUILT: 1902
STYLE: Victorian Eclectic
BUILDER: Harrison A. Hull
ORIGINAL OWNER: William S. and Edith Jones

This two-story Victorian home has a projecting front bay that has a segmental hip roof. There are two corbelled belt courses, one at the top of the second-story windows and the other separating the first and second stories. The front porch has square wooden columns.

Real estate developer Harrison A. Hull built this home and sold it for $3,850 to William and Edith Jones. Mr. Jones operated the Jones Hammer Advertising Agency with his next door neighbor, Paul Hammer. The agency advertised and produced programs for local theaters. Mr. Jones also owned the Grand Theatre. This home was a rental property from 1912 until 1922 when it was purchased by Thomas and Jessie K. McOwens. Mr. McOwens was an engineer for Salt Lake City.

75 M Street B

BUILT: 1891
STYLE: Victorian Eclectic
ORIGINAL OWNER: John J. Daly

This large, brick, two-story Victorian home has a projecting, hip-roofed front bay. The front porch is not original to the home.

The home was built for John J. Daly, president of the Daly West Mining Company and the First National Bank of Park City. It was held as a rental property and is an example of early absentee ownership in the Avenues. The first resident owners were Paul and Annie D. Hammer. Mr. Hammer had a sixty-year career in theater in Salt Lake City, holding many jobs in the industry including actor, stage manager, theatre advertiser, and vice president of the Salt Lake Amusement Association. The home has remained a rental property for much of its existence.

89 M Street   B

BUILT: 1908
STYLE: Bungalow
ORIGINAL OWNER: Louis M. Smith

This one-and-one-half-story bungalow has a hip roof with front and side dormers. The front porch is supported by tapered wood columns.

This home was built as an investment property for Louis M. Smith, president of the Smith Jewelry Manufacturing Company. The home was held as a rental property until 1921 when Hans and Adna Flo bought and occupied the home. Mr. Flo was a clerk for the Federal Reserve Bank while Adna Flo was a well-known voice teacher in Salt Lake City. From 1936 until the mid-1950s, Merrill C. and Louise Conklin owned the home. Mr. Conklin was an employee of the Grand Hotel.

123 M Street   B

BUILT: 1887
STYLE: Victorian Eclectic
ORIGINAL OWNER: John H. Miller Jr.

This one-and-one-half-story Victorian home has a gable roof. The face of the gable is covered in wood-shingle siding and has two diamond-shaped windows. The original front porch had been replaced by a noncompatible metal shed porch in the 1950s, but it has since been restored.

This home was built for John H. Miller Jr., a barber who operated his shop out of the home after 1897. The home was purchased in 1900 by Hugo D. E. Peterson, a Swedish immigrant to Utah. He was a printer for the *Deseret News* and, from 1914 until 1923, the editor of the *Utah Posten*, a Swedish-language weekly newspaper. The home is currently a duplex.

128 M Street   B

BUILT: 1900
STYLE: Victorian Eclectic
ORIGINAL OWNER: James A. Alcorn

This one-story Victorian home has a hip roof and a front gable with Palladian window. The front porch was added around 1915. This home is more typical of the Bungalow style popular during that time.

The home was built for English immigrant and carpenter James A. Alcorn. When he moved to Midvale in 1904 to operate the West Jordan Lumber Company, the home was purchased by Alfred E. Pritchard, a longtime employee of the U.S. Postal Service. He moved to 529 Sixth Avenue in 1920 and sold the home to Clarence A. Foulger. The Foulger family operated a general store at 70 K Street. Mr. Foulger worked in the store as a young man before becoming a clerk with the ZCMI department store.

135–137 M Street B

BUILT: 1909
STYLE: Victorian Eclectic
ARCHITECT: Richard K. A. Kletting
BUILDER: Tako Company
ORIGINAL OWNER: Tako Company

This two-story duplex apartment building was built in a Victorian row-house style, a style that is rare in Salt Lake City. The building has a parapet roof with a corbelled cornice in front. The front porch has its original wood Doric columns.

The development of this building by a real estate firm known as the Tako Company represents the increase in multifamily housing during the early part of the twentieth century. Prominent Utah architect Richard K. A. Kletting designed this building. Mr. Kletting was also the architect of the Utah State Capitol.

163 M Street B

BUILT: 1910
STYLE: Bungalow
BUILDER: Joseph R. Walker
ORIGINAL OWNER: Joseph R. Walker

This bungalow has a high hip roof with front and side dormers. The front porch has its original iron balustrades and tapered wooden columns. Noncompatible stairs were added to the north side of the home to access an upstairs apartment.

Joseph R. Walker built this home as well as 165 M Street. Mr. Walker was the grandson of one of the four Walker brothers who founded Walker Brothers Department Store and the Walker Bank Company. Mr. Walker became a real estate developer after working in his grandfather's department store. In 1924 the home was purchased by George D. Guiver, a meat cutter. The Guiver family built several homes and a store on T Street.

204 M Street B

BUILT: 1906
STYLE: Victorian Eclectic
BUILDER: Angus McKellar
ORIGINAL OWNER: William L. Squier

This Victorian cottage is probably a pattern-book design. The home has a large, gable-roofed front bay. The gabled porch has a decorative oval-shaped window. The porch was restored in 1996.

Angus McKellar built this home as well as 803 Fourth Avenue, 214 M Street, and 216 M Street for investment purposes. William L. Squier, the manager of the Salt Lake Package Delivery Company, was the first resident owner. Charles B. and Emiline Kent were the resident owners from 1921 until 1937. Mr. Kent was a vocalist in Vaudeville theaters, taught music in Salt Lake City, and was a soloist with the Mormon Tabernacle Choir. A later resident owner, Graham Stork, won a Heritage Award in 1996 for restoring the front window and replacing a 1950s-era porch.

221 M Street   B

BUILT: 1907
STYLE: Victorian Eclectic
BUILDER: Theodore Bussman
ORIGINAL OWNER: Theodore Bussman

The design of this Victorian cottage is commonly found throughout the Avenues. There is a lunette window in the main gable. The front porch gable has returns and is supported by iron posts that replaced the original columns. This home is similar to the adjacent 217 and 229 M Street.

The cottage was built by Theodore Bussman, who lived in the home for one year. In 1908 the residence was purchased by John G. and Amy H. Giles. Mr. Giles owned a grocery store in Magna. From 1911 until 1924, the home was owned by George H. James, a traveling salesman and a member of the Salt Lake City Elks Lodge. After 1924, the home changed hands numerous times and was also held as a rental property.

224 M Street   B

BUILT: 1921
STYLE: Prairie Bungalow
ARCHITECT: W. A. Stumm
BUILDER: Roscoe M. Tew
ORIGINAL OWNER: George B. Gudgell

Prairie-style bungalows such as this home are commonly found throughout Utah's early twentieth-century neighborhoods. This home has a hip roof and offset front porch.

Building contractor and stone mason Roscoe M. Tew built this home as an investment. In 1924 George B. Gudgell became the first resident owner. Mr. Gudgell was a clerk at the R. E. Price Grocery Store at 700 South and 700 East in Salt Lake City. From 1926 until 1934 the home was owned by Fred and Geraldine Alkire. Mr. Alkire was the owner of the Alkire-Smith Auto Company.

229 M Street   B

BUILT: 1905
STYLE: Victorian Eclectic
BUILDER: Theodore Bussman
ORIGINAL OWNER: Frank W. and Lena C. Olmstead

This is a common Victorian cottage design found throughout the Avenues. There is a boarded-up lunette window in the main gable, while the front porch gable has returns and is supported by tapered wood columns.

This cottage was built by Theodore Bussman for Frank and Lena Olmstead. Mr. Olmstead worked for the Fidelity Casualty Company in Salt Lake City. From 1915 until 1967 the home was owned by the Straup family. Daniel N. Straup was a prominent Salt Lake City attorney, instructor at the University of Utah Law School, and a Utah Supreme Court justice. His wife, Della Straup, was active in community organizations including the Ladies Literary Club.

230 M Street   B

BUILT: 1890
STYLE: Victorian Eclectic
ORIGINAL OWNER: Richard B. Whitemore and
William H. Shearman

This Victorian home has a main hip roof and a projecting, two-story, gabled front bay. A unique triangular window is found in the gable. The upper walls are covered in patterned, wood-shingle siding which flares out over the first floor. The stucco finish of the first floor may not be original to the home. The large, first-floor picture window replaced the original detailed front window.

Richard Whitemore and William Shearman built this house as an investment property. The home was occupied from 1898 to 1904 by J. William Edmunds, a certified public accountant and member of the Chamber of Commerce. Dr. Samuel H. Allen purchased the home in 1904. He would later build a Prairie-style house on the corner of Eighth Avenue and A Street.

232 M Street   B

BUILT: 1903
STYLE: Victorian Eclectic
BUILDER: James P. Kjergard
ORIGINAL OWNER: James P. and Thora Kjergard

This one-and-one-half-story, gable-roofed home has large side dormers. The gables have returns and the upper walls of the house are covered in wood-shingle siding. There is a small gable above the entrance to the Doric-columned front porch.

James and Thora Kjergard were Danish immigrants who came to Utah in 1895. Mr. Kjergard was a contractor who built several homes in this portion of the Avenues. The Kjergards were also early members of Salt Lake City's Danish Evangelical Lutheran Church. They lived in this home until 1907. From 1907 until 1938 the property was owned by Lynda M. McCarty, who maintained the home as a rental property. From 1938 until 1971, Harvey and Elva Hansen owned the house.

234 M Street   B

BUILT: 1905
STYLE: Victorian Eclectic
BUILDER: James P. Kjergard
ORIGINAL OWNER: Burton O. and Missie E. Curtis

This two-story Victorian home has a projecting, gabled front bay. The one-story front porch has wood-shingle siding in the gable and wood Doric columns.

James P. Kjergard built several homes in this portion of the Avenues including the adjacent 232 M Street. Upon completion of this home, it was purchased by Burton O. and Missie E. Curtis. Mr. Curtis was an assistant engineer for the Oregon Short Line Railroad. In 1909 the home was sold to Martha S. Duncan, who taught English at West High School from 1900 until 1941. She owned the home until 1957.

280 M Street   B

BUILT: 1918
STYLE: Prairie Bungalow
ARCHITECT: H. McKean
BUILDER: Joshua M. Worthen
ORIGINAL OWNER: Joshua M. and Alfreda F. Worthen

This brick, one-story bungalow exhibits the horizontal lines of Prairie-style architecture. It has a low hip roof and front porch supported by paired brick columns.

Joshua M. Worthen, a contractor, built this home for his family at a cost of two thousand dollars. In 1920 he sold the home to Olaf and Edna Erickson. Mr. Erickson was employed as a freight and passenger agent for the Southern Pacific Railroad. The Erickson family lived in this home until 1952.

307 M Street   B

BUILT: 1879/1910
STYLE: Craftsman
ORIGINAL OWNER: Ephraim Caffall

This Craftsman-style home is covered in wood-shingle siding. The gable roof has supporting brackets at the ends. The cobblestone chimney, front porch railing, street wall, and pergola supports bring in natural elements important to the Craftsman style.

This home most likely incorporates an 1879 vernacular structure built by Ephraim Caffall. In 1910, Rachel McMaster, a real estate speculator, purchased the property and expanded the home to its present proportions. The residence remained a rental property until 1914 when it was bought by Asa S. Kienke, head of the Mechanical Arts Department at the old LDS College. He was the last surviving member of the Brigham Young Academy expedition to the lands of the Book of Mormon. This was the first Mormon group to travel to Central America and Mexico.

312 M Street   B

BUILT: 1890
STYLE: Victorian Eclectic
ORIGINAL OWNER: Harry E. and Fanny. Bailey

This small Victorian cottage with several rear additions has a gabled roof with chimneys at each end. The small front porch has turned columns and scroll-sawn brackets and trim.

This home is typical of the older remaining Avenues' homes built by new residents to Salt Lake City late in the nineteenth century. Harry E. Bailey and his wife Fanny came to Utah in 1887 after converting to the Mormon faith in England. They built this home in 1890. Mr. Bailey was a conductor for the Salt Lake City Railway Company. Descendents of the Bailey family maintained ownership of this property for nearly one hundred years. This is a rare example of long-term, single-family homeownership in the Avenues.

328 M Street [B]

BUILT: 1903
STYLE: Victorian Eclectic
BUILDER: Brewster and Oakley
ORIGINAL OWNER: Charles J. and Alice Dangerfield

This well-preserved, brick Victorian home has a small, gabled front porch supported by wooden Doric columns. Under this front porch is a decorative leaded-glass oval window.

The home was built for Charles J. and Alice Dangerfield. Mr. Dangerfield, an immigrant from England and a tinsmith, was the foreman for the David James Company of tinners. The Dangerfield family remained in the home until 1930 when it became a rental property. In 1945 Albert T. and Alice A. Shepherd purchased the home from Alice Dangerfield. Mr. and Mrs. Shepherd were noted Utah violinists. They taught music and played in symphonies throughout the Intermountain West. Alice Shepherd remained in this home until her death in 1965.

340 M Street [B]

BUILT: 1898
STYLE: Victorian Eclectic
BUILDER: Croxford Brothers
ORIGINAL OWNER: Joseph M. Lindsey

This historic Avenues home, originally Victorian Eclectic, has been extensively remodeled twice in its history. Few architectural elements remain from the original home. A dominating, shingle-covered mansard roof was added to the home in the 1960s. In 2002 the home's exterior was changed to a French Country style.

Joseph M. and Rose A. Lindsey had this home built on the corner across from his family's former resort. Lindsey Gardens, established by Joseph Lindsey's parents, was Utah's first amusement park and playgrounds. The Gardens were established in 1865 and later sold to Salt Lake City after failing financially. Mr. Lindsey, a streetcar operator, built this home on land still owned by the Lindsey family. Rose Lindsey remained in the home until her death in 1956.

N STREET

25 N Street   B

BUILT: 1909
STYLE: Bungalow
ARCHITECT: Bernard O. Mecklenburg
ORIGINAL OWNER: Edward A. Althoff

This one-story bungalow has been stripped of most of its original architectural details. This home and the adjacent 21 N Street were designed by prominent Salt Lake City architect Bernard O. Mecklenburg, who was known for several large homes designed on South Temple Street.

The home was built as a rental property for realtor Edward A. Althoff. In 1912 Archibald E. Tomlinson, vice president and director of the Smith Faus Drug Company, bought and occupied the house. In 1920 the home was purchased by H. Eugene Glenn, a printer for the *Salt Lake Tribune* newspaper. His wife, Rose Marie Young, was a great-granddaughter of Brigham Young.

78 N Street   B

BUILT: 1909
STYLE: Bungalow
BUILDER: Agatha P. Schettler
ORIGINAL OWNER: Grace C. Stratton

This one-and-one-half-story bungalow has a gable roof with a large, front center dormer window. The full-faced front porch has wooden columns and the front entrance is marked by a small gable.

Agatha P. Schettler built this home and the nearly identical 74 N Street for investment purposes. Upon completion the property was purchased by Grace C. Stratton, an osteopathic physician. She served in the Utah State Legislature in 1916 and 1918. In 1914 the home was sold to Casten and Ella Olsen. Mr. Olsen, a Norwegian immigrant, was one of the largest ranch dealers in the Intermountain West.

83 N Street   B

BUILT: 1890
STYLE: Victorian Eclectic
BUILDER: Henry A. Ferguson
ORIGINAL OWNER: Alexander and Ivy Cowie

This one-and-one-half-story, ornate Victorian cottage was most likely built from a pattern-book design. The front porch has a small gable over the entrance and turned columns, and the first floor is covered in shiplap siding.

A carpenter, Henry A. Ferguson, built this home and immediately sold it to Alexander and Ivy Cowie. Mr. Cowie was also a carpenter. In 1932 the home was sold to Ole L. and Mary C. Shumway, who had rented the residence since 1930. By the early 1980s the home was in an advanced state of disrepair, but in the mid-1980s the home was restored by Bryan Sirstins. The restoration included the rebuilding of the front porch.

89 N Street   B

BUILT: 1889
STYLE: Dutch Colonial Revival
ORIGINAL OWNER: Amos Cardwell

This Dutch Colonial Revival cottage has a gambrel roof. The front façade of the roof is covered in wood-shingle siding and the small front porch has wood Doric columns. The stucco finish covers brick and may not be original to the home.

This residence was built for Amos Cardwell, a shoemaker who practiced his trade on the premises. The home is representative of the numerous neighborhood commercial services found in the Avenues in the late nineteenth century. In 1906, ownership of the home was transferred to Amos Cardwell's son, Alfred. He was also a shoemaker employed by the Harding Shoe Company. The Cardwell family owned the home until 1935, at which time John Baker, an engineer, purchased the property. His wife Josephine operated a beauty supply store out of the home.

118 N Street   B

BUILT: 1895
STYLE: Victorian Eclectic
ARCHITECT: Daniel H. Bero
BUILDER: Daniel H. Bero
ORIGINAL OWNER: Grant Swan

This two-story, brick Victorian home has a projecting, front, three-sided gable. The front windows have rough-faced stone sills and lintels. An arched opening graces the small, one-story front porch.

Architect and builder Daniel H. Bero built this home as an investment. Soon after completion, it was purchased by Grant Swan, a livestock dealer. He lived in the home until 1903 when he moved to Los Angeles, but he maintained the residence as a rental property until 1945. At that time, Alonzo R. Leavitt, a real estate agent, bought the home.

123 N Street   B

BUILT: 1890
STYLE: Victorian Eclectic
BUILDER: Frank E. McGurrin and Elmer E. Darling
ORIGINAL OWNER: Charles H. Brink

This two-story Victorian home has a hip roof and gabled front bay. The gable is covered in patterned, wood-shingle siding. A first-floor, front bay window projects from the façade. The original wood porch columns were replaced by iron posts in the 1960s and have been recently restored.

Avenues developers Frank E. McGurrin and Elmer E. Darling built this home and the now demolished 125 N Street. Charles H. Brink, manager of Joslin and Park Jewelers, purchased the property upon completion. In 1906 Mr. Brink sold the home to Howard H. Lawson, who was involved in the livestock business. In 1927, a cabinetmaker for Dinwoody's Furniture Store, Peter Moss, bought the home.

167 N Street

BUILT: 1892
STYLE: Queen Anne
BUILDER: Miller and Miller
ORIGINAL OWNER: Charles E. Stevens

This Queen Anne Victorian home has an irregular plan, complex roof shape, an asymmetrical façade, and detailed exterior woodwork.

The Miller and Miller Mortgage Company built this home and sold it to Charles E. Stevens, who held on to the property as a rental home. Successive owners up until 1935 both occupied and rented out the home. At that time, Holger P. V. and Anna Hansen purchased the property. Mr. Hansen was a Salt Lake City policeman and security guard at the University of Utah.

182 N Street B

BUILT: 1898
STYLE: Victorian Eclectic
ORIGINAL OWNER: Carl O. Johnson

This two-story Victorian home is covered in shiplap wood siding. The front gable has returns, and a simple wood cornice runs under the eaves. The original front porch and a second-story door have been removed from the home.

Carl O. Johnson, owner of the adjacent Salt Lake Monument Company, had this home built as an investment. In 1915 he moved from the building that housed his business into this home and lived here until his death in 1940. At that time, ownership passed to his son, Gus H. Johnson. The home was converted into apartments in the 1950s.

273 N Street B

BUILT: 1905
STYLE: Victorian Eclectic
ORIGINAL OWNER: Albert E. Buckwell

This is a one-and-one-half-story, gable-roofed Victorian home. The main gable and porch gable have patterned, wood-shingle siding.

Albert E. Buckwell, a clerk at the ZCMI department store, was the first resident owner of the property. Mr. Buckwell was a member of the Mormon Tabernacle Choir and sang at the dedication of the Salt Lake City Temple. His wife lived in this home until her death in 1964.

275 N Street   B

BUILT: 1890
STYLE: Victorian Eclectic
ORIGINAL OWNER: Walter C. Farrow

This frame cottage has a front gable with re-turns. The large front window has wooden lintel decoration with dentil molding. The house is covered in shiplap siding.

Walter C. Farrow, a motorman for the Salt Lake City Railroad, sold this home soon after completion to Samuel J. and Ann E. Coombs. Mr. Coombs was a painter who lived at the adjacent 277 N Street. Mr. Far-row continued to live in the home until 1911. The Coombs family maintained ownership of the home as a rental until 1930. The resi-dence was restored in the late 1990s.

325 N Street   B

BUILT: 1918
STYLE: Prairie Style Bungalow
ORIGINAL OWNER: Carl A. Miller

This hip-roofed bungalow is one of the most common bungalow designs found through-out Utah. The low hip roof is typical of the Prairie style of architecture.

This home was built at a cost of three thousand dollars for Carl A. Miller, a stone-cutter and long-time partner in the nearby Salt Lake Monument Works. A leader in the LDS Church's Twenty-seventh Ward, he laid the cornerstone of their building in 1902 and the cornerstone of the recreation hall in 1927. Mr. Miller lived in this home until his death in 1943. His wife, Clara Miller, lived here until 1956.

20 O Street   C

BUILT: 1909
STYLE: American Four Square
ORIGINAL OWNER: Charles A. and Matilda J.
Herman

This two-story, Four Square–type home has a hip roof with a center dormer. A contemporary remodel of this home occurred in the 1960s, stripping the building of its original detailing and including the removal of the original front porch. The front porch has since been rebuilt.

This home was built at a cost of four thousand dollars for Charles and Matilda Herman. Mr. Herman was a U.S. deputy land surveyor. His family continued to maintain ownership of the home into the 1950s. In the mid-1990s the home was restored to represent the original design. The owners won a Utah Heritage Foundation preservation award for their efforts.

69 O Street   B

BUILT: 1902
STYLE: Victorian Eclectic
BUILDER: Anderson Realty Company
ORIGINAL OWNER: Edgar R. Wood

This home is among a number of similar residences developed by the Anderson Realty Company in this portion of the Avenues. Under the cornice is a corbelled brick belt course that surrounds the second-floor window arches. The porch has a gable roof and wooden Doric columns.

Edgar R. Wood, a teller for Wells Fargo Bank, purchased the residence upon completion. In 1903 he sold the home to Belle and Frank Browning. Mr. Browning was a bookkeeper for the Royal Baking Company and later secretary-treasurer of the King Browning Hardware Company. The home stood vacant for several years during the Great Depression.

75 O Street   B

BUILT: 1898
STYLE: Victorian Eclectic
ARCHITECT: Walter E. Ware
BUILDER: A. L. Namlin
ORIGINAL OWNER: Henry C. Phipps Jr.

This large Victorian home has patterned, wood-shingle siding on its dormer and gables. A corbelled brick belt course separates the first and second stories. The wide, Doric-columned front porch has a center gable.

Prominent Salt Lake City architect Walter E. Ware designed this home as well as 77, 79, and 81 O Street. The four homes were built for Henry C. Phipps Jr. as investment properties. This one was initially leased for five years. In 1907 Frank and Lucretia H. Kimball purchased the property. Mr. Kimball was a prominent merchant banker and civic leader.

77 O Street [B]

BUILT: 1898
STYLE: Victorian Eclectic
ARCHITECT: Walter E. Ware
BUILDER: A. L. Namlin
ORIGINAL OWNER: Henry C. Phipps, Jr.

This Victorian home has patterned, wood-shingle siding on its dormer and gables. A corbelled brick belt course separates the first and second stories. The wide, Doric-columned front porch has a center gable.

Prominent architect Walter E. Ware designed this home as well as 75, 79, and 81 O Street for Henry C. Phipps Jr. as investment properties. The building was initially leased to Casper L. Robertson, secretary of the Diamond Mining Company. In 1907 the home was sold to Thomas and Alice Callister. Mr. Callister was a realtor. George A. and Isabelle S. Critchlow purchased the property in 1913. Mr. Critchlow was an attorney. The Critchlow family occupied the home for several decades.

78 O Street [C]

BUILT: 1884
STYLE: Vernacular
ORIGINAL OWNER: Alice Williams

This one-story Vernacular cottage is one of the older homes standing in this portion of the Avenues. It has an L-shaped floor plan with two gable-roofed wings. The small front casement windows are not original to the home.

Ownership of this property changed frequently until 1890 when Zealous and Emma Wormuth purchased the home. Mr. Wormuth was the proprietor of the Manitou Hotel located at 125 East Third South in Salt Lake City. The home was rented out while the Wormuths lived at the hotel. In 1909 Fred H. and Anna M. Blomquist purchased the residence. Mr. Blomquist was a bartender. In 1922 the home was purchased by Sidney D. and Alice Flood, who lived here for several decades. Mr. Flood was a conductor for the Los Angeles and Salt Lake Railroad.

79 O Street [B]

BUILT: 1898
STYLE: Victorian Eclectic
ARCHITECT: Walter E. Ware
BUILDER: A. L. Namlin
ORIGINAL OWNER: Henry C. Phipps, Jr.

This Victorian home has patterned, wood-shingle siding on its dormer and gables. A corbelled brick belt course separates the first and second stories. The wide, Doric-columned front porch has a center gable.

Prominent architect Walter E. Ware designed this home as well as 75, 77, and 81 O Street for Henry C. Phipps Jr., who had the homes built as investments. The house was leased to Ernest Bamberger. He was heavily involved in mining, banking, insurance, and land development, and ran for U.S. Senate in 1928. The home was sold in 1907 to Edwin G. Woolley, who worked as a clerk for the State Board of Land Commissioners. E. Vernon and Margaret Thiriot purchased the home in 1927 and lived here for several decades. Mr. Thiriot was a salesman for the Carpenter Paper Company.

81 O Street [B]

BUILT: 1898
STYLE: Victorian Eclectic
ARCHITECT: Walter E. Ware
BUILDER: A. L. Namlin
ORIGINAL OWNER: Henry C. Phipps, Jr.

This Victorian home has patterned, wood-shingle siding on its dormer and gables. A corbelled brick belt course separates the first and second stories. The wide front porch has paired Doric columns and a small center gable.

Prominent architect Walter E. Ware designed this home as well as 75, 77, and 79 O Street for Henry C. Phipps Jr., who had the homes built as investments. The house was initially leased to David S. Murray, general manager of the Rocky Mountain Bell Telephone Company and later the Pacific States Telephone Company. In 1910, brothers William H. and Frederick H. Sweet purchased the home as an investment. Frederick Sweet was president of Standard Oil of Utah. Margaret D. Blackburn bought the home in 1920 and it would remain in the Blackburn family for five decades.

111 O Street [B]

BUILT: 1906
STYLE: Craftsman
ARCHITECT: Walter E. Ware and Alberto O. Treganza
ORIGINAL OWNER: Charles Read

This home, designed by prominent architects Walter E. Ware and Alberto O. Treganza, is the best example of English Arts and Crafts design in the Avenues. The art glass windows, heavy, rounded exposed joints, and doubled or tripled porch posts are typical of the style. The half-timbered gable and steep roof are Tudor or English Arts and Crafts elements. The interior woodwork has been well preserved. The exterior wood shingle siding was covered by asbestos shingles for several decades but has since been restored.

Realtor Charles Read built this home and held it as a rental property until 1913 when he sold it to Abraham Cline, who owned both I. Cline and Sons and the Broadway Shoe Store. Nicholas Meagher purchased the property in 1931. Since the late 1970s, the house has been maintained and restored by Bernard Simbari and Bill Barnett.

116 O Street [C]

BUILT: 1896
STYLE: Victorian Eclectic
ORIGINAL OWNER: James K. Shaw

This two-story, brick Victorian home has a hip roof and a two-story porch on the southwest corner supported by wood columns. The upper portion of the porch is enclosed and the windows are not original to the home.

This home was built for a realtor named James K. Shaw. It was held as a rental property by three different realtors until 1913. Stanley W. Wade purchased the home that year and became the first resident owner. He was a sales agent for the Utah Coal Company. The home changed hands several times during the Great Depression. In 1934 Theodore H. and Louisa Brossard became the owners. Mr. Brossard was a mechanical engineer. Louisa remained in the home until the late 1950s.

118 O Street `C`

BUILT: 1895
STYLE: Victorian Eclectic
ORIGINAL OWNER: Oscar Eliason

This is a plain Victorian cottage covered in asbestos shingle siding. The porch is supported by metal porch posts from the 1960s. While the front bay window is not original, it adds character to the façade.

Oscar Eliason, a jeweler, purchased this home upon completion for two thousand dollars. In 1898 Patrick E. and Annie M. Connor owned the property. Mr. Conner was a draftsman for Salt Lake City. He was also the son of General Patrick E. Connor, who commanded the Utah Military District and had a major influence on early Utah history. In 1906 Frank and Belle R. Heginbotham became the home's owners. Mr. Heginbotham was the Salt Lake City auditor, while Belle was the president of the Ladies Literary Club of Salt Lake City and director of the Sarah Daft Retirement Home.

119 O Street `B`

BUILT: 1890
STYLE: Victorian Eclectic
BUILDER: Thomas Allen
ORIGINAL OWNER: Thomas Allen

This one-story Victorian cottage is most likely a pattern-book design. The home is covered in wooden, shiplap siding with the gable covered in shingles. The front porch has wood Doric columns.

This small home was built by Thomas Allen, a carpenter, who lived here until 1923. At that time the home was purchased by Isabel M. Sears, the widow of prominent Salt Lake City businessman Septimus W. Sears. Mrs. Sears, who was born in a covered wagon in Salt Lake Valley in 1848, was a charter member and president of the Daughters of Utah Pioneers. She maintained ownership of the home until her death in 1941. The home was restored in the 1990s.

120 O Street `C`

BUILT: 1907
STYLE: Bungalow
BUILDER: James Mulyran
ORIGINAL OWNER: Anna S. and N. Edward Liljenberg

This one-story bungalow has been significantly altered through the decades to reflect the Mission style with its stucco finish and arched front windows.

This small home was most likely built by James Mulyran. He and his wife, Mary, sold the property to Anna and Edward Liljenberg for $1,950. Mr. Liljenberg, a Salt Lake City architect, designed several prominent residences and schools including some of the original buildings at Westminster College. In 1912 the home was sold to Albert E. and Emma T. Bennett, who maintained the home as a rental property for several decades.

P STREET

38–40 P Street `C`

BUILT: 1909
STYLE: American Four Square
ARCHITECT: W. Pack
ORIGINAL OWNER: Daniel F. and Agnes H. Morgan

This two-story brick duplex has a front center dormer window projecting from the hip roof. The one-story front porch has square, tapered wood columns.

The duplex stands as an example of the trend away from single-family residences in the Avenues during the first half of the twentieth century. The building was built for Daniel and Agnes Morgan, who lived for several decades in one side of the building while renting out the other side. Mr. Morgan was a postmaster. The building has since been split into additional apartment units.

67 P Street `C`

BUILT: 1896
STYLE: Queen Anne
ARCHITECT: S. W. Druce
ORIGINAL OWNER: John R. and Nellie J. Foulks

This well-preserved Queen Anne–style home has a tower on the southeast corner covered in wood-shingle siding and topped with a conical roof. A corbelled brick cornice runs under the eaves.

This home was built for John and Nellie Foulks. Mr. Foulks was a mining entrepreneur who had previously worked for the American Falls Canal Company and the Lyman Seed Company. After 1900, the home was briefly held as a rental property by Charles O. Merrill. In 1904 John G. and Amy A. Giles purchased the house. Mr. Giles operated a store and dairy in Magna while living here.

68 P Street `C`

BUILT: 1891
STYLE: Victorian Eclectic
BUILDER: Frank E. McGurrin and Elmer E. Darling
ORIGINAL OWNER: Frank E. McGurrin and Elmer E. Darling

This home has been heavily remodeled and stripped of its historic detailing. The front porch is enclosed with a mansard roof, and the exterior is covered in aluminum siding. The home is an example of the modernization of Avenues properties which took place in the 1950s, 1960s, and 1970s.

Frank McGurrin and Elmer Darling built this home as part of the Darlington Place development, and it was maintained as a rental property by several owners. Clem C. and May H. Carhart bought the home in 1920. Mr. Carhart worked for the State Road Commission. The home was owned by several banks in the 1930s and held again as a rental property. For several decades after the Depression, Tessie L. and Davis S. Edwards owned the house.

70 P Street　C

BUILT: 1893
STYLE: Queen Anne
BUILDER: John C. Shipp
ORIGINAL OWNER: Charles L. Rood

This home exhibits massing and detailing typical of the Queen Anne style. A large gable-roofed dormer and two-story corner bay project from the front of the home. The front porch is supported by turned wood columns. For many years in the twentieth century the house was covered in aluminum siding.

John C. Shipp, deputy clerk of the Utah Supreme Court, built this home and 74 P Street as investment properties. He sold this property to Charles L. Rood, who held many positions including superintendent of the Ontario Silver Mine in Park City and secretary-treasurer of the *Salt Lake Herald* Company. The home was sold in 1909 to Frank E. Marcy who lived next door at 74 P Street. The property was held as a rental home until 1934 when it was purchased by art dealer Diran T. Broun.

74 P Street　C

BUILT: 1893
STYLE: Victorian Eclectic
BUILDER: John C. Shipp
ORIGINAL OWNER: J. C. Elliot King

This two-story, shingle-sided Victorian home has a main hip roof and projecting, hip-roofed front bay. The arched front porch may be an early twentieth-century modification.

John C. Shipp, deputy clerk of the Utah Supreme Court, built this home and 70 P Street. He sold this property to J. C. Elliot King. A prominent Salt Lake City physician and surgeon, Mr. King owned the Colorado Beach Sanitarium. In 1906 the home was sold to Frank E. and May S. Marcy. Mr. Marcy owned the Mine and Smelter Supply Company. In 1919 P. Carl and Martha J. Evans purchased the home. Mr. Evans owned a book-binding business. The home was converted into a duplex during the Great Depression, but in 2005 it was restored to a single-family residence.

75 P Street　C

BUILT: 1891
STYLE: Victorian Eclectic
BUILDER: Frank E. McGurrin and Elmer E. Darling
ORIGINAL OWNER: Frank E. McGurrin and Elmer E. Darling

This single-story Victorian cottage has a unique, large arched window with corbelled brick molding above and decorative panes in the transom. The front porch has wooden Doric columns.

Avenues developers Frank McGurrin and Elmer Darling built this home as part of their Darlington Place development. Initially it was held as a rental property until 1894 when Francis E. and Emily Shafer became the first resident owners. Mr. Shafer was the chief clerk for the Utah Central Railroad. In 1899 Russell D. and Laura A. Woodruff purchased the property and lived here until 1928.

77 P Street

BUILT: 1890
STYLE: Queen Anne
BUILDER: Frank E. McGurrin and Elmer E. Darling
ORIGINAL OWNER: Frank E. McGurrin and Elmer E. Darling

The mixed material and massing of this home shows influence of both the Queen Anne and Shingle styles. The southeast corner of the home is dominated by an octagonal bay, while the northeast corner features a two-story, recessed porch with an enclosed second story. Several first-floor windows have been replaced with aluminum windows.

Frank McGurrin and Elmer Darling built this home as part of the Darlington Place development. The home was maintained as a rental property by several owners until 1901 when it was bought by John A. Reeves, a freight agent for the Oregon Short Line Railroad. William F. Bulkley purchased the property in 1934. He was an ordained Episcopal minister and head of the Utah Episcopal Mission.

79 P Street

BUILT: 1901
STYLE: Victorian Eclectic
ORIGINAL OWNER: Mary A. Craig

This two-story Victorian home is covered in multicolored bricks. Two front windows have leaded-glass transoms, and there is a second-story, oval front window. The front porch has wooden Doric columns.

This home was built for Mary A. Craig as an investment rental property. In 1905 Walter B. and Lucy N. Wingate purchased the home. Mr. Wingate was a salesman for the J. G. McDonald Candy Company. A later owner, Devoe Woolfe, was a long-time principal at South High School.

131 P Street

BUILT: 1904
STYLE: Victorian Eclectic
ORIGINAL OWNER: D. William and Anna H. McAllister

This well-preserved, one-and-one-half-story Victorian home has complex roof massing. The front gable is covered in patterned, wood-shingle siding. The large, first-floor front window in the bay has a leaded-glass transom. The front porch columns were recently restored, replacing 1950s iron posts. The home is similar to 125 P Street, and both homes were most likely built by the same developer.

William and Anna McAllister were the first resident owners of this property. Mr. McAllister was an agent for the Tootle Wheeler and Motter Mercantile Wholesale Dry Goods Company. In 1929 the home was sold to Fred C. Rossiter, an insurance salesman, who lived in the home for only two years. In 1931 Edwin D. and Erma S. Hatch purchased the home. Mr. Hatch was a lawyer.

133 P Street   `C`

BUILT: 1903
STYLE: Dutch Colonial Revival Bungalow
BUILDER: Adolf and Lucy Richter
ORIGINAL OWNER: Hattie V. Trunnell

This Dutch Colonial Revival bungalow has a gambrel roof, typical of the style, and two front dormer windows. The porch stretches across the front of the home and is supported by Doric columns.

Avenues developers Adolf and Lucy Richter built this home. Upon completion it was sold to Hattie V. Trunnell for $4,400. The home changed hands several times until 1917 when it was purchased by Annie L. Sands. Mrs. Sands was a vocal teacher and had her studio in the house. In 1922 she sold the house to Albert W. Srefert, an auto repairman, who lived in the home until 1960. The home was restored in 2006.

149 P Street   `C`

BUILT: 1903
STYLE: American Four Square
BUILDER: Adolf and Lucy Richter
ORIGINAL OWNER: Adolf and Lucy Richter

This brick, Four Square–type home has a small, one-story front porch with a gable roof and returns. It is supported by wood Doric columns. The home was restored in 2005.

Avenues' developers Adolf and Lucy Richter built this home for investment purposes and maintained it as a rental until 1910. At that time Albert and Nellie Weber, the current tenants, purchased the home. In 1921 they sold it to Alfred D. Tobin, who operated a furniture store.

170 P Street   `C`

BUILT: 1891
STYLE: Queen Anne
ORIGINAL OWNER: Eli B. Kelsey

This two-story home shows the influence of the Queen Anne style. There is a southeast corner tower, and the one-story front porch curves in to meet the tower. The home is covered in shiplap siding.

Real estate developer Eli B. Kelsey had this home built as an investment. It was held as a rental property by several owners including Russel L. Tracy, president of Tracy Loan and Trust, until 1904. At that time, James D. Harrison, a salesman for the Consolidated Wagon and Machinery Company, purchased the home and lived there until 1910. Later owners included Elmira M. and Thomas S. Kinnersley, who bought the home in 1937. Mr. Kinnersley was a superintendent for the Union Pacific Railroad.

180 P Street

C

BUILT: 1891
STYLE: Victorian Eclectic
ORIGINAL OWNER: John H. and Rosaline G.
Woodmansee

This is a Victorian cottage with a main hip roof and a projecting, gabled front bay. Elaborate, cut-wood brackets support the wood-shingle-sided gable. The original front porch has been removed from the home.

This home was built for John H. Woodmansee, who came to Utah in 1874 and found success in the mining industry. He was also an active leader of the LDS Church, serving on the Quorum of the Seventy. His wife, Rosaline, remained in the home after his death until 1962. The Woodmansee family maintained ownership of this property into the 1980s. It is a rare example of long-term, one-family ownership of an Avenues property.

Q STREET

22 Q Street [c]

BUILT: 1909
STYLE: Bungalow
BUILDER: George C. Greene
ORIGINAL OWNER: Michael and Anna Ryan

This bungalow's façade was heavily remodeled in the 1960s altering its original architectural character. It is a remaining example of attempts to modernize Avenues' homes during the long period of neighborhood decline. The general layout of the home is typical of many common middle-class bungalows built in Utah between 1908 and 1925.

Developer George C. Greene built this home and 26 Q Street. Michael and Anna Ryan were the first resident owners. Mr. Ryan was employed by the Salt Lake City Water Department. William and Alice Shepherd purchased the property in 1923. Mr. Shepherd was the chief clerk to the presiding bishop of the LDS Church. The Shepherds lost the home in a sheriff's sale during the Great Depression.

26 Q Street [c]

BUILT: 1909
STYLE: Bungalow
BUILDER: George C. Greene
ORIGINAL OWNER: Arthur D. and Linda M. Smith

This one-and-one-half-story bungalow has half-timber decoration on the front gable. The full-faced front porch is supported by square, tapered columns. A compatible addition was made to the second story of the home in 2008.

Developer and builder George C. Greene built this home and 22 Q Street. Arthur D. and Linda M. Smith became the first resident owners in 1911. Mr. Smith was the president of the Intermountain Coal Company and a purchasing agent for the Utah Power and Light Company. After being a rental home from 1916 until 1920, Minerva A. Ray purchased the residence. She was a widow who raised her four children in the home. She lived here until 1944.

27 Q Street [c]

BUILT: 1897
STYLE: Victorian Eclectic
ORIGINAL OWNER: Robert E. McConaughy

This two-story Victorian home has a main hip roof with a gabled front bay. The front porch is supported by square, tapered wooden columns and has a wood-paneled bay window above.

The home was built for Robert McConaughy as an investment property. He and his wife resided at the now-demolished 25 Q Street. Mr. McConaughy was involved in the lumber industry as well as mining and land investment. The first resident owners of the property were George and Matilda Williams, who purchased the home in 1900. Mr. Williams was an associate operator of the Palace Laundry Company. After 1906 the home was a rental property for most of the twentieth century.

73 Q Street   C

BUILT: 1900
STYLE: American Four Square
BUILDER: Joseph G. Jacobs
ORIGINAL OWNER: Joseph G. Jacobs

This two-story home is an early version of the popular Four Square–type residence. The second floor is covered by wood-shingle siding. A small Victorian cottage can be found in the rear of the home.

Joseph G. Jacobs owned this entire block and built several homes on the property. This house was built in 1900 and held as a rental property. Mr. Jacobs was the vice president and manager of the Salt Lake and Mercur Railroad Company. In 1904 Charles B. and Emma C. Heikes bought the property. Mr. Heikes was a real estate agent. They lived in the cottage to the rear of this house.

87 Q Street   C

BUILT: 1897
STYLE: Victorian Eclectic
BUILDER: Bothwell and McConaughy
ORIGINAL OWNER: Adolf and Lucy Richter

This two-story Victorian home has a main hip roof and projecting, hip-roofed front bay. A Doric-columned front porch runs the length of the house, and the original Crager Iron Works fence still runs along Q Street.

The construction firm of Bothwell and McConaughy built this home along with the nearly identical homes at 79 and 83 Q Street. Adolf and Lucy Richter occupied the home upon completion. The Richters owned the A. Richter Real Estate Company. They developed numerous properties in this portion of the Avenues. Upon the death of Mrs. Richter in 1930, the home passed to her brother, Robert Deokin. The home was split into apartments during the Great Depression.

88 Q Street   C

BUILT: 1898
STYLE: Commercial
ORIGINAL OWNER: Augusta and Andrew Mortenson

This well-preserved, flat-roofed, brick commercial structure is similar to many other corner markets found in the Avenues. It is attached to the house at 82 Q Street.

Augusta and Andrew Mortenson opened their grocery business here in 1898. The Mortenson family added the adjacent home in 1902. In 1909 Maria Moench purchased the property. She occupied the home and rented the store to Charles A. and Burt J. Caldwell. In 1914 William A. Gregory took over the store and operated it as the Table Supply Company. It continued to operate under this name for several decades. The restored commercial structure is now the Q Street Gallery.

110 Q Street [C]

BUILT: 1921
STYLE: Bungalow
BUILDER: Adolf and Lucy Richter
ORIGINAL OWNER: William A. Hilton

This bungalow has a jerkin-head roof, half-timbered decorative framing, and battered wood columns supporting the front porch. The home is similar to a typical bungalow design found in architectural pattern books.

Avenues developers Adolf and Lucy Richter built this home and 116 Q Street as investments. William A. Hilton was the first resident owner. From 1910 until 1941 Mr. Hilton practiced law in Salt Lake City. In 1927 the property was sold to William J. Lyons, who was assistant adjutant general of the Utah National Guard from 1927 until 1944.

166 Q Street [C]

BUILT: 1916
STYLE: Prairie Bungalow
BUILDER: Avery N. Timms
ORIGINAL OWNER: Avery N. Timms

This is an excellent example of a one-story, brick, hip-roofed Prairie-style bungalow. The cement belt course on the exterior emphasizes the horizontal aspects of this style. The front porch is supported by paired brick columns.

Avery N. Timms built this home for himself. Mr. Timms came from a family of builders that built several homes in the Avenues. At the time of this home's construction, Mr. Timms was the foreman of the Garfield Smelter. He built a nearly identical home on Virginia Street. In 1923 the residence was sold to Frederick Beesley, whose family owned Beesley Music Company in Salt Lake City. Mr. Beesley was a member of the Mormon Tabernacle Choir for fifty-five years. He also played the piano, organ, and bass, and was a founding member of the Salt Lake Philharmonic Orchestra.

175 Q Street [C]

BUILT: 1891
STYLE: Victorian Eclectic
BUILDER: Frank A. Grant
ORIGINAL OWNER: Luther B. Sutton

This is a two-story, gable-roofed Victorian home. The full-faced front porch with Craftsman-style columns replaced the original porch around 1920. The large shingles used for siding are not the original exterior finish.

Frank A. Grant built this home and several others on the block. Upon completion the property was purchased by Luther B. Sutton, who worked as a streetcar conductor for thirty years. In 1928 a plumber named Peter W. Stam became the owner, and he lived in the home until his death in the late 1950s.

180 Q Street   [C]

BUILT: 1896
STYLE: Victorian Eclectic
BUILDER: Frank A. Grant
ORIGINAL OWNER: Albion W. Caine

This Victorian home has a high gable roof. The Colonial-style trim around the front door and second-story window shutters was added in the mid-twentieth century. The front porch has been restored to replicate the original structure removed from the home in the 1960s.

Developer Frank A. Grant built this home and several others on the block. Albion W. Caine became the first resident owner. He owned a bicycle shop called the A. W. Caine Company. In 1906, he sold the home to Charles Letchfield, who owned a business that sold fireplace mantles. Herman Bruschke purchased the home in 1916. After a career as secretary for a chemical company, Mr. Bruschke worked for many years as a gardener at the nearby City Cemetery. He and his wife, Frieda, lived in the home through the 1950s.

198 Q Street   [C]

BUILT: 1896
STYLE: Victorian Eclectic
BUILDER: Frank A. Grant
ORIGINAL OWNER: John P. Eckers

This two-story Victorian home features a hip roof and a front, gabled, attic-vent dormer. The small front porch has a jerkin head roof and wooden columns. The house was covered with asbestos siding in the 1950s but the exterior has been recently restored.

Real estate developer Frank A. Grant built this home and several others on the block. John P. Eckers, who worked at Smith's Drug Store, purchased the property upon completion. In 1901 he sold the home to Mary E. Cannon, a former plural wife of LDS church leader Abraham H. Cannon. In 1912 Joseph V. and Annie Peterson bought the home and lived there until 1940. Mr. Peterson was an automobile mechanic.

R STREET

25 R Street   C

BUILT: 1892
STYLE: Victorian Eclectic
ARCHITECT: Frederick A. Hale
BUILDER: Elmer E. Darling
ORIGINAL OWNER: Joseph P. Bache

This well-preserved Victorian home has scroll-sawn cutouts on the gables. The second floor's siding flares out over the clapboard-sided first story. The front bay window was added in 1936. The front porch was also altered in the 1936 remodel.

This home, designed by prominent architect Frederick A. Hale for Elmer E. Darling, was most likely part of Elmer Darling and Frank McGurrin's Darlington Place development. Joseph P. Bache was the first owner and held the home as a rental property. Gustave Nelson, a brick mason, purchased the home in 1923 and became the first resident owner. From 1936 until 1999 successive owners maintained the house as a rental unit. The building was restored in 1999.

69 R Street   C

BUILT: 1899
STYLE: Victorian Eclectic
BUILDER: N. W. Baysinger
ORIGINAL OWNER: William and Mary Craig

This Victorian cottage has hip roofs and a gabled front porch. The porch gable has wood-shingled fascias and siding. Iron posts replaced the original, slim, paired Doric columns in the 1970s. This home is similar to the adjacent 77 R Street.

The home was built for William and Mary Craig as an investment and rental property. Mr. Craig was a mining entrepreneur. They owned numerous small homes in the area as rental units. In 1909, Harper J. and Sarah O. Dininny bought and occupied the home. Mr. Dininny served on the Salt Lake City Police and Fire Board. From 1905 until his death in 1917, he was the Salt Lake City attorney. After his death, Mrs. Dininny sold the property to Henry W. and Ruth Schuetter. Mr. Schuetter was a motorman for the Utah Light and Traction Company.

72 R Street   C

BUILT: 1891
STYLE: Victorian Eclectic
BUILDER: Frank McGurrin and Elmer Darling
ORIGINAL OWNER: William E. Firman

This two-story Victorian home has a main hip roof and a projecting, gabled front bay. The front windows were changed and the porch altered in the 1950s.

This home was built as part of Frank McGurrin and Elmer Darling's Darlington Place development and was sold upon completion to William E. Firman, vice president of the Salt Lake City Soda Water Company. He lived in the home until the mid-1890s when the property became a rental unit. In 1890 Alan T. Sanford purchased the home and continued to rent it to Mr. Firman. Mr. Sanford, an attorney, was active in local politics, holding positions in the anti-Mormon American Party, Republican Party, and Democratic Party. After 1917 the home was mostly occupied by renters. It is currently divided into a duplex.

131 R Street [C]

BUILT: 1903
STYLE: Victorian Eclectic
ARCHITECT: David C. Dart
BUILDER: Aaron Keyser
ORIGINAL OWNER: David C. Dart

This Victorian home has gable roofs, with the gable ends covered in wood-shingle siding. A projecting brick belt course runs around the house at the tops of the windows. The front porch is supported by wood columns.

Avenues developer Aaron Keyser built this home. It was most likely designed by noted Salt Lake City architect David C. Dart, who was the first owner of the home. Soon after the house was completed, Mr. Dart sold it to Harvey D. Heist for four thousand dollars. Mr. Heist, a civil engineer and surveyor for the Department of the Interior, platted Federal Heights and many other subdivisions in Salt Lake City. He also conducted the engineering for irrigation projects, railroads, and water systems throughout Utah. The home remained in the Heist family into the 1950s.

187 R Street [C]

BUILT: 1897
STYLE: Victorian Eclectic
BUILDER: Frank A. Grant
ORIGINAL OWNER: Peter W. Madsen

This one-and-one-half-story Victorian home has a tall gable roof. Patterned wood shingles cover the front and rear gable ends. The arched opening of the front porch may not be original to the design. A large dormer has been added on the south side.

Avenues developer Frank A. Grant built this home along with 185 and 189 R Street. Upon completion it was sold to Peter W. Madsen, the owner of P. W. Madsen Furniture Company and the Utah Stone and Hardware Company. In 1902 he sold the home to Noble Waterman, who owned Waterman Brothers Loan Company. From 1924 until 1935 Tracy Loan and Trust Company held the property as a rental house.

S STREET

30 S Street `C`

BUILT: 1900
STYLE: Shingle Style
ARCHITECT: Frederick A. Hale
ORIGINAL OWNER: Charles B. Markland

This Shingle-style building was the carriage house for the Markland Mansion at 1205 South Temple. The carriage entry was in the center of the west façade, and the second story served as a hay loft.

The carriage house was built around 1900 and possibly designed by prominent architect Frederick A. Hale, who also designed the Markland Mansion. The carriage house was converted into a dwelling in 1931 by Margaret Wicks, the daughter of Joseph Walker who owned the adjacent mansion. Mrs. Wicks brought paneling, flooring, and a fireplace mantel from her grandfather's mansion on Main Street. The property was not legally separated from the Markland Mansion until 1969. The home was extensively restored in 2010.

36 S Street `C`

BUILT: 1899
STYLE: Victorian Eclectic
ARCHITECT: David C. Dart
BUILDER: Rachel McMaster
ORIGINAL OWNER: Rachel McMaster

This small Victorian home has a hip roof, a front dormer window, and a gabled front porch. The dormer and porch gables have wood-shingled fascias and siding.

The home was designed by prominent architect David C. Dart, who designed homes of varying styles for several years in the Avenues. Developer Rachel McMaster built this home and lived in it briefly before renting it out. In 1908, Walter C. Shipp became the owner. Mr. Shipp gave his sister, Milfordetta Neville a lifetime lease. Her husband, Joseph, was the superintendent of the Los Angeles and Salt Lake Railroad. The Neville family remained in the home until 1940.

40 S Street `C`

BUILT: 1895
STYLE: Victorian Eclectic
ORIGINAL OWNER: William H. Dale

This heavily altered Victorian home has a main hip roof and a small, gabled front bay. While the upper walls have their original wood-shingle siding, the first story was covered in large-shingle siding in the 1970s. The Bungalow-style front porch was most likely added in the 1920s.

William H. Dale, manager of the Middlesex Banking Company, was the original resident of this property. Mr. Dale served as Salt Lake County treasurer and was a member of the Salt Lake City Council. The home is currently divided into apartments.

69 S Street C

BUILT: 1904
STYLE: Victorian Eclectic
ARCHITECT: Bernard O. Mecklenburg
ORIGINAL OWNER: Bernard O. Mecklenburg

This well-preserved Victorian home has a main hip roof, front dormer window, and a gabled front bay with a lunette window and returns. Upper walls have wood-shingled siding while the first floor is brick. The adjacent garage is a recent structure that replaced a smaller Victorian home.

This home was designed by and built for prominent Utah architect Bernard O. Mecklenburg. Mr. Mecklenburg's most important work was the completion of the Cathedral of the Madeleine. He also designed several prominent homes on South Temple. In 1907 Mr. Mecklenburg sold the home to David R. and Nannie Gray. Mr. Gray was a local railroad executive with the Oregon Short Line Railroad. They lived in the home briefly before it became a rental property.

76 S Street C

BUILT: 1898
STYLE: Victorian Eclectic
ARCHITECT: Daniel H. Bero
BUILDER: Daniel H. Bero
ORIGINAL OWNER: Sumner Washburn

This Victorian home has projecting front and north gabled bays. A corbelled brick cornice runs under the eaves. At the bottom of the windows are stone sills with corbelled brick dentils. The front porch is not original to the home.

Architect and builder Daniel H. Bero built this home as well as 78, 80, and 86 S Street. He built this home for Sumner Washburn, a carpenter, who only lived in the home briefly. The property continued to change hands every few years until Charles Dawson, a salesman for the National Band Mortgage Company, purchased the home. In 1939, an employee with the Salt Lake City Board of Health, Eric C. Pollei, purchased the residence.

77 S Street C

BUILT: 1891
STYLE: Victorian Eclectic
ARCHITECT: F. H. Perkins
BUILDER: F. H. Perkins
ORIGINAL OWNER: William B. and Ella Andrew

This Victorian home has a main hip roof and projecting front and north gabled bays. The front gable has unique lattice and bargeboard siding. A bracketed cornice with dentil molding runs under the eaves. The first-floor front porch was partially enclosed for several decades.

Architect and builder F. H. Perkins built this home and 81 S Street. William B. and Ella Andrew were the first owners and occupied the home until 1913. Mr. Andrew was a realtor, mining developer, and stockbroker. Lawrence Hammell, who sold restaurant equipment, purchased the home from them. The home was restored in the late 1990s by Lori Campbell and again in 2010 by Glenda Fullerton.

79 S Street [C]

BUILT: 1892
STYLE: Victorian Eclectic
ARCHITECT: F. H. Perkins
BUILDER: F. H. Perkins
ORIGINAL OWNER: F. H. Perkins

This two-story Victorian home has a mix of hip and gable roofs. The front gable has paneled bargeboards and a horizontal cornice with shamrock-like ornament. The upper portion of the home has been covered in asbestos siding, and the front windows are not original to the home.

Architect and builder F. H. Perkins built this home along with 77 and 81 S Street. Title to the home passed through several owners until 1898. At that time, Lulu and Lucian H. Smyth purchased the property. Mr. Smyth was a chief deputy U.S. Marshal. He and his wife remained in the home until 1927.

80 S Street [C]

BUILT: 1897
STYLE: Victorian Eclectic
ARCHITECT: Daniel H. Bero
BUILDER: Daniel H. Bero
ORIGINAL OWNER: Austin H. and Lena H. Bemis

This two-story Victorian home has a main hip roof and a projecting, hip-roofed front bay. Upper walls are covered in patterned, wood-shingle siding. The main floor is buff-colored brick which is now painted. The full-face front porch has Doric columns.

Architect and builder Daniel H. Bero built this home along with 76, 78, and 86 S Street. He transferred ownership to developer Frank E. McGurrin who sold the property to Austin and Lena Bemis. Mr. Bemis was involved in mining. The home passed through several owners until 1909 when it was purchased by John W. and Florence H. Ensign. He was an attorney and founder of the Ensign Abstract Company. The Ensign family remained in the home into the 1940s.

84 S Street [C]

BUILT: 1898
STYLE: Victorian Eclectic
ARCHITECT: Daniel H. Bero
BUILDER: Daniel H. Bero
ORIGINAL OWNER: John Brown

This two-story Victorian home has a main hip roof and a projecting, hip-roofed front bay. The front porch is not original to the home.

Architect and builder Daniel H. Bero built this home along with 76, 78, and 80 S Street. He transferred ownership to carpenter John Brown. The home was maintained as a rental property by several owners until 1925 when Edward and Sarah Taylor purchased the home. Mr. Taylor was a physician who worked as a narcotics agent. In 1935 James and Oneita Ellison bought the home. Mr. Ellison was the manager of Miller and Ellison's Flowers. The home is currently divided into apartments.

176 S Street   C

BUILT: 1897
STYLE: Victorian Eclectic
BUILDER: Frank A. Grant
ORIGINAL OWNER: James X. Ferguson

This Victorian home has a main gable and projecting, front gabled bay. The upper portion of the house is covered in patterned wood siding while the first floor is covered in shiplap siding. A sunburst design adorns the gable on the front porch.

Avenues developer Frank A. Grant built this home along with 180, 184, and 190 S Street. He sold the home to James X. Ferguson for $3,500. Mr. Ferguson was a merchant, mining entrepreneur, and member of Utah's first state legislature. John J. Deveraux, a freight agent for the Atchison, Topeka, and Santa Fe Railroad, purchased the property in 1902. John R. Van Cline, a mechanic for the Denver and Rio Grande Railroad, bought the home in 1922. The home was restored in the late 1990s.

190 S Street   C

BUILT: 1897
STYLE: Victorian Eclectic
BUILDER: Frank A. Grant
ORIGINAL OWNER: Edwin L. Carpenter

This is a two-story Victorian home with a main jerkin-head roof and a projecting, gabled front bay. The front gables have bargeboard and bull's-eye molding. Asbestos siding covers the original shiplap wood siding.

Avenues developer Frank A. Grant built this home along with 176, 180, and 184 S Street. He sold the home to Edwin L. Carpenter, a sales agent for the Pleasant Valley Coal Company. In 1902 Jeremiah D. Kenworthy, a freight agent for the Denver and Rio Grande Railroad, purchased the home. In 1929 Art Price became the owner. Mr. Price was a draftsman for the LDS Church. The home remained in the Price family into the 1980s.

T STREET

68 T Street   C

BUILT: 1895
STYLE: Victorian Eclectic
BUILDER: E. W. Druce
ORIGINAL OWNER: George and Amanda Guiver

This one-and-one-half-story Victorian cottage has a front gable with patterned, wood-shingle siding. It is similar to many small Avenues Victorian homes of pattern-book design. The original front porch columns have been replaced by iron posts, and there is evidence that a second door may have existed in place of the south front window. This would indicate that the home may have been split into a duplex at one time.

E. W. Druce built the home for George and Amanda Guiver at a cost of $950. Mr. Guiver was a butcher. The Guiver family built six homes on T Street. Several members of the family lived in this home, and it remained in the family into the 1940s.

82 T Street   C

BUILT: 1889/1919
STYLE: Vernacular/Craftsman
ORIGINAL OWNER: Jacob and Katie Ann Chatterton

This cottage incorporates an older vernacular structure. The front porch exhibits characteristics of the Craftsman style.

Jacob and Katie Ann Chatterton built a frame home on the land holdings of Benjamin and Mary Ann Guiver, who built several homes on this block. In 1892, William H. Guiver bought the two-room house and property for $1,750. He lived at 96 T Street and maintained this house as a rental. He also owned the adjacent W. Guiver and Company Meat and Grocery store at 1206 Second Avenue. The home and store were expanded and the Guiver family moved into this residence in 1919. The store has since been demolished. Decedents of the Guiver family maintained ownership of this property into the early 1980s.

107 T Street   C

BUILT: 1909
STYLE: Craftsman
ORIGINAL OWNER: George E. Airis

This Craftsman-style home has large, faceted brackets and unique geometric patterns in the windows. Unlike most Avenues homes on corner lots, the main entrance faces the side of the lot on T Street. This home may have been designed by Walter Ware and Alberto Treganza as it appears to be a more modest, smaller version of 111 O Street.

This home replaced an older, pre-1898 dwelling. George E. Airis had this residence built and moved into it from 1047 Third Avenue. Mr. Airis was then secretary of the Camp and Log Coal Company. He sold the home to Hiram B. Pratt in 1913, who then sold the residence in 1920 to Art Stone, an engineer for the U.S. Smelting Company. He lost the property in a tax sale during the Great Depression. The home was used for boarding U.S. Army officers during World War II.

124 T Street `C`

BUILT: 1896
STYLE: Victorian Eclectic
BUILDER: Herbert G. Button
ORIGINAL OWNER: Robert N. Pipes

This two-story Victorian home has a main hip roof, a south-side dormer window, and a projecting gable front. A corbelled brick course separates the first and second floors.

Herbert G. Button built this home and 132 T Street for investment purposes. Robert N. Pipes, an insurance salesman, was the first resident owner. In 1907 he sold the home to another insurance salesman named Alfred H. Ensign. William T. and Ruth Ingleheart purchased the property in 1919. Mr. Ingleheart was the managing editor of the *Salt Lake Herald* newspaper, and Mrs. Ingleheart was president of the Ladies Literary Club. She remained in the home until 1937.

132 T Street `C`

BUILT: 1896
STYLE: Victorian Eclectic
BUILDER: Herbert G. Button
ORIGINAL OWNER: Herbert G. Button

This two-story Victorian home has a unique, projecting, hip-roofed front bay. The front porch is supported by Doric columns.

Herbert G. Button built this home and 124 T Street for investment purposes. Mr. Button rented out the home for ten years. It is an example of the increasing amount of absentee ownership in the Avenues during this period. In 1906 Albert P. Spitko purchased the home. Mr. Spitko was a salesman and later the manager for the Carpenter Paper Company. In 1921 the home was bought by Samuel C. Baldwin, who was a physician in Salt Lake City for fifty years. He lost the home in a tax sale in 1932. Throughout the Great Depression the home was used as a boarding house.

168 T Street `C`

BUILT: 1911
STYLE: Craftsman Bungalow
BUILDER: C. W. Heastrup
ORIGINAL OWNER: Charles R. Pike

This is a one-story Craftsman Bungalow–style home. Vinyl siding covers the front gable and its original wood-shingle siding. The heavy, decorative support brackets and rafter ends have also been covered in siding. The wide front porch rests on wood-paneled corner columns.

This bungalow was built by C. W. Heastrup for Charles R. Pike. Mr. Pike was a manager at Hewlett Brothers, a store that sold coffee, tea, and spices. He later became partners in the firm of John, Pike, and Tuckett, a bakery and confectionary. A later owner, Charles H. Ketchum, secretary of Ketchum Builder's Supply, rented out the home. This is an example of the growing absentee ownership of Avenues homes during the Great Depression.

173 T Street `C`

BUILT: 1902
STYLE: Victorian Eclectic
ORIGINAL OWNER: Julius E. and Eleanora A. Anderson

This small Victorian home is most likely a pattern-book design. The front gable has fish-scale-patterned, wood-shingle siding. The front porch is supported by square, tapered wood columns.

This home was built for Julius E. and Eleanora A. Anderson. Mr. Anderson was a salesman. In 1921 the home was purchased by Wilson H. and Margaret W. Dusenberry. Mr. Dusenberry was a long-time educator in Utah County and the first secretary-treasurer of Brigham Young Academy. He also held many political offices including mayor of Provo and Utah state legislator. He moved to Salt Lake City in 1920 and died in this home in 1925. His wife, Margaret, was the sister of Utah senator Reed O. Smoot. The Dusenberry family owned the home into the 1950s.

179 T Street `C`

BUILT: 1916
STYLE: Bungalow
BUILDER: Orson Allen
ORIGINAL OWNER: Sterling B. Talmage

This brick bungalow with its front center dormer is a common home design built throughout Utah during this time period.

Orson Allen built this home and the adjacent 185 T Street. Sterling B. Talmage purchased the property from Mr. Allen. From 1915 until 1918, he was a mining consultant for many Intermountain West refining and mining companies. He received a Master's degree from Lehi University and a PhD from Harvard University in the 1920s. He is known for developing a new quantitative scale for mineral hardness. He went on to teach at Northwestern University and the University of New Mexico. He returned to Salt Lake City in 1946 and moved back into the home. He maintained ownership of the house until his death 1956.

185 T Street `C`

BUILT: 1916
STYLE: American Four Square/Prairie Style
BUILDER: Orson A. Allen
ORIGINAL OWNER: Orson A. and Edith S. Allen

This brick, two-story, Four Square–type home shows the influence of the Prairie style with its low hip roof and wide, projecting eaves. There were originally horizontal bands of casement windows on the second floor. The one-story front porch has a hip roof that echoes the main one.

This home and the adjacent 179 T Street were built by Orson A. Allen, a prominent contractor in Salt Lake City. He kept this home for his family, and his wife, Edith, remained in the home until the early 1970s.

U STREET

18 U Street

C

BUILT: 1908
STYLE: Craftsman Bungalow
ARCHITECT: Joseph Don Carlos Young and Don Carlos Young
ORIGINAL OWNER: William and Elizabeth Dern Cunningham

This bungalow has unusual and elaborate decoration. The dormer opens up onto a second-floor balcony with scroll-sawn in-serts reminiscent of designs by architects Louis Sullivan and George Elmslie. The front porch has paired tapered columns.

This home was designed by Joseph Don Carlos Young and his son, Don Carlos Young. Joseph would later become the LDS Church's head architect. The home was built in 1908 for William and Elizabeth Cunning-ham. Mr. Cunningham was active in rail-roads, mining, and insurance. The property was sold to Warren C. and Kate C. Snow in 1913. Mr. Snow was first secretary and buyer for the Central Utah Wool Company and also had business interests in banking and utilities.

30 U Street

C

BUILT: 1898/1902
STYLE: American Four Square
ORIGINAL OWNER: David A. and Martha A. Coombs

This large home has a hip roof with a front center dormer window. The exterior walls are covered with beveled wood siding. The wide, one-story front porch that runs the length of the house has been restored to represent the original structure. The building incorpo-rates an earlier frame home.

David and Martha Coombs had a small frame structure built on this site in 1898 for a rental property. Mrs. Coombs was the daughter of butcher John H. Picknell, who owned a large portion of this block and lived at 1216 First Avenue. James Goodwin bought the home and tripled its size in 1902. He owned the Goodwin Advertising Company and the Utah Publicity Company. He lived in the home with his stepfather, Charles C. Goodwin, the *Salt Lake Tribune* editor.

76 U Street

C

BUILT: 1911
STYLE: Eclectic
ARCHITECT: W. J. Cannonville
BUILDER: George S. Smith
ORIGINAL OWNER: George S. Smith

This unique, two-story home has a gable roof and two-story porch supported by heavy square columns typical of the Craftsman style. Half of the first-floor porch has been enclosed.

This home was designed by W. J. Can-nonville and built by George S. Smith, a prominent builder at that time in Salt Lake City. He lived in the home briefly before selling it to Agatha P. Schettler, who held it as a rental property. In 1917 Andrew M. and Darl H. Hanson purchased the prop-erty. Mr. Hanson was a buyer for the Rosen-baum Brothers Clothing Wholesaler. In 1938 Leland H. and Verana M. Creer bought the home. Mr. Creer was a professor at the Uni-versity of Utah.

87 U Street

C

BUILT: 1904
STYLE: Craftsman
ARCHITECT: Walter E. Ware and Alberto Treganza
ORIGINAL OWNER: Charles T. and Nan Little

This two-story home exhibits elements of both the Craftsman and Prairie styles. The horizontal bands that separate the different exterior surfaces and the hip roof are typical of Prairie-style architecture. The heavy brackets that support the eaves belong more to the Craftsman tradition.

Charles and Nan Little hired the prominent architectural firm of Ware and Treganza to design this home. Mr. Little was a realtor. They sold the house to George and Susan Bacon in 1907. Mr. Bacon worked in land reclamation and became a recognized authority on water resource control on the Colorado River. From 1933 until 1935, he was the Utah State Engineer. Louis and Maria Arnold bought the home in 1923.

98 U Street

C

BUILT: 1890
STYLE: Vernacular
ORIGINAL OWNER: James H. Taylor

This home is a vernacular structure with several later additions. The home incorporates a log structure built before 1890. The second-story dormers are a late 1970s addition.

James H. Taylor, a motorman for one of the city's streetcar companies, is the first listed owner of the home. He sold the property in 1903 to William J. Heckman, who owned a small grocery store. The home had multiple owners through the 1940s. From 1932 until 1936 the LDS Church's Young Men's Mutual Improvement Association owned the property for their secretary-treasurer, Alma H. Pettigrew.

115 U Street

C

BUILT: 1904
STYLE: Victorian Eclectic
BUILDER: Houston Real Estate Investment Company
ORIGINAL OWNER: Charles J. Brown

This one-story Victorian cottage has a front porch with Doric columns and a small gable over the entry.

The cottage was built on speculation by the Houston Real Estate Investment Company. The home passed through several owners that did not live in the residence. Around 1909, William B. Fisher purchased the property and moved into the house. Mr. Fisher was the manager of the Utah Copper Company, which figured prominently in the development of the Bingham Copper Mine. In 1911 Howard M. North, an engineer for the Oregon Short Line Railroad, purchased the home.

116 U Street · C

BUILT: 1908
STYLE: Bungalow
ORIGINAL OWNER: Wesley E. King

This one-story bungalow has a main hip roof and front center dormer window typical of the style. The home is covered in wood-shingle siding. It may have been designed by notable architect David C. Dart as it is similar to other Dart-designed bungalows in the area, including 123, 124, and 129 U Street.

This home was built for Wesley E. King. A prominent Salt Lake City lawyer and businessman, Mr. King was the founder of the Wesley King Insurance Agency, vice president of the Holloron Judge Trust Company, and vice president of the Jersey Creamery Company. In 1930 he sold the home to a mining engineer named William K. Mordock.

124 U Street · C

BUILT: 1909
STYLE: Craftsman Bungalow
ARCHITECT: David C. Dart
ORIGINAL OWNER: Sarah H. Taylor

This one-story bungalow is covered in wood-shingle siding. It has a main hip roof and front center dormer window typical of the Bungalow style. The home was designed by notable Salt Lake City architect David C. Dart and is similar to 123 and 129 U Street. The front porch has an arching, wood-shingled cornice supported by paired square columns.

This home was built for Sarah H. Taylor. It was maintained as a rental property until 1917 when Bertha Wagener became the owner. She was an artist and owner of the Bertha Wagener China Shop. She owned the house until 1938 when it was sold to an accountant named Leland J. Farrer.

136 U Street · C

BUILT: 1907
STYLE: Victorian Eclectic
ORIGINAL OWNER: John R. and Annie R. Sands

This two-story, late Victorian home has a restored porch supported by paired Doric columns. There is a two-story curved bay on the north side of the home.

This home was built for John and Annie Sands. Mr. Sands was the owner of the Walker Hotel in downtown Salt Lake City. He later became involved in mining interests and was also the local representative of the P. F. Collier and Son Publishing Company. Following his death in 1917, Mrs. Sands sold the home to John R. Powell, who was a clerk at the Walker Brothers Bank.

168 U Street C

BUILT: 1904
STYLE: Victorian Eclectic
BUILDER: Thomas J. Armstrong
ORIGINAL OWNER: Sarah E. Farrell

This one-and-one-half-story, brick Victorian home has partial cornice returns and a shingled gable.

This home and 172 U Street were built by Thomas Armstrong and sold upon completion to James J. and Sarah E. Farrell. Mr. Farrell owned his own plumbing company. The Farrell family remained in the home until 1928. From then until 1945 the house had several owners, one of whom was George P. Delury, an engineer for the Union Pacific Railroad and a local union leader. In 1945 Vaughn A. Cutler, an auditor for the Utah State Tax Commission, bought the residence.

172 U Street C

BUILT: 1904
STYLE: Victorian Eclectic
BUILDER: Thomas J. Armstrong
ORIGINAL OWNER: Sarah E. Farrell

The gable on this Victorian home has wood-shingle siding and returns. The front porch has a bracketed cornice and a small gable over the entry.

This home and 168 U Street were built by Thomas Armstrong. It was sold upon completion to James J. and Sarah E. Farrell. The Farrells deeded the property back to Mr. Armstrong in 1909. Ephraim and Mary Gowans purchased the house that same year. The Gowans had lived in the home since its completion. Mr. Gowans, educated as a physician, was the head of the State Industrial School and later state superintendent of public instruction. He ran for office several times as a member of the Socialist, Progressive, and Democratic Party. Eldred Beckstead, an employee of the Utah Liquor Control Commission, purchased the property in 1924.

FIRST AVENUE

136 First Avenue

BUILT: 1905
STYLE: American Four Square with Victorian Elements
ORIGINAL OWNER: John A. Groesbeck

This Victorian house with a distinct curved bay window on the front retains its original architectural character.

John A. Groesbeck was an employee of the Studebaker Company in Salt Lake City for many years. He also held positions as secretary-treasurer of the Utah Fire Clay Company, Jordan Fur and Reclamation, and the Alta Club. From 1908 to 1912 he served as Salt Lake County treasurer. Mr. Groesbeck married Tessi Clawson, a granddaughter of Brigham Young. He took out a permit to build this house in 1905 and lived at this residence until his death in 1930. Successive owners maintained the property as a single-family residence. The home was an early example of Avenues restoration as William and Nancy Nicholls restored the home in the 1970s.

218 First Avenue

BUILT: 1918
STYLE: Craftsman/Prairie
BUILDER: McCormick Company
ORIGINAL OWNER: Stephen L. Richards

This unique home exhibits elements of Prairie-style design late in that architectural time period. The house has a low hip roof with projecting eaves, a band of windows on the first-floor bay, and a front porch with large corner piers. This home appears to be architecturally designed but no architect of record has been found.

Stephen Richards, a member of the Quorum of the Twelve Apostles for the LDS Church, bought this house from the McCormick Company and lived here until 1925. Fred H. Worsley, who held high-level positions in Salt Lake City for several railroads, lived in the home from 1932 until 1956. In 1958 the home was converted into a rest home. In the late 1990s, the home was restored back to a single-family residence.

265–269 First Avenue

BUILT: 1928
STYLE: Spanish Colonial Revival
ARCHITECT: Slack Winburn
BUILDER: Sidney E. Mulcock
ORIGINAL OWNER: H. J. Stewart

This three-story apartment block was built in the Spanish Colonial Revival style, a style not common in Salt Lake City. The columned entries with their broken pediments are inspired by Spanish Baroque architecture.

Builder Sidney E. Mulcock was chairman of Prudential Federal Savings and Loan, director of Granite Furniture Company, and director of the Foothills Development Company. A real estate pioneer in the Salt Lake Valley, he built this building at a time when the Avenues' transition to multifamily residences was accelerating.

The building's architect, Slack Winburn, is better known for his modernist-style buildings in Salt Lake City. His work includes the University of Utah Union building and the Northwest Pipeline (Salt Lake City Fire and Police) Building.

315 First Avenue A

BUILT: 1904
STYLE: American Four Square
ORIGINAL OWNER: John Clark

This Four Square has a distinct projecting bay window on the second story, quoined corners with capitals, and paired columns with ionic capitals.

This home and the one next door at 317 First Avenue were built as investment properties by prominent Salt Lake City business and political leader John Clark. It is an example of the investment rental properties that became common in the Avenues during this time period. Mr. Clark was treasurer and assistant Manager of ZCMI, and went on to serve on the Salt Lake City Council from 1869 until 1888. He spent three terms in the Utah State Legislature before becoming Salt Lake City mayor in 1897. Clark lived at 305 First Avenue (demolished) prior to moving into this residence. Later owners maintained the home as a rental property. It was eventually divided into several apartments.

320 First Avenue A

BUILT: 1906
STYLE: Victorian Eclectic
ORIGINAL OWNER: E. Curtis Warren

This small Victorian cottage is most likely a pattern-book design and is a good example of early 1900s middle-class housing in the Avenues.

Lydia D. Alder purchased this house from E. C. Warren soon after construction. Mrs. Alder was active in the international women's movement. She was the first president of the National Women's Suffrage Association and spoke at the 1904 International Conference of Women. She was also a writer who spent time in the Holy Land writing a book on the region. She was an active member of the Church of Jesus Christ of Latter-day Saints, helping to organize Relief Societies throughout Utah. Lydia lived in this house until 1921. During the 1930s the home was converted to apartments and today remains a multifamily residence.

360 First Avenue A

BUILT: 1897
STYLE: American Four Square
ORIGINAL OWNER: Edward H. Airis

Edward H. Airis, secretary of the Mercur Gold Mining and Mineral Company and president of Northern Light Mining and Mineral Company, took out a building permit for this house in 1897. Architecturally, this home reflects more of an early twentieth-century style. It may have been built later than the permit or altered early in its history.

Mr. Airis sold the home in 1904 to William C. McDonald, head salesman for the J. G. McDonald Chocolate Company. The home passed through numerous owners until it was converted into apartments in 1944. The exterior has been restored and is in excellent condition.

379 First Avenue [A]

BUILT: 1907–1911
STYLE: Gothic Revival
ORIGINAL OWNER: United Danish Evangelical
Lutheran Church

The narrow arched windows, corner bell tower, stained-glass windows, and vertical massing of this neighborhood church indicates a Gothic Revival style.

In 1902 the United Danish Evangelical Lutheran Church in Denmark sent missionaries to Utah in order to convert Mormon Danes back to their original faith. The church was built in stages and not dedicated until 1911. The congregation was led by Danish Pastor Harold Jensen, who built the Victorian home at 61 E Street connected to the rear of the church. Tabor Lutheran Church, the only non-Mormon church in the Avenues, continued to use this building until 1963 when it was sold to the Central Baptist Church. In 1987, that church sold the building to Mahood Engineering which converted it into offices.

418–420 First Avenue [A]

BUILT: 1906
STYLE: American Four Square
ORIGINAL OWNER: John C. Sharp

This two-story home with a low hip roof, projecting eaves, and a front center dormer window is a typical box design popular in the early twentieth century. The home is unique in that it was built as a duplex. It is representative of the advent of investment and rental property in the Avenues.

John C. Sharp, a member of the High Council of the Ensign Ward, built this home solely as a rental unit. Subsequent owners have rarely lived on either side of the duplex.

422–424 First Avenue [A]

BUILT: 1903
STYLE: Row House
ARCHITECT: Dallas and Hedges
ORIGINAL OWNER: George F. Gibbs

This apartment block is similar to row houses found in other cities. This design is not typically found in Salt Lake City. Two-story bay windows project from the façade, with a one-story porch between them. Brick quoins emphasize the first-floor corners.

George F. Gibbs, originally from South Wales, built this duplex row house. He lived with his family in 424 until his death in 1924. He rented out the other half of the building. Mr. Gibbs served as secretary to LDS Church leadership for fifty-five years. He was a pioneer member of the Twentieth Ward and was in the bishopric for twenty-six years. In 1925, Clarence L. Schettler moved into the duplex. The Schettler family built several homes in the Avenues. This duplex row house was converted into apartments in 1930.

423 First Avenue   A

BUILT: 1904
STYLE: Victorian Eclectic/Bungalow
ARCHITECT: Walter E. Ware and Alberto O. Treganza
BUILDER: Allen and Rocnisek
ORIGINAL OWNER: Arthur Lynn

This is a one-and-one-half-story home designed by prominent Salt Lake City architects Alberto Treganza and Walter E. Ware. Originally built as a Victorian cottage, a 1920s remodel added a Craftsman-influenced, low-gabled, full-width porch.

Arthur Lynn, the original owner, was president of the Sierra Nevada Mill Company. The company was one of the pioneer lumber companies in Salt Lake City and was established in 1871. In 1912, the home was sold to Hermann Harms, the state chemist and proprietor of the Brigham Street Pharmacy. In 1942, the home was converted into apartments.

427 First Avenue   A

BUILT: 1907
STYLE: Craftsman/Bungalow
ORIGINAL OWNER: Joseph H. Patrick

This is an excellent example of a one-and-one-half-story Craftsman-style bungalow. The paired wooden columns, knee braces, large projecting dormer, and exposed rafters are typical of this style.

Joseph H. Patrick, a teller for the McCormick Company, built this house in 1907, adding the garage in 1914. Mr. Patrick later became treasurer of the Decker-Patrick Company, a wholesale dry goods and clothing store. Mr. Patrick lived in the home until 1919. In 1920, George M. Cannon Jr. moved into the house. Mr. Cannon was president of Cannon Realty Company and director of Deseret Federal Savings and Loan. Cannon lived in this bungalow until 1940, and the following year the home was converted into apartments. The exterior of the home has been recently restored. The building remains a multifamily residence.

465–467 First Avenue   A

BUILT: 1901
STYLE: Victorian Eclectic
ORIGINAL OWNER: James P. Sharp

This home and the home to the rear are typical examples of the many small Victorian cottages built in the Avenues between 1890 and 1905. These cottages were most likely pattern-book designs. The front gable with patterned wood shingles and small attic window at 465 First Avenue is a common feature. The original front porch has been partially enclosed.

James P. Sharp, a stockman, built the homes in 1901. He most likely rented out the cottages until 1907 when he moved into 465 with his wife Olive Emily Sorenson. He continued to rent out 467. Mr. Sharp served as director of the Pleasant Grove Canning Company and worked at times for Standard Furniture Company and the State Bank of Park City. He was also a writer of early Utah history. Mr. Sharp also owned the home at 188 D Street.

503 First Avenue B

BUILT: 1903
STYLE: Originally a Victorian Four Square
ORIGINAL OWNER: Obed A. Palmer

The present appearance of this apartment block dates to its extensive 1940s renovation. Originally this building was a Victorian mansion. A third story and a large east-side addition have completely altered the original features of the building. The apartments serve as an example of the accelerating transition from single-resident housing to multifamily housing in the Avenues after World War II.

A store existed on this lot until 1903 when Obed A. Palmer replaced it with the residence. He sold the home to prominent Salt Lake City businessman James A. Hogle, a fellow mining engineer and broker, in 1913. Mr. Hogle lived in this house until 1920 when he moved to a now-demolished mansion at 548 South Temple. In 1940, the apartment conversion was completed by the Henderson Investment Company.

531 First Avenue B

BUILT: 1900
STYLE: American Four Square
ORIGINAL OWNER: David Miner

This is a well-preserved example of an American Four Square–type home in the Avenues. The second story is decorated with bands of rough-faced brick. The front entry has a Federal-style carved oval fan panel which may not be original to the home. The front porch, which had been removed for many years, was restored in the late 1990s.

Salt Lake City physician David Miner had this home built in 1900. He lived at this address for only two years before selling it to Ernest A. Greenwood, an employee of the Denver and Rio Grande Railroad. Mr. Greenwood later spent twenty-five years as secretary of the Utah Fuel Company. Grant McFarlane purchased the home in 1930. He was a successful Salt Lake City businessman and politician, serving in both the Utah State House and Senate.

535 First Avenue B

BUILT: 1903
STYLE: Victorian Eclectic
ORIGINAL OWNER: Wilson I. Snyder

This well-preserved, two-and-one-half-story Victorian home shows the transition between Victorian flamboyance and the restraint of Colonial Revival architecture. The octagonal hip-roofed tower is a holdover from Queen Anne style. The entrance porch has a pedimented gable and square, fluted columns.

William I. Snyder purchased the property in 1901 and two years later replaced the existing 1860 home. Mr. Snyder was a well-known Salt Lake City and Park City attorney who served as president of the Utah Bar Association in 1908. For a brief period during the mid-twentieth century the home was split up into apartments.

587 First Avenue B

BUILT: 1909
STYLE: American Four Square
ORIGINAL OWNER: William H. Nutting

William H. Nutting built this Four Square–type home around 1909. It is a large and well-preserved example of this popular type of home.

Mr. Nutting was a mining entrepreneur and secretary-treasurer of the Green River Development Company. Around 1919 Mr. Nutting sold the home to the Lucy D. Parkinson family. Two generations of the Parkinson family lived in the home until the mid-1930s. Parley D. Parkinson, an officer in the United States Army, sold the home to a fellow army officer, Major William T. Yount. After Major Yount was killed in World War II, his widow, Elizabeth, remained in the home until 1951.

603–607 First Avenue B

BUILT: 1937
STYLE: Art Moderne
ORIGINAL OWNER: Charles E. Wymer

The small Wymer apartment building is one of Salt Lake City's best examples of Art Moderne architecture. This streamlined modern design was popular in parts of the United States from the mid-1920s until World War II. Art Moderne was not a common style in Salt Lake City. Rounded stairwell towers with glass-block windows project from the front of the building. The moldings above the doors sweep around the building accentuating the streamlined design. The apartment building retains its industrial, sash-metal horizontal windows.

Charles E. Wymer bought the land from the Sterling Apartment Company in 1936 and started construction soon after the purchase. The building documents both the architectural diversity found in the Avenues and the increase of multifamily housing in the 1930s. The Wymer apartment block retains its original architectural character.

615 First Avenue B

BUILT: 1889
STYLE: Italianate
ORIGINAL OWNER: John J. Duke

This two-story home is an excellent example of Italianate-style architecture. It has low hip roofs that most likely once had a balustraded "widow's walk." Above the windows are corbelled brick arches with drip-molding decoration. The one-story front porch is not original and is missing architectural details.

The house was built in 1889 for John J. Duke, who ran a millinery goods business and later became a policeman. He lived here a few years and then sold the property to Agnes and John T. Rich in 1894. Mr. Rich was a local banker. The home exchanged hands several times until it was converted into apartments in the 1940s. In the early 1990s the home was restored back to a single-family residence.

688 First Avenue `B`

BUILT: 1901
STYLE: Victorian Eclectic
ORIGINAL OWNER: Daniel Eyer

This brick home is typical of late-Victorian design. The gables have strong window cornices with classical-type returns. The east front gable has a brick, arched attic window, while the west front gable has wood-shingle siding.

The home was built by mining professional Daniel Eyer. In 1906, Eyer's son sold the home to John J. McClellan, an internationally known musician and organist. He was a member of the music faculty at the University of Utah and Brigham Young University. In 1906, he was named organist for the Mormon Tabernacle Choir and held that position until his death in 1926. He founded the Utah Conservatory of Music and also conducted the Salt Lake Opera Company and the Salt Lake Symphony Orchestra. Mr. McClellan composed many well-known LDS hymns. The home's exterior has been restored to its original condition.

723 First Avenue `B`

BUILT: 1882
STYLE: Greek Revival
ORIGINAL OWNER: Angus L. Davis

This Greek Revival cottage is historically significant for two reasons. The home stands as one of the oldest remaining structures in this part of the Avenues, and the home's second resident was the owner of a landmark Salt Lake City restaurant. The front porch of this residence has been partially enclosed and wire porch posts have replaced the original posts.

Teamster Angus L. Davis was the original owner and builder of the cottage. After Angus died, his son Art took ownership of the house. Art Davis started a small fruit market. In the evenings his friends would visit him and eat snacks from the market, tossing him some change for the food they had eaten. This gave Art the idea for the Grabeteria, a self-service restaurant with no fixed prices, which became a landmark establishment in downtown Salt Lake City.

751 First Avenue `B`

BUILT: 1897
STYLE: American Four Square
ORIGINAL OWNER: Hubbard W. Reed

This Four Square home is a pattern-book design popular in the late nineteenth and early twentieth centuries. Note the quoin-like panels of corbelled brick decorating the edges of the front windows and the corners of the house that give the house architectural character.

The home was built by real estate speculator Hubbard W. Reed around 1897. Mr. Reed also built the homes at 757, 763, and 769 First Avenue. In 1920, the home was sold to Lehi E. Cluff, a Salt Lake City attorney who served several years as assistant state attorney general. He was a director of the Fisher Banking Company and attorney for the cities of Sandy and Bingham. In the early 1960s, this home was converted into apartments. This conversion documents the continuing trend toward multifamily housing in the mid-twentieth century.

760 First Avenue B

BUILT: 1890
STYLE: Victorian Cottage
ORIGINAL OWNER: Danish Lutheran Church

This small cottage documents the presence of organized non-Mormon religious groups in the Avenues. It was originally built as a chapel and parsonage for a small Danish Lutheran congregation, with F. W. Blohm listed as the first pastor. Apparently by 1895 the congregation had disbanded. A new Danish Evangelical Lutheran mission would establish a church and parsonage at 387 First Avenue in 1902.

The building has been much altered. In the 1920s a front porch with "battered" Craftsman-style columns was added. A new porch with turned Victorian-style posts has since replaced the earlier version. Mid-twentieth-century siding covers the home's exterior. It has remained a single-family residence since the demise of the church congregation.

801–805 First Avenue B

BUILT: 1880s
STYLE: Vernacular and Commercial
ORIGINAL OWNER: Richard Tilt

This one-story cottage with an attached two-story commercial wing is one of the few stone homes built in the Avenues. There is no confirmation on the original construction date of the home. Richard Tilt was listed as a resident at this property beginning in 1869. However, the vernacular style of the cottage was popular in the Avenues in the 1880s. The commercial wing was added in the 1890s.

Richard Tilt lived in the eastern portion of the house and ran the store on the west side of the property until 1903. The home and store, which often operated as the "First Avenue Grocery," passed through successive owners until the late 1930s. Helen and William A. Reilley added the second story to the commercial wing and converted the entire property to apartments around 1939.

810 First Avenue B

BUILT: 1905
STYLE: Victorian Eclectic
ORIGINAL OWNER: Peter N. Rourke

This small Victorian home was built as a speculation property by Peter N. Rourke. Its design was most likely taken from a pattern book. The front of the home is covered by a wide front porch with Doric columns. The two large front windows have leaded-glass transoms and oval leaded-glass windowpanes.

In 1905 Claud W. Mills sold this property to speculator Peter N. Rourke. After completion, the home changed hands twice before it was purchased by Clarissa Dougall. Clarissa married Hyrum Bergstrom, manager of Crescent Loan Company. The Bergstroms only lived in the house for a year before selling it to Edwin J. Kearns, who owned several rental properties in the Avenues. In 1910 the home was sold to the Evans family. They continued as owners into the late 1970s.

815 First Avenue B

BUILT: 1891
STYLE: Victorian Eclectic
BUILDER: Betts and Horton
ORIGINAL OWNER: John Connelly

This large Victorian building is an example of early multifamily housing in the Avenues. Built originally as a two-and-one-half-story duplex, it now contains multiple units. On the top story are mansard dormers with wrought-iron cresting flanking a central hipped dormer. The two-story front porch is an addition to the original building. The style indicates that it was most likely added in the early twentieth century.

The original owner of the house was John Connelly, an immigrant from England. He lived in the building until 1939, and his family retained ownership of the property until 1943.

823 First Avenue B

BUILT: 1888
STYLE: Victorian Eclectic
ORIGINAL OWNER: Hyrum Covey

This one-story Victorian home has a front porch with brick columns added between 1910 and 1920.

The home was built by Hyrum Covey, a teamster who had previously lived at 829 First Avenue (now demolished). The home passed through several owners before being purchased by Royal Daynes in 1910. His father was a musician and watchmaker who brought musical instruments to Salt Lake City by ox cart and established the first music and jewelry store in Utah. Royal Daynes was a trained ophthalmologist and practiced in the city until 1908 when he joined his father's business. He eventually became president of Daynes Music Company. He was also a member of the Mormon Tabernacle Choir, founder of the Musical Arts Society, and organizer of the first symphony orchestra in Utah. Mr. Daynes lived in the home until 1922.

860 First Avenue B

BUILT: 1895
STYLE: Tudor Revival
ORIGINAL OWNER: Samual E. Woodmansee

This two-story home was built from a pattern-book Victorian design in 1895. In the 1920s it was remodeled into an English Tudor–style home. European styles of architecture gained popularity after World War I, and this home is a rare example of a complete remodel for the early twentieth century.

The home passed through five owners during its first fifteen years. It was continually maintained as a rental property by those early owners. From 1900 to 1910 William L. Pickard Jr., president of the American Laundry Company, was the home's tenant. In the 1920s Enoch Cornia, a salesman for the National Tea Importing Company, purchased the property and resided there. During the Great Depression, the home was converted into several small apartments. It has since become a single-family residence again.

861 First Avenue [B]

BUILT: 1903
STYLE: American Four Square
BUILDER: John Dorius Jr.
ORIGINAL OWNER: John Dorius Jr.

This two-story home is a fine example of American Four Square–type, popular in home building across America in the first two decades of the twentieth century. The oval window on the second-floor façade reflects the late-Victorian period of architecture.

John Dorius Jr. built this home in 1903 as an investment. The property was sold to Henry Arthur Schweikart, a sales manager for the Salt Lake Hardware Company, in 1905 for $6,500. Dorius built a number of homes on the east end of First Avenue, including those at 853, 857, and 867 First Avenue.

868 First Avenue [B]

BUILT: 1895
STYLE: Victorian Eclectic
BUILDER: E. G. Woodmansee
ORIGINAL OWNER: James M. Easton

This Victorian home is a pattern-book design built in 1895. The front bay is decorated by extending the bricks beyond the corners of the walls to emphasize the edges.

James M. Easton purchased the residence from the builder in 1895. He is listed as a manufacturer's agent and lived in the home until 1899. Milton E. Lipman became the second resident owner. A prominent civic, business, and political leader in Salt Lake City, Mr. Lipman was founder of the Mercantile Investment Company, an original member of the Salt Lake Rotary Club, an active Mason, and the Salt Lake City treasurer. The home was converted into apartments in the 1930s, but in the early 1970s it was converted back to a single-family home.

877 First Avenue [B]

BUILT: 1901
STYLE: Victorian Eclectic
BUILDER: Anderson Realty Company
ORIGINAL OWNER: Emerson F. Root

This home is among a number of similar residences developed by the Anderson Realty Company in this area of the Avenues. The pedimented front gable features wood-shingled siding. Under the gable is a two-story brick bay window. The center window on the second story of the large bay has corbelled decoration of rough-hewn bricks.

Emerson F. Root was the first resident owner in 1902. He was a well-known medical doctor in Salt Lake City. During his career he was president of the Salt Lake County Medical Society, president of the Utah State Medical Society, and chief of staff of Holy Cross Hospital. His son Frank, also a physician, purchased the home in the early 1920s. The property was converted to apartments during the Great Depression.

881 First Avenue [B]

BUILT: 1902
STYLE: Victorian Eclectic
BUILDER: Anderson Realty Company
ORIGINAL OWNER: Lawrence F. Harr

This home is among a number of similar residences developed by the Anderson Realty Company in this part of the Avenues. This Victorian's decorative façade includes corbelling and partially dentiled brickwork between the first and second stories.

Former army officer Lawrence F. Harr was the first resident owner of this property. He became a well-known cigar dealer. In the early 1920s, he sold the home to Alexander G. Rizos, a Greek immigrant who came to Salt Lake City in 1910 to establish a drugstore serving Utah's Greek community. He also owned a drug store in Bingham Canyon. From 1937 until the 1960s, the home was split into apartments. The original front porch was replaced by the current metal-roofed one, most likely in the late 1950s.

903 First Avenue [C]

BUILT: 1893
STYLE: Victorian Eclectic
ORIGINAL OWNER: Madison B. Whitney

This Victorian home has a truncated hip roof and some unique carved sandstone work. Metal awnings once covered the windows on the west side and front porch but have since been removed. The home's original porch inside the south and west arches has been enclosed.

The home was built in 1893 for Madison B. Whitney, secretary-treasurer of the Utah Implement Company and founder of both the Mount Nebo Irrigation Project and the Utah Lake, Land, Water, and Power Company. In 1912 he sold the house to Dr. Pan Kassinikos. A practicing physician and surgeon in Greece, he immigrated to Utah in 1906. Two years later he founded a weekly Greek newspaper, *The Light*. In the 1940s the home was separated into several small apartments. It currently has one residence on the main floor and an apartment in the basement.

914 First Avenue [C]

BUILT: 1896
STYLE: Victorian Eclectic
BUILDER: Woodmansee Brothers
ORIGINAL OWNER: Daniel H. Bero

This two-story Victorian house exhibits ornate woodwork in the front gable. The yellow brick walls have window arches and quoin-like corner decoration of dark brown brick. The wood-paneled front door's design matches that in the gable.

The house was built in 1896 for Daniel H. Bero, a Salt Lake City architect. He had the house built as an investment property by the Woodmansee Brothers, whose firm built several homes in the area. In 1902 Mr. Bero sold the house to William G. Grimsdel. The Grimsdel family occupied the house for the next sixty years. From 1900 until his death in 1958, Mr. Grimsdel owned and operated the Grocer Printing Company.

915 First Avenue `C`

BUILT: 1895
STYLE: Victorian Eclectic
BUILDER: Andrew Boyle
ORIGINAL OWNER: Madison B. Whitney

This two-story house exhibits many of the typical Victorian elements found throughout the Avenues. The home also has a two-story porch. The upper level was once enclosed and most likely used as a summer sleeping porch.

This residence and 919 First Avenue were constructed in 1895 by Andrew Boyle. Madison B. Whitney purchased the home soon after construction. He lived two doors down at 903 First Avenue but maintained this second home as an investment and rental property. In the early 1920s the residence was purchased by Edward Frank Soderburg, a salesman for the Franklin Building and Loan Company. During World War II, the home was converted into small apartments. In the 1990s the home was restored to a single-family residence.

925 First Avenue `C`

BUILT: 1910
STYLE: American Four Square
ARCHITECT: David C. Dart
BUILDER: McCormick and Gray
ORIGINAL OWNER: Milton E. Lipman

This large home is a good example of the popular American Four Square–type. It exhibits Craftsman and Tudor architectural features, including half-timbering on the second story. The foundation and chimney are made of cobblestones.

The home's architect, David C. Dart, designed many homes in the Avenues in the late nineteenth and early twentieth centuries. This residence was built for Milton E. Lipman. An original member of the Rotary Club and on the board of directors of the Chamber of Commerce, Lipman was appointed city treasurer in 1932. In 1954, the home became a commercial nursery and day care center. The look of the home changed considerably during the late twentieth century when it was painted pink and the porch was fully enclosed. It has since been restored to a single-family residence.

928 First Avenue `C`

BUILT: 1922
STYLE: Bungalow
BUILDER: Joseph A. Adamson
ORIGINAL OWNER: Sidney E. Mulcock

This small brick bungalow is typical of many small homes built in Salt Lake City around 1920.

The home was built by real estate speculator Sidney E. Mulcock in 1922. Mr. Mulcock also built 932 First Avenue, 938 First Avenue, and 23 P Street. All four homes are very similar in design. Carroll C. Hummell, a clerk with the Oregon Short Line Railroad, was the first resident owner.

931 First Avenue   C

BUILT: 1890
STYLE: Victorian Eclectic
ORIGINAL OWNER: Ferdinand Beyle

This two-story Victorian home is covered in stucco on the first level and shingles on the upper exterior walls. This home has unusual details and massing. It is unknown if this is by design or from alterations during the home's history.

The home was built in 1890 for Ferdinand Beyle, a partner in the F. Beyle and Company real estate firm. Later Mr. Beyle operated a secondhand goods store at 310 South State Street. The third owner of the home, from 1920 until 1937, was Forrest Mathez. Mr. Mathez was the superintendent of the Silver King Coalition Mines of Park City and later a mining consultant for a number of Utah mining companies. In 1937, Mr. Mathez moved to California and sold the home to Henry W. Burnham, parts manager of the General Motors Truck Division of Salt Lake City.

953 First Avenue   C

BUILT: 1890
STYLE: Victorian Eclectic
ORIGINAL OWNER: Cyrus L. Hawley

This two-story home retains much of its Victorian detailing. Upper walls are covered in patterned wood-shingle siding and are flared out over the brick first floor. The restored front porch has Victorian millwork and turned columns. The original finials can still be found on the home's gables and corner turret.

This home was built for Cyrus L. Hawley, chief teller at the Utah National Bank. In 1907 Lewis A. Copeland purchased the home. Manager of the Taylor and Brunton Ore Company, Mr. Copeland would later start the Pioneer Ore Sampling Company. In 1923 Mr. Copeland sold the home to William B. Secrest, a physician. From the early 1950s until the mid-1970s, the home was split into small apartments but has been restored to a single-family residence.

957 First Avenue   C

BUILT: 1891
STYLE: Shingle
ORIGINAL OWNER: V. M. C. Silva

This two-story Shingle-style home is most likely a pattern-book design. The front gable has an oval window and wavy-patterned shingles that continue down to shade the second-floor window. Under the bell-cast hipped-roof porch is a large window with a semicircular transom. The rebuilt front porch is missing its original detailing.

The home was built in 1891 for V. M. C. Silva, an agent for the Red Line Transit Company. In 1898, he sold the home to Henry P. Henderson. Henderson was a lawyer who had moved to Salt Lake City when he was appointed chief justice of the Utah Supreme Court in 1866. In 1897, he was the unsuccessful Democratic candidate for the U.S. Senate. By 1950, the home had been converted into apartments. In the late 1970s it was converted back to a single-family home. It was recently damaged by a severe fire but has once again been restored.

961 First Avenue [C]

BUILT: 1900
STYLE: Victorian Eclectic
BUILDER: Anderson Realty Company
ORIGINAL OWNER: Anna H. Calder

This home is a well-preserved, two-story Victorian cottage of pattern-book design. The home retains its original detailing including the large first-floor window with transom and broad front porch.

John G. Anderson built this home in 1897 as an investment and quickly sold the property to Anna H. Calder. Mr. Anderson built many houses in this portion of the Avenues. Mrs. Calder was the widow of David H. Calder, who had been Brigham Young's chief clerk, Utah territorial treasurer from 1859 to 1879, business manager of the *Deseret News*, and a member of the board of directors of ZCMI. Noting her death in 1906, the *Deseret News* said the "death marks the passing of another of the true and sturdy pioneers of 1847."

970 First Avenue [C]

BUILT: 1900
STYLE: Victorian Eclectic
ORIGINAL OWNER: James E. Talmage

This two-story Victorian home has wood-shingled siding on the front gables. The corners of the bay windows are emphasized with rough-faced brick. The front porch's original columns were replaced by iron posts most likely in the 1960s.

This residence was built for James E. Talmage, an internationally known scientist, prominent Utah educator, and leading member of the LDS Church. Mr. Talmage was president of the Latter-day Saints College in Salt Lake City and president of the University of Utah from 1894 until 1897. He was a fellow of numerous scientific societies in the United States and Great Britain. A member of the Council of the Twelve Apostles for the LDS Church after 1911, he became the church's leading authority on technical theological questions. The home was converted into four apartments in 1964.

974 First Avenue [C]

BUILT: 1898
STYLE: Victorian Eclectic
BUILDER: Anderson Realty Company
ORIGINAL OWNER: George H. Reynolds

This Victorian cottage is one of four consecutive homes on First Avenue built by John G. Anderson in 1898, all of which were most likely pattern-book designs. The corner window near the porch was added in the 1930s.

John Anderson built this home as well as 976, 978, and the demolished 980 First Avenue. The first resident owner of this property was George H. Reynolds, president of the Reynolds-Harwood Mining Company. In 1905 the home was purchased by James H. Knowles, an engineer for the Union Pacific Railroad. After 1955 the home was split into small apartments but has since been restored to a single-family residence.

975 First Avenue [C]

BUILT: 1899
STYLE: Victorian Eclectic
ORIGINAL OWNER: Lucius Hayes Curtis

This two-story home retains many Victorian architectural details. The front gable has curved fascia with a sunburst carving, a round attic vent, and half-timber detailing. The upper walls are covered with patterned wood-shingle siding that flares out at the bottom.

This residence was built in 1899 for Lucius Hayes Curtis. Mr. Curtis worked in the mining industry until his death in 1920. His son, Foster J. Curtis, assumed ownership of the house. A well-known Salt Lake City physician, Dr. Curtis joined the staff of the Salt Lake City Veterans Hospital when it opened in 1932. He served as its chief medical officer from 1935 until 1945. When he moved to 1379 Third Avenue in 1930, Dr. Curtis held this property as a rental. The home was converted into apartments in the 1950s.

1002 First Avenue [C]

BUILT: 1920
STYLE: Prairie Bungalow
ORIGINAL OWNER: John H. Johnson

This is a one-story, hip-roofed, Prairie-style bungalow, the most common type of middle-class housing built in Utah between 1910 and 1920. The two concrete belt courses below and above the window line accentuate the horizontal elements of the home's architecture. The attached garage is very rare for a home of this age. The unusual second story above the garage may not be original to the home.

This home was built in 1920 by John H. Johnson as an investment and held as a rental property for many decades. The first tenant, Frank Moormeister, was a physician. According to his obituary, "his wife, Dorothy, was murdered on Feb 21, 1930." The crime was never solved by the Salt Lake City police or sheriff's office.

1007 First Avenue [C]

BUILT: 1893
STYLE: Shingle
ARCHITECT: Ware and Cornell
BUILDER: F. E. McGurrin
ORIGINAL OWNER: Newell Beeman

This large residence is a good and rare example of Shingle style in the Avenues.

The home was built as part of Frank McGurrin and Elmer Darling's Darlington Place development for Newell Beeman, who owned the Salt Lake Photo Supply Company. Railroad executive Hoyt Sherman purchased the residence in 1902. He served on the Utah Commission, which was established by the federal government to suppress the practice of polygamy. In 1916, the home was sold to Claud W. Freed, known as the "father of golf" in Utah and a founding member of the Salt Lake Country Club. The home was converted into apartments in 1938.

1015 First Avenue C

BUILT: 1893
STYLE: Victorian Eclectic
ORIGINAL OWNER: John T. Donnellan

This well-preserved Victorian home has a unique one-story turret-roofed front porch with wooden balustrades and Doric columns.

The home was built in 1893 for John T. Donnellan, a partner in the insurance and loan company, Conway and Donnellan. In 1898, the home was purchased by Henry P. Henderson. Mr. Henderson came to Utah in 1866 when he was appointed chief justice of the Supreme Court for the Utah Territory. After his term, he remained in Salt Lake City and practiced law. He unsuccessfully ran for the U.S. Senate in 1897. Mr. Henderson moved to 957 First Avenue in 1899 and sold the home to Mary McCauley. It then became a rental property for two decades.

1022 First Avenue C

BUILT: 1905
STYLE: American Four Square
ARCHITECT: T. J. Stringer
BUILDER: Oscar Engdahl/Salt Lake Security and Trust Company
ORIGINAL OWNER: James J. Burke

This Four Square–type home has a full-face front porch with a railing on top. The stone porch columns are unique but have unfortunately been painted.

The Salt Lake Security and Trust Company built this home on speculation in 1905. James J. Burke became the first resident owner. Mr. Burke was a successful industrial engineer and contractor during the first three decades of the twentieth century in Salt Lake City. His firm built the former *Salt Lake Tribune* Building, the demolished Medical Arts Building, the former South High School, and numerous industrial plants throughout Utah, Idaho, Montana, and Nevada. Mr. Burke sold the home to George W. Mackay in 1939. Mr. Mackay, a real estate salesman and former director of the Utah State Liquor Control Commission, lived in the home for the next forty years.

1024 First Avenue C

BUILT: 1892
STYLE: Victorian Eclectic
BUILDER: Elmer E. Darling
ORIGINAL OWNER: Joseph P. Bache

This Victorian home was part of the Darlington Place development. The home's detailing was once covered in asbestos shingles from the 1950s. The columns on the second-story porch are an example of what once was found on the first story of the porch.

Joseph P. Bache, the Utah territorial librarian and Supreme Court clerk, owned this home until 1894 when it was sold to Russel L. Tracy, founder of the Tracy Loan and Trust Company. Portions of his banking enterprises would survive into the 1980s. He was active in community affairs and financed the Tracy Wigwam Boy Scout Camp as well as the Tracy Aviary in Liberty Park. The home was converted into apartments in the 1960s but returned to a single-family home in the late 1970s.

1031 First Avenue `C`

BUILT: 1892
STYLE: Shingle
BUILDER: Elmer E. Darling
ORIGINAL OWNER: Elmer E. Darling

This architecturally unique home was built as part of the Darlington Place development by Elmer E. Darling, who chose to retain the home for himself. Underneath the asbestos siding are the original wood shingles, which flare out over the stone foundation.

In addition to home building, Elmer E. Darling held interest in over twenty companies in Utah. During his later years, he devoted most of his attention to his Motor Mercantile Automobile Company. In 1925, Mr. Darling moved out of the Avenues to a home on Highland Drive. From 1931 until 1968, the home passed through numerous owners. In 1968 Jan H. Brunvand purchased the property. Mr. Brunvand, a professor of English at the University of Utah, was known for publishing many books on the subject of folklore.

1037 First Avenue `C`

BUILT: 1896
STYLE: Queen Anne
ORIGINAL OWNER: Edwin C. Coffin

This residence is one of the most elaborate Queen Anne designs in the Avenues. Three projecting bays on the house are articulated and roofed differently. A sweeping curved porch with paired Doric columns covers the southeast corner of the home. Another prominent feature is the onion-domed turret with its pressed metal roof and iron finial intact. The original iron fencing surrounds the property as well. The home's architect, Frederick Hale, designed many prominent buildings in Salt Lake City including the Alta Club and the old Salt Lake City Library.

Edward C. Coffin was the first resident owner of this home. He was a successful business executive and investment broker, owned a hardware store, and was involved in mining. In 1900, the home was purchased by Benjamin F. Caffey, a member of the Salt Lake Stock Exchange with active mining interests. While the exterior of this home possesses nearly all of its original architectural features, they are showing prolonged signs of decay.

1055 First Avenue `C`

BUILT: 1890
BUILDER: Elmer E. Darling
STYLE: Queen Anne
ORIGINAL OWNER: Elmer E. Darling

This two-story Queen Anne–style home is distinguished by its tall, thin tower with a bell-cast pyramidal roof. A broad first-floor porch wraps around the front of the home. A 1908 addition extended the length of the building on its west side. Much of the home's ornate detailing is covered by asbestos siding, most likely added in the 1950s.

This residence was one of the first homes built in Frank E. McGurrin and Elmer Darling's Darlington Place development. Mr. Darling retained ownership of this home and held it as a rental until 1900. Henry C. Hoffman, a realtor, purchased the home at that time. In 1906, John W. Hall, a long-time employee of the Railway Express Company, purchased the home.

1063 First Avenue   C

BUILT: 1891
BUILDER: Elmer E. Darling and Frank McGurrin
STYLE: Victorian Eclectic
ORIGINAL OWNER: John H. Hughes

This two-story home was part of the Darling-ton Place development. The front segmental bay window is capped by an octagonal tent roof with overhanging eaves and brackets creating the appearance of a large turret. The home was covered in asbestos shingles in the 1950s, which have since been removed. The porch posts and decorative trim have been replaced by iron posts.

John H. Hughes purchased the home and rented out the house, an early example of absentee ownership in the Avenues. In 1906, Paul J. Daly, the assistant city attorney for Salt Lake City attorney, purchased the home. In the 1950s, the residence was converted into apartments. It has since reverted back to a single-family home.

1083 First Avenue   C

BUILT: 1914
STYLE: Prairie
BUILDER: Charles A. Newton
ORIGINAL OWNER: Herbert P. Megeath

This hipped-roof Prairie-style bungalow is an example of the most common type of middle-class home built in Utah between 1915 and 1925. The brick exterior has been painted, and the front door is a recent replacement. 1077 First Avenue was built by the same builder at the same time.

The home was built for Joseph P. Mege-ath who sold the home to Herbert M. Chamberlain the same year. Mr. Chamberlain was an employee of the Walker Bank Company for fifty years. He started as a messenger boy at the age of fifteen and retired as executive vice president. He was also active in the Rotary Club and the Utah State Bankers Association. Mr. Chamberlain sold the home to fellow banker Art Davies in 1922. Davies was an employee of the Bankers Trust Company of Salt Lake City.

1087 First Avenue   C

BUILT: 1903
STYLE: Queen Anne
ORIGINAL OWNER: Marvin W. Newcomb

This two-story Queen Anne home is dominated by the square tower on the southeast corner. The home retains its architectural details.

Marvin W. Newcomb, a commercial photographer, had this home built in 1903. Two years later he sold the residence to James Christiansen, who was the Utah state treasurer at the time. In 1914, Glenn Miller became the owner. He was president of the Home Savings and Investment Company. The former U.S. marshal for Utah, he had also been an editor for the *Salt Lake Tribune*. In 1937, the managing editor of the *Salt Lake Tribune*, Kenneth S. Conn, purchased the home.

1105 First Avenue [C]

BUILT: 1903
STYLE: Victorian Eclectic
ORIGINAL OWNER: Orson Howard

This Victorian home has a gable roof with a front dormer window and a projecting segmental front bay with gable roof. The original porch was removed, most likely during the 1960s, and parts of the exterior decorated with Colonial-style trim. In 2000, a historically compatible front porch and front door were restored to the home. A small addition was added to the building's rear.

Orson Howard had this home built in 1903. Mr. Howard was a professor of natural science and English literature at the University of Utah. He organized the University Alumni Association and was its first president. He would later earn a medical degree and return to the university as a professor of natural history and curator of the University Museum of Natural History.

1119 First Avenue [C]

BUILT: 1913
STYLE: Eclectic
ORIGINAL OWNER: Albert H. Walsh

This three-story apartment block exhibits mixed architectural elements. The two-story front porch has four large Doric columns that support a decorated entablature. Unique lattice-work columns support the entablature's roof.

Built in 1913, the Emma apartment building is an example of the growing number of multifamily residences built in the Avenues in the early twentieth century. The original owner, Albert H. Walsh, was founder of the A. H. Walsh Plumbing Company. He named the building after his wife, Emma. Mr. Walsh was also the owner of the adjacent Drayton apartments. The building is currently undergoing a condominium conversion.

1128 First Avenue [C]

BUILT: 1908
STYLE: American Four Square
BUILDER: John Dorius
ORIGINAL OWNER: Albert E. Kimball

This two-story home has a low hip roof and the typical lines of a Four Square–type home. The building is missing its original front porch.

John Dorius built numerous homes in the Avenues, and this home is identical to the adjacent 1122 First Avenue. Albert E. Kimball was the first resident owner. President of the Utah Fire Clay Company, Mr. Kimball also served on the board of directors of the First National Bank and First Security Bank. In 1922 Orson P. Soule purchased the home. Mr. Soule was an owner of regional radio stations and a Salt Lake City attorney.

1136 First Avenue [C]

BUILT: 1907
STYLE: American Four Square
BUILDER: John Dorius
ORIGINAL OWNER: John Dorius

This two-story home has a low hip roof and the typical lines of a Four Square–type home. A massive front porch dominates the building.

Avenues builder and developer John Dorius built this home for himself in 1907. He only lived in the home for two years prior to renting it. In the early 1920s, the home was sold to Edgar L. Newhouse, the manager of the American Smelting and Refining Company in Murray, which operated the state's largest smelter. In the 1930s, Robert C. Williams purchased the property. He was an accountant at the Utah Oil Refining Company. The rear garage was added in 2006.

1171 First Avenue [C]

BUILT: 1893
STYLE: Victorian Eclectic
BUILDER: O. C. Brown
ORIGINAL OWNER: Morris L. Ritchie

This Victorian home is nearly identical to the adjacent 1177 First Avenue. They were built the same year by the same developer, O. C. Brown. The home has a two-story segmental bay window with decorative brickwork. The current porch is not original to the home.

This residence was built for Morris L. Ritchie, an attorney who served from 1896 until 1915 as Salt Lake City's Third Judicial District judge. Edward Zalinski purchased the home in 1919. Mr. Zalinski studied petrography, geology, physics, and chemistry and was a valued consultant in the local mining industry. He lived in the home until the early 1960s. The home was converted into apartments upon his death. It has since been restored to a single-family home.

1180 First Avenue [C]

BUILT: 1908
STYLE: Craftsman Bungalow
ARCHITECT: David C. Dart
ORIGINAL OWNER: Oran W. Ott

This is a small, hip-roofed, one-story bungalow. It may originally have had a side porch on the east side.

This small home was designed by noted Salt Lake City architect David C. Dart for Oran W. Ott in 1908. Mr. Ott was a draftsman for the U.S. Smelting, Refining, and Mining Company. In 1920, the home was sold to Francis B. Critchlow, a Salt Lake City attorney. He owned the home until 1951, leasing it out from 1931 to 1951. In 1951, Henry Dinwoodey, president of the Dinwoodey Furniture Company, purchased the home. At that time, Dinwoodey Furniture was one of the largest furniture stores in the Intermountain West.

1184 First Avenue [C]

BUILT: 1906
STYLE: Dutch Colonial Revival
ARCHITECT: Walter E. Ware
ORIGINAL OWNER: Walter E. Ware

This well-preserved home stands as one of the best examples of Dutch Colonial architecture in the Avenues. The house has a gambrel roof and large front porch with paired square columns.

Prominent Salt Lake City architect Walter E. Ware designed this home for himself. Mr. Ware came to Salt Lake City in 1891 after practicing architecture for the Union Pacific Railroad. In 1901, he began a successful partnership with Alberto Treganza. The Ware and Treganza firm's commissions included schools, churches, warehouses, and residences of all sizes. Mr. Ware occupied the home until his death in 1951, at which time his daughter, Florence, became the owner and resident. Florence Ware was a well-known Utah artist. Her studio was built onto the rear of the home.

1204 First Avenue [C]

BUILT: 1901
STYLE: Victorian Eclectic
ARCHITECT: J. A. Headlund
ORIGINAL OWNER: Charles M. Bell

This two-story Victorian house has a projecting front bay with pilasters at the corners and a curved front of rough-faced brick. The home's original front porch is missing.

The home, designed by Salt Lake architect J. A. Headlund, was built for Charles M. Bell, a traveling salesman. In 1938, he sold the home to Sherman B. Neff, who was the chairman of the English Department at the University of Utah from 1926 until 1952.

1216 First Avenue [C]

BUILT: 1866
STYLE: Vernacular
ORIGINAL OWNER: John H. Picknell

This vernacular structure is one of the oldest homes remaining in the Avenues. This section of the neighborhood was once known as "Butcherville" as the city's slaughter yards were in this area.

John H. Picknell was a butcher and settled in this area to be near the new slaughter yards. Mr. Picknell was also an active member of the Church of Jesus Christ of Latter-day Saints and a member of the Quorum of the Seventies. He originally arrived in Utah in 1862 as a member of the Homer Duncan handcart company. The home remained in the extended Picknell family until 1930.

SECOND AVENUE

169 Second Avenue

BUILT: 1890
STYLE: Victorian Eclectic
ORIGINAL OWNER: Henry P. Richards

This two-story home is one of the older large Victorian homes in the Avenues. Its front gable has decorative wood trim and a triple attic window. A large, two-story wing has been added at the southeast corner of the house. The addition can be identified by the change in brick texture.

Henry P. Richards had this residence built around 1890. Mr. Richards was an employee of the ZCMI department stores and, at one time, head of the wholesale dry goods department. Mr. Richards was one of the first LDS missionaries to go to the Hawaiian Islands. He was also president of the Josepha Agricultural Stock Company, a corporation which was established to care for a colony of Pacific Islanders settled in Tooele County, Utah. The home's second owner converted the building to apartments in 1922.

205 Second Avenue

BUILT: 1930
STYLE: Gothic and Jacobethan Revival
BUILDER: Larson Building Company
ORIGINAL OWNER: Paul E. Keyser

This three-story apartment block shows the influence of both the Gothic and Jacobethan Revival styles popular during this period. The truncated hip roof has a steep center gable with half-timber decoration. The entrance is framed in carved stone with a flamboyant Gothic arch.

This apartment building was built during the period of accelerating shift from single- to multifamily dwellings in the Avenues. Paul E. Keyser, a prominent Salt Lake City business and civic leader, developed the property replacing a pre-1900s two-story building. He and his brothers, George D. and Malcolm A., held many properties in the Avenues as investments. The building remains in good condition.

215–217 Second Avenue

BUILT: 1901
STYLE: Victorian Eclectic
ARCHITECT: David C. Dart
ORIGINAL OWNER: Lutie T. Lynch

This two-story Victorian home was an early design by prolific Avenues architect David C. Dart. While the home retains elements of its original Victorian design, some of the late 1930s additions such as the second-story bay window can be clearly identified.

This home's original owner was Lutie T. Lynch. She financed a number of properties in the Avenues and was one of several women who speculated in Avenues real estate early in the twentieth century. In 1907 the home was purchased by James Rogers, president of the Utah State Association of Fire Insurance Agents and manager of the Garrick Theatre. He died in this home in 1938. After his death the home was remodeled into a duplex.

221 Second Avenue [A]

BUILT: 1906
STYLE: Dutch Colonial Revival
ORIGINAL OWNER: Elbridge L. Thomas

This home is a fine example of the Dutch Colonial Revival style in the Avenues. The large gambrel roof has a wood-shingled façade. A broad porch with square columns covers the front of the home. Adjacent to the sidewalk is the original Crager Iron Works fence. The house is similar to others designed by prominent Salt Lake City architect Walter Ware. However, there is no evidence that he was the architect of this home.

Elbridge L. Thomas was a second-generation non-Mormon political and mining leader in Salt Lake City. His father, Arthur L. Thomas, was territorial secretary and briefly served as interim governor. Elbridge built this home next to the family's mansion at 105 B Street. The family home is now demolished. In 1921, Thomas L. Woodbury, a salesman for the National Biscuit Company, purchased the residence.

257 Second Avenue [A]

BUILT: 1907
STYLE: American Four Square
BUILDER: Heber J. Grant
ORIGINAL OWNER: Joseph S. Wells

This two-story home has a hip roof with a center dormer window. The first-floor front has a curved brick bay window. The original large front porch remains intact.

Heber J. Grant, who would later become president of the LDS Church, built this home. He was president of Heber J. Grant and Company, which built several homes in the Avenues. Joseph S. Wells, Mr. Grant's brother in-law and general manager of the Utah Light and Railway Company, purchased the home from Grant's company. His sister, Edna Wells Sloan, lived next door at 261 Second Avenue. Leon B. Hampton purchased the home around 1918. He was the son of Brigham Young and Mary Jane Hampton and an executive with the Crane Company. The home has been converted into apartments.

261 Second Avenue [A]

BUILT: 1889
STYLE: Italianate
ORIGINAL OWNER: George Curley

This two-story home reflects Italianate styling, which is rare in the Avenues. The eaves of the hip roof have been left open to expose decorated rafter tails. Windows are topped with brick arches and the double front doors have arched transoms.

George Curley, a brick and stone contractor, built this home for himself in 1889 and the Curley family lived here briefly. In 1901 Emily Grant, wife of Avenues' real estate developer and LDS church leader Heber J. Grant, purchased this home. She lived here until 1906 when she sold the home to her sister, Edna Sloan, whose husband, Thomas Watts Sloan, was also a real estate executive. In 1918 John Henry Walker, son of Salt Lake City business and banking leader Matthew Walker, purchased the home. John Henry succeeded his father as president of M. H. Walker Realty Company. He died in this home in 1941.

267 Second Avenue   A

BUILT: 1886
STYLE: Victorian Eclectic
ORIGINAL OWNER: Robert Patrick Jr.

This Victorian home has unusual massing. A single-story hipped-roof section is joined to a dominating two-story east bay. The building exhibits classic Victorian detailing. The east bay has decorative brick work including a corbelled belt course and a large, round, arched first-floor front window.

Robert Patrick Jr., manager of the ZCMI department store, built this home in 1886. His wife, Caroline, sang for the Mormon Tabernacle Choir. After Robert Patrick's death, Caroline continued to live in the home for many years. She converted the residence into several apartments for her daughters. At one time, the ornate front porch was enclosed. The home was restored to a single-family residence in the early 1990s.

271 Second Avenue   A

BUILT: 1911
STYLE: American Four Square
ARCHITECT: Walter E. Ware and Alberto O. Treganza
BUILDER: Schuyler Building
ORIGINAL OWNER: Henry Wallace

This well-preserved, two-story brick Four Square–type home has a broad front porch with brick arched openings. The hip roof has exposed rafter tails consistent with Craftsman architecture.

This home replaced an older frame structure in 1911. Salt Lake City architects Alberto O. Treganza and Walter E. Ware designed this residence for Henry Wallace, founder of the Utah Cracker Company. He eventually sold the company to the American Biscuit Manufacturing Company and served as manager of American Biscuit and the National Biscuit Company until 1915. His daughter, Mary Ellen Wallace, remained in this home until 1965. She was a member of the LDS Young Women's Mutual Improvement Association.

272 Second Avenue   A

BUILT: 1907
STYLE: Victorian Eclectic
ORIGINAL OWNER: Harriet Price

This Victorian home has a two-story front bay with a hip roof. There is a small second-story bay window below the off-center dormer window. The front porch has a cornice with dentil molding and is supported by paired Doric columns.

Harriet Price bought the home in 1907 for three thousand dollars. Mrs. Price was the wife of Well L. Price, a grocer and store clerk. Otto Harbach, who purchased the residence in 1910, became a playwright after careers in teaching and newspaper advertising. He wrote several Broadway musicals including *No No Nannatee* and *Rose Marie* with Oscar Hammerstein. He maintained the property as a rental unit until his sister, Sadie Poulton, purchased the home in 1939. She converted the building into apartments in 1942 and lived in one of the apartments until 1974.

299 Second Avenue　A

BUILT: 1907
STYLE: American Four Square/Colonial Revival
ORIGINAL OWNER: Willard Young

This home shows some Colonial Revival influence in the paired modillion brackets under the broad eaves, the oval front window, and the curved, first-floor bay windows. The front porch has been enclosed.

Willard Young, a son of Brigham Young, built this home, which may have been designed by the architectural firm Cannon and Fetzer. Willard Young was a prominent LDS Church educator and served as superintendent of LDS Church building activities. Anthony W. Ivins purchased the home in 1913. He was a member of the Quorum of the Twelve Apostles of the LDS Church. Later residents included state legislator Richard W. Young Jr. and state treasurer Oliver Ellis. Mr. Ellis converted the home to apartments. The building was restored to a single-family residence in the late 1990s.

301 Second Avenue　A

BUILT: 1902
STYLE: American Four Square
ORIGINAL OWNER: Union Worthington

This tall, Four Square–type home features a hip roof with dormer windows and a wood-framed and half-timbered bay window on the first floor. The side porch has been enclosed, and the east third-floor dormer is not original to the home.

This home was built by one of Utah's early prominent physicians. Union Worthington was a member of the staff of Saint Mark's Hospital. He formed a medical partnership with Albert L. Castleman in 1907 and together they worked to modernize medical practices in Utah. They provided critical medical care to the many immigrants brought to the state for the mining industry. In 1928, the home was purchased by Warwick A. Tyler, a Christian Science medical practitioner. His office was in this home. The building was converted into apartments during the Great Depression but was restored to a single-family residence in the 1990s.

307–309 Second Avenue　A

BUILT: 1886
STYLE: Victorian Eclectic
BUILDER: Edward and Charles J. Brain
ORIGINAL OWNER: Charles J. Brain

This home has a stucco-covered front gable with half-timbering. A small, enclosed entrance, also with half-timbering, projects from the front of the structure. The residence was remodeled with additions in 1910 and again in the 1930s.

Charles J. Brain and his father, Edward, built this home in 1886, and Charles was its first resident. He was the builder of the now-demolished Eighteenth Ward amusement hall and the Lafayette School. His wife, Georgiana, was the daughter of George Romney, a property developer, political leader, and ecclesiastical leader in the Avenues. In 1930, Mary Maggie purchased the home but lost it to Zion's Savings and Loan during the Great Depression in 1933. In 1935, the home was converted to apartments.

315 Second Avenue A

BUILT: 1877
STYLE: Victorian Eclectic
BUILDER: Edward Brain
ORIGINAL OWNER: William F. Nelson

This one-story Victorian cottage has an oval window on the front gable and dentiled, raking cornices. There is a segmental front bay window. This home faced demolition in 1993 due to structural failure. As one of the oldest standing structures in the Avenues, the adobe walls had seriously deteriorated. The home was structurally rebuilt and retains its historic character.

Edward Brain built this home, along with 309 and the now-demolished 303 Second Avenue. Mr. Brain was the owner of the former Brain Brickyard located at Fourth Avenue and Virginia Street. The first resident-owner was William F. Neslon, superintendent of the S. P. Teasdale Department Store. His second wife, Mary Maria Evans, continued to live in the home after William's death. She was a charter member of the Westminster Presbyterian Church.

318 Second Avenue A

BUILT: 1890
STYLE: Victorian Eclectic/Italianate
BUILDER: C. N. Christiansen and Charles Worthin
ORIGINAL OWNER: Charles F. Sansom

This Victorian home has tall, narrow windows with brick arched openings and carved wooden frames. A prominent feature is the flat-roofed, segmental front bay. The small porch has Doric columns.

Charles F. Sansom owned homes at 86 C Street and 316 Second Avenue. He sold both properties to build this residence. Herbert and Ida Hirschman purchased the home in 1901. The Hirschmans, German Jewish immigrants, owned the Hirschman Shoe Company on Main Street in Salt Lake City. They were active in the local Jewish community, donating time and money for building projects and social welfare activities. The home was converted into a duplex in the late 1960s. It has since been restored to a single-family home.

323 Second Avenue A

BUILT: 1891
STYLE: Victorian Eclectic/Italianate
ORIGINAL OWNER: Lydia and Susan Alley Wells

This Victorian cottage has a projecting front gabled bay. The cornice on this bay has returns and paired brackets typical of the Italianate style. A wooden bay window projects out from the main bay with brackets, thin pilasters, and arched windows. The attached garage is a late-twentieth-century addition.

This home was built for the plural wives of prominent civic and ecclesiastical leader Daniel H. Wells. His third and fourth wives, Lydia Ann and Susan Alley, lived here with their six children. Both women lived in this home until their deaths. The property remained in the family as a rental unit until 1945.

337 Second Avenue A

BUILT: 1899
STYLE: Victorian Eclectic
ORIGINAL OWNER: William Lloyd

This one-story Victorian home of pattern-book design is typical of many working-class homes in the Avenues. The home has a main hip roof with south and east gabled bays. The gables are shingled, and the east gable has a Palladian-style window. The small front porch has turned columns.

William Lloyd, a retired local and professional baseball player, built this modest home in 1899 for $1,050. Mr. Lloyd owned the local market across the street at 89 D Street. He remained in this home until 1926 when he moved next door to 335 Second Avenue. He also owned the home at 121 D Street which he maintained along with this residence as rental properties. William Lloyd's sister, Elizabeth Lloyd Pratt, purchased the home from William in 1937. Her husband, Alonzo Platt, was a leather craftsman and saddle maker.

376 Second Avenue A

BUILT: 1920
STYLE: English Cottage
ARCHITECT: Lewis Telle Cannon
ORIGINAL OWNER: Martha H. Cannon

This bungalow, inspired by the English cottage, has a long, sloping roof with a notch cut out on the northeast corner for the entry. There is a small, semicircular porch roof. Some of the home's original front casement windows have been covered by siding. The garage and sleeping porch are original to the home.

The home was built for Martha H. Cannon, wife of Lewis Telle Cannon, senior partner of the prominent Salt Lake City architecture firm Cannon and Fetzer. The firm designed many notable buildings in the city including the First Security Bank tower, at First South and Main Street, and West High School. Mr. Cannon was an active civic and LDS Church leader. Martha continued to live in the home until her death in 1968. The residence was later converted into apartments.

405 Second Avenue A

BUILT: 1893
STYLE: Queen Anne
ORIGINAL OWNER: Emanuel A. Hartenstein

This two-and-one-half-story home has a conical tower on the southwest corner with its original metal finial. The upper gable and the tower share a bracketed cornice. The second story of the home has patterned wood shingles that flare out over the brick first story.

Emanuel A. Hartenstein built this Queen Anne–style home in 1893. Mr. Hartenstein was an active member of the early Jewish community in Salt Lake City. In 1905 he sold the residence to John H. McChrystal. A mining engineer, Mr. McChrystal became the manager of the Gemini Mining Company, the Ridge and Valley Mining Company, and the Godiva Mining Company in Eureka, Utah. At times during his ownership, the home was a rental property.

411 Second Avenue

BUILT: 1892
STYLE: Victorian Eclectic
BUILDER: Thompson and Wegal
ORIGINAL OWNER: William C. Dunbar

This Victorian home has a projecting front gabled bay, wood shingles on the second story, and shiplap siding on the first story. Most of the original front porch columns were replaced by iron posts in the early 1970s. Two of the original Doric columns are found along the house.

This residence was built for William C. Dunbar, a successful businessman who was cofounder and manager of the *Salt Lake Herald* newspaper. He was also a well-known bagpipe player, sketch reader, and singer. His daughter, Belle, inherited the home and maintained it as a rental property. Harry and Margaret Thomas purchased the home in 1923. Mr. Thomas was the owner of the Thomas Electric Company. The home was converted into apartments in the 1950s and has since been restored to a single-family home.

420 Second Avenue

BUILT: 1900
STYLE: Victorian Eclectic
ORIGINAL OWNER: Charles H. and Susan R. Wells

This Victorian home has front and side gables faced with fish-scale shingle siding. Below each gable is a shallow, projecting two-story bay. From the mid-1950s until the late 1990s, permastone brick covered the entry. The original porch was replaced by a metal shed porch in the 1950s. An awning currently covers the porch.

Charles H. and Susan R. Wells had this home built for $2,700. Mr. Wells was the receiving teller at the State Bank of Utah and also worked for the Salt Lake City Engineer's office. Lynn A. McKinlay, an early producer for KSL Television, lived in the residence from 1945 until 1953. In 1955, James and Jessie Caldwell purchased the home, dividing it into apartments in 1969. The home was restored to a single-family residence in the late 1990s.

424 Second Avenue

BUILT: 1891
STYLE: Queen Anne
ORIGINAL OWNER: William Bateman

This residence is a good example of Queen Anne architecture in the Avenues. At the northeast corner is a three-story octagonal tower with a high, domed roof topped with a small finial. The upper part of the building is covered in patterned shingles that flare out over the shiplap siding of the first floor.

William Bateman had this home built at a cost of five thousand dollars. Mr. Bateman was an officer in several local companies, including the Spencer-Bateman Company, Sears Glass and Paint, the Saltair Railway Company, and Western Hardware. Prior to his successful business career, he was a telegrapher for the Utah Southern Railway. Mr. Bateman lived in this home until his death in 1947. The building was converted into four apartments in 1960.

461 Second Avenue

BUILT: 1892
STYLE: Victorian Eclectic
ARCHITECT: Walter E. Ware
BUILDER: H. E. Redfield
ORIGINAL OWNER: William C. and Lillias T. Staines

This Victorian home shows influence of Romanesque style. The front gable has a decorated bargeboard with floral pinwheel carvings. A dentiled belt course separates the first and second floors. This motif is repeated above the large, arched, first-floor front window with its ornate, art glass top panel.

William C. and Lillias Staines built this home. This residence is one of the oldest homes designed by prominent architect Walter E. Ware. Mr. Staines was the vice president of the Cunnington Company and Cane Spring Consolidated Mining Company. His wife, Lillias, was active in real estate development in the Avenues. The building was split into apartments in the 1920s. The Staines family continued to own the home until 1944. The home has been restored in recent years.

474 Second Avenue

BUILT: 1888
STYLE: Victorian Eclectic
ORIGINAL OWNER: Howe C. Wallace

This is a one-story ornate Victorian cottage with bell-cast, truncated hip roofs. The corners of the front bay have been cut out. The roof is supported by elaborate, built-up, scroll-sawn brackets with turned pendants.

Howe C. Wallace, a carpenter, pharmacist, and building contractor in Salt Lake City, built this cottage in 1888. In 1912 he sold the home to Katherine and Henry Meyer. Mr. Meyer was involved in mining. The residence passed through several owners until 1952 when it was purchased by Nels Benjamin Lundwall, the author of Latter-day Saints Church books and secretary to the Quorum of the Seventy.

514 Second Avenue

BUILT: 1900
STYLE: Victorian Eclectic
ARCHITECT: David C. Dart
ORIGINAL OWNER: Wilford S. Barnes

This is a two-story Victorian home designed by notable Salt Lake City architect David C. Dart. The home's one-story porch has paired Doric columns on brick piers.

Wilford S. Barnes, a bookkeeper for the ZCMI department store for twenty-five years, had this home built in 1900. In 1924 Henry W. Blake, a postal inspector, purchased the home. In 1932 the building was converted into apartments. It has since been restored to a single-family residence.

516 Second Avenue   B

BUILT: 1898
STYLE: Victorian Eclectic
ARCHITECT: David C. Dart
BUILDER: Baysinger and Jenkins
ORIGINAL OWNER: John Kelly

This Victorian home was designed by noted architect David C. Dart. The Craftsman-style front porch with exposed wooden roof structure replaced the original porch around 1915.

This home had three owners before the first resident owner purchased the property in 1903. Among the home's early owners were Albert Fisher and Aaron Keyser, who owned the Fisher Brewing Company. James and Lillian Marshall became the resident owners in 1903. Mr. Marshall was the secretary of the A. H. Boxrud Company, a wholesale dry goods store. In 1906 they sold the house to Willard T. Cannon, vice president of the Utah-Idaho Sugar Company. The home continued to pass through several owners before being converted into apartments in 1938.

517 Second Avenue   B

BUILT: 1909
STYLE: Bungalow
ARCHITECT: C. B. Onderdonk
BUILDER: Merrill and J. B. Nibley
ORIGINAL OWNER: Merrill and Belua Nibley

This unique one-and-one-half-story bungalow has a large, front dormer window with wood-shingle siding. The dormer cornice and main cornice below both have dentil molding. The broad front porch is stuccoed with arched openings.

Merrill and J. F. Nibley, partners in a wholesale lumber company, built this home. Mr. Nibley and his wife, Belua, lived in the house until 1922. The next resident owner was George D. Keyser, vice president of the M. S. Fireproof Storage Company. He would later serve as manager of the A. Keyser Investment Company. Mr. Keyser was also active in civic affairs serving as a Salt Lake City park commissioner. The Keyser family lived in the home until 1934 and maintained the home as a rental property until 1945.

535 Second Avenue   B

BUILT: 1905
STYLE: American Four Square
ARCHITECT: Walter E. Ware and Alberto O. Treganza
ORIGINAL OWNER: Clarence Warnock

This two-story Four Square–type home has classical detailing. The corners of the house are accented with brick quoins topped by carved Ionic capitals. From the 1950s into the 1980s the large front porch was enclosed with vertical siding that destroyed the original character of the home. The building has since been restored and is in excellent condition.

This home, designed by the notable Salt Lake City firm of Ware and Treganza, was built for Clarence Warnock, an accountant and partner in the Knight and Warnock Company. Mr. Warnock and his wife, May, lived in the house until 1930. They continued to maintain it as a rental property until 1939.

607 Second Avenue　B

BUILT: 1906
STYLE: Georgian Revival
ARCHITECT: Walter E. Ware and Alberto O. Treganza
ORIGINAL OWNER: Adrian C. Ellis Jr.

The design of this large residence reflects the Georgian Revival style. Pronounced modillions mark the Classical cornice, pediment, and portico. The home's style is unique for the architectural firm of Ware and Treganza.

The home was built for lawyer Adrian C. Ellis Jr., who specialized in mining law and owned numerous mining properties. He sat on the board of directors of several Utah enterprises, including the First Security Bank Corporation and the Columbia Steel Company. During the 1950s and 1960s, the Alta Rest Home occupied the building. It was slated for demolition in 1976 along with the rest of the block to build a Safeway grocery store. Community opposition stopped the project and helped create the Avenues' Historic District.

624 Second Avenue　B

BUILT: 1888
STYLE: Victorian Eclectic
ORIGINAL OWNER: George W. Reed Jr.

This one-story Victorian cottage with hip roofs is similar to many small, Victorian middle-class homes in the Avenues. The heavy front porch was an early twentieth-century addition.

The residence was constructed for George W. and Clara T. Reed. Mr. Reed was a long-time employee of the ZCMI department store and ultimately became manager of the drug department. The home's second owner, Roy E. Cline, remained in the house until the early 1970s. He was a machinist for the Union Pacific Railroad.

627 Second Avenue　B

BUILT: 1898
STYLE: Dutch Colonial Revival
ORIGINAL OWNER: William H. Nutting

This one-and-one-half-story home is a well-preserved example of Dutch Colonial Revival–style architecture in the Avenues. The building's gambrel roofs are typical of this style. Although the recorded date of construction of this home is 1898, the interior reflects a later Craftsman style.

William H. Nutting, an owner of numerous mining properties in northern Utah, was the home's original owner. In 1920 Joseph H. Weiner purchased the property. Mr. Weiner was the manager of the Goodyear Tire and Rubber Company in Salt Lake City. In 1976 a local developer planned to demolish this home along with the rest of the block for the construction of a Safeway grocery store. Community activism saved these homes.

637 Second Avenue B

BUILT: 1880
STYLE: Victorian Eclectic
ORIGINAL OWNER: Amos J. Lucas

This well-preserved Victorian cottage was built in two stages. The original adobe home was built in 1880, with a Victorian brick addition in 1891. Over the windows there are arched stone lintels.

Amos J. Lucas was the home's original owner. Mr. Lucas was a butcher who later operated the A. J. Lucas Company Meat Market at 633 Second Avenue with Thomas A. Mulholland of 218 K Street. In 1900 Mr. Lucas sold the home to Louis L. Terry, the owner of the Troy Laundry Company. From 1929 until the late 1960s Patrick Hession owned the property. Mr. Hession was an inspector for the Oregon Short Line Railroad. In 1976 this home was scheduled for demolition along with the rest of the block in order to build a Safeway grocery store. Community activism stopped the demolition.

663 Second Avenue B

BUILT: 1880
STYLE: Greek Revival
BUILDER: William J. Tuddenham
ORIGINAL OWNER: William J. and Mary Ann Tuddenham

This home is a one story "L"–plan Greek Revival cottage. The home has been covered with siding and stripped of many of its original details including the porch columns.

William J. Tuddenham built this home for his family in the early 1880s. He was one of Salt Lake City's best-known building contractors. During his partnership with Charles Brain, he built the Hotel Utah, LDS Hospital, Deseret Gymnasium, Deseret National Bank, and numerous school buildings. In the 1930s Mr. Tuddenham moved next door to 669 First Avenue. This home was briefly split into small apartments from the 1930s until 1950 when James C. McGarry, a police officer, converted it back to a single-family residence.

669 Second Avenue B

BUILT: 1899
STYLE: Victorian Eclectic
ORIGINAL OWNER: James E. Darmer

This two-story Victorian home has a heavy cornice that runs around the house under the eaves. The large, first-floor front window has a transom. The home was restored in 2007.

This pattern-book-designed residence was built for James E. Darmer, who was active in the American Political Party and served as its chairman in 1909. The American Party was organized by powerful non-Mormon Utah residents including former U.S. senator Thomas Kearns. The party objected to the Mormon influence in Utah politics. In 1906 the home was purchased by John Q. Critchlow, treasurer of the Dow and Kelley Clothing Company.

687 Second Avenue   B

BUILT: 1908
STYLE: American Four Square
ORIGINAL OWNER: Jeremiah E. Langford

This distinguished residence has a front porch topped with a metal balustrade, a brick round corner bay, and paired roof dormers. The home has been altered to accommodate multiple apartments. An intrusive stairwell cuts through the front eave.

This home was built for Jeremiah E. Langford. Mr. Langford developed a procedure to produce commercial salt from the Great Salt Lake and became an executive of the Inland Crystal Salt Company. He was also the general manager of the Saltair Beach Company. Along with Charles Nibley and Nephi Clayton, he purchased the resort from the LDS Church in 1906. Mr. Langford would patent a design for a metal railroad tie in 1915. In 1916, he sold the home to the new manager of the Saltair Resort, Joseph Nelson, whose wife, Dr. Pearl Udall, practiced osteopathic medicine.

711 Second Avenue   B

BUILT: 1903
STYLE: Victorian Eclectic
BUILDER: Robert E. McConaughy
ORIGINAL OWNER: Anne H. Perkins

This Victorian home has a two-story front bay of rough-faced brick. The home's front porch has been removed and the Colonial Revival entry is not original. The center second-story window has been filled in with bricks.

Anne H. Perkins purchased this home from mining entrepreneur Robert E. McConaughy. He built four similar homes on this block. The residence was later purchased by Dr. Ellis R. Shipp, the first of the four plural wives of Milford B. Shipp. Dr. Shipp trained to be a physician in Philadelphia and, upon returning to Salt Lake City, established a school for nurses and midwives. She traveled throughout the Utah Territory establishing additional training programs. Dr. Shipp was also a delegate to the National Council of Women, a published poet, and president of the Utah Women's Press Club.

728 Second Avenue   B

BUILT: 1925
STYLE: Bungalow
ORIGINAL OWNER: Sidney G. Saville

This is a late-period Bungalow-style home. As most of this area of the Avenues had been built up by the mid-1920s, this home filled in a remaining small empty lot. It is representative of common middle-class housing in the lower Avenues. The porch has paired Doric columns on brick bases.

The home's original owner, Sidney G. Saville, was an employee of the Utah State Tax Commission. He later served as director of the Motor Vehicle Department. In 1929, the home was sold to a stockbroker named George M. Groesbeck.

740 Second Avenue [B]

BUILT: 1891
STYLE: Victorian Eclectic/Commercial
ORIGINAL OWNER: Castleton Brothers

This corner commercial block is representative of the many neighborhood stores found in the Avenues. After remaining empty for nearly fifty years, the building and west-wing addition have been preserved and converted into a residence.

The Castleton Brothers General Merchandise Store operated from 1891 until 1940, first in the two-story building and later also in the 1905 west addition. During the later years of operation, the store narrowed sales to meat and groceries. Most of the six Castleton brothers lived in the Avenues near the store.

768 Second Avenue [B]

BUILT: 1903
STYLE: Victorian Eclectic
ORIGINAL OWNER: Issac Montegomery Fisher

This two-story Victorian home of pattern-book design features corbelled brick detailing under the eaves. A large first-floor window has corbelled drip molding. The current porch is not original to the home.

This home was built for Salt Lake County auditor Issac Montegomery Fisher. In 1920 a salesman named Orson J. Hyde purchased the property. During the 1960s the building served as the Bethesda Nursing Home. The home was left vacant for several years in the 1970s. It is currently a single-family residence.

803 Second Avenue [B]

BUILT: 1889
STYLE: Victorian Eclectic
ORIGINAL OWNER: John Henry Miller

This pattern-book-designed Victorian cottage has a rectangular, front bay window built of brick. The front porch is not original.

This cottage was built for John Henry Miller, who was a "circulator" for the *Salt Lake Tribune*. In 1903 the home was sold to James Reilley. He and his brother Charles owned the Buffalo Bar and the Elks Saloon in Salt Lake City. Mr. Reilley lived here until 1923. The home was maintained as a rental property until 1931.

863 Second Avenue   B

BUILT: 1906
STYLE: Victorian Eclectic
ORIGINAL OWNER: Glenn R. Bothwell

This one-story Victorian cottage features a gabled front bay with patterned wood-shingle siding in the gable. This is a common design for Victorian cottages found in Salt Lake City.

Gleen R. Bothwell acquired the south half of Avenues' lot 2 from Timothy Egan in 1902. He broke it up into four sections for investment purposes, building homes on two of the sections and selling the other two sections. This home and 859 Second Avenue were maintained as rental properties. Mr. Bothwell, a mining entrepreneur, was one of many to use their money in Avenues' real estate speculation. In 1907 Alma O. Soderberg became the first resident owner. He was a clerk for the Utah Light and Railway Company.

868 Second Avenue   B

BUILT: 1900
STYLE: American Four Square
ORIGINAL OWNER: John W. Delano

This two-story Four Square–type home replaced an earlier adobe structure. The front porch is not original and the garage is a non-historic addition.

This home has had several significant owners including Ernest Van Cott, who practiced as a physician in Salt Lake City and for the Oregon Short Line Railroad. George H. and Alice Merrill Horne purchased the property in 1924. She was one of the founders of the LDS Church's children's organization, The Primary Association. She was elected to the Utah state legislature in 1898 and was responsible for Utah becoming the first state to own its own fine arts collection. A founder of the Utah Arts Colony, she housed the colony's art gallery in this home. Her son, Dr. Lyman Horne, was one of the first obstetricians in Utah and practiced medicine in the state for over fifty-four years.

870 Second Avenue   B

BUILT: 1898
STYLE: Victorian Eclectic
BUILDER: Henry C. Phipps Jr.
ORIGINAL OWNER: Henry C. Phipps Jr.

This two-story Victorian home is similar to 75, 77, and 79 D Street. All four homes were built by the same builder, Henry C. Phipps Jr., for investment purposes. This home features an off-center window and front gable. A corbelled brick course separates the first and second floors. The original front porch has been removed from the building and the Colonial Revival trim around the front door is not original decoration.

Henry C. Phipps Jr. leased the property to tenants until 1919. The first resident owner of the house was George Hoffman, founder of the George Hoffman Hardware and Sporting Goods Company. An avid golfer, he won the Utah State Amateur Golf Championship four times.

879 Second Avenue B

BUILT: 1897
STYLE: Victorian Eclectic
BUILDER: Albert B. Farley
ORIGINAL OWNER: Joseph E. Frick

This is a Victorian home dominated by its front porch, which has octagonal columns. There are gables on the south and west sides.

A carpenter and contractor, Albert B. Farley built this home for Joseph E. Frick, who founded the law firm of Frick and Edwards in 1897. In 1906 he was appointed to the Utah State Supreme Court, where he served for eighteen years. Following his death in 1930, William H. Hassard purchased the property. Mr. Hassard was a traffic analyst for the Utah State Road Commission. In 1964 the home was converted into apartments. It has since been restored to a single-family residence.

881 Second Avenue B

BUILT: 1892
STYLE: Victorian Eclectic
ARCHITECT: Harrison and Nichols
BUILDER: Salt Lake Building and Manufacturing Company
ORIGINAL OWNER: Orson P. Miles

This two-story brick Victorian home has a front gable supported by decorative brackets. The porch is a 1920 addition to the home. The property's original iron fencing is found atop sandstone blocks.

This home was built for Orson P. Miles at a cost of $3,500. Mr. Miles was a clerk for a grocery and hardware firm known as the Cunnington Company. Following his death in 1910, ownership of the property passed to his daughter, Luetta P. Miles, one of Utah's early women physicians. The home was bought in 1947 by Kindred L. Storrs, who owned the Storrs International Chemical and Refining Company. His wife, Gladys C. Storrs, continued to live in the home until the late 1970s.

903 Second Avenue C

BUILT: 1887
STYLE: Victorian Eclectic
ORIGINAL OWNER: Samuel J. Coombs

This large Victorian home dominates the corner lot. Multiple hip roofs, gables, and dormers express the architectural style of this house. The home suffered from many years of neglect before being fully restored back to a single-family residence in 2009. The restoration included the stripping of multiple layers of paint from the exterior of the home. The porch was rebuilt to represent the original porch demolished in the 1950s.

The home was built for Samuel J. and Ann E. Coombs. Mr. Coombs owned a painting company. In 1896 real estate entrepreneur James K. Shaw purchased this property and 116 O Street. The property was rented to John F. Cowan, who acquired title to the property in 1902. Mr. Cowan owned mining properties throughout Utah, Nevada, Idaho, California, and Montana. The home was converted to apartments in the 1940s.

909 Second Avenue `C`

BUILT: 1908
STYLE: Craftsman Bungalow
ARCHITECT: David C. Dart
BUILDER: F. E. Thatcher
ORIGINAL OWNER: Frank E. Dole

This well-preserved, one-and-one-half-story bungalow has a gable roof and shed dormer. The home is clad in shingle siding. The front porch is one broad, arched opening supported by paneled wooden posts.

The home was designed by noted Salt Lake City architect David C. Dart and built by F. E. Thatcher for Frank E. Dole. Mr. Dole was a member of the board of directors of the First Security Bank, operator of the Palace Laundry Company, and vice president of the People's Finance and Thrift. In 1929 he sold the home to Cecil E. McCartey, an engineer for the Oregon Short Line Railroad. In 1932 the home was purchased by an accountant named August Glissmeyer.

917 Second Avenue `C`

BUILT: 1891
STYLE: Victorian Eclectic
ORIGINAL OWNER: Alfred F. Kendell

This two-story, hip-roofed Victorian home has a brick first floor. Shingle siding on the second story flares out over the first floor. The front porch of the home has been re-built to represent the original porch. In 2007 multiple layers of paint were stripped from the soft yellow brick walls.

Alfred F. Kendell, a veterinarian, was the home's original owner. He and his wife, Margaret, owned the property until 1941. The home has had four additional owners since that time.

918 Second Avenue `C`

BUILT: 1884 and 1916
STYLE: Bungalow
ORIGINAL OWNER: David Fields

This two-story residence has been significantly altered twice in its history. The home was originally built as a small, Vernacular-style home. It was remodeled in 1916 into a bungalow. In the late 1970s a gambrel-roofed second story was added. The front of the house has two wood-paneled bays with casement windows. The entrance is under the porch on the west side of the house.

David Fields, who was listed in the Salt Lake City Directories as a laborer, was the first owner of this home. In 1914 a lawyer, William A. Hilton, purchased the property and undertook the conversion to a bungalow.

921 Second Avenue   `C`

BUILT: 1907
STYLE: American Four Square
BUILDER: Adolf and Lucy Richter
ORIGINAL OWNER: H. S. Scott

This two-story home is an American Four Square–type design which was popular throughout America between 1895 and 1920. The wide eaves of the hip roof and those of the first-floor front porch have modillion brackets. On the west side of the house is a curved, wooden bay window.

Adolf and Lucy Richter built this home on speculation. A surgeon, H. S. Scott, was the first resident owner. In 1926 the home was sold to Oliver R. Dibblee, vice president of the Commercial Real Estate Company and manager of the State Reclamation Company. He was also known as a promoter of rock asphalt for city streets and the inventor of a well-known trench machine. In 1939 he sold the home to Otto P. Rubisch, the brewmaster of the Fisher Brewing Company.

924 Second Avenue   `C`

BUILT: 1897
STYLE: Victorian Eclectic
ORIGINAL OWNER: William F. Hilton

This one-story Victorian cottage has a truncated hip roof with a small dormer and large front gable. In the gable is a plaque with the words "Myrtle Cottage." The origin of the sign is not known. The original front porch wrapped around the northwest front corner of the home. The porch posts are not original but most likely match those of the original porch.

The home was built for Salt Lake City policeman William M. Hilton. After his death in the late 1920s, his wife, Annie, continued to live in the house. In 1938 Hagew R. DePriest, a conductor for the Union Pacific Railroad, bought the house.

925 Second Avenue   `C`

BUILT: 1906
STYLE: Dutch Colonial Revival
ORIGINAL OWNER: Howard S. Stowe

This Dutch Colonial Revival bungalow has two front dormers and a front porch covering the face of the home. The house has been covered in aluminum siding and asbestos shingles.

Howard S. Stowe, a real estate salesman, built this home and occupied it for just one year. Samuel R. Neil, a stockbroker, owned the home from 1907 until 1925. Mr. Neil sold the home to Frank Slaats, a contractor, who briefly lived in the home before renting it out. In 1926 Otto P. Rubisch purchased the residence. Mr. Rubisch, the brewmaster for the Fisher Brewing Company, lived next door at 921 Second Avenue. He rented the home out until 1940 when it was sold to Samuel R. Wynn, an employee of the Union Pacific Railroad.

933 Second Avenue `C`

BUILT: 1903
STYLE: Dutch Colonial Revival
ORIGINAL OWNER: Elliott Kelly

This Dutch Colonial Revival bungalow has a large gambrel roof typical of the style. There is shiplap wood siding on the first floor and wood shingles above. A cut in the siding on the west end of the first-story façade reveals the location of a second door that existed when the home was split into apartments. The exterior of this home remains in good condition.

This property had multiple owners during construction. The first resident owner was Elliot Kelly, editor and general manager of the *Salt Lake Telegram* newspaper. In 1919 the home was sold to a physician named Frank D. Spencer. The home was divided into small apartments in 1951. In the early 1990s the building was restored to a single-family residence.

937 Second Avenue `C`

BUILT: 1902
STYLE: Victorian Eclectic
ORIGINAL OWNER: Hugh L. Thomas

This Victorian home has wood-shingle siding that flares out over the brick first floor. The original wraparound front porch was stuccoed in a Mission style in the 1920s. The home's exterior was in a state of extensive deterioration by the late 1970s but has since been restored.

This home was built for Hugh L. Thomas, an executive with the Rocky Mountain Bell Telephone Company. He sold the property to Herbert J. Westmore in 1907. Mr. Westmore was the vice president and general manager of the Western Dental Supply Company. In 1925, the home was purchased by Wilber E. DeWitt, an early and long-time motion picture projectionist in Salt Lake City. He worked at both the Orpheum and Uptown Theaters during his career. Folksinger Rosalie Sorrels lived in the home in the 1960s.

951 Second Avenue `C`

BUILT: 1890
STYLE: Vernacular
ORIGINAL OWNER: John and Isabella Gibson

These frame buildings are two of the few wood-frame structures built in the Avenues. The L-plan cottage was extensively restored in 2006 and included a complete rebuilding of the home's foundation. A compatible addition and garage were added to the rear of the original home. Current homeowners Jim and Jennifer Levy received a Utah Heritage Foundation Preservation Award for the restoration and addition.

The buildings were most likely built for Scottish immigrant John Gibson, who purchased the property in 1890 for one thousand dollars. Mr. Gibson established his tailor shop in the one-story building. His daughters, Margaret and Isabella, continued to own the property until 1967.

965 Second Avenue [C]

BUILT: 1905
STYLE: Victorian Eclectic
ARCHITECT: David C. Dart
BUILDER: Adolf and Lucy Richter
ORIGINAL OWNER: William D. and Elizabeth MacLean

This home was designed by noted architect David C. Dart. The front façade has a projecting center gabled bay. The roof is flared out at the ends to cover broad eaves. The original front porch once covered the full width of the home.

Elizabeth and William Maclean purchased this home for $6,300 from Adolf and Lucy Richter. Mr. Maclean was the chief clerk of the state's largest supplier of coal, the Utah Fuel Company. He was later the president of the Maclean Coal Company. His family maintained ownership of this property into the 1970s. The home was converted into apartments in 1974. It was extensively restored by owners Rachel Sweet and Scott Martin in 2003 and is once again a single-family residence.

979 Second Avenue [C]

BUILT: 1911
STYLE: American Four Square
BUILDER: Adolf and Lucy Richter
ORIGINAL OWNER: William K. and Estella D. Mordock

This large, Four Square–type home has a hip roof with a pedimented front center window. Between the large, double-hung second-floor windows is a small window with art glass. A broad front porch with Doric columns covers the façade. The home's entrance is on the west side instead of the more common front porch entrance. The current porch exactly replicates the original one that collapsed in 2005.

William and Estella Mordock purchased this home for $9,250 and moved here from 964 First Avenue. Mr. Mordock was a mining engineer. In 1920, the property was sold to Fred E. Rolopp, president of a wholesale coal company, Rolopp-Romney. During much of the 1960s, the home was known as "Pat's Friendly Boarding House."

1009 Second Avenue [C]

BUILT: 1914
STYLE: American Four Square
ARCHITECT: David C. Dart
BUILDER: Adolf and Lucy Richter
ORIGINAL OWNER: Adolf and Lucy Richter Company

This Four Square–type home has a hip roof with a front center dormer. A small porch with iron balustrade is on the south side. The original porch on the building's west side has been enclosed. A noncompatible addition has been added on top of the west-side porch.

This home was built as and has remained a rental property through most of its history. The building was designed by noted architect David C. Dart. Avenues developers Adolf and Lucy Richter built the home and rented it through their company until 1929. Mose Lewis, an owner of a wholesale ladies furnishing company and resident at 1017 Second Avenue, purchased the property and continued to maintain it as a rental house. It was converted into apartments in the 1950s.

1012–1014 Second Avenue C

BUILT: 1898
STYLE: Victorian Eclectic
ORIGINAL OWNER: Andrew Mortenson

This Victorian duplex is dominated by a two-story gabled porch. The building's original detailing is well preserved.

The duplex was built by Andrew Mortenson, who operated the small grocery next door at 88 Q Street. The grocery was known as the Table Supply Company. In 1906 he sold the building to Henry J. Plumhoff, a secretary for the Oregon Short Line Railroad. Currently each side of the duplex is used as office space.

1025 Second Avenue C

BUILT: 1891
STYLE: Victorian Eclectic
ORIGINAL OWNER: Fred A. Rowe

This Victorian home is most likely a pattern-book design. The dominating rock front porch was added in the 1920s replacing the original Victorian porch.

Fred A. Rowe, a clerk, had the home built in 1891. In 1900 I. Montgomery Fisher purchased the property. Mr. Fisher was active in Utah politics as a member of the Liberal Party, an anti-Mormon party formed to challenge Mormon political, social, and economic domination. Mr. Fisher served as Salt Lake County auditor and as accountant for the Utah State Road Commission. The home passed through several owners before being converted into apartments in 1958. The home currently is a duplex with a basement apartment.

1029 Second Avenue C

BUILT: 1891
STYLE: Victorian Eclectic
BUILDER: Elmer E. Darling and Frank McGurrin
ORIGINAL OWNER: John A. Barker

This two-story Victorian house has a hip roof and a fish-scale-shingled front gable. A band of vertical boards separates the first and second floors. The home no longer has its original front porch.

In 1890 Elmer Darling and Frank McGurrin acquired this section of the Avenues for their Darlington Place development. 1029, 1033, and 1037 Second Avenue were part of this development. John A. Barker purchased the home for $4,800 in 1891. Little is known about him or the subsequent six owners. For much of the period between construction and 1925, the home was a rental property. In 1925 Fredrick Wrathall, a former renter of the home, purchased the property. He was a taxidermist and operated the business out of the home.

1065 Second Avenue C

BUILT: 1909
STYLE: Craftsman Bungalow
ORIGINAL OWNER: Eugene Giles

This is an excellent example of a one-story, gable-roofed Craftsman bungalow. The front gable has broad, projecting eaves supported by heavy brackets. Half-timbering is found on the front of the gable. The large porch rests on three brick columns, and the front of the home features a wooden bay window.

The home was built for Eugene Giles. Mr. Giles came to Salt Lake City in 1909 to be cashier at the National Copper Bank. In 1924 he was named vice president of Continental National Bank and sold the residence that year to David R. Pingree. Mr. Pingree was the manager of the Fuller Brush Company and would later form his own company, the Morlite Lamp and Shade Manufacturing Company.

1073 Second Avenue C

BUILT: 1909
STYLE: Bungalow
ARCHITECT: Headlund and Wood
ORIGINAL OWNER: Elmer E. Casady

This is a one-and-one-half-story, gable-roofed bungalow. The front gable has patterned wood shingles and a unique, projecting three-part window. The home's original porch posts were replaced by iron posts most likely in the 1960s.

Elmer E. Casady had this home built as an investment property. It is an early example of absentee ownership in the Avenues. Mr. Casady was a real estate developer who built several Avenues' homes. The home's architect, J. A. Headlund, is best known for his design of Salt Lake City's Emanuel Baptist Church. In 1920 a contractor, Charles J. Hutcherson, bought the residence. He lost the property in a tax sale during the Great Depression.

1077 Second Avenue C

BUILT: 1909
STYLE: Craftsman Bungalow
ORIGINAL OWNER: Fred W. Meakin

This is a one-story, gable-roofed brick bungalow with broad eaves supported by brackets. The front of the home is dominated by a large, wood-shingle-sided gable covering a porch with square wooden columns and balustrades.

The home was built for a prominent Utah dentist and businessman, Fred W. Meakin. During his life, Mr. Meakin was president of the Utah State Dental Supply Association and founder of the Western Dental Supply Company. He was also well known as a bicyclist and often raced at the old Salt Palace Saucer Track. In 1928 he sold the house to Rudolph Orlob, manager of the Mountain States Rubber Company.

1089 Second Avenue [C]

BUILT: 1908
STYLE: Bungalow
ORIGINAL OWNER: Lilith A. Pinkerton

This one-story bungalow features a hip roof and front center dormer window, a common bungalow design found in Utah.

Real estate broker Edward M. West built three houses on property owned by his wife. 1081 and 1085 Second Avenue are similar in design. Lylith A. Pinkerton purchased the home from Mr. West for $5,750 in 1908. Mr. Pinkerton was the consulting physician to the Standard Coal Company and the Peerless Coal Company. In 1922 the home was sold to Leslie S. Squires, a long-time employee of the Utah Fire Clay Company who eventually became its executive vice president. He also served as president of the Utah Manufacturers Association and director of the Salt Lake City Chamber of Commerce.

1103 Second Avenue [C]

BUILT: 1900
STYLE: Victorian Eclectic
ORIGINAL OWNER: Donald Rose

This one-and-one-half-story Victorian cottage has an octagonal tower on the southwest corner. On the west side there is a small, second-floor balcony cut into the wall behind the tower. The home's stucco finish may not be original. Stucco was not a common exterior finish in Utah when this home was built.

Donald Rose, a commercial agent for the Illinois Central Railroad, was the first resident owner of this property. He remained in the home until 1909. The residence passed through several owners until 1924 when Wilkie H. Blood bought the home. Mr. Blood was a physician and the brother of Utah governor Henry Blood. During his career, he was a member of the staff of the LDS Hospital School of Nursing and a medical advisor at the Primary Children's Medical Center.

1119 Second Avenue [C]

BUILT: 1906
STYLE: Dutch Colonial Revival
ORIGINAL OWNER: Louis A. Bailey

Gambrel roofs are typical of the style of this one-and-one-half-story Dutch Colonial Revival cottage. The original front porch posts were replaced by iron posts in the late 1960s. This home is nearly identical to 1121 Second Avenue. The two houses were most likely built by the same developer.

Louis A. Bailey, a well-known local businessman, was the first resident owner of this home. Mr. Bailey operated a brokerage business representing many manufacturers in the city. In 1917 he formed the Horseshoe Auto Tire Company. He was an active member of the Salt Lake City Elks Club and directed many charitable activities. He moved from the home in the early 1920s but continued to own and maintain the property as a rental unit. Renting homes in the Avenues was a growing practice throughout most of the twentieth century.

1120 Second Avenue <kbd>C</kbd>

BUILT: 1892
STYLE: Victorian Eclectic
ORIGINAL OWNER: Henry A. Ferguson

This home is an ornate and well-preserved one-and-one-half-story Victorian cottage. A carved sunburst adorns the front gable. On the first floor, the corners of the bay are cut away to form a bay window. The whole bay is covered with a variety of patterned wood-shingle siding. First restored in 1977, this home is an early example of Avenues' restoration. The brick, two-story shop building at the rear was built in 1909.

A carpenter, Henry A. Ferguson, built this home. In 1899 the property was purchased by Albert H. Walsh, founder of the A. H. Walsh Plumbing Company. The home would remain in the Walsh family for the next seventy years. Mr. Walsh also built two large apartment buildings on First Avenue, "The Drayton" and "The Emma," the latter named after his wife, Emma Wiscombe.

1127 Second Avenue <kbd>C</kbd>

BUILT: 1909
STYLE: American Four Square
ARCHITECT: Bernard O. Mecklenburg
ORIGINAL OWNER: Benjamin A. and Grace Stewart McMillan

This home is a Four Square–type residence with Craftsman detailing. The paired squared columns, exposed rafter tails, cobblestone porch foundation, and broad eaves are typical details of the Craftsman style.

Benjamin and Grace McMillan had this home built in 1909. The architect, Bernard O. Mecklenburg, was the architect of the Cathedral of the Madeleine. The McMillans owned the McMillan Paper and School Supply Company. Grace McMillan also worked for the Western Union Telegraph Company after Benjamin's death. In 1918 the home was sold to Arch H. Cook, owner of the Cook Tea and Coffee Company. The home was damaged by fire in 2007 but has since been restored.

1135 Second Avenue <kbd>C</kbd>

BUILT: 1908
STYLE: Bungalow
ORIGINAL OWNER: Fred R. and Francis O. Davis

This stuccoed, hip-roof bungalow features a front center dormer window and full-width porch.

The original resident owners of this home were Fred and Francis Davis. Mr. Davis was the president of the Davis, Short, and Elliot Company. The property was sold in 1910 to Fred A. Conely, a clerk at a national plumbing supplier called the Crane Company. Lonis B. Felt purchased the home in 1920. She had been the president of the LDS Church's Primary Association since 1880. From 1935 until 1971 the home was owned by Louis Zucker, a professor of English at the University of Utah. He conceived and helped fund the Judaica Library at the university. Mr. Zucker was an active leader of Salt Lake City's Jewish community.

1153 Second Avenue

BUILT: 1905
STYLE: American Four Square
ARCHITECT: S. W. Sears
BUILDER: L. W. Ritter
ORIGINAL OWNER: Noble Warrum

This home is an excellent example of the popular Four Square–type home. The building has a hip roof with a center dormer. Doric columns support a wide front porch.

This house is associated with two prominent, politically active Utahns. The home's first owner, Noble Warrum, served on the editorial board of the *Salt Lake Herald* and *Salt Lake Tribune*. A member of the Utah State Constitutional Convention, he also served terms as the city postmaster, a state senator, and city recorder. He wrote two books on Utah history including *Utah Since Statehood*. Harold P. Fabian purchased the property in the 1920s. He was a member of the Republican National Committee during the Herbert Hoover administration and served on Hoover's unemployment relief committee. Appointed by Governor George D. Clyde, he organized the Utah State Park and Recreation Commission.

1163 Second Avenue

BUILT: 1912
STYLE: Bungalow
BUILDER: Quinn and Schmeirer
ORIGINAL OWNER: Hyrum and Minerva Woolley

This one-story bungalow has a hip roof with a front center dormer window, a common bungalow style found in Salt Lake City.

Jack Quinn and Walter Schmeirer built this home on speculation. The residence is an example of the growing number of homes built for investment purposes. Hyrum and Minerva Woolley were the first resident owners of the property. Little is known of Mr. Woolley other than that he worked in the mining industry. In 1921 they sold the home to James H. Wolfe, who served from 1917 to 1921 as assistant attorney general of Utah. In 1928 he was appointed judge for Salt Lake City's Third Judicial District. After 1934 Mr. Wolfe was a member of the Utah State Supreme Court and for many years was chief justice of the court.

1172 Second Avenue

BUILT: 1912
STYLE: Craftsman Bungalow
BUILDER: Anson Lee
ORIGINAL OWNER: Edgar M. West

This is a one-and-one-half-story, gable-roofed brick bungalow. The porch gable has fascia boards supported by brackets and wood-shingle siding. The frame garage was built in 1921. The home has a compatible upper-story addition.

A real estate broker, Edgar M. West, built this home. Mr. West maintained the property as an investment and rental unit. In 1938 a prominent Utah lawyer, Knox Patterson, purchased the residence. Mr. Patterson, an active Democrat, served two terms in the Utah State Senate. In 1945 the property was bought by Ralph H. Stringham, manager of the Stringham Lumber Company.

1175 Second Avenue | C

BUILT: 1902
STYLE: Shingle
ARCHITECT: Alberto O. Treganza
ORIGINAL OWNER: James H. Taylor

This large home includes a gable roof, a wood-shingled hood over the second-floor windows, and an indented front porch. The casement windows are grouped to form horizontal bands. The house has gone through considerable remodeling throughout its history.

The home was built for James H. and Susan O. Taylor as a rental property. George Steiner purchased the residence in 1911. He was the founder of the American Linen Supply Company, a director of Walker Bank and Trust, and president of the Salt Lake Chamber of Commerce. By the 1930s, the American Linen Supply Company was the largest of its kind in the United States. In 1945 the home was converted into five apartments. The building was restored to a single-family residence in the 1970s.

1187 Second Avenue | C

BUILT: 1909
STYLE: Bungalow
ARCHITECT: W. H. Lepper
BUILDER: John Allen
ORIGINAL OWNER: Karl Spinner

This is a one-and-one-half-story, gable-roofed brick bungalow. There is a large, gabled, front dormer window with wood-shingle siding. Heavy brick columns support the front porch. There is a curved bay window with art glass windows on the east side of the home. The west end of the porch has been enclosed.

Karl Spinner, a German immigrant to Utah and a realtor, built this bungalow in 1909. Following his death in 1920, the house was sold to Mahlon E. Wilson, who practiced law in Salt Lake City for forty years. In the late 1940s Alex M. McDonald bought the home. Mr. McDonald, a geologist, worked in the mining industry throughout the western United States.

1205 Second Avenue | C

BUILT: 1901
STYLE: Classical Revival/Shingle
ORIGINAL OWNER: William C. and Martha H. Jennings

This large, two-story home shows influence of both Classical Revival and Shingle styles. Both styles are rare in the Avenues. The gabled west end of the home has a cornice with modillions, and returns in the Classical manner. There is an oval window on the gable. The porch, which wraps around the west and south sides of the home, has a dentiled cornice, Doric columns, and a wooden balustrade. The eastern portion of the home is a 1922 addition.

Martha and William Jennings had this unique Avenues home built. Mr. Jennings was a land attorney in Salt Lake City. In 1922 the home was sold to Robert R. Hampton, a doctor specializing in ear, nose, and throat disorders. In 1941, William S. Worthington, foreman at the Utah Fire Clay Company, became the owner.

1225 Second Avenue C

BUILT: 1903
STYLE: Victorian Eclectic
ORIGINAL OWNER: Earl T. Harvey

This two-story home features Victorian and Classical detailing on the exterior. The hip roof has front and side dormers, and modillion brackets are found in the eaves. On the southwest second floor, there is a curved brick corner window. Bay windows are found on the front and west sides of the home. The porch is supported by Ionic columns.

Real estate salesman Earl T. Harvey had this home built. He lived in the residence for several years and then rented it out until 1921. That year, he sold the home to Christopher B. Diehl, a corporate attorney for the Union Pacific Railroad. From 1925 until 1948, Alexander E. Eberhardt owned the property. He was an executive with the Salt Lake Mattress and Manufacturing Company. He also served terms as head of the Utah Manufacturers Association and was on the Salt Lake Board of Education.

1235 Second Avenue C

BUILT: 1890
STYLE: Victorian Eclectic
ORIGINAL OWNER: William Hoffman

This two-story Victorian home's exterior is in excellent condition. On the front of the building are a decorated cornice with brackets and a projecting gabled bay with curved, paneled fascia boards. The house is covered in wood shingles which flare out over the wooden novelty siding on the first floor. The front porch has square wooden columns, a scroll-sawn baluster panel, and lattice work underneath. The garage was built in 1922.

William Hoffman, an insurance salesman, built this home. In 1904 he sold the residence to William P. S. Hawk, superintendent of the Postal Telegraph Cable Company. In 1909 the home was purchased by John W. Dyer, a salesman for the Standard Furniture Company.

THIRD AVENUE

131–135 Third Avenue   A

BUILT: 1890–1895
STYLE: Victorian Eclectic
ORIGINAL OWNER: Seldon Irwin Clawson, Mary A. Sears, and J. Wash Young

Buildings such as this two-story row house of Victorian design are rare in Salt Lake City. It has a stamped metal cornice with corbelled brickwork below. Corbelled brick pilasters separate the three sections of the building and mark the corners.

The structure was built in three sections over a six-year period. Seldon Irwin Clawson, a grandson of Brigham Young, built the first section in 1890. Mr. Clawson installed the first electric lights in the Salt Lake City Tabernacle and invented a way to reduce ore using chlorine gas. Mary A. Sears, a widow, built the second section in 1893. J. Wash Young, also a grandson of Brigham Young, built the third section in 1895. He was a pioneer in the motion picture industry. The building has remained rental units throughout its history.

142 Third Avenue   A

BUILT: 1888
STYLE: Victorian Eclectic
ORIGINAL OWNER: George D. Pyper

This is a two-story Victorian home with a one-story west wing. The main section of the home has a projecting three-sided front bay with segmental hip roof. The front porch columns have been restored to their original design.

George D. Pyper had this home built in 1888. Mr. Pyper, a prominent Salt Lake City citizen in the fields of art literature, drama, and music, was a long-time general superintendent of the LDS Sunday School Program. In 1892 Henry C. James purchased the property. Mr. James was the manager of the Utah Plumbing Supply Company. This home has been a rental property for most of the past hundred years.

152 Third Avenue   A

BUILT: 1922
STYLE: Prairie Bungalow
BUILDER: Carl F. Buehner
ORIGINAL OWNER: Ezra T. Stevenson

This is a Prairie-style brick bungalow. Such bungalows were commonly built in Utah between 1910 and 1925. As this home is built on a hill, there is an additional front basement entrance.

Ezra T. Stevenson, an agent for Western State Life, had this home built as an investment property. He lived at 125 A Street at the time of construction. In 1924 Thomas A. Clawson, a dentist, purchased the property. After his death, ownership transferred to his son, Thomas Jr., who was a physician.

158 Third Avenue

BUILT: 1929
STYLE: Tudor
BUILDER: Gaskett Romney
ORIGINAL OWNER: Charles and Caroline Hatch

This is an example of a small, brick, Tudor-style home, a common home style built in Salt Lake City in the 1920s. It represents the transition away from the Bungalow style.

Contractor Gaskett Romney built this home for Charles and Caroline Hatch. Mr. Hatch was known as a prominent sheepman. His wife, Caroline, was a long-time Salt Lake Temple ordinance worker. She remained in the home until her death in 1967. The bottom floor of the home has always been a rental unit.

183 Third Avenue

BUILT: 1870s
STYLE: Vernacular/Bungalow
ORIGINAL OWNER: Abbie Wells Young

The original portion of this home is one of the oldest remaining structures in the Avenues. A simple vernacular cottage is surrounded by a Craftsman-style porch. The porch with cobblestone columns was added between 1910 and 1920.

The first resident of this home was Emmeline Free Young, who had married Brigham Young in 1845. She died a few years after moving into this home. Her niece, Abbie Wells Young, was listed as the property owner. She was the second wife of LDS Church leader Seymour B. Young. She was also a resident of the home starting in the mid-1870s. One of her daughters, Hanna Young, and her husband, A. A. Clark, resided in the home after Abbie Young's death.

223 Third Avenue

BUILT: 1910
STYLE: Classical Revival
ARCHITECT: Charles. B. Onderdonk
BUILDER: O. M. Engdahl
ORIGINAL OWNER: Joseph S. Peery

This apartment block is representative of the growing number of rental properties built in the Avenues during the second decade of the twentieth century. It has a parapet roof with a broad, Classical Revival–style cornice supported by paired brackets and dentil molding. The original exterior detailing of the building remains intact. The tall porches were enclosed by siding from the 1950s until the 1990s. The adjacent Wesley Apartment building is similar in design but has been stripped of architectural details.

Joseph S. Peery built these apartments at the same time as E. Wesley Smith built the Wesley Apartments next door. The two owners agreed to install a joint heating plant. Charles B. Onderdonk, the architect of both buildings, designed numerous public schools in Salt Lake City that have all been demolished.

253 Third Avenue A

BUILT: 1888
STYLE: Victorian Eclectic
ORIGINAL OWNER: Ichel Watters

This two-story home has had several additions and was heavily remodeled in the 1930s or early 1940s.

Ichel Watters, a leading early Jewish merchant in Salt Lake City, was the first resident owner of this home. Ichel and his brother Abraham set up a jewelry store in Salt Lake City in 1866, where Ichel also trained artisans. He served as the grand master of the Independent Order of Odd Fellows in Utah. His wife, Augusta Graupe, was president of the Ladies Hebrew Benevolent Society. They were some of the earliest members of the B'nai Israel Congregation. From 1907 until 1927 the home passed through several owners who rented out the property. In 1927 Ray B. McKinnon, a clerk at the ZCMI department store, divided the home into apartments.

261 Third Avenue A

BUILT: 1907
STYLE: American Four Square
ORIGINAL OWNER: Hyrum L. Nelson

The square porch columns, broad overhanging eaves, and decorations of this yellow brick home are all typically found in Craftsman or Prairie-style design.

This home was built for Salt Lake City business leader Hyrum L. Nelson. Among the many businesses that Mr. Nelson was involved with were the New York Life Insurance Company, the Utah-Idaho Sugar Company, and the Utah Oil Refinery Company. In 1923 he sold the home to Downie D. Muir Jr., who was vice president and general manager of the Utah State Refining, Smelting, and Mining Company. He also served as president of the Salt Lake City Chamber of Commerce in 1934. In 1926 Mary T. Smith, widow of LDS Church president Joseph F. Smith, purchased the home.

267 Third Avenue A

BUILT: 1882
STYLE: American Four Square
ORIGINAL OWNER: John Dull

This two-story, cube-shaped home could be considered an early version of the popular Four Square–type residence.

John Dull had this home built on a piece of Avenues property that had been recently subdivided from its original owners. Mr. Dull worked for the Hanauer Smelting Works. Members of his family lived in the house until about 1896. The home passed through several owners until 1931 and was maintained continuously as a rental property during that period. The home's renter from 1897 until 1903 was James T. Hammond, Utah's first secretary of state. Rose Thomas and her husband, David, purchased the home in a foreclosure auction in 1931, and Rose converted it into apartments in 1955.

275 Third Avenue A

BUILT: 1916
STYLE: Bungalow
BUILDER: Eardley and Elkins
ORIGINAL OWNER: Lucy M. Branning

This unique, one-story bungalow is a rare early example of concrete block construction. The front gable has half-timbering decoration created by using precast aggregate beams.

Lucy M. Branning had this house built in 1916, then immediately sold it to William B. Sage, who was the secretary-treasurer for the Utah Oil Refining Company. In 1927 the home was purchased by Oscar W. Rawlings, a deputy sheriff for Salt Lake County. In 1932 Earl Wagner Pierce became owner of the property. Mr. Pierce was vice president and treasurer for the Beneficial Life Insurance Company.

305 Third Avenue A

BUILT: 1873 and 1909
STYLE: Eclectic
ORIGINAL OWNER: Levi Richards

This large, two-story stucco structure has a double-gabled wing with unusual tapered pilasters. The 1909 building incorporates an 1873 adobe home, but none of the nineteenth-century elements are visible.

The original adobe structure was most likely built by Levi Richards, a physician. His son, Levi W. Richards, inherited the property in 1877. A real estate entrepreneur, Mr. Richards lived in this home with his two wives, Louise Lula Greene and Persis Louiza Young.

333 Third Avenue A

BUILT: 1922
STYLE: Bungalow
BUILDER: Jesse H. Newton
ORIGINAL OWNER: Robert H. Wallis

This home is a good example of a common, early 1920s Bungalow-style built in Utah. Similar in style to 339 Third Avenue, both homes were built by the same builder, Jesse H. Newton.

The first owner of the home was Robert H. Wallis, a lawyer in Salt Lake City. Two years after purchasing the home, Mr. Wallis sold the property to Thomas M. Douglas Jr., who owned the Yellowstone Specialty Company. In 1939 the home was sold to Joseph R. Rozzelle, manager of the Cullen Garage.

339 Third Avenue   A

BUILT: 1922
STYLE: Bungalow
BUILDER: Jesse H. Newton
ORIGINAL OWNER: Ernest N. Carlquist

This one-story bungalow is similar to 333 Third Avenue, and both homes were built by contractor Jesse H. Newton. This home is representative of the Bungalow style commonly built in Utah in the early 1920s.

The first resident owner of this property was Ernest N. Carlquist, a real estate salesman for several companies including the Ashton-Jenkins Company and the American Land Company. Mr. Carlquist was an active member of the Salt Lake Masonic Lodge. In 1931 John W. Lawson purchased the home. Mr. Lawson was a clerk for the Union Pacific Railroad. Members of his family continued to own the home into the 1980s.

361 Third Avenue   A

BUILT: 1890
STYLE: Victorian Eclectic
BUILDER: Taylor, Romney, Armstrong Company
ORIGINAL OWNER: George E. Romney

This one-story Victorian cottage is similar in design to the adjacent 367 Third Avenue. The front porch was recently restored. The large front window on the projecting bay has been altered.

George E. Romney built this home for himself in 1890 at a cost of $2,500. Mr. Romney was secretary-treasurer of the Taylor, Romney, Armstrong Construction Company. He later owned the Pacific Lumber Company, the New State Lumber Company, and the Ogden Lumber Company. He lived in this home until 1903 when it became a rental property. His brother, William S. Romney, lived next door. This home won a Utah Heritage Foundation preservation award in 2012.

367 Third Avenue   A

BUILT: 1890
STYLE: Victorian Eclectic
BUILDER: Taylor, Romney, Armstrong Company
ORIGINAL OWNER: William S. Romney

This one-story Victorian cottage is similar in design to the adjacent 359 Third Avenue. The large front porch retains its dentiled cornice. The original porch posts have been replaced by 1960s iron posts.

William S. Romney built the home and maintained it as a rental property while he continued to live at the now-demolished Romney family home. Mr. Romney worked for the ZCMI department store for forty-four years. He was director of the Heber J. Grant Company and the First National Bank, and was also an officer in the many Romney family businesses. Mr. Romney moved into the home in 1902 and lived there until his death in 1932. The Romney family continued to maintain ownership of this property into the 1980s.

375 Third Avenue

BUILT: 1902
STYLE: Victorian Eclectic
BUILDER: Robert Rogers
ORIGINAL OWNER: James Rogers

This Victorian cottage is probably a pattern-book design and is typical of many small Victorian homes in the Avenues. The original front porch columns were replaced by iron posts most likely in the 1960s. The porch columns have since been restored.

Robert Rogers built this home for his brother James, who was president of the Rogers and Evans Insurance Company and the Utah State Association of Fire Insurance. In 1907, James moved to 215 Second Avenue. The home passed through several owners and was a rental property for a brief time. Cornelius and Rose Salisbury purchased the home in 1933. Mr. Salisbury was a well-know artist and art instructor in Utah, teaching at Brigham Young University and West High School. His family continued to own this property into the 1980s. The home was restored in 2001.

401 Third Avenue

BUILT: 1891
STYLE: Victorian Eclectic
BUILDER: Henry Luff
ORIGINAL OWNER: Henry Luff

This is a small Victorian cottage of pattern-book design. The home has truncated hip roofs, corbelled brick arches with drip molding around the windows, and a projecting front bay.

Henry Luff, a carpenter, built this home for himself. He both resided in this residence and rented it to tenants between 1891 and 1913. Mr. Luff was a carpenter on the Salt Lake City LDS Temple and LDS Tabernacle, as well as many nineteenth-century Salt Lake City residences. Brigham Young deeded this portion of the Avenues to him. He also lived at 409 Third Avenue and 162 E Street. In 1913, Alma A. Harris purchased the property. He operated a confectionary from this home and then built a small store next door at 405 Third Avenue. This building was restored in 2001.

409 Third Avenue

BUILT: 1870/1888
STYLE: Vernacular
BUILDER: Henry Luff
ORIGINAL OWNER: Henry Luff

The frame portion of this cottage was built in 1870 with an addition completed in 1888. This home is one of the oldest standing residences in the Avenues.

Henry Luff built the home for himself and maintained it mostly as a rental property until he sold it in 1907. Mr. Luff was deeded this section of the Avenues by Brigham Young. This home was the first structure built by Henry Luff on this block. He is best known as one of the leading carpenters on the Salt Lake City LDS Temple and Tabernacle. The home was a rental property from 1907 until 1931 when Milton and Ella Dority purchased the residence. The Dority family continued to own this home into the late 1970s.

431 Third Avenue

BUILT: 1902
STYLE: Victorian Eclectic
ARCHITECT: John Alfred Headlund
ORIGINAL OWNER: Louis A. Amsden

This Victorian home with its steep gable roofs shows influence from the Gothic style. The front porch has broad eaves and is supported by Doric columns. The stucco finish may not be original to the home.

Louis A. Amsden, secretary of the Blackbird Copper-Gold Mining Company, built this home as well as three others on the block. Salt Lake City architect John A. Headlund designed all four homes. This home has been a rental property throughout most of its history.

434 Third Avenue

BUILT: 1898
STYLE: Victorian Eclectic
ORIGINAL OWNER: Lillias Hilton Staines

This unique Victorian building has a flat parapet roof. There is an ornamental wooden cornice and wide segmental bays on the front and north sides.

Lillias Hilton Staines inherited this property in 1892. She had the multifamily home built a few years later and maintained it as a rental property. Mrs. Staines was the daughter of pioneers Allan and Annie Lyon Hilton. The Hiltons owned several plots of land in the Avenues during the nineteenth century. Her husband, William C. Staines, was a prominent Salt Lake City business and mining entrepreneur. The Staines lived at 461 Second Avenue. In 1922 their son, Fred Chisholm Staines, inherited the home. He and his wife, Carol, lived in part of the home and maintained the rest of the property as rental units.

437 Third Avenue

BUILT: 1902
STYLE: Victorian Eclectic
ARCHITECT: John Alfred Headlund
ORIGINAL OWNER: Louis A. Amsden

This two-story Victorian home is built of buff brick, with hip roofs and a front eyelid dormer window. The front porch has Doric columns and square posts on the corners. There is a decorative carving under the bay's second-story window.

Louis A. Amsden, secretary of the Blackbird Copper-Gold Mining Company, financed and built this home as well as three others on the block. Salt Lake City architect John A. Headlund designed all four homes. Mr. Amsden maintained this home as his residence and rented out 431 Third Avenue, 159 F Street, and 161 F Street. His wife, Emma, remained in this home until 1934. From 1938 until 1973 the home was split into several apartments.

454–458 Third Avenue A

BUILT: 1913
STYLE: Eclectic
BUILDER: J. M. Morris
ORIGINAL OWNER: Ernest N. Hill and Lorenzo Price

This three-story brick building is a well-preserved apartment block. The flat roof is surrounded by a brick parapet. Below the parapet is a cornice with dentil molding and paired modillions. A stone belt course separates the second and third floors.

Ernest N. Hill and Lorenzo Price financed the construction of this apartment building. The building represents the increasing trend toward multifamily housing in the Avenues during the early twentieth century. The building was originally named the Hill Apartments after Ernest N. Hill. From 1917 until 1960 the apartments were named the Murray Hill Apartments. Since 1960, the building has been the Chapel Hill Apartments.

459 Third Avenue A

BUILT: 1895/1919
STYLE: Vernacular/Bungalow
ORIGINAL OWNER: Robert H. Irvine

This stucco bungalow incorporates an older adobe structure. The building has a large front dormer window with a combination of shed and gable roofs. The front porch has a curved central entry. The internal chimneys are most likely from the original adobe structure. An additional apartment entrance has been added to the east side of the home.

In the mid-1890s Robert H. Irvine built an adobe-and-frame structure on this lot. Sanborn Insurance maps indicate further additions made to the building in 1911 and 1919. Mr. Irvine worked for the Oregon Short Line Railroad. He also operated a small grocery store at this address for a period of time. In 1919 the property was sold to Gomer Morgan Richards, who transformed the building into a bungalow. Mr. Richards was an assistant auditor for the state of Utah.

465 Third Avenue A

BUILT: 1880/1898
STYLE: Vernacular/Victorian Eclectic
ORIGINAL OWNER: Harry G. Naisbitt

This one-and-one-half-story Victorian home incorporates an older vernacular structure. The front gable has decorative fish-scale wood-shingle siding. The front porch wooden columns have an unusual square convex shape.

Harry G. Naisbitt, the manager of the LDS Twentieth Ward Co-op, converted a small vernacular structure into this Victorian home and lived here until 1923. Hogan Michael Hearley purchased the home in 1925. At the time he was general manager of the Salt Lake Ice Company. In 1926 he moved to Park City but maintained this home as a second residence. In Park City, he owned a general merchandise store and was active in civic affairs. He was also a founding member of the Benevolent and Protective Order of the Elks in Salt Lake City. He owned this home until his death in 1964.

468 Third Avenue   A

BUILT: 1907
STYLE: American Four Square
ORIGINAL OWNER: Charles J. Fowlger

This two-story home is representative of the popular Four Square–type found across the United States in the early twentieth century. The hip roof flares out at the eaves, and corbelled brick quoins accent the corners of the house. The original wooden columns of the front porch have been replaced.

This home represents the trend toward absentee ownership of properties in the Avenues. It has been owner occupied for only a brief period of time. The residence was built for Charles J. Fowlger, who owned the adjacent grocery and meat market at 476 Third Avenue. In 1909 he and his wife, Hannah, moved to 819 Tenth Avenue but continued to own this home and rent it out. The home was converted in 1945 into apartments by the owners, William and Cora Farley.

479 Third Avenue   A

BUILT: 1903
STYLE: Queen Anne
ORIGINAL OWNER: Charles E. Madsen

This one-and-one-half-story, well-preserved, Queen Anne–style cottage features a prominent round tower on the southeast corner. The tower has a conical roof and retains its original metal finial.

Charles E. Madsen was the original owner of the property. He was a clerk who worked at various Salt Lake City department stores including ZCMI, Auerbach Brothers, and Brown, Terry, and Woodruff. He died in this home in 1913, and Earnest Quayle purchased the home from Madsen's estate. Mr. Quayle was a prominent sheep rancher in Utah and Wyoming. His family continued to maintain ownership of the home until 1964.

505 Third Avenue   B

BUILT: 1899
STYLE: Victorian Eclectic
ARCHITECT: Walter E. Ware
BUILDER: Salt Lake Building Company
ORIGINAL OWNER: John R. Tierman

This Victorian home has elaborate Colonial Revival detailing. The front gable has an oval window and patterned wood-shingle siding. The porch gable has an ornate carved panel. A swan's neck pediment adorns the front dormer. The original Crager Iron Works fencing remains across the front of the yard.

The home was designed by prominent architect Walter E. Ware. John R. Tierman, an assayer and manager of the Miner Assay Office, was the first resident owner of the property. He lived in the home only three years, then ownership passed through several more persons until 1920 when Frank B. Scott purchased the house. He was a patent and copyright attorney, and was also a member of the Socialist Party in Utah.

509 Third Avenue   B

BUILT: 1899
STYLE: Victorian Eclectic
ARCHITECT: Edgar W. Bruce
BUILDER: Salt Lake Building Company
ORIGINAL OWNER: William G. Phillips

This Victorian home is a common design found throughout the Avenues. The original Crager Iron Works fence runs along the sidewalk.

The home's first two owners lived here briefly before Anton Pederson purchased the property in 1904. He was the director of the Salt Lake Philharmonic Orchestra and founded the first symphony in Utah. His wife, Mary Olive, was a member of the Mormon Tabernacle Choir. Arthur Pedersen Freber lived in the home from 1913 until 1951. A child prodigy violinist, Mr. Freber assumed many of his father's duties as a musical leader in Utah. His wife, Virginia, was a prominent organist. She lived in the home into the late 1970s. Mr. Freber's sisters also lived in this home during portions of their lives.

515 Third Avenue   B

BUILT: 1895/1915
STYLE: Victorian/Bungalow
BUILDER: Orson D. Romney
ORIGINAL OWNER: Nicholas W. and Annie M. Miller

This home was originally built as a Victorian cottage. In 1915 the exterior was remodeled into a bungalow style. The front gable is supported by heavy beams with curved ends. Similar beams are found below the second-story window. Octagonal columns support the front porch. The gable end is stuccoed with decorative half-timber framing.

Orson D. Romney, of the prominent Romney family of builders and developers, built this home. Nicholas and Annie Miller were the first resident owners. In 1920, the home was purchased by Perry E. Burnham, who was known for developing a number of water-measuring devices related to irrigation and agriculture. He was the regional manager of the Crop Production Loan Office and president of the Bountiful State Bank.

521 Third Avenue   B

BUILT: 1909
STYLE: American Four Square
BUILDER: Hartwell and Godd
ORIGINAL OWNER: Heber K. Burton

This is a two-story Four Square–type home. Under the broad eaves there are modillion brackets. The original front porch that covered the full width of the home was removed from the façade and replaced by an aluminum awning in the 1950s. The current porch was placed on the footprint of the 1950s porch.

Heber K. Burton was the first owner of this residence. Mr. Burton was a long-time employee of the Salt Lake City Water Department and eventually became the superintendent. He lived in this home until his death in 1949. There were numerous other owners until 1957 when Rueben E. and Andrean A. Whitney purchased the property. They lived in the home into the 1980s.

531 Third Avenue **B**

BUILT: 1909
STYLE: Bungalow
ORIGINAL OWNER: Edwin E. and Florence B. Wilcox

This is a well-preserved one-and-one-half-story bungalow. The upper walls have heavy stick-style framing while the first floor is brick. On the east side of the house is an unusual two-story bay window.

Edwin E. Wilcox was the first owner of this property. Mr. Wilcox was a surgeon in Salt Lake City from 1903 until 1936. His wife, Florence Burton Wilcox, was a charter member of the Salt Lake City Shakespeare Club. Lynn W. Raybould, an engineer at the Clearfield Naval Base, purchased the home in 1946 and lived here into the 1980s.

559 Third Avenue **B**

BUILT: 1894
STYLE: Queen Anne
ARCHITECT: H. H. Anderson
BUILDER: J. J. Chapman
ORIGINAL OWNER: Edwin E. and Florence B. Wilcox

This ornate Queen Anne Victorian home has at the southeast corner a three-story octagonal tower with a bell-curved hip roof, wood-shingle siding, and round windows on the third floor. The second floor of the gable once had a balcony. The front façade on the second floor has a carved stone plaque. The home's porch has been restored to its original condition.

This home was built for Joseph Johnson, who managed the accounting department at the Consolidated Wagon and Machinery Company. In 1902, he sold the home to John Farrington, owner of the Farrington Livery Stable at 162 South State Street. He later converted the business to the Farrington Auto Service. John J. Galligan, a physician, bought the home in 1918. The home remained in the Galligan family for several decades.

566–568 Third Avenue **B**

BUILT: 1888
STYLE: Vernacular
ORIGINAL OWNER: Isabella M. Jones

This is a small vernacular cottage with a modified saltbox roof at the rear. A small commercial structure was added to the front. A large window has been cut out of the façade of the west unit.

This small home was built as a duplex for Isabella M. Jones. She lived on one side of the home and rented out the other. In 1916 Norman P. Bales purchased the property and added the commercial structure to the front of the building. It served as Mr. Bales's barbershop. He was active in the Barber's Union and left-wing politics. He was an officer in the Utah branch of the Socialist Party and later joined the Communist Party. The building has remained a barbershop throughout its history.

613 Third Avenue [B]

BUILT: 1888
STYLE: Victorian Eclectic
ORIGINAL OWNER: Marcellus S. Woolley

This one-and-one-half-story Victorian home exhibits elements of French Second Empire style. The home has a Mansard-like roof, and there is a front dormer window with a small pediment. The exterior of the home including the porch has been restored.

This home was built for Marcellus S. Woolley, a local LDS Church leader and realtor who was also a member of the Salt Lake City Board of Education and Salt Lake City Council. In 1909 he moved to 637 Third Avenue and maintained this house as a rental property. In 1921 another realtor, Heber Charles Kimball, purchased the home. He continued to rent out the house until 1926. From 1948 into the 1980s, Joseph S. Schonfield owned the home.

624 Third Avenue [B]

BUILT: 1908
STYLE: American Four Square
ORIGINAL OWNER: David A. Affleck

This two-story home is a restored Four Square–type residence. The front windows have decorative glass transoms. There are prominent side chimneys with wrought-iron braces.

This home was built for David A. Affleck, who operated a grocery store at 801 First Avenue for many years. During the Great Depression he left the grocery business and became a purchasing agent for the Salt Lake City government. He later worked for the Salt Lake City Water Commission. Following his death in 1953, his wife and daughter remained in the home. In the early 1970s the home was purchased by the Safeway Corporation. It was their intent to demolish this home along with the rest of the block for a large grocery store. Community opposition ended the effort. The home was restored in 2002.

633 Third Avenue [B]

BUILT: 1898
STYLE: Victorian Eclectic
ORIGINAL OWNER: Albert M. Cherry

This one-and-one-half-story Victorian home is most likely a pattern-book design. The home has a three-sided, hip-roofed front bay.

This home was built for Alfred M. Cherry, who served as judge in Salt Lake City's Third Judicial District from 1897 until 1901. In 1904 he sold the home to Walter C. Orem, founder of the Salt Lake and Utah Railway Company. Mr. Orem had mining interests in Bingham Canyon, Carbone County, and Nevada. He was a founding member of the First Baptist Church of Salt Lake City. In 1920 the home was bought by Walter L. Drager, an engineer with the U.S. Reclamation Service. In the mid-1930s the home was converted into apartments.

653 Third Avenue   B

BUILT: 1906
STYLE: American Four Square
ORIGINAL OWNER: J. Fewson Smith Jr.

This is a Four Square–type home with elements of Victorian decoration. The building was significantly altered for multiple apartments starting in the 1930s. It was restored to a single-family residence in 2000. The first-floor decorative glass was added during the recent restoration.

The home was built for mining engineer J. Fewson Smith Jr., who worked for the U.S. Smelting, Mining, and Refining Company for thirty-eight years. He was also the designer of Salt Lake City's first sewage system. In 1914 Mr. Smith moved from this home and maintained it as a rental property. The residence was purchased in 1924 by Harry Logan, a conductor on the Oregon Short Line Railroad. Upon the death of his wife, the home was converted into apartments.

654 Third Avenue   B

BUILT: 1890
STYLE: Victorian Eclectic
ORIGINAL OWNER: Samuel Woolf

This is a well-preserved wood-frame Victorian home. The walls have wide shiplap siding with corner boards. A one-story porch wraps around the north and west sides of the house. Small gables mark the entry on the northwest corner.

This home and 658 Third Avenue were built for Samuel Woolf. A prominent Jewish business leader in Salt Lake City, Mr. Woolf owned and operated a wholesale cigar business at 150 South Main Street. From 1899 until 1924 several successive owners would live at 654 Third Avenue and rent out 658 Third Avenue. After 1924 the home was owned by the Fred R. Nuslein family and descendents for the next six decades.

668 Third Avenue   B

BUILT: 1899
STYLE: Victorian Eclectic
ARCHITECT: David C. Dart
BUILDER: G. Arnold
ORIGINAL OWNER: John D. Owen

This one-story Victorian cottage has a gabled front bay and a hip-roofed west bay. The front gable has patterned wood-shingle siding and is supported at the corners by brackets and scroll-sawn decoration.

This small home was designed by noted Salt Lake City and Avenues architect David C. Dart and built for John D. Owen. Mr. Owen was an active member of several Salt Lake City musical groups, including the Mormon Tabernacle Choir and the Harmony Glee Club. The home remained in the Owen family until 1947.

673 Third Avenue B

BUILT: 1884
STYLE: Victorian Eclectic
ORIGINAL OWNER: Oliver S. and Mary Ann Walsh

This one-story Victorian cottage has gable roofs and a projecting front bay. The window in the bay has a wooden Italianate pediment. The home's front porch, eave treatment, and stucco finish are later alterations.

This home was built for Oliver and Mary Ann Walsh. Mr. Walsh ran a tin and hardware shop at 77 West 100 South. Following Oliver's death, Mary Ann continued to live in the home until 1924. A later owner, Andrew Jacobsen, was a researcher at the University of Utah and part owner of the Gem Grocery and Meat Market at Third Avenue and K Street. In 1941 Francis and Lena Urry bought the house. Mr. Urry was a producer for KSL Radio.

676 Third Avenue B

BUILT: 1899
STYLE: Queen Anne
ARCHITECT: David C. Dart
BUILDER: William Asper
ORIGINAL OWNER: Rachel McMaster

This Queen Anne–style home has a main hip roof with small front and east-side gables. There is an octagonal tower on the northeast corner. The upper level of the home is covered in wood shingles and the main floor in brick.

This home was designed by noted Salt Lake City architect David C. Dart and built on speculation for Rachel McMaster, a draftsman for the Oregon Short Line Railroad. Mr. McMaster sold the property to Ernest F. and Grace Ashby Hawch in 1900. There is evidence that the home was split into apartments briefly. It was restored in the 1990s.

681 Third Avenue B

BUILT: 1896
STYLE: Victorian Eclectic
BUILDER: John G. Anderson
ORIGINAL OWNER: John G. Anderson

This two-story Victorian home has a projecting, gabled front bay similar to many of the Avenues homes of this era. The front gable has dentiled raking cornices, paneled barge boards, and returns. The front porch columns were replaced by iron posts in the late 1960s but have since been restored.

This home's builder, John G. Anderson, built several similar homes in this portion of the Avenues. Mr. Anderson kept this home for himself and lived here until 1899. At that time, James E. Darmer purchased the property. Mr. Darmer was a well-known Salt Lake City attorney and political leader. He was an organizer and eventual chairman of the anti-Mormon American Party.

683 Third Avenue   B

BUILT: 1897
STYLE: Victorian Eclectic
BUILDER: John G. Anderson
ORIGINAL OWNER: Charles O. Veness

This two-story Victorian home has projecting front and west-side gabled bays. The front gable has ogee-arched fascia with wood-shingle siding. The front porch has been restored.

The home's builder, John G. Anderson, built several similar homes, including 681 Third Avenue, in this portion of the Avenues. Charles O. Veness, who was in the livestock business, purchased the property upon completion for $3,500. In 1905 the home was sold to John A. Edwards, who was the Utah state auditor from 1905 until 1908 and later served as secretary of the Utah State Senate. He spent thirty years in the insurance business. Mr. Edwards remained in this home until 1933.

687 Third Avenue   B

BUILT: 1896
STYLE: Victorian Eclectic
ORIGINAL OWNER: Stephen O. Snyder

This two-story Victorian home has a curved second-floor bay window of rough-faced brick with unusual curved brick corbelling below the window. All corners of the house are accented with rough-faced brick. The garage was built in 1923.

This home was built for Stephen O. Snyder, the assistant superintendent for the Denver and Rio Grande Western Railroad. He later became president of the Swanisea Mining Company in Utah's Tintic Mining District. After his death in 1915, his son-in-law, Jay Eliot Johnson, moved into the home. Mr. Johnson was an agent for the New York Life Insurance Company and an active Mason in Salt Lake City. From 1962 until 1975 this home was known as the Cloverleaf Rest Haven.

729 Third Avenue   B

BUILT: 1904
STYLE: Victorian Eclectic
ORIGINAL OWNER: Frank M. Castleton

This two-story Victorian home has a shallow, two-story curved bay front. The front porch has modillion brackets and Doric columns.

This residence was built for Frank M. Castleton. He and five of his brothers operated the Castleton Brothers General Store on Second Avenue. The Frank Castleton family lived in the home until the late 1940s when it was converted into apartments. In the early 1960s, a University of Utah professor, Elmer Young, restored the home back to a single-family residence. This home is a rare example of an Avenues residence being restored at a time when many homes were being neglected, demolished, or converted to apartments.

730 Third Avenue [B]

BUILT: 1899
STYLE: Dutch Colonial Revival
ARCHITECT: Edgar Druce
BUILDER: William C. Steers
ORIGINAL OWNER: William C. Steers

This Dutch Colonial Revival cottage has a gambrel roof and a curved, wooden front bay window with a leaded glass transom. The home is similar to 728 Third Avenue which was built at the same time by the same developer.

William C. Steers built this home as a rental property. He held several homes in the Avenues as investment rental homes. In 1905, he sold this residence to Henry M. McCune, a conductor for the Utah Light and Railway Company. Eight years later, the home was sold to G. Wesley Browning, who was secretary of the Silver King Coalition Mines in Park City. During the Great Depression, the home was converted into several apartments. It has since been returned to a single-family home.

735 Third Avenue [B]

BUILT: 1890/1903
STYLE: American Four Square
ORIGINAL OWNER: William J. Castleton

This two-story brick home has a front center dormer window. The one-story front porch has Doric columns with a small gable to mark the entrance. The brick exterior was sandblasted in the late 1970s.

This home incorporates an earlier 1890 structure built for William J. Castleton. Mr. Castleton operated the Castleton Brothers General Store with five of his brothers on Second Avenue. Mr. Castleton moved to 107 J Street in 1902 and sold the property to Josiah and Harriet Burrows. Mr. Burrows operated the William Longmore and Company Clothing Store on Main Street in Salt Lake City. In 1948 the home was purchased by William and Cornelia Riet, who remained in the residence for the next thirty years.

759 Third Avenue [B]

BUILT: 1901
STYLE: Victorian Eclectic
BUILDER: William C. Steers
ORIGINAL OWNER: William C. Steers

This Victorian home of pattern-book design has a two-story brick front bay. The original wooden front porch columns have been replaced with iron posts.

Mason and contractor William C. Steers built this home for himself. He and his wife Ann lived the balance of their lives here until 1929. At that time Archie and Susie John De St. Jeor became owners. Mr. John De St. Jeor was a mining executive and later a radio salesman. Ownership of this home remained in the family into the 1980s.

765 Third Avenue B

BUILT: 1905
STYLE: Bungalow
ARCHITECT: Erkine and Liljenberg
BUILDER: J. L. Eckert
ORIGINAL OWNER: George H. and Euphemia Smith

This bungalow has unique Classical Revival styling in its decoration. The front dormer has a large broken pediment, a lunette window, and Ionic columns.

This early bungalow was built for George and Euphemia Smith. Mr. Smith was a lawyer for the Oregon Short Line Railroad. They lived in the home until 1915 when it was sold to Jacob H. and Eva L. Provol. Mr. Provol founded a local branch of the Hudson Fur Company. One year after buying the home, Mr. Provol died. Eva continued to live here, and five years later married Sidney S. Fox, general manager of the Intermountain Broadcast Network and KDYL radio station. KDYL was one of the most powerful stations in the United States at that time.

787 Third Avenue B

BUILT: 1906
STYLE: American Four Square
BUILDER: Anna K. and Louis P. Kjergard
ORIGINAL OWNER: William M. and Sarah A. Havenor

This home has a hip roof and front center dormer window that are typical of the American Four Square–type. The house is nearly identical to the adjacent 783 Third Avenue.

The home is one of five built on this block by Anna K. and Louis P. Kjergard. Upon completion, it was sold to William and Sarah Havenor. Mr. Havenor was a member of the Salt Lake Stock Exchange and former employee of the Denver and Rio Grande Railroad. In 1929 ownership passed to their son-in-law, Ray T. Woolsey. From 1925 until 1945 Mr. Woolsey was the assistant Salt Lake County physician, and in 1935 he was president of the Salt Lake County Medical Society. He was also a charter member of the Wasatch Presbyterian Church.

821 Third Avenue B

BUILT: 1892
STYLE: Victorian Eclectic
BUILDER: Miller and Miller Investment Company
ORIGINAL OWNER: Paul Hawther Jr.

This is a one-and-one-half-story Victorian home. The gable that faces the street has dentil molding and curved fascia boards. The front porch has dentil molding and turned columns. The home was covered in asbestos siding in the 1950s.

This residence is one of four homes built on this block by the Miller and Miller Investment Company. Upon completion, the home was purchased by Paul G. Hawther, treasurer of the Salt Lake Theater. In 1896 the home was sold to Anton Pederson. Mr. Pederson was known as a prominent musician in the Intermountain West. He was the music director at All Hallows College for seventeen years.

881 Third Avenue [B]

BUILT: 1895
STYLE: Victorian Eclectic
BUILDER: Herbert North
ORIGINAL OWNER: John T. Dick

This is a one-and-one-half-story, gable-roofed Victorian home. The home retains much of its decorative exterior woodwork including scroll-sawn applied trim, lattice-like wood paneling above the attic window, and fish-scale wood-shingle siding.

Herbert North built three houses on this block. John T. Dick purchased the home for $2,500 and became the first resident owner. Mr. Dick was a partner in the blacksmith and wagon repair firm of Jones and Dick. A year after purchasing the home, he sold it to William T. Atkin, a real estate executive. The home was maintained as a rental property until 1932, when Zions Bank assumed ownership. It is possible that Mr. Atkin lost ownership of the home to the bank due to the Great Depression.

888 Third Avenue [B]

BUILT: 1901
STYLE: Victorian Eclectic
BUILDER: Bothwell and McConaughy
ORIGINAL OWNER: William S. Higham

This one-and-one-half-story Victorian home features a high gable roof covered in fish-scale siding. The original front porch posts have been removed.

The construction firm of Bothwell and McConaughy built this home for investment purposes. William S. Higham was the first resident owner. Mr. Higham was an executive with the Higham-Burton Plumbing Company and from 1928 until 1934 was a Salt Lake City plumbing inspector. He lived in this home until 1958.

903 Third Avenue [C]

BUILT: 1908
STYLE: Dutch Colonial Revival/Bungalow
BUILDER: Adolf and Lucy Richter
ORIGINAL OWNER: Hezekiah E. Van Housen

This bungalow exhibits elements of the Dutch Colonial Revival style. The main portion of the home has a gambrel roof typical of the style. The front dormer, which covers the second-story balcony, has a gable roof with returns and a lunette window. The front porch has a gable similar to that found on the dormer. The windows on each side of the chimney have been altered.

Adolf and Lucy Richter developed a significant amount of property along this portion of Third Avenue. Hezekiah E. Van Housen, the supervisor for the Salt Lake and Los Angeles Railroad, was the first resident owner of this home. He lived in the home briefly and then maintained it as a rental. In 1919, Russell K. Woodruff, who owned the Woodruff Automobile Company, purchased the home.

907 Third Avenue C

BUILT: 1906
STYLE: Victorian Eclectic
BUILDER: Adolf and Lucy Richter
ORIGINAL OWNER: Adolf and Lucy Richter

This two-story, late-Victorian home was built during the transition from Victorian to Craftsman style. The front gable has classic returns and wood siding. The front porch has Doric columns and an unusual mansard roof.

Adolf and Lucy Richter developed a large portion of this section of the Avenues. The Richters rented out the property until 1915. At that time, J. Fred Daynes purchased the home. Mr. Daynes was president of the Daynes Jewelry Company, Daynes Optical Company, and the J. Fred Daynes Building Company. In 1931, he sold the home to one of his employees, Alf Burrell. In the mid-1950s, the home's owner, Vernon E. Jarman, converted the building into five apartments. It remains an apartment building today.

911 Third Avenue C

BUILT: 1906
STYLE: Dutch Colonial Revival/Bungalow
BUILDER: Adolf and Lucy Richter
ORIGINAL OWNER: Imogene J. and James A. Melville

This is a one-and-one-half-story Dutch Colonial Revival bungalow. The home has a gambrel roof typical of the style.

Adolf and Lucy Richter built this home as they developed this portion of Third Avenue and sold it to Imogene and James Melville. James was the manager of the Irrigated Lands Company. They sold the home in 1908 to Alice E. Houghton, who practiced medicine from 1905 until 1955. She partnered for many years with Dr. Pearl Udall Nelson. In 1947 she sold the home to John McReynolds, who worked at Hill Air Force Base and lived at this residence until 2003. Ms. Houghton continued to live in the home with the McReynolds family until 1957. A 2005 restoration included the removal of aluminum siding from the front gable.

915 Third Avenue C

BUILT: 1905
STYLE: American Four Square
ARCHITECT: David C. Dart
BUILDER: Adolf and Lucy Richter
ORIGINAL OWNER: Adolf and Lucy Richter

This two-story Four Square–type home is representative of a popular home style found across the United States in the early twentieth century.

Adolf and Lucy Richter developed this portion of Third Avenue. Upon completion of this home, the Richters rented out the property. In 1915 the home's tenant, Ellen P. Ferris, purchased the home. James J. Ravanaugh bought the residence in 1918. He was the Salt Lake City general freight agent for the Missouri Pacific Railroad. In 1927 he sold the home to Herbert A. Dyer, an engineer for the Western Pacific Railroad. The Dyer family remained in the home until 1966. The home's exterior was restored in the late 1990s.

918 Third Avenue `C`

BUILT: 1907
STYLE: American Four Square
ORIGINAL OWNER: Benjamin and Elizabeth Snyder

This two-story, Four Square–type home is representative of a popular home style found across the United States in the early twentieth century. The wide front porch has Doric columns.

Benjamin and Elizabeth Snyder purchased the home upon its completion in 1907. He worked for the Consolidated Wagon and Machinery Company for fifty years, ultimately becoming foreman of the company. In 1934 Bryan E. Blackwell purchased the home. Mr. Blackwell was a salesman for the Remington Rand Company. In the mid-1950s the home was converted into several apartments. It has since been restored to a single-family home.

923 Third Avenue `C`

BUILT: 1906
STYLE: Bungalow
ARCHITECT: David C. Dart
BUILDER: Adolf and Lucy Richter
ORIGINAL OWNER: Joseph W. and Isabel Gates

This home has a large, gabled front dormer and a front porch with tapered columns. The residence is an early example of the Bungalow style in the Avenues.

This home was designed by noted architect David C. Dart for developers Lucy and Adolf and Lucy Richter. The Richters developed numerous properties in this portion of the Avenues. Joseph W. and Isabel Gates rented the home until 1911 when they became the owners. Mr. Gates was the manager for the Mine and Smelter Supply Company. He was also the designer of the first Alta ski lift. William and Leela Hard purchased the home in 1918. Mr. Hard was the assistant traffic manager for the Denver and Rio Grande Railroad.

927 Third Avenue `C`

BUILT: 1906
STYLE: American Four Square
BUILDER: Adolf and Lucy Richter
ORIGINAL OWNER: Sidney W. Nicholle

This two-story, brick Four Square–type home has a full-width front porch. The porch was restored to the home after 2000.

This home may have been designed by noted Salt Lake City architect David C. Dart for developers Lucy and Adolf and Lucy Richter. The Richters developed numerous properties in this portion of the Avenues. Upon its completion, they sold the property to Sidney W. Nicholle, an employee of the Mine and Smelting Supply Company. In 1926, Marlow L. Cummings purchased the property. Mr. Cummings, a realtor and active local politician, served as Salt Lake County assessor from 1920 until 1926. In 1940, Calvin Dalton bought the home and converted it into a duplex. The home was recently restored by Jack and Carolyn Chase.

967 Third Avenue   C

BUILT: 1891
STYLE: Queen Anne
BUILDER: Frank A. Grant
ORIGINAL OWNER: Joseph P. Bache

This two-and-one-half-story, Queen Anne–style home features a southwest corner tower with a high hip roof. The front gable and top walls of the tower have wood-shingle siding.

The home was built by Frank A. Grant, who developed this block face. He sold the home upon completion to Joseph P. Bache for $4,300. Mr. Bache was the Utah territorial librarian and clerk of the Utah Supreme Court. In 1902 the home was sold to John A. and Emma Street. Mr. Street was a mining executive with the Wabash Mining Company. In 1926 the home was purchased by Dwight M. Newton, a ticket agent for the Union Pacific Railroad for thirty-one years. The home has been converted into four apartments.

983 Third Avenue   C

BUILT: 1904
STYLE: American Four Square
ORIGINAL OWNER: Lafayette Hanchett

This Avenues mansion can best be described as a large American Four Square. It has a hip roof with exposed rafters. The front porch and southwest second-story balcony were enclosed for many years.

The home was built for Lafayette Hanchett, who came to Utah in 1904 to manage the Boston Consolidated Mining Company. In 1910 he began his involvement in the power industry, eventually serving as president and chairman of the Utah Power and Light Company. Mr. Hanchett was also an influential banking leader in Salt Lake City. From 1919 to 1935 he was director of the Federal Reserve Bank of Salt Lake City. Following his death in 1955, the home was turned into a nursing home and remained so until 1978. It has been restored to a single-family home.

986 Third Avenue   C

BUILT: 1891
STYLE: Victorian Eclectic
ORIGINAL OWNER: Edward D. Woodruff

This large, well-preserved, brick Victorian home has gable roofs with patterned wood-shingle siding in the gables. There is a wooden, two-story wraparound porch, a one-story brick bay window on the east, and a third-floor enclosed porch on the west.

Edward D. Woodruff came to Salt Lake City in 1890 and moved into this home the following year. He was a former physician, part owner of the Troy Laundry Company, and president of the Salt Lake Savings and Trust Company. In 1906 the home was sold to Peter A. and Martha J. Dronbay. Mr. Dronbay retired to the city after controlling large ranching interests in Tooele County. John N. Erickson converted the home to six apartments in the 1920s. It is a rare example of a well-maintained apartment conversion.

1006 Third Avenue C

BUILT: 1898
STYLE: Victorian Eclectic
ARCHITECT: John M. Anderson
BUILDER: John G. Anderson
ORIGINAL OWNER: William H. Tibbals

This two-story Victorian home has a one-story front porch with wooden Doric columns. Beneath the front gable is a three-sided bay and beneath the west gable is a curved bay. This home is similar to 1010 and 1014 Third Avenue. All three homes were built by John G. Anderson.

This home's first resident owner was William H. Tibbals. Mr. Tibbals came to Utah as an educator but soon became involved in mining. He had large holdings in the Tintic and Beaver mining districts. In 1916 the home was purchased by Ernest Gaylord, a nationally known mining engineer. He was a partner in the General Engineering Company and eventually became its president. He remained with the company until 1940.

1010 Third Avenue C

BUILT: 1898
STYLE: Victorian Eclectic
ARCHITECT: John M. Anderson
BUILDER: John G. Anderson
ORIGINAL OWNER: William H. Needham

This two-story brick Victorian home has shingle-faced gables. There is a small, one-story front porch with Doric columns. This home is similar to 1006 and 1014 Third Avenue. All the homes were built by John G. Anderson.

William H. Needham was the first resident owner of this property. He was the manager of the ZCMI retail dry goods department. In 1906 George F. Richards Sr. purchased the home and lived there until his death in 1950. Mr. Richards was a member of the LDS Church's Council of the Twelve Apostles.

1014 Third Avenue C

BUILT: 1898
STYLE: Victorian Eclectic
ARCHITECT: John M. Anderson
BUILDER: John G. Anderson
ORIGINAL OWNER: Francis M. Lyman

This two-story brick Victorian home has a hip roof and projecting front bay. There is a corbelled belt course separating the first and second stories. The home's front porch was recently rebuilt.

Francis M. Lyman, a member of the LDS Church's Council of the Twelve Apostles, purchased this home from the builder, John G. Anderson. Mr. Lyman was a prominent political and church leader in central Utah before moving to Salt Lake City in the 1880s. The home has been restored in the past ten years.

1018 Third Avenue C

BUILT: 1903
STYLE: Victorian Eclectic
ORIGINAL OWNER: John G. Klink

This two-story Victorian house has a hip-roofed front dormer window. Upper walls have wood-shingle siding above a brick first story. The front porch roof is a sweeping extension of the main roof and is supported with wooden Doric columns.

The first resident owner of this property was John G. Klink, co-owner of the F. E. Schoppe and Company hardware store. Following his death in the 1920s, the M. H. Walker Realty Company purchased the home and maintained it as a rental property. It is representative of the growing number of rental properties at that time in the Avenues. In 1936 a postmaster, Ernest J. Mansfield, bought the home. This home has been extensively restored over the past ten years.

1059 Third Avenue C

BUILT: 1895
STYLE: Queen Anne
ORIGINAL OWNER: Arthur O. Clark

This home is an excellent example of a Queen Anne Victorian cottage. The home has a small tower with a domical roof and original metal finial. Fish-scale-patterned wood siding covers the tower and gables. The gables have ornate fascia and bracketed returns.

This home was built for Arthur O. Clark, the principal at Salt Lake City High School. In 1901 Frantz J. Hyde purchased the property. Mr. Hyde was a manager at the Creditor's Commercial Agency. In 1913 a music teacher, Philander N. Cook, became the home's owner.

1084 Third Avenue C

BUILT: 1898
STYLE: Victorian Eclectic
BUILDER: Frank A. Grant
ORIGINAL OWNER: Frank A. Grant

This Victorian home has a hip roof and a three-sided, hip-roofed front bay. The bungalow-style front porch replaced the original porch around 1915.

Frank A. Grant built this home along with 1083, 1087, and 1088 Third Avenue. He lived at 1103 Third Avenue. Charles Felt became the first resident owner in 1900. As a member of the American Party, he was elected city auditor in 1905 and 1907. He sold the home to Richard R. Lyman in 1905. Mr. Lyman was a nationally known educator, engineer, and member of the LDS Church's Council of the Twelve Apostles. He founded the University of Utah's Civil Engineering Department and was a consulting engineer on many projects around the West including the Grand Coulee Dam. He was excommunicated from the LDS Church in 1943 for chastity violations. His father, who was also an LDS apostle, lived at 1014 Third Avenue.

1088 Third Avenue   C

BUILT: 1895
STYLE: Victorian Eclectic
BUILDER: Frank A. Grant
ORIGINAL OWNER: Frank A. Grant

This two-story brick Victorian home has a hip roof and projecting north gable. The broad front porch with brick piers is more typical of Bungalow style. It most likely replaced the original porch around 1915.

Frank A. Grant built this home along with 1083, 1087, and 1084 Third Avenue. He lived at 1103 Third Avenue. This home was maintained as a rental property until 1900. General William H. and Harriet Penrose were the first resident owners. General Penrose was a career army officer and former commander of Fort Douglas. He retired in 1900 and spent the next three years in mining speculation. After his death in 1903, the home passed through several owners through the late 1930s.

1103 Third Avenue   C

BUILT: 1893
STYLE: Victorian Eclectic
BUILDER: Frank A. Grant
ORIGINAL OWNER: Frank A. Grant

This Victorian home has a cross-gable roof. An indented porch wraps around the side of the home. Recent exterior restoration includes the replacement of mid-century metal posts and the removal of metal awnings.

The home was built for prominent real estate developer Frank A. Grant, who lived at this property until 1900. Mr. Grant built several homes in this part of the Avenues. He was president of the Atlantic Mining and Milling Company and founder of the Frank A. Grant Real Estate Company. The next owner of the home was James F. Dunn, who was the superintendent of the Oregon Short Line Railroad and later the president of the Reed's Peak Consolidated Mining Company. In 1939, the home was split into several small apartments.

1105 Third Avenue   C

BUILT: 1894
STYLE: Queen Anne
ORIGINAL OWNER: William R. and Anna Hutchinson

This Queen Anne Victorian home has a small southwest corner tower with a pyramidal roof flared out at the eaves. The second story walls are covered in patterned wood shingles.

The home was built for William and Anna Hutchinson. Mr. Hutchinson was a lawyer in Salt Lake City and an active local member of the Republican Party and Presbyterian Church. William Hutchinson died in 1934 and Anna continued to live in the home until 1939. In 1939 a contractor named Byron C. Monson bought the home. From 1943 until the late 1970s, Erich H. Mittelsteadt, a butcher, owned the home.

1111 Third Avenue   C

BUILT: 1894
STYLE: Victorian Eclectic
ORIGINAL OWNER: Harry C. Burnett

This well-preserved, ornate, one-and-one-half-story Victorian home retains its elaborate woodwork. The front gable has curved bargeboards, curved wood trim in the peak, and latticework. Below the cornice is a wide band of patterned, wood-shingle siding and additional lattice framing. The first floor is covered in shiplap siding.

Harry C. Burnett, Salt Lake City general agent for the Atchison, Topeka, and Santa Fe Railroad, was the first resident of this home. After just two years, Mr. Burnett sold the home to Ralph Zwicky. He was the secretary treasurer of the W. P. Noble Mercantile Company and also owned mining properties in Mercur and Bingham Canyon. In 1915 the home was purchased by Edgar M. Ledyard, a trained zoologist employed by the U.S. Smelting, Refining, and Mining Company.

1115 Third Avenue   C

BUILT: 1892
STYLE: Victorian Eclectic
ORIGINAL OWNER: Emmett G. Hunt

This one-and-one-half-story Victorian home has been stripped of much of its original detailing. The home is similar to the elaborately decorated 1111 Third Avenue. The two homes, along with 167 N Street, were most likely built by the same developer.

Emmett G. Hunt, the pastor of the Liberty Park Methodist Episcopal Church, was the first owner of this property. He maintained it as a rental property until 1901 when James G. Buswell became the first resident owner. Mr. Buswell, an optometrist, owned the property until 1924 when his son, also an optometrist, inherited the home.

1124 Third Avenue   C

BUILT: 1897
STYLE: Victorian Eclectic
BUILDER: Avery W. J. Timms
ORIGINAL OWNER: Alfred H. Ensign

This one-story Victorian cottage exhibits excellent exterior detailing. The home is similar to 1128 Third Avenue. Both homes were built by the same developer. For most of the second half of the twentieth century, the two homes were covered in aluminum siding. In the late 1990s the removal of the siding revealed the original detailing.

Avery W. J. Timms built this home for Alfred H. Ensign, an insurance executive. His insurance firm became one of the largest in the Intermountain West in the early 1900s. In 1919 Mr. Ensign left the insurance field and started an engineering sales firm. In 1904 Robert E. McConaughy purchased the home. His real estate company, Bothwell and McConaughy, held the home as a rental property for the next twenty years.

1129 Third Avenue [C]

BUILT: 1904
STYLE: Victorian Eclectic
BUILDER: Abner F. Callison
ORIGINAL OWNER: Edward W. Delano

This one-story cottage was built at the end of the Victorian period in the Avenues. The house is similar to 1133 Third Avenue and built by the same developer.

Abner F. Callison built this home and 1133 Third Avenue as investments. Upon completion he sold the home to Edward W. Delano, a salesman for the A. H. Boxrud Company. In 1918 Stephen S. Buckwalter purchased the property and lived here until the mid-1940s.

1153 Third Avenue [C]

BUILT: 1910
STYLE: Dutch Colonial Revival
ORIGINAL OWNER: Larett S. Wilson

This home has a cross-gambrel roof typical of the Dutch Colonial Revival style. The first story is covered in brick. The front porch was enclosed for much of the twentieth century. There is a large addition off the rear of the house dating to the 1950s.

Larett S. Wilson took out a building permit for this home in 1910. He lived at 133 U Street and rented out this property until 1913 when he sold it to Walter Wright, who was the first resident owner. Joseph W. Musser became the owner in 1941. He was a practicing polygamist and leader of an organization of 2,500 fundamentalists in the Intermountain West. He was arrested for illegal cohabitation and imprisoned in 1945. He was released after seven months and agreed to terms allowing him to live with only one wife in this home.

1156 Third Avenue [C]

BUILT: 1906
STYLE: Victorian Eclectic
BUILDER: Peterson Real Estate Company
ORIGINAL OWNER: Edwin C. Penrose

This one-story Victorian cottage is similar to many pattern-book homes in the Avenues. The front gable has wood-shingle siding and rests on a segmental bay. The front porch has Doric columns.

This home, along with 1152, 1160, and 1164 Third Avenue, were built by the Peterson Real Estate Company speculatively and sold upon completion. Edwin C. Penrose, a well-known reporter for the *Deseret News*, purchased the completed home in 1906. In 1923 Isaac A. Clayton Jr. purchased the property. Mr. Clayton was the secretary of the Inland Crystal Salt Company.

1165 Third Avenue [C]

BUILT: 1910
STYLE: American Four Square
ORIGINAL OWNER: Theodore A. Bussman

This is a good example of a two-story, American Four Square–type home. The second story has three-part bowed windows set into the walls. The front porch has large, square, wood-paneled columns.

Theodore A. Bussman, a carpenter, built this home for himself and lived in it until 1918. Harry Coombs then owned the property until 1940. Mr. Coombs was the owner of the Coombs Drug Store in Salt Lake City. Alan M. and Marion B. Lipman purchased the property in 1940. The home was restored in 1999.

1169 Third Avenue [C]

BUILT: 1922
STYLE: Prairie Bungalow
BUILDER: John F. Miller
ORIGINAL OWNER: Fred M. and Grace M. Francis

This one-story bungalow is typical of the Prairie-style design found throughout Utah. There is a dominating hip roof and full-width porch.

This home was built by John F. Miller as a speculative property. Fred and Grace Francis purchased the house for $5,750 in 1922. Mr. Francis was an accountant for the Continental Oil Company. In 1924 they sold the home to Thomas L. Walden, manager of the New Park Mining Company. He died in the house in 1933. His family continued to own the property until 1943.

1177 Third Avenue [C]

BUILT: 1920
STYLE: Prairie Bungalow
BUILDER: Samuel Campbell
ORIGINAL OWNER: Charles T. Worley

This one-story bungalow is a common Prairie-style design found throughout Utah. It features a dominating hip roof and wide porch supported by paired brick columns.

This home and 1171 Third Avenue were built by Samuel Campbell as speculative properties. Upon completion, the house was purchased by Charles T. Worley, the manager of the Standard Fuel Company and later president of the MacLean Coal Company. Hector R. Sindait, a travel agent for the Milwaukee Road Railroad, purchased the home in 1925. He lived in this house for thirty years.

1203 Third Avenue

C

BUILT: 1908
STYLE: Craftsman
ARCHITECT: Alberto O. Treganza and Walter E.
Ware
ORIGINAL OWNER: Wiggo F. Jensen

This is a large, shingle-sided home with Craftsman detailing. There are brackets under the eaves. On the west side of the house is a porte cochere with wood-paneled columns and a sleeping porch above.

This home was designed by the prominent architectural firm of Treganza and Ware and built for Wiggo F. Jensen, founder of the Jensen Creamery Company and the Mutual Creamery. He was the Utah State Food Administrator during World War I. Gibon A. Marr purchased the property in 1924. He was an attorney and general counsel to the Utah Bankers Association. He divided the home into apartments during the Great Depression. A later owner, Dr. Ralph G. Pendleton, restored the home to a single-family residence. The Pendleton family maintained ownership of the property into the 1980s.

1218 Third Avenue

C

BUILT: 1909
STYLE: Bungalow
ARCHITECT: W. J. Cannonville
BUILDER: William M. Kronner
ORIGINAL OWNER: James E. and Fannie M.
Woodard

This one-and-one-half-story home is a bungalow with some Victorian design elements. By 1909, most bungalows were being built in the Craftsman style. Thus, this home may be one of the last homes built in the Avenues with Victorian details.

William M. Kronner built this home for James and Fannie Woodward. Mr. Kronner built his own home a block away. He was also the builder of the original Salt Palace and the Kearns St. Ann's Orphanage. Mr. Woodward was a Salt Lake City police officer. This home was held as a rental property until 1920, at which time Harold M. and Virginia A. Stephens purchased the home. Mr. Stephens was an attorney and judge in the Third Judicial District.

1225 Third Avenue

C

BUILT: 1910
STYLE: Craftsman Bungalow
ORIGINAL OWNER: Eugene Walter Baysinger

This is a one-story Craftsman-style bungalow. The home has a hip roof with exposed rafter tails. The full-width front porch is supported by brick columns.

This small bungalow was built for Eugene Walter Baysinger, who was the deputy Salt Lake City auditor. Vera I. Felt purchased the property in 1918. Ms. Felt was the co-owner of the Felt-Knowlton Art Shop. In 1920 the home was bought by James H. Housely, who owned and operated the Exchange Barber Shop in Salt Lake City's Boston Building.

FOURTH AVENUE

175 Fourth Avenue   A

BUILT: 1909
STYLE: Craftsman/American Four Square
ARCHITECT: Joseph Don Carlos Young and Don Carlos Young
ORIGINAL OWNER: Alonzo and Mary Young

This is a two-story, Four Square–type home with Craftsman detailing. The rafter ends are left exposed and treated as decoration. The front porch has paired wooden square columns set on brick posts. The east side of the house has a bay window and a brick, arched stair window.

The home was designed by Joseph Don Carlos Young and his son, Don Carlos Young. Joseph would later become the LDS Church's head architect. Alonzo Young, son of Brigham and Emeline Free Young, was the first resident owner of the property. Alonzo Young spent his entire career working for the ZCMI department store, eventually becoming manager of the shoe department. Mary Young remained in the home until 1926. At that time it was converted to apartments.

181 Fourth Avenue   A

BUILT: 1902
STYLE: Classical Revival
ORIGINAL OWNER: Matthew and Rose Noall

This sandstone-and-brick house has neoclassical features such as the portico, symmetrical fenestration on the façade, and cornices. The front porch was extended in 1912 and a second tier was added. The corners of the home are rounded and extend out from the main frame. The rear barn was constructed in 1903.

This home was built by Matthew and Rose Noall. Mr. Noall, a carpenter, was a partner in the Noall Brothers Lumber Company. The company built many late-nineteenth-century Salt Lake City buildings. The home was converted into apartments in 1913. The Noall family owned the building until 1967. The home was purchased in 1991 by Robert Blackhurst. It has since been restored, including stripping the white paint off the exterior bricks.

184 Fourth Avenue   A

BUILT: 1913
STYLE: Prairie Style
ARCHITECT: Walter Ware and Alberto Treganza
ORIGINAL OWNER: Alexander R. Irvine

This is a brick Prairie-style home. The stucco found on the second floor creates a horizontal band around the building and is typical of this style. The enclosed east porch was originally open.

This home was built for Dr. Alexander R. Irvine for seven thousand dollars. Dr. Irvine was one of the founders of the Salt Lake Clinic. He practiced medicine in Utah until 1922, then moved to Los Angeles and became a noted eye specialist and head of the USC Medical School ophthalmology department. David A. Skeen, an attorney, purchased the home in 1925. He helped organize the Lions Club in Utah and was president of the Lions International in 1944. The home was converted into apartments in 1943 and restored to a single-family residence in 2003.

203 Fourth Avenue A

BUILT: 1909
STYLE: Craftsman Bungalow
ORIGINAL OWNER: Roscoe M. and Molly S.
Breeden

This excellent example of a Craftsman bungalow is clad in wood shingles. The front porch is supported by large wooden posts. Exposed rafter tails and brackets are typical of the style.

This home replaced an earlier brick structure owned by the Schettler family, who had several homes on this block. Roscoe and Molly Breeden were the first residents of the bungalow. Mr. Breeden managed the Breeden Office Supply Company. They lost the home to their bank in 1914. Ernest Schettler, secretary-treasurer of Intermountain Electric Company, purchased the property from the bank in 1920. The Schettler family occupied the home until 1967. Elizabeth and Theodore Gurney purchased the home in 1974. They have restored and maintained the architectural character of this residence.

207 Fourth Avenue A

BUILT: 1909
STYLE: Classical Revival
ORIGINAL OWNER: Peter and Frank Evans

The design of this two-story duplex is rare for Salt Lake City. The two front corners of the home are rounded. The symmetrical brick-and-stucco façade is divided horizontally by continuous bands of sandstone.

Attorneys Peter and Frank Evans purchased two adjoining lots in 1907. Their intent was to build two homes, but neighbors prevented the construction of the second home. The Evans brothers lived on each side of the duplex until 1913. Peter would go on to become a district judge while Frank was a state senator and insurance executive. They traded this property for a farm in Taylorsville with Joseph and Preston Cannon, the sons of LDS Church president George Q. Cannon. The Cannon brothers were both associated with the National Savings and Trust Company. The home was later divided into apartments but was restored to a duplex in the 1970s.

211 Fourth Avenue A

BUILT: 1919
STYLE: Prairie Bungalow
BUILDER: J. E. Roberts
ORIGINAL OWNER: Nathaniel Wolfe

The low hip roof, broad eaves, and band of casement windows on this one-story bungalow are characteristic of the Prairie style.

Prominent merchant Nathaniel Wolfe purchased this home upon completion. He was president of the Utah Surplus Army Goods Store at the time. He had also established the Wolfe Grand Leader Store and N. Wolfe and Company. In 1926 O. Fredrick and Agnes Hansen purchased the home. Mr. Hansen was the foreman of the Arthur Plant of Kennecott Copper. William and Wilhelmina Hagemann became the home's owners in 1935. Mr. Hagemann was a candy maker for the Sweet Candy Company.

219 Fourth Avenue A

BUILT: 1910
STYLE: Craftsman Bungalow
ARCHITECT: W. J. Cannonville
BUILDER: Eardley and Ball
ORIGINAL OWNER: Hugh W. Dougall

This one-and-one-half-story bungalow has a large dormer and recessed front porch supported by paneled wood columns. Rafter tails and brackets are left exposed as is typical of the Craftsman style. The cobblestone wall along the street and stairs was part of the Cobble Knoll development.

This home was designed by W. J. Cannonville and built by the firm of Eardley and Ball for Hugh W. Dougall, an instructor at the Utah Conservatory of Music. After 1919 the Laker family maintained the property as a rental unit. The home sat empty for much of the 1930s and early 1940s.

223 Fourth Avenue A

BUILT: 1911
STYLE: Prairie
ARCHITECT: C. B. Onderdonk
BUILDER: J. M. Silver
ORIGINAL OWNER: Horace B. and Rebecca Nibley Whitney

The low hip roof and broad eaves of this home are typical of the Prairie style. The wide, first-story front porch has rusticated brick columns and a dentiled wooden cornice. Stone walls from the Cobble Knoll development run along the street.

The home, designed by C. B. Onderdonk, replaced an earlier adobe brick structure occupied by Elizabeth Perry Schettler, one of the wives of Bernard H. Schettler. Horace and Rebecca Whitney had the home built. Mr. Whitney spent his entire career in the banking business with First Security Bank. At the time of his death in 1964, he was the manager of the Deseret Banking Building owned by First Security Bank. Mrs. Whitney remained in the home until 1968.

237 Fourth Avenue A

BUILT: 1898
STYLE: Victorian Eclectic
ORIGINAL OWNER: Cornelius D. Schettler

The gable of this one-and-one-half-story Victorian home has a Palladian window and fish-scale, wood-shingle siding.

The brick cottage was built for Cornelius D. Schettler. The Schettler family owned several houses on this block. Mr. Schettler was a music teacher and prize-winning guitarist. His wife Florence Adler remained in the home after his death.

253 Fourth Avenue [A]

BUILT: 1908
STYLE: Dutch Colonial Revival
ARCHITECT: David C. Dart
ORIGINAL OWNER: Sarah E. Karrick

The gambrel roof of this home is typical of the Dutch Colonial Revival style. The enclosed addition on top of the porch is not original to the home. The porch posts have been recently restored, replacing 1950s iron posts.

This home was designed by noted architect David C. Dart. Thomas and Mary Shannon were the first residents of this home. Mr. Shannon was a partner in a retail clothing store. Herman E. Boorman, a liquor proprietor, bought the home in 1913. In 1917 the property was purchased by Winnefred Bernhardt. She initially maintained the house as a rental unit until she married Reynolds Cahoon and they moved into the home. He was an executive with the Salt Lake Pressed Brick Company and Cahoon Lumber Company. The home was converted into apartments in 1939. It is once again a single-family home.

271 Fourth Avenue [A]

BUILT: 1891
STYLE: Victorian Eclectic
ORIGINAL OWNER: William G. Romney

A prominent front bay window with a dentiled cornice characterizes this hip-roofed Victorian home. The front porch is supported by Doric columns.

The home was built for William and Carrie Romney. Mr. Romney had spent part of his youth in a polygamy colony in Mexico. A printer by trade, Mr. Romney partnered with John Q. Ryan to open the Romney and Ryan Printing Company. They owned the first linotype machine in Utah. His wife, Carrie, remained in the home after his death in 1931.

303 Fourth Avenue [A]

BUILT: 1890
STYLE: Victorian Eclectic
ORIGINAL OWNER: Henry E. Phelps

This tall Victorian home has been stripped of much of its original details. The front porch, scalloped window trim, and stucco finish are not original.

The home was built for Henry E. Phelps, a blacksmith, merchant, and employee of the LDS Church Historian's office. In 1895 the Phelps family lost the property in a tax sale. Brigham S. Young, grandson of Brigham Young, bought the home in 1902 and sold it in 1904 to Elbert D. and Martha A. Thomas. Mr. Thomas became a professor at the University of Utah and eventually a three-term U.S. senator from Utah.

319 Fourth Avenue [A]

BUILT: 1897
STYLE: Victorian Eclectic
BUILDER: J. O. Taft
ORIGINAL OWNER: Nancy Williams

This home is more elaborately decorated than typical Avenues Victorians. There is a pedimented front gable with wood-shingle siding and a cornice with modillion brackets under the broad eaves. Beneath the gable is a recessed second-story window above a first-story brick segmental bay window. The pedimented front porch has triplicate turned columns of a unique shape.

Nancy Williams, the widow of Moses Williams, had this home built as a rental property. She lived at 385 Fifth Avenue. It remained a rental property until Mathius and Emma Connelly bought it in 1908. Mr. Connelly had worked in the mining industry throughout the West. Members of the Connelly family owned the home until 1946.

329 Fourth Avenue [A]

BUILT: 1904
STYLE: Victorian Eclectic
ORIGINAL OWNER: Sidney and Maude Reynolds

This Victorian cottage has a central block with a projecting front bay. The gables are covered in wood-shingle siding.

This house was built on a portion of land acquired in the land grants of 1866 by Sidney Reynolds's father, George, who was a secretary to Brigham Young. Sidney and Maude Reynolds lived in this home for nearly thirty years. They were prominent in local politics, and Sidney served as Salt Lake County sheriff.

369 Fourth Avenue [A]

BUILT: 1899/1912
STYLE: American Four Square
BUILDER: B. E. Smith
ORIGINAL OWNER: Joseph C. and Jane Bennett Sharp

The large, one-story front porch dominates the façade of this American Four Square–type home. The home incorporates an earlier Victorian cottage.

Jane Bennett Sharp received the lot from her father, Richard Bennett, in 1899. She and her husband, Joseph Sharp, had a Victorian home similar to 371 Fourth Avenue built by B. E. Smith that year. They expanded the residence to its present size in 1912. Mr. Sharp, who was the Salt Lake County sheriff when the home was built, was also involved in the sheep industry. He lived here until his death in 1934. His son, LaVon, owned the home until 1943.

371 Fourth Avenue A

BUILT: 1902
STYLE: Victorian Eclectic
ORIGINAL OWNER: Richard and Maria F. Bennett

The complex roof massing of this Victorian cottage is typical of the Queen Anne style. Scroll-sawn brackets support the front gable. The curved front porch is supported by Doric wood columns.

This was the second home built on this lot for Richard and Maria F. Bennett. Richard was an engineer for the Taylor, Romney, and Armstrong Company. The Bennetts' son, John F., was the founder of the Bennett Paint and Glass Company. His grandson was U.S. Senator Wallace Bennett, and his great-grandson was U.S. Senator Robert Bennett. Members of the Bennett family owned this home until 1943 when it was purchased by Lamar and Faye Peterson. Mr. Peterson was a piano and organ teacher.

381 Fourth Avenue A

BUILT: 1898
STYLE: Victorian Eclectic
ORIGINAL OWNER: Hanna S. Capish

This brick Victorian home has detailed woodwork and brickwork. The front gable has diamond-shaped, wood-shingle siding. The front porch has octagonal wood columns, brackets with scroll-sawn decoration, and a wood-shingled railing wall.

Hanna S. Capish moved into this home from Salina, Utah, and lived there with her three children. She was a leader of the Women's Suffrage movement in Utah, serving as a Suffrage delegate from Utah at both national and international conventions. Her son, Joseph, served in the Utah state legislature in 1901. Hanna lived in this home until her death in 1924. Alonzo W. and Elizabeth L. Platt purchased the home and the cottage to the rear in 1942. He was an employee of Kennecott Copper Corporation.

385–389 Fourth Avenue A

BUILT: 1910
STYLE: Craftsman Bungalow
ARCHITECT: T. Hirst
BUILDER: E. M. Mauer
ORIGINAL OWNER: John J. Hicks

This is a multifamily structure built in the Craftsman Bungalow style. The broad gable roof is supported by brackets on the front gable end. Rafter ends are left exposed for decorative effect. The front porches have paired wood columns on brick posts. The building was covered in asbestos shingles in the 1950s.

This apartment house was built as an investment for John J. Hicks, who was a butcher at the Palace Meat Market. In 1913 he moved into one of the apartments in this building and remained in the home until 1944. He spent many of those years as a food inspector for the Utah Board of Health.

413 Fourth Avenue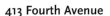

BUILT: 1889
STYLE: Victorian Eclectic
ORIGINAL OWNER: Albert W. Felt

This Victorian cottage has a front porch supported by turned-wood columns.

Portions of this structure may have been built as early as the mid-1870s. The residence was remodeled in 1889 by Albert W. Felt, a traveling salesman and then a manufacturing agent for M. D. Wells and Company, which produced and sold shoes. Mr. Felt remained in the home until 1903 when he moved to 113 Second Avenue. Theron J. and Josephine Smith purchased the property that year. Mr. Smith sold real estate. From 1907 until 1927 Mary Ann Rothlisberger resided in the home. The residence was converted to a duplex in the late 1920s.

414–416 Fourth Avenue

BUILT: 1902
STYLE: Victorian Eclectic
ORIGINAL OWNER: Ernest A. Lambourne

The irregular roof massing of this Victorian home shows the influence of the Queen Anne style. The home also features an oval entry window and square front porch columns.

Ernest A. Lambourne owned a floral shop when he became the first owner of this home. He also worked nights as a doorkeeper at the Salt Lake Theater. He and his wife, Belle, lived here until 1907. From 1908 until 1923 the home was occupied by William H. and Evelyn Weyher. Mr. Weyher was president of the Plantry Gold Mining Company and secretary-treasurer of the Sedo Mining Company. From 1935 until 1971 the home was owned by Maude B. Kimball, who was an active leader of the Democratic Party in Utah. She also worked for the Federal Housing Administration and the Salt Lake General Hospital. She remodeled the home into a duplex in 1970.

422–426 Fourth Avenue

BUILT: 1901
STYLE: Victorian Eclectic
BUILDER: George T. Luff
ORIGINAL OWNER: George T. Luff

This Victorian apartment block has minimal detailing except for the dentiled cornice and square porch columns.

George T. Luff built this apartment block for three thousand dollars in 1901. It is an early example of the transition to multifamily housing in the Avenues. Mr. Luff was a prominent late-nineteenth-century contractor in Salt Lake City.

423–425 Fourth Avenue

BUILT: 1884/1887
STYLE: Vernacular/Mission
ORIGINAL OWNER: William Willes

This is a one-story vernacular cottage combined with a commercial structure nearer to the street. The storefront was most likely remodeled into a Mission style in the 1920s.

William and Elizabeth Willes had the cottage built about 1884. The store was added possibly in 1887 and operated by the Willes family as the W. and E. Willes Grocery Store. After 1899 the operators and owners of the store changed numerous times. The store did remain open under various names until 1952. The combined buildings have been split into four apartments.

435 Fourth Avenue

BUILT: 1904
STYLE: Victorian Eclectic
ORIGINAL OWNER: William Broadbent

This is a Victorian home of pattern-book design. The front porch is supported by wooden Doric columns, and there is a diamond-shaped window next to the front door. The gables are faced with wood-shingle siding.

This home is nearly identical to 437 Fourth Avenue and was built by the same developer. William and Florence Broadbent purchased the home upon completion. Mr. Broadbent was a dentist. They lived here until Florence died in 1909. The next resident owners were James and Edith Karr. Mr. Karr operated the Salt Lake Barber Supply Company at 25 East 100 South in Salt Lake City. Margaret and James Ogilvie purchased the property in 1924. Mr. Ogilvie was a local leader in the Masonic order. Cathy and Rodney Fritch restored the porch and exterior of the home in 1992.

457 Fourth Avenue

BUILT: 1894
STYLE: Vernacular
ORIGINAL OWNER: Harriet Belle

This vernacular cottage in adobe covered in stucco features the popular L-shaped floor plan. A serious fire in 1977 nearly destroyed the home. The front porch is a late 1970s addition.

Harriet Belle was the widow of Millard P. Belle when this home was built. She was one of many widowed women living in the Avenues in the late nineteenth century. The home changed hands several times between 1899 and 1904, when Mary A. Richards bought the home. The second plural wife of Samuel W. Richards, she worked at the Salt Lake LDS Temple.

467 Fourth Avenue   A

BUILT: 1924
STYLE: Prairie Bungalow
BUILDER: Thomas L. Newton
ORIGINAL OWNER: Henry T. McEwen

This brick bungalow is a common design found throughout Utah. The low hip roof and overall profile of the home show the influence of the Prairie style of architecture.

Thomas L. Newton built several homes in the Avenues in the early 1920s. Henry T. McEwen purchased this property upon completion and lived here until he retired in 1932. He had lived next door at 473 Fourth Avenue. Mr. McEwen was the president of McEwen Brothers Incorporated, which sold tea and coffee. John L. and Marie M. Jones purchased the home from Zion's Savings and Loan in 1942. Mr. Jones was secretary of the Utah State Board of Health. John K. and Naomi Fetzer bought the home in 1944. Mr. Fetzer was the manager of the Salt Lake Cabinet Company.

501 Fourth Avenue   B

BUILT: 1889
STYLE: Victorian Eclectic
ORIGINAL OWNER: Mary J. and Brigham Young Hampton

A wooden cornice runs under the eaves with returns and bargeboards in the front gable of this home. Projecting drip molding is found around the windows. There is a one-story, segmental front bay window.

This home was built for Mary J. and Brigham Young Hampton. Mr. Hampton served the LDS Church as a detective investigating federal officials for sexual corruption in an effort to counter their anti-polygamy activities. Arthur Pratt purchased the home in 1901. He was the chief of police for Salt Lake City at the time. The home then changed hands several times before the Great Depression when it was converted into apartments.

522 Fourth Avenue   B

BUILT: 1901
STYLE: Victorian Eclectic
ORIGINAL OWNER: Alfred A. Isom

This two-story Victorian home's gable faces the street and is covered in diamond-shaped, wood-shingle siding. The balance of the home was covered in asbestos shingles in the 1950s which have since been removed. This home is similar to 524 Fourth Avenue.

Alfred A. Isom and members of his family worked for the Salt Lake Mattress and Manufacturing Company. He lived at 177 H Street before he moved to this house in about 1904. He lived here until 1934. In 1941 the home was bought by Harold C. Aubrey, who was employed by the Mountain Fuel Supply Company.

531 Fourth Avenue   B

BUILT: 1890
STYLE: Queen Anne
ORIGINAL OWNER: Joseph Johnson

Although this two-and-one-half-story brick home is similar to other large Avenues residences built during the period, it is distinguished by fine detailing. There are brick dentil ornaments on the octagonal corner tower. Eastlake molding decorates the corners of the main gable and the pediment over the porch. A decorative panel on the second floor is surrounded by brick laid on edge.

Joseph Johnson, who had recently moved to Salt Lake City from Logan with his wife, Emma Cope, built this house next to his brother-in-law's home at 535 Fourth Avenue. Three years later they sold the property to George W. Philips.

560 Fourth Avenue   B

BUILT: 1902
STYLE: Victorian Eclectic
ORIGINAL OWNER: Vashni H. Pease

This one-story Victorian home has a hip roof and a square, projecting front bay. The front porch of the home has been enclosed.

This is one of several homes built for Vashni H. Pease in the Avenues. Mr. Pease had been a mail carrier over stagecoach routes throughout the West. He held this home as a rental property until 1914, when it was purchased by Oliver M. Holding, a prominent resort director in Utah. Over the years he directed the Saltair Resort, Lagoon Resort, Pinecrest Resort in Emigration Canyon, the Hermitage Hotel in Ogden Canyon, and Vivian Park in Provo Canyon. He also served as superintendent of the state fairgrounds. He was employed as an engineer at the State Crippled Children's Hospital at the time of his death. He died at his home in 1954.

675 Fourth Avenue   B

BUILT: 1885/1889
STYLE: Victorian Eclectic
ORIGINAL OWNER: Vashni H. Pease

This Victorian home was built in two stages between 1885 and 1889. The home has a projecting front bay, and patterned wood siding covers the front of the gable. The Bungalow-style front porch was added around 1915.

The rear section of the home was built in 1885 for Vashni H. Pease. Mr. Pease had been a postal carrier over numerous stage coach routes around the West. He lived in this home until 1908. Thomas F. and Clara L. Snowball resided here from 1908 until 1956. Mr. Snowball was a meat cutter and had managed the Royal Meat Market and George Wood Market.

715 Fourth Avenue `B`

BUILT: 1891/1909
STYLE: Prairie/American Four Square
ORIGINAL OWNER: Cornelius West

The broad projecting eaves, low hip roof, and horizontal banding are characteristics of the Prairie style of architecture. The home's exterior is covered in stucco. A wooden belt course separates the smooth and rough surfaces.

Cornelius West built a Victorian home on this site in 1891. Around 1909 the original home was either heavily remodeled in the Prairie style or demolished. Carl Samuelson was the owner of the property at that time. An actor and singer, he was a member of the Mormon Tabernacle Choir and Orpheus Choir. He also performed for the Salt Lake Theater. From 1919 until 1924 the home was owned by Phillip J. Purcell, director of the Utah State National Bank, the Utah Red Cross, and the local YMCA. The home then changed hands seven times between 1935 and 1978.

758 Fourth Avenue `B`

BUILT: 1921
STYLE: Prairie Bungalow
BUILDER: Edward A. Johnston
ORIGINAL OWNER: Edward A. and Jane I. Welch

This hip-roofed brick bungalow is a common design found throughout Utah. The Prairie style was prevalent from 1910 to 1925.

Developer Edward A. Johnston built this home along with 754, 764, and 768 Fourth Avenue. Edward and Jane Welch purchased the property upon completion. Mr. Welch was a long-time employee of the Denver and Rio Grande Western Railroad. The Welch family still owned this home into the 1980s, representing a rare case of long-term, single-family ownership of an Avenues property.

763 Fourth Avenue `B`

BUILT: 1907
STYLE: Victorian Eclectic
BUILDER: Salt Lake Security and Trust Company
ORIGINAL OWNER: Jessie G. Smith

This cottage was built at the end of the Victorian design period in the Avenues. Just one year later, most homes built in the area were Craftsman bungalows. The porch is supported by Doric wood columns.

Jessie G. Smith purchased this home from the Salt Lake Security and Trust Company upon completion. He maintained the home as a rental property until 1925. Famed Salt Lake City sports reporter John C. Derks purchased the home in 1938. He worked in the city's sports market for thirty years. He helped found the baseball rookie Pioneer League and assisted the city in obtaining its first baseball franchise in the Pacific Coast League. After his death in 1940, the city's new baseball stadium was named Derks Field. His family owned this home until 1972.

764 Fourth Avenue   B

BUILT: 1921
STYLE: Prairie Bungalow
BUILDER: Edward A. Johnston
ORIGINAL OWNER: Orson F. Whitney

This hip-roofed brick bungalow is a common design found throughout Utah. These homes were built between 1910 and 1925. Angled iron posts added in the 1960s support the center of the porch.

Developer Edward A. Johnston built this home along with 754, 758, and 768 Fourth Avenue. Orson F. Whitney purchased the property upon completion. He was active in local politics and in the LDS Church. He was the author of a number of books including a four-volume history of Utah while associated with the LDS Church Historian's office. He also served terms as clerk to the territorial legislature, as a state senator, and as Salt Lake City treasurer. He lived most of his life at 160 Fourth Avenue, only spending his last eight years at this address.

768 Fourth Avenue   B

BUILT: 1921
STYLE: Prairie Bungalow
BUILDER: Edward A. Johnston
ORIGINAL OWNER: Thomas and Anastasia Vaughan

This brick bungalow is a common design built throughout Utah between 1910 and 1925.

Developer Edward A. Johnston built this home along with 754, 758, and 764 Fourth Avenue. Upon completion this home was purchased by Thomas Vaughan, who was the superintendent of the Catholic Church's Mount Cavalry Cemetery for fifty-two years. He was an active member of the Cathedral of the Madeleine. Two of his sons became Catholic priests. The Vaughan family owned this home into the 1980s.

777 Fourth Avenue   B

BUILT: 1908
STYLE: Bungalow
BUILDER: Salt Lake Security and Trust Company
ORIGINAL OWNER: Charles V. Worthington

This is a one-story bungalow with a hip roof and front center dormer. Most of the front porch has been enclosed.

The Salt Lake Security and Trust Company built numerous homes in the Avenues, including nearly all the homes on this block face. Charles V. Worthington purchased the home upon completion. Mr. Worthington had been a political cartoonist for the *Chicago Tribune* and *Salt Lake Tribune*. When he purchased the home he was the advertising manager for Keith-O'Brien's Department Store. He worked for the company until 1950, eventually becoming the store manager. The Worthington family owned this property until 1962.

779 Fourth Avenue `B`

BUILT: 1910
STYLE: American Four Square
ORIGINAL OWNER: James C. and Jennie W. Climo

This brick, two-story, Four Square–type home has a hip roof and front center dormer. The corners of the home have quoin-like decoration. The front porch is supported by brick corner columns and wood Doric columns.

This home was built for James and Jennie Climo. Mr. Climo was the director of the Meteor Electric Company. They lived in this home for just two years, after which they maintained it as a rental property until 1930. In 1938 H. Hartland and Camille Halliday purchased the home. Mr. Halliday was an attorney, while Camille taught at the Columbus School.

803 Fourth Avenue `B`

BUILT: 1906
STYLE: Victorian Eclectic
BUILDER: Angus McKellar
ORIGINAL OWNER: Walter Manning Williams

This is a rambling Victorian home on a corner lot. It has a truncated hip roof and projecting, gable-roofed bay on the west. The original front porch columns were replaced by iron posts and the home covered in asbestos shingles in the 1950s. In 1985 the porch was restored.

The first resident owner was Walter Manning Williams, who owned a garden supply store in Salt Lake City named Vogelers Inc. He lived in this home until 1913. Gilbert V. and Frankie L. Heal purchased the property in 1921. Mr. Heal was a major figure in the Utah newspaper industry. At various times he was a reporter, editorial writer, and editor for the *Salt Lake Herald*, *Salt Lake Telegram*, and *Salt Lake Tribune*.

816–818 Fourth Avenue `B`

BUILT: 1905
STYLE: Victorian Eclectic/Commercial
ORIGINAL OWNER: Joseph J. Paul

This two-story Victorian home has a commercial-style, one-story east wing. The home has a gable roof with returns and a Palladian-style window in the front gable. The exterior of the store and home have been altered from their original condition.

Joseph J. and Sarah Ann Paul lived in the residence and operated a grocery store at this location starting in 1905. Mr. Paul was also a contracting carpenter and active leader of the LDS Twenty-seventh Ward. In 1948, the Paul family sold this property to George P. Fivas. Ownership of the property changed hands numerous times over the next fifty years. It was mostly maintained as a rental property. The combined buildings were restored as a single-family residence in the late 1990s.

825 Fourth Avenue   B

BUILT: 1909
STYLE: Bungalow
ARCHITECT: N. Edward Liljenberg and Emil Maesar
BUILDER: National Real Estate Investment Company
ORIGINAL OWNER: John N. and Dora A. Taggart

This is a rather plain, one-story, hip-roof bungalow with front center dormer. The original front window has been replaced by a picture window.

The National Real Estate Investment Company built this home as well as 829, 833, and 837 Fourth Avenue, and all four homes were designed by N. Edward Liljenberg and Emil Maeser. John N. and Dora A. Taggart purchased the property from the company in 1912. Mr. Taggart, a professional piano tuner, was often called upon when a major artist appeared in Salt Lake City. Theresa Leaver purchased the home in 1921 and owned the residence until 1938.

833 Fourth Avenue   B

BUILT: 1909
STYLE: Bungalow
ARCHITECT: Edward N. Liljenberg and Emil Maeser
BUILDER: National Real Estate Investment Company and Emil Maeser
ORIGINAL OWNER: William T. Atkin

This is a one-and-one-half-story, hip-roofed bungalow. The front porch is supported by brick columns, and there is a large addition on the rear of the home.

The National Real Estate Investment Company built this home designed by Emil Maeser and Edward N. Liljenberg. The firm also built 825, 829, and 837 Fourth Avenue. William T. Atkin, manager of the firm, owned the home as a rental property until 1917. The first tenant, Maria Angell Woolley, was the daughter of Salt Lake LDS Temple architect Truman O. Angell. Maria eventually became the owner of the home. Members of the Woolley family remained in the residence until 1967.

837 Fourth Avenue   B

BUILT: 1909
STYLE: American Four Square
ARCHITECT: Edward N. Liljenberg and Emil Maeser
BUILDER: National Real Estate Investment Company
ORIGINAL OWNER: William T. Atkin

This is a two-story, brick American Four Square. The porch is supported by paired Doric columns, and its original iron balustrade remains. The interior of the home maintains much of its original character.

William T. Atkin, owner of the National Real Estate Investment Company, built this home designed by Emil Maeser and Edward N. Liljenberg for himself. Between 1928 and 1937 the house was owned by Zion's Bank. It was rented out to various individuals and also remained vacant for extended periods of time during the Great Depression. Robert S. and Alice A. Folland were the owners and residents from 1942 until 1973. Mr. Folland owned the Folland Drug Company on Sixth Avenue.

870 Fourth Avenue B

BUILT: 1891
STYLE: Victorian Eclectic
ORIGINAL OWNER: John D. and Julia Ford

This Victorian home was built in several stages starting in 1891. A smaller front bay and gable covers the east façade of the home. The front porch is supported by Doric wood columns.

The home was built for John D. and Julia Ford, who would maintain ownership until 1950. Mr. Ford was a long-term employee of the *Deseret News*. He worked for the paper from the time he was eighteen until he was eighty-three years old. He was also an early member of the Utah National Guard, eventually attaining the rank of lieutenant colonel.

976 Fourth Avenue C

BUILT: 1934
STYLE: Commercial
ORIGINAL OWNER: Spiker Tile and Pottery
Company

The front façade of this two-story commercial building is covered with brick and tile. The large center window has replaced the original sliding door.

This structure was built for the Spiker Tile and Pottery Company. Owned by John E. Spiker, the company operated at this address as a leading tile producer in the state until 1945. Bronze Craft Memorial Company, maker of graveyard plaques, moved into the building at that time. In 1953 Rex W. Williams purchased the property. Mr. Williams restored the building in 1978.

1128 Fourth Avenue C

BUILT: 1898
STYLE: Victorian Eclectic
ORIGINAL OWNER: Hames Maxwell

This one-and-one-half-story Victorian home has a tall gable roof. The original shingles on the gable have been covered in siding. A shed roof covers the front porch.

Hames Maxwell, the first owner of this property, came to Utah as part of the first group of Mormon converts to travel entirely by rail to the state. He was employed as a brick maker and was awarded a prize at the 1894 World's Fair in Chicago for making the world's best red brick. Later in life he served as the custodian of the Salt Lake City and County Building. In 1939 his daughter, Jessie L. Beans, bought the home. She retained ownership of the property into the 1980s.

1202 Fourth Avenue

BUILT: 1908
STYLE: Bungalow
ARCHITECT: David C. Dart
BUILDER: Thomas J. Armstrong
ORIGINAL OWNER: Thomas J. Armstrong

This one-and-one-half-story bungalow also exhibits elements of Colonial Revival style. The steeply pitched gable roof is faced with wood-shingle siding. Doric columns support the front porch.

Noted architect David C. Dart designed this home for builder Thomas J. Armstrong, who maintained the property as a rental unit until 1921. Christian N. and Mary L. Jensen purchased the home that year. A local educator, Mr. Jensen held numerous positions including Utah state school superintendent, superintendent of the Jordan School District, and vice president of the National Education Association. The Jensen family lived in the home until 1934 and maintained ownership of the property until 1945.

1203 Fourth Avenue

BUILT: 1903
STYLE: American Four Square
BUILDER: William Kronner
ORIGINAL OWNER: William Kronner

This Four Square–type home has a hip roof with a front center dormer. A one-story porch runs across the front of the home. The porch is supported by Doric columns and decorated with dentil molding. There is a small gable over the entrance to the porch.

Contractor William Kronner built this home for himself. Mr. Kronner was the builder of the original Salt Palace and Kearns St. Ann's Orphanage. Mary B. Kronner, William's wife, assumed ownership of the property after William's death in 1930. Mrs. Kronner was active in the local Catholic community. The home was divided into apartments in 1948. Members of the Kronner family maintained ownership of the property into the 1980s. The home has since been restored to a single-family residence.

1212 Fourth Avenue

BUILT: 1903
STYLE: Victorian Eclectic
BUILDER: Thomas J. Armstrong
ORIGINAL OWNER: Thomas J. Armstrong

This is a two-story, gable-roofed Victorian home. The gable is covered in wood-shingle siding. The original front porch columns have been replaced by iron posts.

Contractor Thomas J. Armstrong built this home as an investment property. He rented out the house until 1907 when he sold it to Louis O. and Ida H. Dick. Mr. Dick was the manager of the Strevell-Paterson Hardware Company in Salt Lake City. Franz R. Schultze, a long-time postal worker, became the owner of the home in 1925.

1227 Fourth Avenue

BUILT: 1901
STYLE: Victorian Eclectic
ORIGINAL OWNER: Charles M. Freed

This Victorian home was most likely a pattern-book design. The front gables have wood-shingle siding and returns. The original wooden porch columns and balustrades have been replaced by iron posts.

This home was built as a speculative rental property. The first owner, Charles M. Freed, was a prominent businessman and owner of the Freed Furniture and Carpet Company. After his death in 1910, his son, Claud W. Freed, briefly owned the home. Claud, known as the "father of Utah golf," sponsored the first Utah Open Golf Tournament. He was involved in the furniture, finance, and automobile businesses in Salt Lake City. Charles E. and Rose Whiteman became the first resident owners in 1911. Mr. Whiteman was a pipefitter for the Denver and Rio Grande Railroad. The Whitemans remained in the home until 1938.

FIFTH AVENUE

207 Fifth Avenue

BUILT: 1913
STYLE: American Four Square
ORIGINAL OWNER: Robert R. Anderson

This is a large Four Square–type home. Brick pattern work at the corners of the house resembles quoins. There are two wooden second-floor bay windows above the front porch. The porch has a wooden cornice with modillion brackets and square wooden columns.

Robert R. Anderson was one of the original settlers on the north bench of Salt Lake City. He moved to this home from 211 Fifth Avenue. He had been a private accountant for Brigham Young and manager of Dinwoodey Furniture Company. He also served as the first state bank examiner. After his death in 1935, his daughter and her husband, Bessie and William Winder, lived in the home until 1958. Mr. Winder, a proponent of tourism in the state, was a director of the Utah Department of Publicity and Industrial Development.

216 Fifth Avenue A

BUILT: 1907
STYLE: Victorian Eclectic
ORIGINAL OWNER: Ella S. Sears

This late Victorian home has a two-story gabled front bay. The front porch is supported by Doric wood columns. This was one of the last Victorian homes built in the Avenues before the Bungalow style became popular.

Ella S. Sears had this home built along with 214 and 218 Fifth Avenue as investment properties. Six other property owners held this home as a rental property until 1918 when Brigham Spencer Young Jr., a son of Brigham Young, purchased the home. He lived here until 1922. In the late 1930s the home was split into several apartments. Lynn and Ruth Morgan purchased the property in 1981 and converted it back to a single-family residence.

225 Fifth Avenue A

BUILT: 1902
STYLE: Victorian Eclectic
ORIGINAL OWNER: Simon Grieve

This Victorian home has a large gable roof that faces the street. The gable is covered in patterned wood-shingle siding. The first floor has a bay window on the front. The entrance is on the east side of the home.

Simon Grieve was a carpenter and patternmaker for the Silver Brothers Iron Works Company when this home was built. After his death in 1915, his wife and children remained in the home until 1923. From 1935 until 1971 Arno A. Steinicke owned the home. Mr. Steinicke emigrated from Germany in 1928 and was a deputy sheriff. He also was a sculptor, and some of his works can be found in the Salt Lake City, Logan, St. George, and Manti LDS Temples.

323 Fifth Avenue [A]

BUILT: 1902
STYLE: Victorian Eclectic
ARCHITECT: David C. Dart
ORIGINAL OWNER: Robert R. and Nettie Anderson

The upper walls of this home are covered in decorative wood-shingle siding while the first floor is brick. Corbelled drip molding is found around the first-floor windows. The porch was rebuilt with iron columns and concrete floor in the early 1970s. Turned porch columns have been recently added to replicate the original porch.

Robert R. Anderson was a plumber when he took out a building permit to construct this home. The home's architect was David C. Dart, who designed numerous Avenues homes of various styles. Mrs. Anderson lived in the home until 1930. She converted the home into a duplex. Michael H. and Genevieve M. Bastian purchased the home in 1946 and lived there for over thirty years.

335 Fifth Avenue [A]

BUILT: 1888
STYLE: Queen Anne
BUILDER: John Larsen
ORIGINAL OWNER: R. D. Winters

This mansion shows the influence of the Queen Anne style. The home has a pyramidal tower on the southeast corner. The exterior is covered with decorative brickwork and ornamental woodwork. The original Crager Iron Works fence runs along the perimeter of the property. The home's horse hitch also is found near Fifth Avenue.

John Larsen built this home and sold it upon completion to R. D. Winters, an attorney, who only lived here for one year. Thomas and Hannah Webb were the next owners. Hannah Webb operated the H. and M. M. Webb Bakery. In 1896 the home was purchased by James L. Chipman, a banking and mining executive who was also the first treasurer for the State of Utah. He lived here until 1922. The home was converted into apartments in 1926.

363 Fifth Avenue [A]

BUILT: 1899
STYLE: Victorian Eclectic
ARCHITECT: Edgar Druce
BUILDER: Edgar Druce
ORIGINAL OWNER: George W. Lambourne

This Victorian home has a projecting two-story front bay. The front gable has a lunette window, fish-scale wood-shingle siding, and a dentiled cornice. The Bungalow-style front porch was most likely added in the early 1920s.

Architect Edgar Druce built this home for George W. Lambourne. Mr. Lambourne was active in mining and banking in Park City, holding positions as vice president of the Judge Mining and Smelting Company and vice president of the State Bank of Park City. He moved to 89 C Street in 1907 and his brother, Ernest Lambourne, bought the home. He owned a florist shop. In 1928 the house was purchased by Nathan W. Tanner, the foreman for the Shirley Plumbing Supply Company. The Tanner family would maintain ownership of this home for the next fifty years. The building was subdivided into apartments in the 1960s.

369 Fifth Avenue　A

BUILT: 1899
STYLE: Victorian Eclectic
ARCHITECT: Edgar Druce
BUILDER: Edgar Druce
ORIGINAL OWNER: Orson P. Arnold

This Victorian home has a projecting front bay. The front gable has a lunette window, fish-scale wood-shingle siding, and a dentiled cornice. The Craftsman-style front porch was added in the early 1920s. The glass-block window on the façade is not original to the home.

Architect Edgar Druce built this home for Orson P. Arnold, superintendent of the Salt Lake City Railroad. Joseph A. Decker purchased the property in 1911. He formed the Decker-Patrick Dry Goods Company along with Will A. Patrick and was president of the company until 1927. He was also the first president of the Utah Automobile Club and three-time director of the Salt Lake Commercial Club. The Decker family maintained ownership of this home into the 1980s. The residence is currently split into a duplex.

373 Fifth Avenue　A

BUILT: 1902
STYLE: Victorian Eclectic
ORIGINAL OWNER: George E. and Mary Ann Wareing

This Victorian home has an L-shaped floor plan. The front gable is faced with patterned wood-shingle siding. The roof has a hip-roofed dormer. The front porch columns have been replaced by iron posts.

This home was built for George E. and Mary Ann Wareing. Mr. Wareing was employed by the ZCMI department store for forty-four years, starting in the shoe department in Ogden at the age of fifteen. He eventually became the manager of the shoe department in Salt Lake City. He remained in this home until his death in 1951. That year the home was bought by Moroni B. Harrison, owner of Harrison Brothers Janitorial Supply. He lived in this residence into the 1980s.

379 Fifth Avenue　A

BUILT: 1874
STYLE: Vernacular
ORIGINAL OWNER: Henrietta Woolley Simmons

The symmetrical façade, gable roof, and brick exterior end chimneys of this small, one-story house are typical of the Vernacular design. The Georgian Revival front door frame is not original. The home's exterior has been recently restored.

This house was built for Henrietta Simmons by her father, Edwin D. Woolley, two years after the death of her husband, Joseph Marcellus Simmons. Her sister, Rachel, also one of Simmons's plural wives, lived next door at 385 Fifth Avenue. Mr. Simmons, who had boarded and worked for the Woolley family as Rachel and Henrietta grew up, was noted for his involvement in local theatrical groups.

385 Fifth Avenue

BUILT: 1874
STYLE: Vernacular/Georgian Revival
ORIGINAL OWNER: Rachel Woolley Simmons

Covered in shiplap siding, this vernacular house runs five bays wide with double-hung windows framed by wide plain trim. Between 1898 and the 1930s, several different porches were added to the home. Originally the home appeared similar to the adjacent 379 Fifth Avenue. Since the original vernacular form was derived from eighteenth-century Georgian architecture, the remodeling shows the same style revived in a more elaborate form.

Edwin D. Woolley built this home for his daughter Rachel two years after the death of her husband, Joseph M. Simmons. She was his first wife, and her sister, Henrietta, who lived next door, was also a plural wife of Mr. Simmons. Rachel Simmons practiced obstetrics after her husband's death. In 1958, the home was converted into apartments.

453 Fifth Avenue

BUILT: 1921
STYLE: Prairie Bungalow
BUILDER: T. A. Bussman
ORIGINAL OWNER: Marcellus Simmons Woolley

This home has a low hip roof, horizontal banding, and a brick exterior. Its Prairie design is typical of many bungalows built in Utah between 1910 and 1925.

Marcellus Simmons Woolley took out a building permit for this home in 1921. Mr. Woolley was heavily involved in local government, serving on the Salt Lake County Commission, as chief deputy sheriff, and as a member of the Utah State Board of Education. He was also involved in real estate development. He died soon after the home was completed but his wife, Mary Ann Woolley, remained in the residence until 1930. The home then became a rental property for most of the next eighty years. In 2008 the house was restored.

475 Fifth Avenue

BUILT: 1905
STYLE: Victorian Eclectic
BUILDER: George Paul
ORIGINAL OWNER: Frank J. Lucas

This one-and-one-half-story Victorian home is of pattern-book design. Both front gables have patterned wood-shingle siding. The home is similar to 473 Fifth Avenue which was built by the same developer.

Frank J. Lucas was a grocer when he became this home's first owner. Eventually he would own a chain of twelve stores. He lived in this home until 1921. From 1928 until 1934 James C. and Joanah E. Jensen owned the property. Mr. Jensen had been the county recorder in both Salt Lake and Wasatch Counties. He also had helped organize the Heber City Bank.

528 Fifth Avenue   `B`

BUILT: 1936
STYLE: Tudor Revival
ORIGINAL OWNER: Joseph A. and Anna Falsetti

This brick cottage was built in the Tudor Revival style popular in Utah neighborhoods between 1925 and 1940. The home has steep gables and is covered in dark red brick. The arched front door is also typical of this style. The main front window has been altered.

Joseph A. and Anna Falsetti moved from 235 H Street into this cottage when it was completed and lived here until Anna's death in 1941. Karl and Mathilda Sennhauser purchased the property in 1948. Mr. Sennhauser was a driver for the Rand Cleaning and Tailoring Company.

531 Fifth Avenue   `B`

BUILT: 1905
STYLE: Victorian Eclectic
BUILDER: James G. McDonald
ORIGINAL OWNER: John S. and Nellie E. Gardner

This two-story Victorian home has a main hip roof and front gabled bay. The gable has wood-shingle siding while the main walls are yellow brick. A one-story front porch runs the length of the house.

James G. McDonald built this home along with 535 Fifth Avenue and 271 H Street as investments. John and Nellie Gardner purchased the property upon completion. Mr. Gardner was assistant secretary and treasurer for the Ohio Copper Company. Virginnies L. and Alice W. Johnson purchased the residence in 1928. Mrs. Johnson was the dean of women at LDS College, while Mr. Johnson was the district agent for the U.S. Fish and Wildlife Service.

535 Fifth Avenue   `B`

BUILT: 1906
STYLE: Victorian Eclectic
BUILDER: James G. McDonald
ORIGINAL OWNER: William G. Williams

This late Victorian home shows elements of the Shingle style on the second floor. There is a projecting front bay. The garage was added to the home in 1916.

William G. Williams purchased this home after it was constructed by James G. McDonald. Mr. McDonald also built 531 Fifth Avenue. Mr. Williams, the founder of Camp Williams, was a brigadier general in the Utah National Guard. Members of the Williams family owned this home until 1962.

553 Fifth Avenue [B]

BUILT: 1913
STYLE: Craftsman Bungalow
BUILDER: H. Henderson
ORIGINAL OWNER: Harold G. Reynolds

Cobblestone frames the main walls below the windows and supports the porch of this excellent one-story Craftsman bungalow. The gable has projecting eaves supported by large purlins.

Harold G. Reynolds owned this house from the time of its construction until his death in 1940. Mr. Reynolds was active in LDS Church administration. As missionary secretary and transportation agent for the church, he was in charge of the transportation of the church's thirty thousand missionaries. He also owned the Hotel Utah Souvenir Shop.

557 Fifth Avenue [B]

BUILT: 1913
STYLE: Prairie Bungalow
BUILDER: Burt and Carlquist
ORIGINAL OWNER: Daniel C. and Lucille Coulham

This one-story brick bungalow with its low hipped roof is a design commonly found throughout Utah. Homes such as this were built between 1910 and 1925 in the state.

Daniel and Lucille Coulham owned this home from the time it was built until 1953. The Coulham family lived in the residence until 1934 when they maintained it as a rental property. Mr. Coulham was employed as the manager of the insurance division of Burt and Carlquist, the real estate development company that built this home.

559 Fifth Avenue [B]

BUILT: 1904
STYLE: Victorian Eclectic
ORIGINAL OWNER: Hyrum and Ida Nelson

The design of this Victorian home was most likely chosen from a pattern book. An enlarged dormer protrudes from the hip roof of the structure. There is a gabled, projecting front bay covered in wood-shingle siding. The front porch was removed in the 1960s. The dormer windows are not original to the home.

Hyrum and Ida Nelson only lived in this home for two years after it was built. Mr. Nelson was an agent for the New York Life Insurance Company. In 1906 the home was purchased by Anna Olson Bourne, widow of George E. Bourne who had helped establish the grocery department at the ZCMI department store. Anna's son, E. LeRoy Bourne, lived in the home as well. He eventually became the editor of the *Deseret News* and *Salt Lake Telegram* newspapers. The home has been split into multiple apartments.

566 Fifth Avenue B

BUILT: 1924
STYLE: Bungalow
BUILDER: H. J. McKean
ORIGINAL OWNER: Julia Ann and Rebecca Almond

This small bungalow has a hip roof, front casement windows, and a bracketed canopy over the entry.

H. J. McKean built this home and 560 Fifth Avenue for the Ellerby Searle Company. Upon completion it was sold to Julia Ann Almond and her sister, Rebecca. Rebecca was a teacher at the McCune School of Music. They lived here for two years and then rented out the home. Former renters Samuel and Afton Kalm purchased the house in 1931.

567 Fifth Avenue B

BUILT: 1905
STYLE: American Four Square
ARCHITECT: Barber and Klatz
BUILDER: Asper Noall and Company
ORIGINAL OWNER: Joseph Johnson

This two-story, Four Square–type home shows Colonial Revival influence in its decoration. It has a gabled front dormer with returns and a Palladian window. Corners of the structure are accented with brick quoins. The wide front porch is supported by Doric columns.

The original owner, Joseph Johnson, was the manager of the accounting department of the Consolidated Wagon and Machine Company. He only lived here for two years before selling the property to William S. M. Bean, who worked for the Utah Implement and Vehicle Company. He lived here until 1923 when C. Bert and Almira F. Peterson bought the residence. They lived here for the next forty years.

573 Fifth Avenue B

BUILT: 1899
STYLE: Dutch Colonial Revival
ARCHITECT: Edgar W. Druce
BUILDER: Edgar W. Druce
ORIGINAL OWNER: John K. Nicholson

This large home has gambrel roofs that are typical of Dutch Colonial Revival style. The wide front porch is supported by octagonal columns. The porch shelters a three-sided, brick bay window with a decorative glass transom.

John K. Nicholson, a department manager at the ZCMI department store, lived in this home until 1903. The next resident owner, Michael Ryan, was employed by Salt Lake City as a carpenter. Charles F. and Nellie J. Jennings bought the property in 1910. Mr. Jennings was a purchasing agent.

575 Fifth Avenue   B

BUILT: 1898
STYLE: Victorian Eclectic
ORIGINAL OWNER: Emanuel R. and Ada R.
Lundquist

This one-and-one-half-story Victorian cottage has an attached commercial structure. The cottage features a main gable roof with a small gable over the front entry.

Emanuel R. Lundquist operated a store from the commercial structure from 1898 until 1925. His wife, Ada, kept the store open until 1933. The Lundquist family lived in the attached home while owning the store. The building has been converted to a duplex.

587 Fifth Avenue   B

BUILT: 1905
STYLE: Victorian Eclectic
BUILDER: Peter G. Hoffman
ORIGINAL OWNER: Peter G. Hoffman

Italianate influences can be seen in this home's boxed massing and bracketed cornice. There is a curved, front bay window with stone sills. The porch has been partially enclosed.

Peter G. Hoffman replaced an older adobe-and-frame home which his parents had owned with this structure. Mr. Hoffman was a contractor and had built several homes in the neighborhood. In 1907 the property was purchased by Robert B. Ketchum, dean of the School of Mines at the University of Utah. In 1927 he sold the home to Hubert and Almeda Hall. Mr. Hall was an engineer for the firm of Caldwell, Richards, and Hall.

588 Fifth Avenue   B

BUILT: 1916
STYLE: Prairie Bungalow
BUILDER: H. J. McKean
ORIGINAL OWNER: Thomas Parry Billings

The low hip roof, brick exterior, and heavy brick columns are characteristics of this bungalow with Prairie-style influences.

Mining pioneer and executive Thomas Parry Billings had this home built for his family. Mr. Billings was instrumental in developing new methods of recovering copper in Bingham Canyon. He eventually became the general manager of the Bingham Copper Mines, and in 1952 he was appointed head of the lead and zinc department at the Department of the Interior. The Billings family lived in this home until 1950.

611 Fifth Avenue [B]

BUILT: 1892
STYLE: Queen Anne
ORIGINAL OWNER: John and Caroline Flowers

This one-and-one-half-story Queen Anne home features a front gable with an arched opening. The gable is covered in fish-scale, wood-shingle siding. There is a pilaster-like decoration on the front corner of the structure. The front porch is supported by turned wood columns.

This home was built for John and Caroline Flowers. Mr. Flowers was a bookkeeper for the Salt Lake Telephone Company and eventually became assistant treasurer for the Rocky Mountain Bell Telephone Company. The home stayed in the Flowers family until 1967 when Seville Flowers, a botany professor at the University of Utah, sold the property to Linda and Kevin Lyman. They were responsible for this early Avenues restoration.

620 Fifth Avenue [B]

BUILT: 1892
STYLE: Victorian Eclectic
BUILDER: James Devine
ORIGINAL OWNER: James and Annie Devine

This is a decorated Victorian cottage with complex roof shapes that show the influence of the Queen Anne style. The dormers all have different ornate trim. In the 1960s an aluminum awning replaced the original ornate porch structure. The awning has been removed but the porch has not been rebuilt.

James Devine built this home for his family. He had multiple careers in his life. He was a contractor who was the superintendent of construction on the Utah State Capitol. He also served as Salt Lake City fire chief from 1894 to 1904. He modernized the department and organized the first large national convention held in Salt Lake City for the International Association of Fire Engineers. He later served as the state prison warden and as an attorney. The home was converted into apartments in 1940.

678 Fifth Avenue [B]

BUILT: 1902
STYLE: Victorian Eclectic
BUILDER: William G. McGinty
ORIGINAL OWNER: Lucian A. Ray

This one-and-one-half-story, gable-roofed Victorian home is most likely of pattern-book design. The main gable and the gable over the front porch have wood-shingle siding. The original porch columns have been replaced by iron posts. The windows in the front gable have been altered.

William G. McGinty built this home along with 674 and 680 Fifth Avenue. He sold it to Lucian A. Ray upon completion. A prominent local businessman, Mr. Ray was a broker for the firm of Ray and Whitney. He lived in this home until 1907. William F. Williams, a bank clerk, owned the home from 1907 to 1916. In 1925 the property was purchased by Hugh C. McDevitt, a Salt Lake City firefighter. He later rose to the rank of captain in the fire department.

704 Fifth Avenue   B

BUILT: 1890
STYLE: Victorian Eclectic
ORIGINAL OWNER: Emily Woodmansee

This simple, frame cottage is covered in shiplap siding with corner boards. There are plain Italianate wood pediments above the front windows.

Emily Woodmansee had this house built in phases starting in 1890. Mrs. Woodmansee, a renowned poet, held this as a rental property. After the home was enlarged in 1897 it was sold to Charles P. and Caroline R. Ringwood. They had twenty-two children. Mr. Ringwood was a veteran of the Indian Wars and was one of the city's first police officers. The Ringwood family owned the home until 1922.

711 Fifth Avenue   B

BUILT: 1893
STYLE: Victorian Eclectic
BUILDER: J. L. Bicknell
ORIGINAL OWNER: Mathew H. and Amy W. Barnes

This Victorian home has an L-shaped floor plan. The front gable has patterned wood-shingle siding. The front porch has turned columns.

W. C. Staines had J. L. Bicknell build this cottage for five hundred dollars. He sold the home to Mathew and Amy Barnes upon completion. Mr. Barnes was a pipe foreman for the Salt Lake Water Works Department. He was also an early volunteer fireman and president of the Veteran Volunteer Fireman's Association. He lived in this home until his death. His wife, Amy, remained in the home until her death in 1955. She was the longest living handcart pioneer in the LDS Church's Twenty-first Ward. The home remained in the Barnes family past 1980. This is a rare case of long-term, single-family home ownership in the Avenues.

753 Fifth Avenue   B

BUILT: 1907
STYLE: Craftsman Bungalow
ORIGINAL OWNER: Albert R. Burns

This is one of the first homes built in the Craftsman Bungalow style. The gable roof is supported by brackets. Square, tapered columns support the front porch.

The home was built for Albert R. Barnes, a prominent lawyer in Salt Lake City. He served as Utah's attorney general from 1908 until 1917. H. B. Whitman purchased the house in 1925 and maintained it as a rental property.

771 Fifth Avenue `B`

BUILT: 1908
STYLE: Craftsman
ARCHITECT: H. Sidney Fredrickson
BUILDER: H. Bittner
ORIGINAL OWNER: Oscar H. Jensen

This unique Craftsman home has half-timber work on the façade typical of the Tudor Revival style. There is a small bay window projecting from that façade. The small front porch has bargeboards, brackets, exposed framing, and paired square columns.

Oscar H. Jensen was a clerk with the U.S. Post Office when he moved into this home. He later worked as an accountant for the firm of Haskins and Sells. He lived here until 1921. The home was then held as a rental property until 1933. James E. King was the resident owner until 1939. In the late 1970s the home was run as a "cooperative residence" known as Blithering Heights.

775 Fifth Avenue `B`

BUILT: 1893
STYLE: Victorian Eclectic
ORIGINAL OWNER: Edward Orson Howard

This two-story Victorian home's façade is dominated by a Bungalow-style front porch added around 1915. The front gables of the home have carved sunburst panels.

Edward O. Howard was a bookkeeper at the Walker Brothers Bank when he moved into this home. He would eventually become director of the bank and of the Salt Lake branch of the Federal Reserve Bank. Other positions held by Mr. Howard included president of the Utah Light and Traction Company, director of Utah-Idaho Sugar, and trustee for Westminster College. After 1898 he continued to own this home but moved to a larger residence on South Temple. He eventually lived at 1219 South Temple.

SIXTH AVENUE

253 Sixth Avenue

BUILT: 1900
STYLE: Victorian Eclectic
BUILDER: John W. A. Timms
ORIGINAL OWNER: John W. A. Timms

The complex massing of this Victorian home is typical of the Queen Anne style. Below each large gable is a curved, paneled, brick bay. The front porch has a dentiled wooden cornice and squat, paired wood columns.

Contractor John W. A. Timms built this home for his family. Mr. Timms was a member of a family of builders in the Avenues. In the 1890s he was a partner in a lumber company, the Phoenix Planing Mill Company. He later established Timms and Sons Contractors, and the business operated from his home until his death in 1916. His wife, Sarah Ann, remained in the residence until 1940. In 1945 the property was purchased by Ping Y. Gin, who owned and operated the Coconut Garden Café and later the Bamboo Garden Café.

259 Sixth Avenue

BUILT: 1890
STYLE: Victorian Eclectic
BUILDER: John W. A. Timms
ORIGINAL OWNER: John W. A. Timms

This small Victorian cottage has extensive exterior decorations. The gable has a wood-paneled sunburst decoration, and the paired front windows are surrounded by ornate trim. The southwest front porch is now enclosed.

John W. A. Timms built this home and 263 Sixth Avenue as rental properties. He lived at 253 Sixth Avenue. Mr. Timms was partnered with Thomas Oakey in the Phoenix Planing Mill, which may explain the lavish exterior. In the early 1920s Jacobus J. and Hillgie Van Langeveld purchased the home. Mr. Van Langeveld was a clerk for several downtown stores.

266–268 Sixth Avenue

BUILT: 1914
STYLE: Prairie Bungalow
ORIGINAL OWNER: Aldridge N. Evans

This is a low, hip-roofed, Prairie-style bungalow duplex. The bungalow design was commonly built throughout Utah during this time period.

This duplex was built in 1914 for Aldridge N. Evans, secretary and assistant manager of the Keeley Ice Cream Company. He would eventually be vice president of the restaurant company known as Keeley's. Mr. Evans lived on one side of the house until his death in 1950. The Evans family still owned the property in the 1980s.

267 Sixth Avenue A

BUILT: 1917
STYLE: Prairie Bungalow
BUILDER: Sidney E. Mulcock
ORIGINAL OWNER: B. Spencer and Edna B. Young

This low, hip-roofed, Prairie-style bungalow is a common design built throughout Utah between 1910 and 1925. The upper walls are covered in stucco while the lower portion is dark brown brick.

Developer Sidney E. Mulcock built several homes in the Avenues between 1917 and 1925. He sold this property to Spencer and Edna Young. Mr. Young was a great-grandson of Brigham Young. He worked in real estate and for the Home Owner's Loan Corporation. He was a member of the Utah legislature from 1932 to 1934.

273 Sixth Avenue A

BUILT: 1897
STYLE: Victorian Eclectic
ARCHITECT: Richard K. A. Kletting
ORIGINAL OWNER: Constance M. Kletting

This is a one-story Victorian cottage with an eyelid window in the front roof. Both the round front and large front windows have colored art glass. The recessed front porch has turned wood columns.

This small home was designed by prominent Utah architect Richard K. A. Kletting for Constance Kletting. Mr. Kletting, known as "the dean of Utah architects," had been the architect of the Utah State Capitol, the original Salt Palace, the original Saltair Pavilion, and several other prominent Utah buildings. Members of the Kletting family owned this home until 1950.

283 Sixth Avenue A

BUILT: 1900
STYLE: Victorian Eclectic
ARCHITECT: Richard K. A. Kletting
ORIGINAL OWNER: William G. and Margaret N. Patrick

This two-story, brick Victorian home has a corbelled belt course that runs along the top of the exterior. The wide front porch is supported by Doric wood columns. All front windows have leaded glass transoms.

This home was built for William G. and Margaret N. Patrick. Mr. Patrick was vice president and cofounder of the Decker Patrick Dry Goods Company and served as president of the Western Garment Manufacturing Company. He was a member of the Mormon Tabernacle Choir. He died in this home in 1936.

287 Sixth Avenue [A]

BUILT: 1912
STYLE: American Four Square
ARCHITECT: David C. Dart
BUILDER: Adolph and Lucy Richter
ORIGINAL OWNER: Ezra J. and Nellie B. Howell

This brick Four Square has wide eaves and a broad front porch. The porch gable has a unique spindled façade. The second story windows have been replaced.

Prolific Avenues developers Adolf and Lucy Richter had David C. Dart design this home. Ezra and Nellie Howell purchased the property upon completion. Mr. Howell was involved in the livestock industry. The Howell family lived here until the mid-1940s.

322 Sixth Avenue [A]

BUILT: 1909
STYLE: Craftsman Bungalow
BUILDER: C. N. Christensen
ORIGINAL OWNER: Milton W. Snow

This is a one-story bungalow with Craftsman details. The eave brackets are left exposed as is typical of the style. The large front window has been replaced by a picture window. Iron posts replaced the front porch's original columns in the 1960s.

This home was built for Milton W. Snow, son of LDS Church president Lorenzo Snow. He was a dentist and later the curator of the LDS Bureau of Information on Temple Square. He lived here until 1912 before moving to 507 Fifth Avenue. He maintained this home as a rental until 1923.

353 Sixth Avenue [A]

BUILT: 1890
STYLE: Victorian Eclectic
ORIGINAL OWNER: Oliver A. and Georgia Jennings

This two-story Victorian home had been covered by aluminum siding and stripped of much of its detailing in the 1950s. In 2001 the exterior of the home was restored.

This home was built for $4,500 for Oliver and Georgia Jennings, who held it as a rental property for the next twenty years. Mr. and Mrs. Jennings also had 361 and 367 Sixth Avenue and 320 D Street as investments. Mr. Jennings was the secretary-treasurer of the Empire Utah Laundry Company. The home's tenants, Samuel and Georgia Williamson, purchased the property in 1910. Mr. Williamson was a grain broker.

374 Sixth Avenue A

BUILT: 1898
STYLE: Victorian Eclectic
ORIGINAL OWNER: Orson D. Romney

This one-and-one-half-story Victorian house is probably of pattern-book design. It has a main gable roof and a smaller, gabled front bay. The front porch is supported by wood Doric columns.

Orson D. Romney, assistant manager and secretary-treasurer of the Taylor, Romney, and Armstrong Company, had this home built as a rental property. Mr. Romney was part of the prominent Romney family of builders and lumber company owners. He sold the home to a nurse named Abbie S. Young, widow of Brigham Young Jr., in 1920. She lived here until 1954. Mrs. Young had been trained by Dr. Ellis R. Shipp and was one of Utah's first trained nurses.

403 Sixth Avenue A

BUILT: 1875
STYLE: Victorian Eclectic
ORIGINAL OWNER: Olof A. T. Forssell

The frame portion of this home was built around 1875 as a vernacular structure. The stucco exterior, small front porch, and front windows are later alterations.

In 1887 Olof Forssell added the brick section to the older frame home. Mr. Forssell had been a teamster and later a janitor at McCornick and Company. The Forssell family lived here until 1909. The property was bought in 1914 by Frank J. Folland, who operated the Sixth Avenue Drug Store located at 402 Sixth Avenue. He later renamed the store the Folland Drug Store. The Folland family owned this home until 1949.

453 Sixth Avenue A

BUILT: 1909
STYLE: Craftsman Bungalow
ARCHITECT: H. S. Fredrickson
BUILDER: H. S. Fredrickson
ORIGINAL OWNER: William J. Leaker

This Craftsman home was extensively damaged by fire in 2006. The home was rebuilt to look nearly like the original structure. The cobblestone chimney and exposed rafters are typical of the Craftsman style. The original posts supporting the porch and gabled entry were square and paneled. The new posts are smaller. The divided windows in the dormer were replaced with undivided windows. The interior of the home has been stripped of nearly all its original woodwork.

William J. Leaker had this home built as an investment. The first resident owner was Emanuel Kempner, who occupied the residence in 1913. Mr. Kempner owned the Kempner Insurance Agency and was a developer of the Park Utah Mines in Park City. He lived here until 1921.

474 Sixth Avenue A

BUILT: 1926
STYLE: Tudor Revival
ORIGINAL OWNER: Louisa Lofgren Larson

The half-timber decoration on the gable ends of this home's façade is typical of the Tudor Revival style. This style was popular in the 1920s in the United States. At the northeast corner of the house is a recessed porch with a heavy brick corner column.

The home was built for Louisa Lofgren Larson, an immigrant from Sweden and convert to the LDS Church. She lived in the home until 1933 and then maintained it as a rental property. From 1946 to 1949 Rex S. Baird lived in the house. Mr. Baird was assistant general manager of Utah Sand and Gravel Corporation.

480 Sixth Avenue A

BUILT: 1905
STYLE: Commercial
ORIGINAL OWNER: Albert and Serena Olson

This wood-frame commercial structure retains most of its original character. The main building had a small addition added in 1908.

Albert and Serena Olson had this store built for their grocery store and operated the business for thirty-five years. They also built a home behind the store at 283 G Street. This building remained a grocery store under various names and owners until 1967. In the 1970s a shoe and boot repair shop operated here.

504 Sixth Avenue B

BUILT: 1904
STYLE: Bungalow
BUILDER: Sidney E. Mulcock
ORIGINAL OWNER: Earl B. Wixcey

This one-story brick bungalow is typical of those built in the early 1920s in Salt Lake City. The porch has fascia boards, returns, and decorative wood framing.

Sidney E. Mulcock built this home and 508 Sixth Avenue. He sold it upon completion to Earl B. Wixcey. A reporter for the *Salt Lake Tribune*, Mr. Wixcey later became a secretary for Senator Elbert D. Thomas. In 1933 the property was purchased by Ralph I. Branning, who owned the Branning Chili Parlor. James E. L. Carey purchased the home in 1946. He had been a county commissioner in Duchesne County and laid out the town of Fruitland. In Salt Lake City he served as a draftsman for the Salt Lake County Recorder's Office. He lived in this home until 1952.

524 Sixth Avenue [B]

BUILT: 1908
STYLE: Bungalow
BUILDER: Andrew Samuelson
ORIGINAL OWNER: Andrew Samuelson

This one-story bungalow has arched openings across its wide front porch. The home is covered in wood-shingle siding.

Andrew Samuelson, a builder with the firm of Schumann and Samuelson, lived in this home until 1914. In 1922 another contractor, Henry Schravens, purchased the property. Mr. Schravens built a number of schools and several prominent Salt Lake City buildings including the old Salt Lake Public Library and the Mountain States Telephone and Telegraph building.

529 Sixth Avenue [B]

BUILT: 1899
STYLE: Victorian Eclectic
ARCHITECT: David C. Dart
BUILDER: Brice W. Sainsbury
ORIGINAL OWNER: David J. and Mary Elizabeth Watts

The front gable on this Victorian home has a bracketed hood over what were originally three tiny double-hung windows. The number of windows has been reduced to two. Below the wooden cornice is a corbelled brick belt course. The front porch is supported by slender columns.

This home was built for David and Mary Elizabeth Watts. Mr. Watts worked for sixty-three years as a barber in the LDS Church's office building. He was the personal barber for LDS Church president David O. McKay. He lived in this home until his death in 1956. This is one of the earliest homes designed by David C. Dart in the city. He was the architect of numerous Avenues homes of varying style.

537 Sixth Avenue [B]

BUILT: 1902
STYLE: Victorian Eclectic
ORIGINAL OWNER: Harry L. and Jean R. Finch

This one-and-one-half-story Victorian cottage on a corner lot has a main hip roof with a front dormer window and east-side gabled bays. The gables, together with their barge-boards and returns, are covered in wood-shingle siding. The original front porch columns have been replaced by iron posts.

Harry L. Finch had this home built for his family. Mr. Finch was partnered with Richard E. Rogers in the ownership of Finch's Café at 20 East 200 South. He later served as a parks commissioner for the city and served as Salt Lake City police chief. He lived here with his wife, Jean, until his death. Their daughter, Nancy E. Finch, inherited the home. She was a manager at the Utah Power and Light Company.

554 Sixth Avenue   B

BUILT: 1908
STYLE: Victorian Eclectic
BUILDER: William McCartney
ORIGINAL OWNER: Hattie J. Selay

This late-Victorian home could be described as a transitional bungalow as it has a bungalow layout with Victorian detailing. Iron posts replaced the original porch posts in the mid-1970s. The front porch was recently restored. The window in the front gable has been altered.

William McCartney built this home along with 558 and 562 Sixth Avenue. He sold this property upon completion to Hattie J. Selay, who lived here with her brother and mother until 1915. That year, Charles C. Davis moved into the home. Mr. Davis was the manager of the Bamberger Coal Company.

564 Sixth Avenue   B

BUILT: 1908
STYLE: Victorian Eclectic
BUILDER: Elmer E. Casady
ORIGINAL OWNER: Frank F. Phelps Jr.

This late-Victorian home could also be described as a transitional bungalow as it has a bungalow layout and Victorian detailing.

Elmer E. Casady built this house and the adjacent 566 Sixth Avenue. Frank F. Phelps Jr., who ran a printing shop, purchased the property upon completion. In 1928, Ada and Jed G. Woolley bought the house. Mr. Woolley, a prominent engineer, had surveyed the Washington Heights area of Ogden and the Ogden Golf and Country Club. After working on major hydroelectric projects in the early 1920s, he eventually became the manager of the Utah Power and Light Company. His wife, Ada, was president of the Ladies Literary Club and the State Federation of Women's Clubs. The Woolley family owned this home into the 1980s.

609 Sixth Avenue   B

BUILT: 1890
STYLE: Victorian Eclectic
ORIGINAL OWNER: Emanuel Olbrick

The façade of this large structure is dominated by a two-story porch added in 1913. The building was originally a large Victorian home and is an example of an early apartment conversion in the Avenues. The heavy tapered wood porch columns and cornice make the building look larger than its actual size.

The original Victorian home was built for Emanuel Olbrick, a realtor. His wife, Nellie, was the matron of the Ladies Turkish Bath Department at the Salt Lake Hot Springs Sanitarium Company.

621 Sixth Avenue B

BUILT: 1899
STYLE: Victorian Eclectic
ARCHITECT: Richard K. A. Kletting
BUILDER: N. J. Dean
ORIGINAL OWNER: Fred M. and Emily W. Stockdale

This one-story Victorian cottage has a projecting bay. The front porch is supported by turned wood columns and decorative corner brackets.

Richard K. A. Kletting designed this home for Fred and Emily Stockdale. Mr. Kletting is known as the "dean of Utah architects" and was the architect of the Utah State Capitol. Mr. Stockdale was a clerk for the R. K. Thomas Dry Goods Company. The Stockdale family lived in this home until 1928.

622 Sixth Avenue B

BUILT: 1900
STYLE: Victorian Eclectic
BUILDER: Frank G. Shepherd
ORIGINAL OWNER: Frank G. Shepherd

This one-and-one-half-story Victorian home has a gable roof covered in shingles. The home also features a three-sided hip-roofed porch supported by Doric columns.

Frank G. Shepherd built this home as a rental property. He lived next door at 626 Sixth Avenue. Annie Bywater bought the property in 1909. Mrs. Bywater was the owner and operator of a clothing factory that supplied the ZCMI department stores. Her husband, William H. Bywater, was the Salt Lake City fire chief from 1904 to 1925.

634 Sixth Avenue B

BUILT: 1898
STYLE: Victorian Eclectic
ORIGINAL OWNER: Joseph J. Coles

This one-and-one-half-story Victorian home has a gable roof and a large, gabled west dormer. In the mid-1950s asbestos shingles covered the original exterior of the gables. The siding has since been removed to reveal the original shingle work. There is a small transom over the entry, and the front porch is supported by Doric wood columns.

This home was built for Joseph J. Coles, who worked for the Salt Lake City Railway Company. He directed the construction of the Emigration Canyon Railway and later served as a building engineer for the *Deseret News*, the Knutsford Hotel, and the Paris Company Department Store. He lived here until 1924.

687 Sixth Avenue `B`

BUILT: 1922
STYLE: Prairie Bungalow
BUILDER: Charles A. Peterson and Company
ORIGINAL OWNER: Paul Walton

This home's low hip roof, brick exterior, and heavy brick porch columns are typical of the common Prairie bungalows built throughout Utah between 1910 and 1924.

Charles A. Peterson and Company built this home along with 681 and 683 Sixth Avenue for the Cannon Real Estate Investment Company. Upon its completion, it was sold to Paul Walton, a rancher from Wyoming and employee of the Baldwin and Utah Radio Company. In 1935 the home was purchased by Ortis L. Skaife, who was a traffic manager at the American Smelting and Mining Company.

703 Sixth Avenue `B`

BUILT: 1908
STYLE: Victorian Eclectic
BUILDER: S. Lester Jr.
ORIGINAL OWNER: James Tate

The style of this Victorian cottage is more typical of homes built in Salt Lake City between 1890 and 1905. However, property records indicate that this home and 709 Sixth Avenue were built in 1908. By then Craftsman-style homes were more commonly being built in the Avenues. The original porch columns have been replaced by iron posts.

William P. Hemphill and James W. Collins of the Russell Collins Trust Company built this home as an investment. James Tate purchased the home upon completion for $3,900 and lived here until 1924. Mr. Tate was employed as a clerk, packer, and foreman during this time period. Lewis and Lucille Williams owned the home between 1928 and 1941. Mr. Williams was the manager of the F. J. Lucas Grocery Store.

709 Sixth Avenue `B`

BUILT: 1908
STYLE: Victorian Eclectic
BUILDER: S. Lester Jr.
ORIGINAL OWNER: Russell Collins Trust Company

The style of this Victorian cottage is more typical of homes built in Salt Lake City between 1890 and 1905. However, property records indicate that this home and 703 Sixth Avenue were built in 1908. By then the Craftsman style was more prevalent in the Avenues.

William P. Hemphill and James W. Collins of the Russell Collins Trust Company built this home as an investment. The first residents were tenants Fred D. and Elizabeth Ulmer. Mr. Ulmer was architect for his father's firm before working for the Union Pacific and Oregon Short Line Railroads. The Ulmer family purchased the home in 1915, and Fred and Elizabeth continued living here until 1929. The home stood vacant for five years during the Great Depression.

711 Sixth Avenue   B

BUILT: 1903
STYLE: Victorian Eclectic
ORIGINAL OWNER: Mary Hull

This Victorian home had a major porch alteration in 1913. That year the Bungalow-style porch covered the entire front façade.

This home was owned by several investors until 1908 when George F. and Carrie G. Strickley bought the property. They had lived in the home as tenants from the time it was built. Mr. Strickley owned the Strickley Candy Company. They lived in the home until 1927. Members of the Strickley family maintained ownership of the home as a rental property until 1944.

715 Sixth Avenue   B

BUILT: 1904
STYLE: Victorian Eclectic
ORIGINAL OWNER: John H. Richards

The front gable of this Victorian cottage was covered in wood siding in the 1970s. A corbelled brick belt course runs along the house at the top of the windows. The original porch columns have been replaced by iron posts.

John H. Richards was the first resident owner of this property. He was a cashier with the Consolidated Wagon and Machine Company. He lived here only a year when he sold the home to Stephen Gillett, an inspector for the Bureau of Animal Industry. Alma W. and Mabel Farnsworth bought the property in 1912. Mr. Farnsworth was a civil engineer. They lived in the home through the 1940s.

718 Sixth Avenue   B

BUILT: 1910
STYLE: Bungalow
BUILDER: Quinn and Son
ORIGINAL OWNER: Orodio C. Hart

This one-story bungalow has a front gable supported by heavy purlins. It is covered in wood-shingle siding and has a dentiled, horizontal cornice.

Contractors John B. Quinn and Marcus Shumann built this home and sold it to Orodio C. Hart, a chemist at the Portland Cement Company. He lived here until 1918 when the residence became a rental property. In 1927 James J. and Hilda S. Ryser bought the home. Mr. Ryser was a long-time employee of the ZCMI department store. He lived here until 1968. The Ryser family maintained ownership of the home into the 1980s.

723 Sixth Avenue

BUILT: 1922
STYLE: Prairie Bungalow
BUILDER: Jesse H. Newton
ORIGINAL OWNER: Rufus K. and Annie E. Hardy

This one-story brick bungalow has an elongated front window to emphasize the horizontal character of the home.

Developer Jesse H. Newton built this home for four thousand dollars and sold it to Rufus and Annie Hardy. Mr. Hardy was the supervisor of the Western States Life Insurance Company. He was also a leader in the LDS Church, serving on the First Council of Seventy. He lived in this residence until his death in 1945.

727 Sixth Avenue B

BUILT: 1903
STYLE: Victorian Eclectic
BUILDER: Walter G. Schmierer
ORIGINAL OWNER: Walter G. Schmierer

This Victorian home has a main hip roof and a projecting, gabled front bay. The front gable has bargeboards and is covered in patterned wood-shingle siding. Triangular window cutouts were added to the gables in the 1980s.

Contractor Walter G. Schmierer built this home and sold it one year later to James William Collins, who was vice president of the Tracy Loan and Trust Company at the time. He worked for the company for fifty-five years, moving up from office boy at age fifteen to chairman of the board. He also held positions with the Federal Reserve Bank of San Francisco and the Independent Coal and Coke Company. His brother, C. Louis Collins, was resident owner of the home from 1914 to 1939.

738 Sixth Avenue B

BUILT: 1910
STYLE: Bungalow
ORIGINAL OWNER: Edward S. Harvey

This one-story bungalow has a low hip roof and front center dormer. The wide front porch is supported by heavy wood columns on brick posts. Rafter ends were originally left exposed in the eaves for decorative effect. They are now covered in bead-board siding.

This home was built for Edward S. Harvey, an engineer with the Union Pacific Railroad and Oregon Short Line Railroad. Mr. Harvey owned the property until 1944.

752 Sixth Avenue   B

BUILT: 1925
STYLE: Commercial
BUILDER: B. A. Rudd
ORIGINAL OWNER: Angus McKellar

This corner commercial structure is typical of the neighborhood markets found throughout Salt Lake City between 1890 and 1950.

Angus McKellar of the McKellar Real Estate Company built this building and leased it to Arnisson Hoskisson, who opened the A. Hoskisson Grocery Store. There were a number of Hoskisson stores in Salt Lake City. This store, No. 8, only operated for three years. The Brimley Brothers Cash Market was located here from 1929 until 1932. Businesses continued to change rapidly in this location for several years. From the 1970s until the late 1990s the building was a laundry.

761 Sixth Avenue   B

BUILT: 1899
STYLE: Victorian Eclectic
ARCHITECT: Edgar W. Druce
BUILDER: Edgar W. Druce
ORIGINAL OWNER: Edgar W. Druce

This Victorian residence is the largest home in this portion of the Avenues. The large front porch has thin, tapered wood columns with decorative brackets at the top. A sandstone wall runs along the street, and the original iron fence sits atop the wall.

Edgar W. Druce designed and built several homes in the Avenues as investment properties. He built this large residence for himself and lived here until 1908. Margaret Nelson, a linotype operator for the *Salt Lake Tribune*, purchased the property in 1913. Her father had been the editor of the paper. She lived in this house until her death in 1953 when her sister, Esther Nelson, inherited the property.

813 Sixth Avenue   B

BUILT: 1907
STYLE: Victorian Eclectic
ORIGINAL OWNER: Ephraim Allen

Both front gables on this one-and-one-half-story Victorian home are covered in patterned wood-shingle siding. The porch columns were replaced by iron posts in the 1960s.

This late-Victorian home was built for Ephraim Allen. Mr. Allen, who was employed by the Utah Ore Sampling Company, lived in this home until 1936. The Allen family then maintained the residence as a rental property for the next forty years.

817 Sixth Avenue

B

BUILT: 1905
STYLE: Victorian Eclectic
ARCHITECT: J. P. Stinger
BUILDER: Oscar Engdahl
ORIGINAL OWNER: Louis H. Stohr

This Victorian home has a front porch with Doric columns. The west side of the home has a curved, brick bay window. The gables are covered in wood-shingle siding and there is a small triangular window in the porch gable.

Oscar Engdahl built several homes including this one in this portion of Sixth Avenue. Louis Stohr purchased the property upon completion. He was a branch manager for the New York Life Insurance Company and was also a director of the Tintic Mining Company. William W. and Cora Farley became the owners in 1944. They rented the home to Marion C. and Betty L. P. Tanner. Mr. Tanner was the shop foreman of O. C. Tanner Jewelry Company. A compatible rear addition was recently added to the second story.

SEVENTH AVENUE

229 Seventh Avenue D

BUILT: 1920
STYLE: Prairie
ARCHITECT: H. J. McKean
BUILDER: H. J. McKean
ORIGINAL OWNER: Hyrum and Claire Bergstrom

This home's horizontal massing with low, hip roof and dark brick are characteristic of the Prairie style.

The house was built for Hyrum and Claire Bergstrom. Mr. Bergstrom, a prominent dentist, worked for the Salt Lake Clinic until 1924 before opening his own practice. He was president of the Utah State Dental Association and the State Board of Dental Examiners. Mr. Bergstrom was also active in the Alta Club and Salt Lake Country Club. He lived here until his death in 1969.

254 Seventh Avenue A

BUILT: 1905
STYLE: Colonial Revival
ARCHITECT: Richard K. A. Kletting
ORIGINAL OWNER: Isaac A. Clayton

This Colonial Revival home has a hip roof and pairs of tall chimneys. There is an eyelid window in the roof. The small west porch has been enclosed and the eaves are covered in aluminum siding.

Utah State Capitol architect Richard K. A. Kletting designed this home for Isaac A. Clayton. Mr. Clayton was the cofounder of the Inland Crystal Salt Company, the first salt manufacturing company in the state. He also played a major role in the development and management of Saltair Resort and the Salt Lake and Los Angeles Railroad. He was married to Fannie Van Cott Young, the youngest daughter of Brigham Young. Stephen L. Richards, an apostle for the LDS Church, purchased the property in 1925.

259 Seventh Avenue D

BUILT: 1896
STYLE: Classical Revival
ARCHITECT: Walter E. Ware
ORIGINAL OWNER: Gill S. Peyton

This Classical Revival mansion is elevated by a stone platform decorated by iron fencing. Four Corinthian columns support the two-story entrance portico. The front doorway is surrounded by a columned pediment shelter and there is a semielliptical porch above. Semicircular bays on each side of the house originally included open, second-story porches.

Known as the McIntyre Mansion, this large residence was built for Gill S. Peyton, manager of the Mercer Gold Mining and Milling Company. William H. McIntyre purchased the home in 1901. He and his brother Samuel established a profitable cattle-drive business as young men and invested money in several Utah mining and business ventures. The home is currently owned and maintained by Intermountain Corporation.

351 Seventh Avenue D

BUILT: 1904
STYLE: Victorian Eclectic
ORIGINAL OWNER: William J. Bennett

The first floor of this home was part of the original Victorian structure. In 1916 heavy re-modeling of the second story included the addition of a Prairie-style hip roof. The second floor was originally wood frame with casement windows. It has since been covered in stucco and the casements have been replaced by large picture windows.

William J. Bennett replaced a pre-1898 frame home with this structure and moved here from 371 Fourth Avenue. He was secretary-treasurer of the Bennett Paint and Glass Company. The Bennett family maintained ownership of the home until 1935. Joseph V. Peterson, owner of the J. V. Peterson Body Building Company, bought the home that year.

361 Seventh Avenue D

BUILT: 1905
STYLE: American Four Square
ARCHITECT: Fred A. Hall
BUILDER: Peter Anderson
ORIGINAL OWNER: George H. and Calaveras M. Davis

This Four Square–type home has Classical Revival decoration on the exterior. Brick quoins accent the corners of the house and are topped by Ionic capitals. The second story has an off-center bay window. The large front porch is supported by Doric columns and square corner posts.

This home was built for George and Calaveras Davis. Mr. Davis had mining interests in Bingham Canyon and was also an owner of the Mullet-Kelley Clothing Store. Sylvester E. and Bernice Pier bought the home in 1918. He was the general manager of the Salt Lake Hardware Company.

369 Seventh Avenue D

BUILT: 1905
STYLE: Victorian Eclectic
ORIGINAL OWNER: Curtis B. Hawley

The front gable of this house was covered in glass in the 1970s. The original art glass transoms above the first-floor door and windows remain. The porch is supported by Doric wood columns.

This home was built for Curtis B. Hawley at a cost of $2,400. Mr. Hawley was secretary and manager of the Utah Electric Company, a large, early electrical supply business for the Intermountain West. Mr. Hawley was also active in civic affairs as president of the Salt Lake City Chamber of Commerce and the Utah Tuberculosis Association. The United Danish Evangelical Lutheran Church bought the home in 1922. The congregation maintained the residence as the parsonage for the church, which was located at First Avenue and E Street.

371 Seventh Avenue [D]

BUILT: 1906
STYLE: American Four Square
ORIGINAL OWNER: Rhoda Welcher

This Four Square–type home has a broad porch with paired, slender square columns standing on paneled posts. The hip roof has a front center dormer window. Rafter tails in the eaves are left exposed as is typical of the Craftsman style.

Alexander and Florence Watson had this home built as an investment and sold it to Rhoda Welker. James Cash and Berta Penney purchased the property in 1909 for seven thousand dollars. They resided in this house during the time that the headquarters for Mr. Penney's Golden Rule Stores was located in Salt Lake City. In 1913 he changed the name to J. C. Penney and moved the headquarters to New York City. His Salt Lake City manager, Frank R. Payne, bought the house in 1918. Wayne Green and Linda Kelly purchased the residence in 1994 and undertook an extensive restoration of the building.

383 Seventh Avenue [D]

BUILT: 1904
STYLE: Victorian Eclectic
ORIGINAL OWNER: George E. and Nettie C. Calder

This Victorian home has a two-story, curved front bay and a three-sided east-side bay. The front porch has been rebuilt to replicate the original structure.

George and Nettie Calder purchased this home upon completion and lived here until 1911. Mr. Calder was a clerk at the ZCMI department store. John and Eliza James acquired the property in 1929. Mr. James was a prominent civic and business leader in Salt Lake City, serving as Salt Lake County clerk, Utah insurance commissioner, and British vice consul. He formed the Utah Cambrian Society and was awarded a King's Medal from England's King George VI. He lived in this home until his death in 1954.

407 Seventh Avenue [D]

BUILT: 1906
STYLE: Transitional Bungalow
ORIGINAL OWNER: Heber C. Wilkes

This is one of the first bungalows in the Avenues, built during a time when Victorian cottages were still being constructed there. The low, hip roof and exposed rafter tails are more typical of the Craftsman style. The home is set farther back on the property, as a frame-structured store once stood near the street.

James E. Wilkes, an emigrant from England and an LDS Church convert, owned the southwest portion of this block. His three sons built homes here. Heber C. Wilkes, who had been a clerk with various companies, opened a store on Seventh Avenue when this home was built. His wife, Lizzette Evans Wilkes, lost the home to Zion's Savings Bank and Trust after Heber's death, but her family helped her regain ownership and she remained in the home until 1948.

471 Seventh Avenue D

BUILT: 1890
STYLE: Victorian Eclectic
ORIGINAL OWNER: John T. Axton

This one-story, wood-frame Victorian cottage has more ornate detailing than is typical of small Avenues homes of this style. The east-side gable has diamond-pattern shingles, and the front porch originally had a small, diamond-shingled gable over the entry. The bulbous, turned porch columns with heavy ornate brackets at the top replicate the original design. The main body of the home is covered in shiplap siding and corner boards.

John T. Axton, whose father lived next door at 473 Seventh Avenue, had this home built. He was a shipping clerk with Co-op Wagon and Machine Company. He and his wife, Jane, lived here for only a few years before moving to Wyoming and maintaining this property as a rental unit. In 1940 Edward M. and Emily Reid purchased the home.

539 Seventh Avenue D

BUILT: 1924
STYLE: Tudor Revival
BUILDER: Elijah Thompson
ORIGINAL OWNER: Edward R. Callister

This one-and-one-half-story Tudor Revival home has a half-timber and brick exterior typical of the style. There is an elongated, south-facing shed dormer above a first-story three-sided bay. The second-floor railing is a recent addition.

Contractor Elijah Thompson built this home for Edward R. Callister, a prominent Salt Lake City attorney. He had lived at 519 Seventh Avenue before moving into this home. Members of the Callister family owned the home until 1942. The home was bought in 1945 by Milton R. Hunter, a historian of the LDS Church.

587 Seventh Avenue D

BUILT: 1909
STYLE: Dutch Colonial Revival
ORIGINAL OWNER: William W. Riter

This is a good example of Dutch Colonial Revival design in the Avenues. The cross gambrel roofs of the home are typical of the style. The front porch has Doric columns.

Avenues developer John Dorius built this home and sold it to William W. Riter, the president of Deseret Savings Bank. He transferred the property to his brother Levi Riter, a mining engineer and manager of the Dragon Consolidated Mining Company. In 1914 Levi moved to 76 B Street and sold this house to Eugene Stacey, who was an engineer with the Union Pacific and Oregon Short Line Railroad.

602–620 Seventh Avenue B

BUILT: 1907
STYLE: Victorian Eclectic
ORIGINAL OWNER: Lucy Watkins

This long, one-story Victorian structure is a unique multifamily apartment building. Each of the six units has its own door facing the street. Small round vents are found above each of the brick, arched windows. The small, gable-roofed porches have been rebuilt to look similar to the original ones. Some of the original Victorian details have been stripped from the building.

Lucy Watkins, the widow of William Watkins, was the original owner. Mrs. Watkins was the proprietor of the Palace Café and owned this property until 1923. E. D. Sorenson was the next owner.

751 Seventh Avenue D

BUILT: 1904
STYLE: Victorian Eclectic
ORIGINAL OWNER: Lorenzo D. and Dora W. Young

This is a one-story Victorian home probably of pattern-book design. Asbestos shingles from the 1960s covered the original siding. The asbestos shingles have been removed from the gables.

This home was part of what was originally called Pratt's subdivision. Lorenzo and Dora Young were the first resident owners of the property. Mr. Young was the second son of Brigham Young's eleventh wife, Emaline Free. He died of pneumonia soon after moving into this home. Mrs. Young continued to own the home until 1946. She had worked for many years as a nurse at Holy Cross Hospital.

757 Seventh Avenue D

BUILT: 1905
STYLE: Victorian Eclectic
ARCHITECT: David C. Dart
ORIGINAL OWNER: William G. Farrell

The front gable of this Victorian cottage has a Palladian window with wood-shingle siding. The front porch is supported by Doric columns.

This home was part of what was originally called Pratt's subdivision. Notable Salt Lake City architect David C. Dart designed this home for William G. Farrell. Mr. Dart designed numerous homes in the Avenues of varying styles. Mr. Farrell was an insurance executive with the Pennsylvania Mutual Life Insurance Company. He also served as managing director of the Commercial Club and Chamber of Commerce. He lived here until 1919.

761 Seventh Avenue   D

BUILT: 1903
STYLE: Transitional Bungalow
ORIGINAL OWNER: Arthur Pratt Jr.

This one-story home, with its hip roof and front center dormer, shows early Bungalow influence. The porch is supported by Doric columns.

This home is one of several residences built as part of Pratt's subdivision. The home was most likely designed by prolific Avenues architect David C. Dart. The first resident owner of the property was Arthur Pratt Jr., who worked for the Salt Lake City Police Department and at the state prison. After he died of a heart attack at the age of thirty-two, his wife, Elsie, continued to own the home until 1944.

767 Seventh Avenue   D

BUILT: 1909
STYLE: Craftsman Bungalow
ORIGINAL OWNER: John Q. Ryan

This is a one-and-one-half-story Craftsman bungalow with a gable roof and gabled front entry. Brackets support the eaves. The porch columns show Craftsman decoration. The shed-roof dormers perched atop the home were added in the mid-1970s.

John Q. Ryan was the first resident owner of this home. Mr. Ryan, a pioneer in the printing industry, operated the Century Printing Company and established the first linotype printing plant west of Chicago. He lived in this home until his death in 1943.

EIGHTH TO ELEVENTH AVENUES

201 Eighth Avenue [D]

BUILT: 1915
STYLE: Craftsman Bungalow
ORIGINAL OWNER: Mary Grant Judd

The brick first story of this residence is topped with wood-frame gables. Craftsman detailing can be seen in the exposed purlins on the full-width front porch and also on the large, faceted bracket on the gables and dormer. All the current windows were installed in 2010. While of the Craftsman style, they are not replicas of the original windows.

Heber J. Grant, president of the LDS Church from 1918 until 1945, lived in this home until his death in 1945. His daughter Mary Grant Judd, owned the property while he lived there. She lived at 420 A Street. Mr. Grant, son of former Salt Lake City mayor and LDS apostle Jedediah Grant, was a successful real estate developer in the Avenues. He was also involved in the development of the sugar beet industry. The home remained in the extended Grant family until 2008. In 2010 the home was extensively restored.

206 Eighth Avenue [D]

BUILT: 1910
STYLE: Prairie
ARCHITECT: Walter E. Ware and Alberto O. Treganza
ORIGINAL OWNER: Samuel H. Allen

The horizontal emphasis of this two-story, Prairie-style building is created by the rusticated dark brick courses, stucco second story, and grouped casement windows. The hip roof includes broad eaves and a small, front center dormer window. Heavy brick columns, railing walls, and paired, exposed rafters ornament the front porch. As in other Prairie-style residences of Ware and Treganza, the architects employed a traditional central hall plan.

This house was one of several fine homes built for Dr. Samuel H. Allen. Educated at Johns Hopkins University, Dr. Allen practiced medicine with Dr. George W. Middleton, and together they formed the Salt Lake Clinic. He also worked on the staff of LDS Hospital. Currently the home is split into a duplex.

765 Eighth Avenue [D]

BUILT: 1919
STYLE: Period Revival
ARCHITECT: Carl W. Scott
ORIGINAL OWNER: Carl W. Scott

The unusual design of this house results from its complex roof massing. Two wings with clipped gable roofs flank the two-story, hip-roofed block. Their separation from the main body is emphasized by the diagonal extension of the center section roof line. Ionic columns frame the gabled entrance.

Architect Carl W. Scott graduated as a mining engineer in 1907 from the University of Utah. He began a career as a draftsman for prominent Utah architect Richard K. A. Kletting, then in 1914 established his own firm, initially in partnership with George W. Welch. He designed and built this home for himself. His best-known Utah works include the Masonic Temple and South High School.

711 Tenth Avenue D

BUILT: 1936
STYLE: Art Moderne
ORIGINAL OWNER: James Rex and Florence Clark
Miller

The projecting forms and modern materials of this now two-story stucco house set it apart as one of the few examples of Art Moderne architecture in the Avenues. Originally, metal sash windows that continued around the front corners of the home emphasized the design's freedom from historical restraint. Those windows have been replaced. The arched front door is set in a receding, round arch opening. The door features a circular window with an abstract, leaded-glass pattern. A two-story addition emerges from the rear of the home.

This home was built for James Rex and Florence Clark Miller. Mr. Miller, a successful local businessman, died in his garden two years after moving into the home. Florence Clark Miller continued to reside in the home.

381 Eleventh Avenue D

BUILT: 1913
STYLE: Prairie
ARCHITECT: Hyrum C. Pope and Harold W. Burton
ORIGINAL OWNER: Malcolm A. Keyser

This home is the best realization of a Prairie-style residence in the Avenues and perhaps all of Utah. The horizontal emphasis of the design results from the long, overhanging eaves. The house is integrated with a series of garden terraces on the sloping lot. Architects Pope and Burton are best known for several Prairie-style LDS Church structures including the Cardston, Alberta, temple.

This home was built for Malcolm A. Keyser, who was president of the M. A. Keyser Fireproof Storage Company, vice president of the Aaron Keyser Realty Insurance Company, and vice president of the Utah Paper Box Company. This residence suffered through a series of alterations over the years. The exterior has been recently restored. The interior of the home was remodeled in the 1930s and no longer retains any reflection of the Prairie style.

533 Eleventh Avenue D

BUILT: 1918
STYLE: Swiss Craftsman
ORIGINAL OWNER: Joseph Nelson

The materials and detailing of this large house follow a Swiss variation of the Craftsman style. Cut-out balcony panels on the first and second floors, as well as the octagonal pattern in the east belt course between the two floors, are among its unique decorative details.

Joseph Nelson, the president of a plumbing supply firm, lived in this house until 1927 when he sold it to Alvin A. and Ruby Pratt Beesley. Alvin Beesley was a director and executive board member of the Hotel Utah. As president and manager of the Beesley Music Company, he organized the Salt Lake local of the American Federation of Musicians union. This home was extensively restored in 2005.

MAPS OF THE SIGNIFICANT SITES

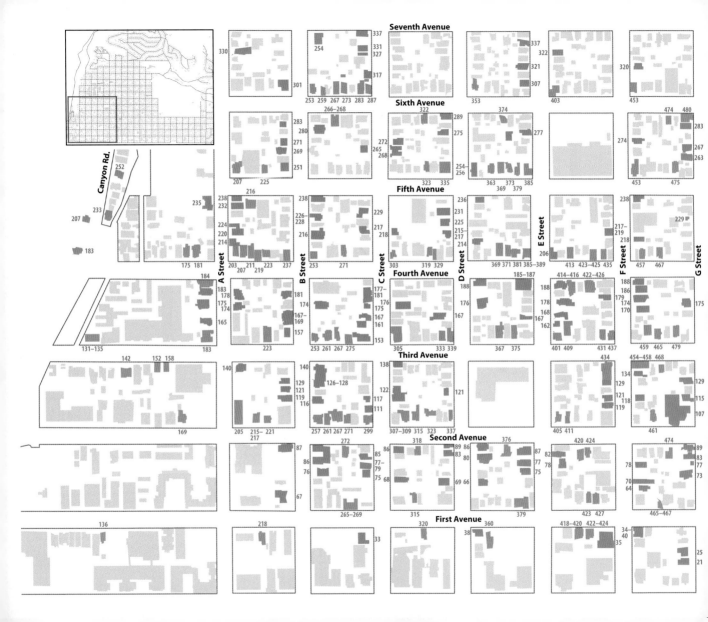

Index to Map A

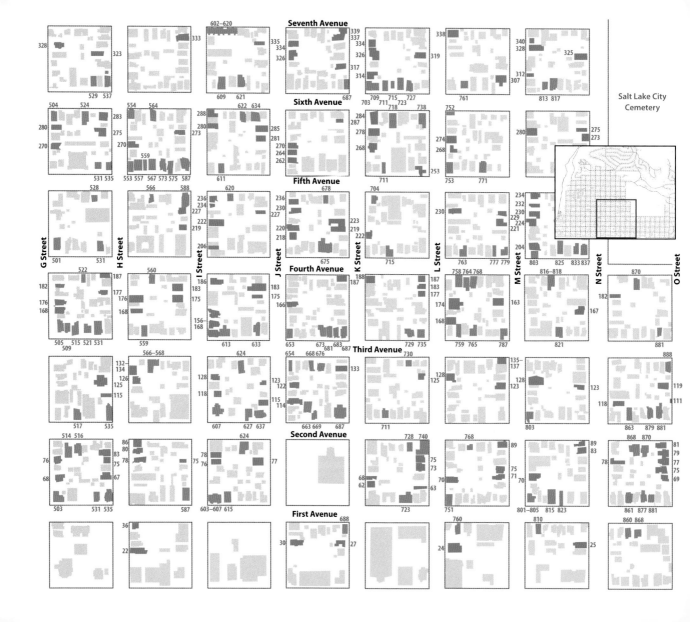

Index to Map B

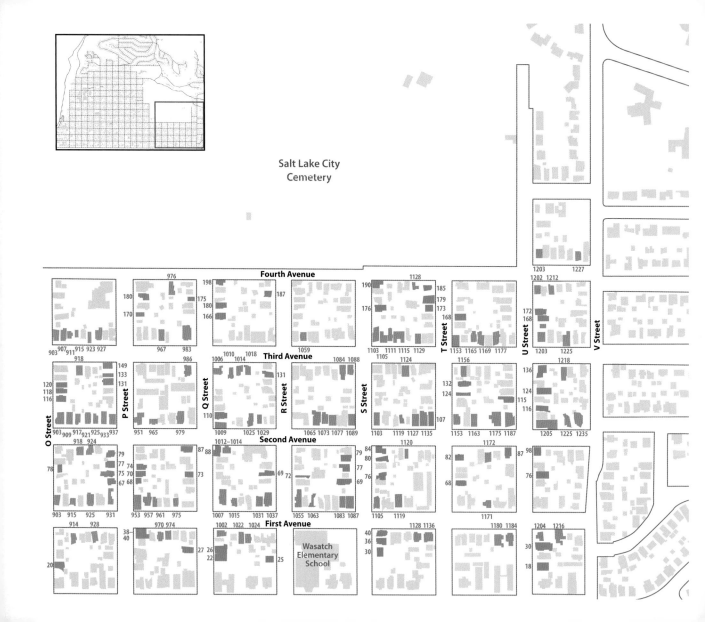

Salt Lake City
Cemetery

Fourth Avenue

Third Avenue

Second Avenue

First Avenue

Wasatch
Elementary
School

O Street
P Street
Q Street
R Street
S Street
T Street
U Street
V Street

Index to Map C

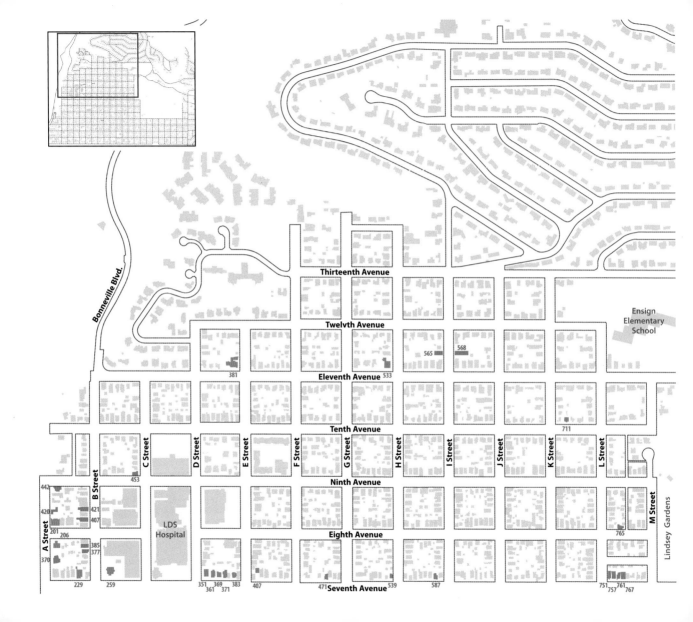

Index to Map D

NOTES

The Patterns of the Past

1. Charles S. Peterson, *Utah: A Bicentennial History* (New York: W. W. Norton, 1977), 36.
2. Nicholas G. Morgan Sr., comp., *Pioneer Map: Plat 'D' and Empire Mill Tract*, Great Salt Lake City, Map #538, Utah State Historical Society.
3. Schuster, "Evolution," in Edward W. Tullidge, *History of Salt Lake City* (Salt Lake City: Star Printing Company, 1886), 79–80. An early description of Salt Lake Valley is found in this same volume, 55–56.
4. Schuster, "Evolution," 80–82.
5. Salt Lake City Directory (1885), 62. No apparent reason for the changes has been found; Nicholas Morgan indicated that A and B streets were named early and provided a "hook up for the others"; "Historical Data," Nicholas G. Morgan Sr., *Pioneer Map: Plat 'D' and Empire Mill Tract* (Salt Lake City: Utah Historical Society). Additional map research has revealed that O Street was originally Hickory, P was named Larch, and Q was known as Box Elder. Fifth Avenue was Prospect, Sixth was named High, and Seventh was once Mountain. See Augustus Koch, *Bird's Eye View of Salt Lake City, Utah Territory, 1870* (Chicago: Chicago Lithographing Co., 1870); Map 587-1, Utah State Historical Society; Engineering Department, *Annual Report of the City Engineer for the Year 1907* (Salt Lake City, 1907), 31; Salt Lake City Directory (1907), 47–65.
6. Leonard J. Arrington, *Great Basin Kingdom* (Chicago: University of Illinois Press, 2005), 112; "The Wall," *Deseret News*, October 1 1853, 2. Each lot around the wall was assessed a tax to help finance the project. Albert Carrington, Parley P. Pratt, and Franklin D. Richards comprised the committee appointed by Mayor Jedediah M. Grant and the City Council to study the wall problem.
7. Daughters of the Utah Pioneers, comp., *Tales of Triumphant People: A History of Salt Lake County, Utah 1847–1900* (Salt Lake City, 1947), 118.
8. Ivy C. Fowler, "Story of City Creek," in Kate B. Carter, ed., *Heart Throbs of the West* (Salt Lake City, 1939–1951), 9:156–57; Daughters of the Utah Pioneers, *Tales of a Triumphant People*, 118. See also, Laura Patrick Nicholson, "The Dry Bench," in Carter, *Heart Throbs of the West*, 9:160–62.
9. Fowler, "Story of City Creek," 157.

10. Ibid.; Charles Brooks Anderson, "The Growth Patterns of Salt Lake City, Utah and Its Determining Factors" (PhD diss., New York University, 1945), 111–12.

11. Kip King Harris, "Return of the City: A Study of Architectural Restoration/Renovation in the Context of the Avenues District of Salt Lake City" (MArch thesis, University of Utah, 1978), 25–26.

12. Anderson, "Growth Patterns," 112.

13. Kate C. Snow, "Dry Canyon Stream," in Carter, *Heart Throbs of the West*, 9:162–63; Daughters of the Utah Pioneers, *Tales of a Triumphant People*, 128–29. Names prominent in the field included John Picknell, Charles B. Taylor, William Word, William Jennings, John Paul Epworth, and George Chandlers.

14. Salt Lake City Directory (1885), 86; Daughters of the Utah Pioneers, *Tales of a Triumphant People*, 129.

15. The titles received through "squatters rights" were deemed legal. July 14, 1884, was the last "Date of Deed" recorded on Morgan's map; "Index of Owners," Morgan, *Pioneer Map*.

16. Morgan, *Pioneer Map*.

17. Paul A. Wright, "The Growth and Distribution of the Mormon and Non-Mormon Populations in Salt Lake City" (Master's thesis, University of Chicago, 1970), 113–14.

18. The information regarding all the homes referred to in this text is taken from their respective site structure information forms, Avenues File, Utah State Historical Society. Filed by address.

19. Harris, "Return to the City," 27. Daughters of the Utah Pioneers, *Tales of the Triumphant People*, 130.

20. Harris, "Return to the City," 28. Ronald R. Boyce, "An Historical Geography of Greater Salt Lake City, Utah" (Master's thesis, University of Utah, 1957), 71.

21. Utah Light and Traction Company, *Overhead System, Diagram of Trolley System and Feeders* (Salt Lake City, April 30, 1915), Map #595, Utah State Historical Society. See also Harris, "Return to the City," 28. Utah Light and Traction Company, "History of Origin and Development," 10, Utah Historical Society.

22. Harris, "Return to the City," 27.

23. Wright, "Growth and Distribution," 9, 24.

24. Boyce, "Historical Geography," 47. Ronald Boyce covers the effects of the "Mormon-Gentile Culture" on pages 47–51 of his study.

25. Ibid., 50–51.

26. Salt Lake City Directory (1869), 87–152.

27. Salt Lake City Directory (1889), 1–264.

28. Salt Lake City Directory (1869), 136. Charles Savage established a partnership with artist George M. Ottinger, a volunteer fireman chief, for whom Ottinger Hall was named.

29. Wright, "Growth and Distribution," 131–34, 140.

30. For a social history of Brigham Street see Margaret D. Lester, *Brigham Street* (Salt Lake City, 1979).

31. Walter Ware's home was located at 1184 First Avenue. Lewis Telle Cannon's bungalow was constructed at 376 Second Avenue.

32. Ralph V. Chamberlin, *The University of Utah: A History of Its First Hundred Years, 1850–1950* (Salt Lake City: University of Utah Press, 1960), 174.

33. 182 G Street is the location of the only remaining home of Heber M. Wells. In 1897 he moved to 61 First Avenue, now the site of the Wells Apartments.

34. Robert S. Olpin, *Dictionary of Utah Art* (Salt Lake City: Salt Lake Art Center, 1980), 200–202, 245–249, 280–283, 285–293.

35. Daughters of the Utah Pioneers, *Tales of a Triumphant People*, 116. Henry Culmer's work is still evident in the William Culmer House, 33 C Street.

36. Anderson, "Growth Pattern," 89.

37. Ibid., 134.

38. Harry R. Browne, "Salt Lake City," 263, Pamphlet #10608, Utah State Historical Society.

39. Ibid., 263–264.

40. *Salt Lake Tribune*, January 1, 1892, 36.

41. Ibid.

42. Ibid., Browne, "Salt Lake City," 267–70, 272.

43. Other homes included Elijah Griffiths, 953 Third; Ernest G. Rognon, 959 Third; James A. Robinson, 70 P Street; Edward D. Woodruff, 986 Third; E. C. Coffin, 1037 First; and Newell Beeman, 1007 First.

44. In 1891 Lettie D. Bach had built two homes and was living at 967 Third, but in 1898 she was boarding at 664 East First South, and boarded elsewhere in subsequent years. Additions and subdivisions were often built in residential areas. In the Avenues the following additions have been identified: Nob Hill Subdivision (Eight and Ninth, between H and I Streets); Grand View Subdivision (Eight and Ninth, between L and M Streets); Pratt's Subdivision, including Vianna (Seventh and Eighth, between K and M Streets); Cooke's Subdivision (Fifth and the north half of Sixth, between L and M Streets); May's Court (First and Second, between C and D Streets); North End Subdivision (Eighth and Ninth between D and E Streets); Victoria Place (off F Street between Ninth and Tenth); and Isom Place (off the north side of H Street between Third and Fourth).

45. Salt Lake City Directory (1905), 72. The company was incorporated on January 29, 1907. See Secretary of State, Articles of Incorporation #6111, Utah State Archives, Salt Lake City.

46. Salt Lake City Directory (1907), 741, 1047. By 1908 M. D. Grash was president, with O. H. Gray as secretary. Gray resided at 74 Virginia. An example of a dwelling built by the Modern Home Building Company is 410 Seventh Avenue, built in 1912. Aaron Keyser Investment Company erected the bungalow at 530 Second Avenue in 1921; Deseret Savings and Loan was responsible for 202, 206, 210, and 214 I Street.

47. Salt Lake City Directory (1909), 797 1128, 312, 142.

48. *Salt Lake Herald*, June 15, 1915, 14; Salt Lake City Directory (1916), 142–43, 339, 349–50, 372–75, 412, 717–18, 889–90. Heber J. Grant served as president of the society, with G. J. Cannon as secretary, and R. T. Badger as treasurer. In 1913 George Romney, originally deeded land in the Avenues, headed Zion's Cooperative Home Building and Real Estate Company. On Grant's business dealings see Bryant S. Hinkley, *Heber J. H. Grant: Highlights in the Life of a Great Leader* (Salt Lake City, 1951), 51–76; and George Frederic Stratton, "The Business End of Mormonism," *Dearborn Independent*, March 27, 1926,

Pamphlet #10288, Utah State Historical Society.

49. The house at 201 Eighth Avenue transferred to Augusta Winters Grant in 1945 after her husband's death. Emily Harris Wells Grant, Heber Grant's third wife, lived at 61 First Avenue in 1892 in a home built by her husband. She later resided at 29 C Street. Another example is 257 Second Avenue, a box-type home built in 1907 by Heber Grant and sold to his brother-in-law, Joseph S. Wells.

50. *Salt Lake City Directory* (1998), interview by author with residents.

51. Four of the Castleton Brothers lived in the Avenues—Charles L., 283 H. Street; Frank M., 729 Third Avenue; James S., 823 Third Avenue; and Wallace C., 73 L Street.

52. *Deseret News*, January 17, 1951.

53. *Deseret News*, August 14, 1967.

54. Ruby K. Smith, *One Hundred Years in the Heart of Zion: A Narrative History of the Eighteenth Ward* (Salt Lake City: *Deseret News* Press, 1960), 36, 41–50; "Through Memory's Halls, Eighteenth Ward Reunion, February 22 to 27, 1953," 12, Pamphlet #3074, Utah State Historical Society; "Eighteenth Ward Chapel," Salt Lake County, State Register File, Utah State Historical Society. The chapel was reconstructed on the site next to Council Hall on Capitol Hill.

55. Several additions have been made to the basic L-shaped structure at 107 G Street. In 1941 the largest addition was completed on the southeast corner, creating a new entry and several classrooms. As mentioned, the Twentieth Ward contained many artists, poets, and musicians. *The Peep O'Day*, a periodical edited by Elias L. T. Harrison and Edward W. Tullidge, was published weekly in the Twentieth Ward and concerned itself with science, literature, and art; *The Peep O'Day* 1, No. 1 (October 20, 1864), Pamphlet #15742, Utah State Historical Society. See also Allen Roberts, "Historic Architecture of the Church of Jesus Christ of Latter-day Saints," photocopy, Preservation Office, Utah State Historical Society.

56. *Historical Sketch of the Twenty-seventh Ward Emigration Stake* (Salt Lake City, 1970).

57. *Salt Lake Tribune*, "Avenues Wards Continue to Lose Members," June 22, 2006.

58. These churches are contributing structure to the South Temple Street National Historic District.

59. Site Structure Report, Utah State Historical Society.

60. The Mount Tabor Lutheran Church constructed a new chapel at 709 East Second South.

61. *The Enterprise*, April 27, 1987.

62. Salt Lake City Directory (1885), 55. *Salt Lake Tribune*, January, 1893, 18; January, 1895. The former article includes a sketch of Lowell School. Salt Lake City Directory (1893), 508; Salt Lake City Directory (1894–95), 52.

63. Salt Lake City Directory (1900), 70. In 1924 an annex for the Longfellow School was listed at 62 J Street. In 1895 the Salt Lake City Board of Education recognized the need for a "first-class school building" in the area. See, *The Fifth Annual Report of the Public Schools of the City of Salt Lake for the Year Ending June 30th, 1895* (Salt Lake City, 1895) 14.

64. *Deseret News*, September 5, 1947.

65. Salt Lake City Directory (2008).

66. "Rowland Hall–Saint Mark's School," Salt Lake County, National Register File, Utah State Historical Society.

67. Ibid.
68. *Deseret News*, May 18, 1999.
69. *Deseret News*, November 22, 2002.
70. "The Dr. W. H. Groves Latter-day Saints Hospital, Salt Lake City," Pamphlet #8721, Utah State Historical Society.
71. *Deseret News*, November 30, 1976.
72. *Deseret News*, June 12, 1996.

A Suburban Cityscape

1. Henry Glassie, *Pattern in the Material Folk Culture of the Eastern United States* (Philadelphia: University of Pennsylvania Press, 1976) 124–33.
2. *Utah Territorial Library Catalog* (Salt Lake City, 1852), 27.
3. For a list of builders' guides and pattern books published before 1895, see Henry Russell Hitchcock, *American Architectural Books* (New York, 1976).
4. Paul Goeldner, ed., *Bicknell's Village Builder: A Victorian Architectural Guidebook* (Watkins Glenn, New York: American Life Foundation & Study Institute, 1976), plate 2, This popular pattern book was originally published in 1872.
5. Salt Lake City, Sanborn Maps, 1898, Special Collections, Marriott Library, University of Utah, Salt Lake City.
6. *Salt Lake Tribune*, January 1, 1892. For examples of Darlington Place transactions see Deeds Book J. 165–67, Salt Lake City Records, City and County Building, Salt Lake City; Deeds Book 3R, 223–24, ibid.; and Deeds Book 3C, 249–50, ibid.
7. Plat Book C, 89, Salt Lake City Records.
8. Salt Lake Security and Trust Company, *Owning Your Own Home* (Salt Lake City, 1908). Booklet courtesy of Mrs. L. A. Dahlstrom.
9. "Final Confrontation on Old Downtown Apartments," *Deseret News*, February 22, 1984.
10. "Modern Clean Apartments," *Salt Lake Tribune*, August 17, 1929.
11. See Ryner Banham, *The Architecture of the Well-Tempered Environment* (Chicago: Architectural Press, 1969); David P. Handlin, *The American Home: Architecture and Society, 1815–1915* (Boston: Little, Brown, 1979), 452–86.
12. Sigfried Giedion, *Space, Time and Architecture* (Cambridge, Massachusetts: Harvard University Press, 1954), 345.
13. Handlin, *American Home*, 4.
14. Catharine E. Beecher and Harriet Beecher Stowe, *The American Woman's Home, or, Principles of Domestic Science* (Hartford, Conn., 1975) 19, 20, 24, 23–42. Handlin, *American Home*, 405–8.
15. Handlin, *American Home*, 4–19.
16. Arthur J. Krim, *Northwest Cambridge: Survey of Architectural History in Cambridge, Report Five* (Cambridge, Mass.: Cambridge Historical Commission, 1977), 85.
17. See Peter L. Goss, "The Prairie School Influence in Utah," *Prairies School Review XII, No. 1* (1975), 5–22. Barry Sanders, *The Craftsman: An Anthology* (Salt Lake City: Peregrine Smith, 1978).

18. Infill construction is building homes on empty lots in well-established neighborhoods.
19. Information on these architects was taken from the Utah Architects File, Utah State Historical Society.
20. Plans for the Warren McArthur concrete apartment project in Kenwood, Chicago, Illinois, are given in Henry Russell Hitchcock, *In the Nature of Materials, 1887–1941: The Buildings of Frank Lloyd Wright* (New York: Da Capo Press, 1975), figures 131, 132.
21. Among the houses Fredrick Hale resided in were those at 125 N Street, 84 R Street, and 318 First Avenue. In 1903 he moved to 223 South Sixth Street, at that time a fashionable boulevard connecting South Temple and Liberty Park.
22. Dale L. Morgan, "Changing Face of Salt Lake City," *Utah Historical Quarterly* XXVII (July 1959), 211.
23. See, for example, Mark P. Leonne, "Archeology as the Science of Technology: Mormon Town Plans and Fences," in Charles L. Redman, ed., *Research and Theory in Current Archeology* (New York, 1972).
24. Deeds Book E, 242, Salt Lake City Records; Deeds Book F, 192–93, ibid.; *Salt Lake Tribune*, June 20, 1948. Mark Lindsey received the patent to the homestead on July 15, 1870, Deeds Book E, 785–86, Salt Lake City Records. For examples of Lindsey's lot sales, see Deeds Book F, 332, 720, 721, ibid.
25. "City Creek Canyon Historic District," Salt Lake County, National Register File, Utah State Historical Society.
26. *Deseret News*, October 22, 1906.
27. Patricia Dougall, "The Shade Trees of Salt Lake City" (MA thesis, University of Utah, 1942), 8.

Decline, Renewal, and Preservation

1. *Deseret News*, "Avenues Plan A Good Start," February 7, 1977.
2. Salt Lake City Building Permit Records.
3. Avenues Community Research Project, Salt Lake City Planning Commission, 1975.
4. *Salt Lake Tribune*, "Developer Gives Choice: Stores or Condominiums," March 26, 1976.
5. *Deseret News*, "Council Votes against Condominium Complex," February 20, 1980.
6. *Deseret News*, "Council Studies Avenues Report," July 13, 1977.
7. *Deseret News*, "Salt Lake Nails Down Rules on Home Building," December 14, 2005.
8. *Salt Lake Tribune*, "Salt Lake City's 1st Neighborhood," January, 1997.

Selected Reading

Charles Brooks. "The Growth Patterns of Salt Lake City, Utah and Its Determining Factors." PhD diss., New York University, 1945.

Arrington, Leonard J. *Great Basin Kingdom: An Economic History of the Latter-day Saints, 1830–1900*. Chicago: University of Illinois Press, 2005.

Banham, Reyner. *The Architecture of the Well-Tempered Environment*. Chicago: Architectural Press, 1969.

Beecher, Catharine E., and Stowe, Harriet Beecher. *The American Woman's Home, or, Principles of Domestic Science*. Boston: H. A. Brown & Co., 1869.

Boyce, Ronald R. "An Historical Geography of Greater Salt Lake City, Utah." Master's thesis, University of Utah, 1957.

Carter, Kate B., ed. *Heart Throbs of the West*. 12 vols. Salt Lake City: Daughters of Utah Pioneers, 1939–1951.

Chamberlin, Ralph V. *The University of Utah: A History of Its First Hundred Years, 1850–1950*. Salt Lake City: University of Utah Press, 1960.

Daughters of the Utah Pioneers. *Tales of a Triumphant People: A History of Salt Lake County, Utah 1847–1900*. Salt Lake City: Daughters of the Utah Pioneers, 1947.

Deseret News. "Avenues Plan a Good Start." February 7, 1977.

———. "Council Studies Avenues Report." July 13, 1977.

———. "Council Votes against Condominium Complex." February 20, 1980.

———. "Salt Lake Nails Down Rules on Home Building." December 14, 2005.

Dougall, Patricia. "The Shade Trees of Salt Lake City." Master's thesis, University of Utah, 1942.

Giedion, Sigfried. *Space, Time and Architecture: The Growth of a New Tradition*. Cambridge, Mass.: Harvard University Press, 1954.

Glassie, Henry. *Pattern in the Material Folk Culture of the Eastern United States*. Philadelphia: University of Pennsylvania Press, 1976.

Goeldner, Paul. *Bicknell's Village Builder: A Victorian Architectural Guidebook*. Watkins Glenn, New York: American Life Foundation & Study Institute, 1976.

Goss, Peter. "The Prairie School Influence in Utah." *Prairie School Review* XII, No. 1 (1975).

Handlin, David P. *The American Home: Architecture and Society 1815-1915*. Boston: Little, Brown, 1979.

Harris, Kip King. "Return of the City: A Study of Architectural Restoration/Renovation in the Context of the Avenues District of Salt Lake City." MArch thesis, University of Utah, 1978.

Hitchcock, Henry Russell. *In the Nature of Materials, 1887–1941: The Buildings of Frank Lloyd Wright*. New York: Da Capo Press, 1975.

Koch, Augustus. *Bird's Eye View of Salt Lake City, Utah Territory, 1870*. Chicago: Chicago Lithographing Co., 1870.

Krim, Arthur J. *Northwest Cambridge: Survey of Architectural History in Cambridge, Report Five*. Cambridge, MA: Cambridge Historical Commission, 1977.

Morgan, Dale L. "The Changing Face of Salt Lake City." *Utah Historical Quarterly* XXVII (July 1959).

Morgan, Nicholas G., Sr. *Pioneer Map: Plat 'D' and Empire Mill Tract*, Map #538. Salt Lake City: Utah Historical Society.

Olpin, Robert S. *Dictionary of Utah Art*. Salt Lake City: Salt Lake Art Center, 1980.

Peterson, Charles S. *Utah: A Bicentennial History*, New York: W. W. Norton, 1977.

Salt Lake City Directory, 1885–2008.

Salt Lake City Planning Commission. Avenues Community Research Project, 1977.

Salt Lake City School District. "The Fifth Annual Report of the Public Schools of the City of Salt Lake for the Year Ending June 30th, 1895." Salt Lake City, 1895.

Salt Lake Security and Trust Company. *Owning Your Own Home*. Salt Lake City: Salt Lake Security and Trust Company, 1908.

Salt Lake Tribune. "Avenues Wards Continue to Lose Members." June 22, 2006.

———. "Developer Gives Choice: Stores or Condominium Complex." March 26, 1976.

———. "Salt Lake City's First Neighborhood." January, 1977.

Sanborn Maps, Salt Lake City, 1898.

Sanders, Barry. *The Craftsman: An Anthology*. Salt Lake City: Peregrine Smith, 1978.

Smith, Ruby K. *One Hundred Years in the Heart of Zion: A Narrative History of the Eighteenth Ward*. Salt Lake City: *Deseret News* Press, 1960.

The Enterprise. Salt Lake City, April 27, 1987.

Utah Light and Traction Company. "Diagram of Trolley System and Feeders." Salt Lake City: Utah Light and Traction Company, 1915.

Utah Territorial Library Catalog. Salt Lake City, 1852.

Wright, Paul A. "The Growth and Distribution of the Mormon and Non-Mormon Populations in Salt Lake City." Master's thesis, University of Chicago, 1970.

Index to Addresses

329; **683,** 329; **687,** 329; **703,** 329;
709, 329; **711,** 330; **715,** 330; **718,**
330; **723,** 331; **727,** 331; **738,** 331;
752, 103, 332; **761,** 332; **813,** 332;
817, 333

Seventh Avenue: **229,** 335; **254,** 335;
259, 12, 41, 42, 335; **351,** 336; **361,**
45, 59, 336; **369,** 336; **371,** 12, 337;
383, 337; **407,** 337; **471,** 338; **473,**
338; **519,** 338; **539,** 338; **587,** 338;
602–620, 339; **751,** 339; **757,** 339;
761, 340; **767,** 340

Eighth Avenue: **201,** 13, 19, 342;
206, 13, 40, 42, 342; **219,** 19; **765,**
46, 342

Tenth Avenue: **711,** 29, 61. 343; **819,**
270

Eleventh Avenue: **381,** 40, 60, 343;
533, 39, 343

INDEX TO NAMES

Farrer, Leland J., 210
Farrington, John, 272
Farrow, Walter C., 178
Felt: Albert W., 297; Charles, 12; Lonis B., 257; Vera I., 289
Ferguson: Ellen Brooke, 11, 77; Henry A., 175, 257; James X., 118, 202
Ferris, Ellen P., 280
Fetzer, John K. and Naomi, 299
Fields, David, 250
Finch: Harry L. and Jean R., 326; Nancy E., 326
Firman, William E., 196
First Avenue Grocery, 220
First Methodist Episcopal Church, 128
First Presbyterian Church, 23
Fisher: Albert, 243; George A., 130; Isaac Montgomery, 247, 254; William B., 209
Fivas, George P., 303
Flo, Hans and Adna, 168
Flohm, F. W., 23
Flood, Sidney D. and Alice, 181
Flowers: John and Caroline, 317; Seville, 317
Folland: Frank J., 324; Robert S. and Alice A., 304
Folland Drug Store, 324
Ford, John D. and Julia, 305
Forssell, Olof A. T., 324
Foster, William H. and Eunice Neslen, 87
Foulger: Arthur, 152; Charlotte M., 160; Clarence A., 168; Edith, 160; Herbert J., 152, 160
Foulger Brothers Grocery Co., 152
Foulks, John and Nellie, 185
Fowler, William and Florence, 99
Fowlger, Charles J. and Hannah, 270
Fox, Sidney S., 278
Francis, Fred and Grace, 288

Freber, Arthur Pedersen and Virginia, 15, 271
Frederickson, H. Sidney, 319, 324
Freed: Charles M., 307; Claud W., 227, 307
Freeman: Clyde B. and Nedra J., 91; Douglas D., 147
Frick, Joseph E., 249
Fritch, Cathy and Rodney, 298
Fullerton, Glenda, 200

Galligan, John J., 272
Galligher, Joseph E. and Violet, 160
Gallivan: Frances W. and Daniel J., 129; Jack, 129
Gamble, Mary G., 137
Gardiner, A. G., 146
Gardner, John S. and Nellie E., 313
Gates, Joseph W. and Isabel, 281
Gateway Apartments, 34, 36
Gaylord, Ernest, 283
Gem Grocery and Meat Market, 275
George Romney and Sons Co., 17–18
Gibbs, George F., 215
Gibson: Isabella, 252; Jeanette, 119; John, 252; Margaret, 252
Gibson's Tailor Shop, 11
Giles: Eugene, 255; John G. and Amy, 170, 185; Petrear, 157
Gillett, Stephen, 330
Gin, Ping Y., 321
Glade: James, 93; William J., 93; William S. and Annie, 92
Gleason, Helena C., 130
Glenn, H. Eugene and Rose Mary Young, 175
Glissmeyer, August, 250
Godbe: Ernest L., 104; Murray C. and Alta Y., 82
Goddard and Co., 11
Goddard Investment Co., 90, 107
Golden Top Baking Co., 152

Goldsmith, Leopold, 131
Goodfellow: John, 153; Lynn and Dorothy, 153
Goodman, Thomas and Harriet, 144
Goodson, Floyd, 165
Goodwin: Charles C., 208; James, 208
Gordon, Andrew M., 89
Gowans, Ephraim and Mary, 211
Grace, William and Isabel, 98
Grant: Brigham Frederick, 19; Emily, 236; Frank A., 17, 193, 194, 197, 202, 282, 284, 285; Heber J., 13, 18, 19, 72, 82, 83, 236, 342
Grant and Bower Building Co., 72
Graupe, Augusta, 264
Gray: David R. and Nannie, 200; George, 83
Greater Avenues Community Council, 53
Green, Wayne, 337
Greene: Charles and Henry, 39, 60; George C., 191; Oliver B., 123
Greenwald, Isadore E., 137
Greenwood, Ernest A., 217
Gregory: Frank A., 139; William A., 192
Grieve, Simon, 309
Griffin, John, 156
Griffiths, Elijah, 18
Grimsdel, William G., 223
Groeber, Charles A., 167
Groesbeck: Ella Brown May, 128; George M., 246; John A. and Tessi Clawson, 213; Leslie H. and Hazel Alice Calder, 128
Groves, William H., 27
Gudgell, George B., 170
Guiver: Benjamin and Mary Ann, 204; George and Amanda, 204; George D., 169; William H., 204
Gunn, John F., 133, 146
Gurney, Elizabeth and Theodore, 292

Haag, Richard T. and Caroline, 115
Hagemann, William and Wilhelmina, 292
Hale, Frederick A., 36, 45, 196, 199, 229
Hall: Fred A., 336; Hubert and Almeda, 316; John W., 229
Halliday: H. Hartland and Camille, 303; Thomas W. and Millicent, 156
Hammell, Lawrence, 200
Hammer, Paul and Annie D., 167
Hammond, James T., 264
Hampton: Grant A. and Catherine, 72; Leon B., 236; Mary J. and Brigham Young, 299; Robert R., 259
Hanchett, Lafayette, 282
Hanks, Howard A. and Dora C., 164
Hansen: Harvey and Elva, 171; Holger P. V. and Anna, 177; O. Fredrick and Agnes, 292; Ole C., 122; Swen, 164
Hanson, Andrew M. and Darl H., 208
Hara, Birdie E. Brey, 112
Harbach, Otto, 237
Hard, William and Leela, 281
Hardman, John R., 161
Hardy: Burton J. and Sarah Ann, 157; John K. and Clare, 165; Rufus K. and Annie E., 331; William and Hannah, 90
Harmer, Earl W., 153
Harms, Hermann, 216
Harper: Thomas E., 124; Thomas E. Jr., 124
Harr, Lawrence F., 223
Harris: Alma A., 267; William D. and Alice N., 101
Harrison: James D., 188; Moroni B., 311
Harrison and Nichols, 249

Kinnersley, Elmira M. and Thomas S., 188

Kjergaard, M., 129

Kjergard: James P. and Thora, 171; Louis P. and Anna K., 147, 278

Kletting: Constance, 322, 328; Richard K. A., 14, 24, 40, 79, 88, 125, 127, 169, 322, 335

Klink, John G., 284

Knowles, James H., 226

Kopp, Joseph A., 111

Kronner: Mary B., 306; William M., 289, 306

Krueger, Chris, 95

Laker family, 293

Lamberson, Annie Evans and Era, 81

Lamberson Apartments, 81

Lambourne: Alfred, 15; Charles A. and Emma, 113; Ernest A. and Belle, 297, 310; Eugene A., 106; George W., 310; Martha Wernham, 105, 106; William, 105

Lang, Daniel J., 70

Langford, Jeremiah E., 246

Larsen, John, 310

Larson, Louisa Lofgren, 325

Larson Building Co., 235

Latimer: Clara, 113; Richard and Emma, 91; Thomas, 113

Lauridsen, Theodore, 23

Lawson: Howard H., 176; John W., 266; Thomas H., 162

LDS Hospital, 26, 27

Leaker: Inez, 112; William J., 112, 324

Leaver, Theresa, 304

Leavitt, Alonzo R., 176

Ledyard, Edgar M., 286

Lee: Anson, 258; Hyrum and Lillian, 70

Leeson, Jeanne Tellier and Delmar, 111

Leland, Davis M., 132

Lepper, W. H., 259

Lester, S. Jr., 329

LeSueur, Walter B., 103

Letchfield, Charles, 194

Levy, Jim and Jennifer, 252

Lewis, Mose, 253

Liljenberg: Anna S., 183; N. Edward, 183, 304

Liljenberg and Sundberg, 72, 155

Lindsey: Joseph M. and Rose A., 173; Mark and Birthiah, 48

Lindsey Gardens (city park), 48

Lindsey Gardens (resort), 6, 48, 173

Lipman: Alan M. and Marion B., 288; Daniel W., 127; Milton E., 222, 224

Little, Charles T. and Nan, 209

Lloyd, William, 97, 240

Logan: Glenn, 121; Harry, 274

Longfellow School, 24

Lowell School, 22, 24, 25

Lucas: Amos J., 245; Frank J., 312

Luff: Fred S., 114; George D. and Sarah, 116; George T., 297; Henry, 104, 267; Lovina, 104

Lund, Herbert Z. and Emma J., 72

Lundquist, Emanuel and Ada, 316

Lundwall, Nels Benjamin, 242

Lutz: Charles G., 163; Clarence O., 163

Lyman: Amy Brown, 12; Francis M., 283; Linda and Kevin, 317; Richard R., 12, 284; Willard H. and Hildegard S., 165

Lynch, Lutie T., 235

Lynn, Arthur, 216

Lyon, Alexander, 145

Lyons, William J., 193

MacKay, George W., 228

MacLean, William D. and Elizabeth, 253

Maddison, Effie R., 83

Madeline Choir School, 27, 75, 76

Madsen: Charles E., 270; Peter W., 197

Maesar, Emil, 304

Magdiels, John H., 80

Maggie, Mary, 238

Mahood Engineering, 215

Mansfield, Ernest J., 284

Mantle, William, 158

Marcy, Frank E. and May S., 186

Marioneaux, Thomas, 103

Markland, Charles B., 199

Markland Mansion, 199

Marr: George E., 71; Gibon A., 289

Marshall, James and Lillian, 243

Martin: Dennie O., 83; Elizabeth E., 16; Lewis and Elizabeth, 77; Scott, 253

Mathez, Forrest, 225

Mauer, E. M., 296

Maxwell, Hames, 305

Mayer, Joseph P. and Loy M., 129

Maynes, John A. and Selina, 122

McAllister, William and Anna, 187

McCartey, Cecil., 250

McCartney, William, 327

McCarty: Lynda M., 171; William H., 13

McCauley, Mary, 228

McChrystal, John H., 240

McClellan, John J., 15, 219

McConahy, William M. and Ella J., 141

McConaughy, Robert E., 191, 246, 286

McCormick Company, 213

McCullough, Derell, 164

McCullough's Market, 164

McCune: Alfred and Elizabeth, 71; Henry M., 277

McDevitt, Hugh C., 317

McDonald: Alex M., 259; James

G., 313; William C., 214; William K., 82

McEwen, Henry T., 299

McFarlane, Grant, 217

McGarry, James C., 245

McGinty, William G., 317

McGregor, Charles R., 110

McGurrin, Frank E., 17, 33, 176, 185, 186, 187, 196, 201, 227, 230, 254

McIntyre: Mrs, Thomas, 11; William H., 12, 41, 42, 355

McIntyre Mansion, 355

McKean, H. J., 315, 316, 355

McKee, William and Edith, 164

McKellar, Angus, 169, 303, 332

McKim, Mead, and White, 58, 59

McKinlay, Lynn A., 241

McKinnon, Ray B., 264

McMaster, Rachel, 167, 172, 199, 275

McMillan, Benjamin A. and Grace Stewart, 257

McMurray, Annie, 128

McOwens, Thomas and Jessie K., 167

McReynolds, John, 280

Meagher, Nicholas, 182

Meakin, Fred W., 255

Mecklenburg, Bernard O., 10, 46, 127, 175, 200, 257

Megeath, Joseph P., 230

Melville, Imogene and James, 280

Memory Grove Park, 48

Meredith, Alfred H. and Anna, 115

Merrill, Charles O., 185

Meyer, Katherine and Henry, 242

M. H. Walker Realty Co., 284

Mickelson, Georgianna and James, 123

Midgley: Anne Grant, 19; Charles W., 147, 148

Midgley-Boedel Co., 115

Midley, J. George, 82

Miles: Luetta P., 249; Orson P., 249